BLACK
COMEDY

AN APPLAUSE ORIGINAL
BLACK COMEDY: Nine Plays A Critical Anthology
with Interviews and Essays
Edited by Pamela Faith Jackson & Karimah
Copyright 1997 © Pamela Faith Jackson

Library of Congress Cataloging-In-Publication Data
   Black comedy classics: a critical anthology of nine plays, with interviews and essays / edited by Pamela Faith Jackson
      p.   cm.
   "an Applause original" --T. p. verso.
   ISBN 1-55783-278-1 (pbk.)
   1. American Drama (Comedy) --Afro-American authors. 2. American drama (Comedy) --Afro-American authors--History and criticism. 4. Afro-American dramatists--20th century--Interviews. 5. Afro-Americans in literature. 6. American drama--20th century. 7. Afro-Americans-Drama. I. Jackson, Pamela Faith.
   PS628.N4b52 1997
   812'.052308896073--dc21   97-9500
                                                                          CIP

APPLAUSE BOOKS
211 West 71st Street
New York, NY 10023
Phone (212) 496-7511
Fax: (212) 721-2856

A&C BLACK
Howard Road, Eaton Socon
Huntington, Cambs PE19 3EZ
Phone 0171-242 0946
Fax 0171-831 8478

First Applause Printing, 1997

BLACK COMEDY:

NINE PLAYS

A CRITICAL ANTHOLOGY

WITH INTERVIEWS
AND ESSAYS

EDITED BY
PAMELA FAITH JACKSON
AND
KARIMAH

APPLAUSE
NEW YORK • LONDON

To my son, David O., David B. and Aunt Odessa — this one's for you because you taught me how to laugh at this mean old world; . . . and to you Danitra Vance because you were so believably funny; . . . and last but not least for my parents. Thanks for your love and understanding — James and Helen Jackson, Sr. I love you much.

—Pamela Faith

ACKNOWLEDGMENTS

I am eternally grateful to my Columbia University Instructor, Evangeline Morphos, for making the creation of an anthology a class assignment; to Woodie King, Jr. who affirmed my vision; to my cousin Camille Howard for her help with formulating my publishing proposal; to Howard Stein for accepting me into the M.F.A. program; to Dr. Paul Jackson who introduced me to the world of drama literature at Spelman College; to Marsha Hudson (executor of the Bert Andrews Collection); to Carman who helped me locate Marsha; to Susan Watson Turner for access to The Negro Ensemble Company Archive; to the Billie Holliday Archive; to Geri Blanchett and Ken McClain for access to the Jomandi Productions Archive; to playwright Charles Fuller who mandates that every black person who can should write a book telling our story; to Kimberly Harding and Valerie Boyd for the Lynda Hill connection; to my colleague Sydne Mahone for letting me pick her brain; to Professor James Hatch for the Abram Hill connection; to NEC Board Member James Frazier for sharing his experience of being a t the theatre to witness the original production of Day of Absence; playwright Cherry Miles for supplying me with a video copy of the NEC documentary; to the Black Comedy Classics contributors Thomas W. Jones, II, L. Kenneth Richardson, Tia Dionne Hodge, Dr. Paul Jackson, Eugene Nesmith, Ed Bullins, Dick Gregory, Floranté Galvez, Jeff Nichols, and Lynda Hill; to Paul Sugarman, Emily Franzosa and Kay Radtke, and to my publisher, Mr. Glenn Young who said yes without hesitation, and most importantly to the restoration playwrights of comedy.

—*Pamela Faith*

CONTENTS

PREFACE

Signifying people slip slidin' on a lyric...

Giving guts to belief in the power of laughter

        "Check you out...lookin' like an old broke down..."

Yeah Signifying cause its our legacy...inherited from sayers signify
ing in days gone by...Slaves in the shanty. Signifying

        "Ain't nobody in here but us chickens..."

Brothers on the block signifying...

"Yo momma so...

"yeah yo momma so black she sweat coffee"

Sisters in the beauty parlor signifying...

        "My man so..."

    "Yeh well my man so poor he can't afford to be broke."

And so it goes from the pain of our living, we signify and give our lives the laughter we needed to survive another day, another week, another life. To find order in chaos is an ethic rooted in the slave experience and passed down to present day gatherings. Black humor, and by that one understands, the full world view that is held by African-Americans translating a new world experience — finds its root in the day to day lives of laborers; workers; migrants; a blues people making sacrifice.

The humor so heavily invested in our lives readily translates to our stages. From the minstrel tradition of Williams & Walker; where our genius lived behind black face...to the comic re-inventors of Rochester, Amos & Andy, Mantan Moreland — humor has been a utilitarian function born from the need of a people to cope, to survive, to give levity to circumstances at once overwhelming and intolerable.

The humor of African-American life is inextricably tied to the humor on the African-American stage. It's character shaped by the contradictions of being Black & Bewildered & Bothered in the new world. It is a humor that breathes sanity & humanity in the midst of profound circumstances.

And so Richard Pryor, Redd Foxx, Bill Cosby...articulate the ethic concerns, values of a people in all its disparate machinations.

Douglas Turner Ward articulates that ethical discourse in *Day of Absence*; George Wolfe further explores the cultural contradictions in *Colored Museum* and there is a connection to the cognitive based organization of African-American life. Each seeks to give clarity to the chaos. Each utilizes an idiom of satire, farce, "signifying" to connect the mythical nature of our living.

To find logic to this existence is at the heart of the African-American comic odyssey.

In the following pages that tradition continues; writers who understand the mythic comic paradigm, articulate the rage; the panic; the contradictions of a new world existence. African-American humor functions to heal, to clarify, to assert, and so the following pages continue the tradition of using humor, comic linguistic based art to bridge reality with mythic possibility. And this work is the work of generations healing the wounds. To laugh is to diffuse the powerful rage burning beneath the soul.

From the street to the stage, black comic invention services the need of a people to hear their voice moving through the centuries without scars. From Langston to Pryor to Wolfe to you . . .

"Did you hear the one about . . . "

Peace in the New Age —

—Thomas W. Jones, II

INTRODUCTION

Snicker. Snicker. Monkey. Aunt Jemima On The Cornbread Box. Coon. Black Sambo. N-i-g-g-a. I didn't understand! The first time I heard these words directed at me was in September 1964, when I along with four black teens integrated an all-white "Dixie-loving" high school in Atlanta, Georgia. The melancholy realization that these tempestuous words were only the tip of the iceberg hit me like the Titanic. My experience never made national headlines like the story of the Little Rock Nine, who broke down the walls of segregation at Central High in Arkansas. Nonetheless, the psychological devastation skewed my perceptions for many years to come. I guess the worse part was being ignored, having no voice, and feeling invisible to the majority of my peers and teachers. Hecklers on the school bus greeted my black skin each morning. The daily nightmare of passing room after room of agitated students chanting and throwing things sank my soul into deep dark depression. Living in the hometown of Dr. Martin Luther King, Jr., dictated that I ignore the turbulence for the sake of a better education. I believed I had successfully ridden the wave of hate until I entered an all-black college and went from being too black to being not black enough. (Say What?) Oh, yes, and I gradually succumbed to the murky waters of anger, self-doubt and mistrust. I realized through my excruciating maturation process, that for sanity's sake I had to discover the beauty and possibility in me and my people.

Black stage comedy coupled with the Holy Spirit helped me do just that by exposing the absurdities in the class, race, and gender-based issues affecting my life. Introduction to outrageous characters who could say and do what I had merely thought or secretly talked about doing turned my frown upside down. White-faced minstrels played by black actors, Purlie with his this-land-is-my-land-too declaration, Mrs. Love and her poison pie, the schizophrenic wigs LaWanda and Janine, and Miss Roj the snap queen of truth all allowed me to take a retrospective look at myself from the inside out. Ossie Davis wrote an essay in 1965 entitled "Purlie Told Me" where he contends that Purlie imparted the following words of wisdom to him:

> "Look at the Negro from outside and all you see is oppression. But look at the Negro from the inside, and all you see is resistance to that oppression. Now oppression, and the resistance to oppression, are universal themes...The profoundest commitment possible to a black creator in this country today—beyond all creeds, crafts, classes and ideologies whatsoever—is to bring before his people the scent of freedom. He may rest assured his people will do the rest."

This first-of-its-kind collection entitled *Black Comedy*, personifies Purlie's scent of freedom in nine stage comedies that span six decades written by Abram Hill, Langston Hughes, Charlie Russell, Douglas Turner Ward, Ted Shine, Don Evans, George C. Wolfe, Thomas W. Jones, II, and Phyllis Yvonne Stickney. Regrettably, *Purlie Victorious* (presented in Atlanta during the 1996 Olympics) is missing from this volume. The works included range from an early examination and critique of American society after World War II to plays that reflect socio-political concerns that kept pace with historical events, like the sit–in demonstrations, the bus boycotts, black nationalism, and the women's liberation movement. A hybrid of comedic forms including satire, farce, comedy of manners, romantic comedy, dark comedy, and tragicomedy are presented through vernacular language, stand-up performance art, masks, broad humor, as well as the minstrel show. Essays, articles and interviews complement this critical edition.

Comedies in the black theatre canon written by other playwrights that merit investigation include: *The Church Fight* by Ruth Gaines Shelton; Zora Neale Hurston's *The First One* and *Mule Bone* (written with Langston Hughes); *Livin' Fat* by Judy Ann Mason; *Hotel Happiness* and *Don't Rock The Boat* by Margaret Ford Taylor; *Plain Folk* by Cheryl Johnson and Traci Reynolds, 227 by Christine Houston, *Steal Away* by Ramona King; *The Fly In The Coffin* and *God Is A Guest What* by Ray McIver; *The Name Game* by J.E. Franklin; *Maggie* by Lillie Marie Redwood; *Skin Game* by Lisa Jones; *Colored People's Time* by Leslie Lee; *Daddy Goodness* by Richard Wright; *Paper Dolls* by Elaine Jackson; and *Remembering Aunt Jemima* by Glenda Dickerson.

Thank God for Black theatre institutions such as The American Negro Theatre co-founded by Hill, The Negro Ensemble Company co-founded by Ward, Jomandi Productions co-founded by Jones, New Federal Theatre, Crossroads Theatre, Karamu, and the National Black Theatre. Artistic homes such as these continue to provide nurturing environments where black comic revolutionaries can develop the work that challenges authority, explodes stereotypes, and eases racial tensions.

I'd be remiss if I did not take this opurtunity to pay homage to the ancestors and their work. Bert Williams and George Walker's musical comedy *In Dahomey* as one critic wrote " . . . was the first time that a piece written by Negroes and performed by Negroes, had been admitted to the boards of a Broadway theatre. The unquestionable success of the enterprise is likely to result in renewed and more ambitious efforts in this direction." W. E. B. DuBois understood the importance of this genre and in Bert Williams *Son of Laughter* (ed. by Mabel Rowland) was quoted as saying:

> "He was one of those who made the world laugh. When in the calm after day of thought and struggle to racial peace we look back to pay tribute to those who helped most, we shall single out for highest praises those who made the world laugh; Bob Cole, Ernest Hogan, George Walker, and above all Bert Williams. For this is not mere laughing: it was the smile that hovered above the blood and tragedy; the light mask of happiness that hid breaking hearts and bitter souls. This is the top of bravery; the finest thing in service."

Black Comedy is an expression of my gratitude to the visionary humorists who voiced my pain, and supplied me with life-saving heart to heart resuscitation performed by the comic spirit.

—Pamela Faith Jackson
May 1, 1997

Abram Hill

ON STRIVERS ROW
A SATIRE

ABRAM HILL

Born in Atlanta, Georgia, the fourth of five children of John and Minnie Weather Hill. He was baptized at the Friendship Baptist Church, under Dr. Benjamin E. Mays and Dr. E. R. Carter. Abram was educated in Atlanta elementary schools and during high school moved to New York City, where he graduated from DeWitt Clinton High School. He attended the City College of New York and then completed his college education at Lincoln University in Pennsylvania. He did graduate study at Columbia University. At a very early age Abram showed a love for drama and his family recalls his portrayal of nursery rhyme characters and his zest for the movies. That love of the theater remained with him throughout his life. In 1938 he became an assistant in the Drama Department at Lincoln and later that year became a consultant to the Federal Theater in New York City. For the next two years he studied play writing and play analysis at the New School of Social Research.

His first produced play was *On Strivers Row*, mounted at the Rose McClendon Workshop and later by the American Negro Theater, which Abram co-founded with Frederick O'Neal. The fledgling American Negro Theater rehearsed in a funeral parlor and some of the early productions were staged at the Abyssinian Baptist Church and then in the basement of the Schomberg Public Library at 135th Street and Lenox Avenue. Ruby Dee, Hilda Simms, Helen Martin, Sidney Poitier, Harry Belefonte, Frederick O'Neal, Clarice Taylor, Maxwell Glanville, Gertrude Jeannette, Hilda Haynes, Alvin Childress, Jacqueline Andra, Earl Hyman, Georgia Burke and Roger Furman are among the ANT alumnae.

"As a director and playwright, I have tried to bring a balance in the Negro theater. Most big-time commercial productions on race themes have dealt with only about 10 percent of the Negro population — as a rule the exotic lower depths. All I'm trying to do is introduce a few of the other types who run the gamut from the professional, middle class and everyday Dicks, Toms and Harrys," explained Abram Hill when asked about his role in the development of black theater.

Anna Lucasta, adapted by Abram for the ANT was a great success. It later moved to Broadway, where it ran for 900 performances and was one of the longest running non-musical plays on Broadway. Abram Hill also authored several other plays, including *Hell's Half-Acre*, and *Walk Hard, So Shall you Reap*, and the much publicized but never produced *Liberty Deferred*, which he co-authored with John Silvera. After leaving the American Negro Theater, Abram taught at Lincoln University and then returned to the New York City public school system, where he taught at

Laurelton High School. He was in great demand as a lecturer and consultant and he greatly enjoyed traveling. He was a member of Riverside Church and served on the board of the Schomberg Corporation. He was delighted to see the revival of *On Strivers Row* at Roger Furman's New Heritage Repertory Company in New York City and in a number of cities across the country.

["Obituary." Services for Abram Hill, October 6, 1986, Riverside Church, NYC.]

CHARACTERS

SOPHIE

DOLLY VAN STRIVEN

PROFESSOR HENNYPEST

TILLIE PETUNIA

CHUCK

COBINA

MRS. PACE

OSCAR VAN STRIVEN

LILY LIVINGSTON

ROWENA

ED TUCKER

LOUISE DAVIS

DR. LEON DAVIS

RUBY JACKSON

BEULAH

JOE SMOTHERS

SCENES

*The action takes place in the reception room and foyer of the Van Striven
Home in Harlem.*

ACT ONE

Scene 1   *A morning in the fall of the 1940s*
Scene 2   *Nine P.M., the same day*

ACT TWO

Scene 1   *A few minutes later*
Scene 2   *Later, the same evening*

BACKGROUND: *The Van Strivens' residence stands high and mighty
in the heart of Harlem on West 139th Street between Seventh and Eighth
Avenues. In bygone days when this and similar homes in the block were
built, [circa 1913], they became the town homes for upper-class whites. As
the complexion of Harlem later changed, the boire bourgeoisie, especially
the socially inclined ones, purchased these properties.*

By the 1920s, the block had become known as Strivers Row, a trim, tree-dotted, exclusive community of "society" Blacks. Fearing slum encroachment, affluent lawyers, doctors, teachers, real estate brokers, business people, and renowned celebrities established a rigid pattern of disciplined living, guarded orderliness, and more than a hint of luxury.

Striving to set an exclusive and fashionable way of living became the order of the day. Neighbor competed with neighbor to outdo one another. Meanwhile less fortunate Blacks developed varying degrees of mockery and hostility. It is no mere coincidence that our story deals with a family by the name of Van Striven.

Musicales, teas, and soirees set the social vogue in these homes; whereas yacht parties, theater–concert–opera attending, weekend retreats at resorts and summer homes, motor trips in high-powered cars, and trips abroad added additional luster to the doings of this tribe.

The Van Strivens consider themselves socially miles above their neighbors. Though their home is a four-story dwelling — the same as the others in the block — Van Strivens have engineered themselves into a position of "second to none." The first floor of the home includes an entrance, sitting room, den, dining room, kitchen, pantry, maid's room, and bath. The second floor includes a foyer, reception room, back parlor and family room. The third and fourth floors have baths and bedrooms.

SCENE: *The scene of the play is the large reception room [front parlor] and the foyer, an elevated entrance area further upstage. Here, the Van Strivens entertain small and informal gatherings. The back parlor off left is reserved for larger and more formal affairs.*

An arch in the center of the upstage wall of the reception room, three steps, flanking wrought-iron rails and an accompanying balustrade separate the room from the foyer. The foyer floor is about two feet above the level of the parlor floor. The walls of the room, heightened by the sunken floor and a spectacular chandelier, enhance a quiet elegance and a hint of pretentiousness.

Upstage off right leads to the front door. It cannot be seen, but it frequently can be heard to slam. Upstage off left leads to the stairwell, the hall, back parlor, and a den. Along the right wall is a pair of French doors, leading to a veranda overlooking the street. Partially drawn drapes and venetian blinds encase the French doors. This wall is indented, allowing a three–quartered viewing of the doors by the audience. Downstage of the left wall is a doorway leading to a passageway to the back parlor. Double swivel doors are suggested for the area, thus allowing easy–flowing exits and entrances.

Clusters of furniture are arranged for easy conversation. Right of center is a stylish loveseat with a small table above holding a lamp. An up-

holstered armchair down left, a cocktail table in front of the loveseat, and a stool extremely down right complete this grouping. A console table with a vase and a French phone plus a radio and record–playing combination along the left wall add luster.

Right and left of the arch are single antique chairs. A classy painting and a delicately carved bench dominate the foyer. Other paintings, furnishings, and minutiae are strategically placed, including rugs and candlelight wall fixtures. The setting is very prim, proper, and affluent. One has to wonder why there is a sign tucked in the French door that makes one wonder about the Van Strivens. The sign reads: ROOM TO RENT.

ACT I

SCENE 1

Before the curtain rises, appropriate music [classical, please] sets the high and mighty tone of Strivers Row. The music is emanating from a radio. Since the blinds are drawn, very little light illuminates the room. Entering from the left foyer is SOPHIE, a rather chic, casual, and extremely informal maid. She is wearing the customary maid's uniform and is carrying a dust mop and a basket of cleaning paraphernalia. She adjusts the venetian blinds; light filters the room. She is humming "When the Saints Go Marching In" and is deliberately drowning out the radio music. Her cleaning begins with her feathered duster and cleaning cloth taking a stroke at the furniture. Shutting off the radio, she sings, synchronizing her strokes with the song.

SOPHIE: Lord, I want to be in that number;
when the saints go marching in.
Oh, when the saints go marching in;
Oh, when the saints go marching in,
[almost prayerfully.]
Lord, I sure wish I'd hit a NUMBER—

DOLLY: [Off stage.] Good morning, Sophie.

SOPHIE: [Now very busy.] Morning. Ma'am.

DOLLY: You sound as if you attended a revival meeting last night instead of a dance. [Entering from left foyer.]

SOPHIE: Ain't no difference. At one you dance with your man. At the other, you dance with the Holy Ghost.

[*Now within full view,* DOLLY *is dressed in a Dior housecoat and is strikingly handsome, well–bred, youthfully fortyish matron of the Afro–American elite that descended from pre–Civil War black and white Romeos and Juliets in downstate New York. Though totally confident of the supremacy of her social status, there is a slight edge of uncertainty — "a hidden dissuader" — that creeps into her manner. She masks this dissuader with wit, but at times frustration makes her a bit daffy. She is carrying a pair of slippers.*]

DOLLY: You must have had fun. You didn't get in until the wee hours this morning. Break these in again for me, please.

SOPHIE: [*Taking the slippers.*] What again! I crucified my feet last night at the Bellhops Ball. I don't feel —

DOLLY: [*Embracing her.*] You also wore my mink cape. Am I annoyed? No!

SOPHIE: [*Changing to slippers.*] When I first took the job, having access to your wardrobe was part of the deal.

DOLLY: [*Very lightly.*] My jewelry and cape were the exceptions. Let's remember not to forget that. [SOPHIE *winces, her feet hurt.*] It's that left one that pinches, isn't it.

SOPHIE: It's the left side of my face that's screwed up, ain't it? In the Flip Flop Boogie we danced, the action was on the right foot.

DOLLY: Where was the left foot?

SOPHIE: In the air, like this — [*Rises, does the Flip Flop Boogie on the right foot, the left stabbing the air.*]

DOLLY: Get the mail. That's no dance. That's some new version of a fit. [SOPHIE *shuffles toward the foyer.*] Stop, Sophie! I'll get it. You shuffle like Uncle Tom after he has swallowed ten beers. [*She goes off foyer right.*]

SOPHIE: [*Sitting on chair arm.*] It's beyond me why some colored people — even "the well–bred ones" — have such unbred feet.

DOLLY: [*Entering with mail and a newspaper.*] Lovely! Lovely! Scores of people have R–S–V–Peed! [*Examining the mail.*]

SOPHIE: Any mail for me?

DOLLY: No, dear. Nobody wrote to you. [*Opening mail.*]

SOPHIE: Who cares. The only male I'm interested in wears pants.

DOLLY: A reply from Dr. Leon Davis and his wife, Louise.

SOPHIE: His hands stray too much on foreign territory. [*Smacks her buttocks.*]

DOLLY: How nice! Judge and Mrs. Tucker, true born aristocrats.

SOPHIE: They may be aristocrats, but that son is a acrobat. He—

DOLLY: And George P. Muzzumer, the undertaker tycoon. Why, the money he has!

SOPHIE: You know, when my fourth husband died, he wouldn't let him down in his grave until I paid a deposit on his funeral.

DOLLY: [*Puzzled at the letter.*] Rita Richpot—Rita Richpot—?

SOPHIE: That's the former Rita Kale. You see, Dr. Kale ain't filling her prescription no more.

DOLLY: What's that?

SOPHIE: He pulled that mink coat off her and put her tail out on the turf.

DOLLY: Heavens! [*Throws reply into waste basket.*] Then I must retract my invitation. I'll telephone her—make some excuse for her not to come. When people drop their morals, I drop them from my guest book. [*Picks up book and scratches name from book.*] Couples are so dizzy now a days. They change one another faster than you can change the bed linen.

SOPHIE: [*Impertinently.*] That do'd it! My salary, please.

DOLLY: [*Sitting* SOPHIE *down.*] Oh—come now, Sophie—there's something between us bigger than salaries.

SOPHIE: It sure is. And that's my bill.

DOLLY: [*Rising.*] Come, Sophie, we have plenty to do.

SOPHIE: [*Rallying.*] We! That bunch of snobs coming here can't appreciate the fact that I've lost ten pounds in ten days getting this house in shape for them tonight.

DOLLY: Tis not in vain, Sophie. Cobina Van Striven's debut will be the debut of the season.

SOPHIE: That child don't want no debut.

DOLLY: But, my dear, debutantes at eighteen always make their bows before society.

SOPHIE: [*Resuming dusting.*] I nearly busted my corset when I debuted.

DOLLY: Hahahahaha—you bowing before society—at eighteen, I suppose!

SOPHIE: What old society at eighteen! I was bowing before the Captain at precinct 32, explaining!

DOLLY: Sophie, you're impossible. But, what would I ever do without you?

SOPHIE: That's what he wants to know.

DOLLY: He?

SOPHIE: Joe.

DOLLY: Joe who? Has he no last name?

SOPHIE: [*Gloatingly.*] Ain't nothin' in a name.

DOLLY: You would love a man without knowing whether he was good or not?

SOPHIE: And will you tell me what a good man can do?

DOLLY: Well, what do you expect in a man?

SOPHIE: Excitement!

DOLLY: [*Disdainfully.*] Oh! Such talk! I hope mother nor Cobina has ever heard you talking like this.

SOPHIE: Cobina would surprise you.

DOLLY: [*Puzzled.*] What do you mean?

SOPHIE: Nothing.

DOLLY: [*She strolls to the window.*] You will see some fine young men here tonight. Unfortunately, one or two have kinky hair.

SOPHIE: Ma Pace ain't gonna have them.

DOLLY: Mother, well — yes — she can be made to — That sign. That awful sign! [*Going to window.*] Why Oscar insists upon putting it there — he is so uncommonly common.

SOPHIE: You know Mr. Van Striven ain't gonna have you taking that thing down.

DOLLY: [*Coming down center with sign* "ROOM FOR RENT".] I cannot have it up now. What will people say? [*Lays it on table near sofa.*] The Van Strivens' palatial residence is not a rooming house.

SOPHIE: Mr. Van Striven's more interested in getting it paid for than he is in getting it palatial. Besides four people don't need no fourteen rooms.

[*Door slams off stage.*]

DOLLY: Get my foot into your shoe — I mean get your foot into my shoe. Hurry!

SOPHIE: [*Rising slowly.*] They seen feet b'fore.

DOLLY: [*Threatening* SOPHIE.] One of these days —

[HENNYPEST *enters through hall door. He is a humble little fat man with a bald head. Somewhere between forty and fifty, he has traded his youth for wisdom — he has gained more than he has lost in the bargain. The apex of his stomach puffs out between a wrinkled vest and his baggy pants.*]

DOLLY: Good morning, Professor — always full of smiles.

HENNYPEST: Smiles — Madame — at home they say, I grin like a "Chessy" cat.

SOPHIE: [*Slyly.*] Well, Professor, down home we still grin, but up North we smile.

DOLLY: That will do, Sophie.

HENNYPEST: [*Folding his hands.*] You have one beautiful home, and a beautiful maid.

SOPHIE: [*Coquettishly.*] Aw, gone.

DOLLY: I say — you catch New York's flattering habit in your first three days. You're quite apt, Professor. How was your morning stroll?

HENNYPEST: I didn't stroll this morning — I was basking in the sunshine out in the backyard...

DOLLY: [*Correcting.*] You mean court!

HENNYPEST: Oh, yes, court. Someone across the way hung out a blanket and blocked out the sunshine.

DOLLY: : [*Abruptly.*] You mean in the next block?

HENNYPEST: Yes, madame.

DOLLY: [*With a feeling of difference.*] Those common nookies are such an envious bunch of hoodlums.

SOPHIE: [*Defensively.*] Hey, my brother lives in that block.

DOLLY: [*Gently.*] Oh, but your brother is different.

SOPHIE: He's an Elk.

DOLLY: I mean that crowd that curses from Monday to Friday, throws those noisy Saturday night gin parties, and cooks pig's feet all day Sunday.

HENNYPEST: You wouldn't happen to have any now, would you?

DOLLY: Heavens, no! Why Professor Hennypest, pig's feet come from the lowest part of the pig. People of class simply do not partake.

HENNYPEST: But, Madame, what I cast into my stomach has nothing to do with class distinction.

DOLLY: Appetites and attitudes will at times get confused. However, Oscar telephoned that you had breakfast at the Hotel Clarissa.

HENNYPEST: [*Sadly.*] Exactly three orders, Madame, and I regret to say that what you New Yorkers call a meal is a gross overstatement.

DOLLY: I am so sorry. Sophie, prepare a big breakfast for Professor Hennypest. A glass of orange juice — an egg and some toast.

SOPHIE: [*To* HENNYPEST.] Two eggs wouldn't kill you, would they?

HENNYPEST: Physically, Sophie, no. Socially, I hope not.

DOLLY: Good gracious, no! This isn't Sugar Hill. Why, fix him as many as — three eggs if you like.

[*The doorbell rings.*]

HENNYPEST: Thank you, madame.

DOLLY: Answer the door!

SOPHIE: [*At second ring,* SOPHIE *rises slowly.*] Take it easy, I'm coming!

DOLLY: Hurry!

HENNYPEST: I will answer it.

DOLLY: Of course not, Professor. Let her do something. [*Pauses — sees her feet.*] Look at her feet! [*Rises.*] Never mind, I will —

SOPHIE: [*Bangs into both from her tilted position.*] Will you make up your —

DOLLY: [*Screams.*] Ouch! Get off my foot! [*Crossing down right.*]

SOPHIE: [*Exiting right.*] This ain't no time for no visitors!

DOLLY: Such a maid.

SOPHIE: [*Off right as doorbell rings again.*] Keep down your dandruff!

TILLIE: [*Offstage.*] Please stay in your place! Such horrible manners!

[*Entering from right in a huff, stopping down center.* SOPHIE *enters, stops and leans nonchalantly against archway.* TILLIE, *dressed fashionably in mink stole and mink hat, is a high-powered fortyish, uppity "do wager" with an SS figure somewhat like a drunken dollar sign. She radiates a disarming superiority that is more calculated than real.*]

TILLIE: Dolly — that maid! Such impertinence. Such undiluted insolence.

DOLLY: What did you say to Mrs. Petunia?

SOPHIE: That her big, white Cadillac looks like a pregnant Frigidaire.

DOLLY: [*Bangs into* HENNYPEST, *both dashing to window right.*] New Cadillac. Tillie, it's magnificent. It must be twenty feet long.

TILLIE: Twenty–two.

SOPHIE: Honey, you could paste a vacancy sign on your bumper and rent that thing out as a floating motel.

TILLIE: And the sign on your bumper should read MAD, not MAID.

DOLLY: Take her stole, Sophie.

[TILLIE *sits upper end of sofa.*]

SOPHIE: [*Takes stole.*] I wonder how many animals would be wearing their own furs this season if it wasn't for the installment... plan?

DOLLY: Suppose you let the skunks do their own worrying and bring tea for us.

[SOPHIE *flings stole on foyer table, exits left after a mean look at* TILLIE.)

TILLIE: Did you say she was from Newark or Noah's Ark?

DOLLY: [*Sitting opposite* TILLIE.] Mrs. Petunia, I want you to meet Professor Hennypest.

HENNYPEST: How are you, Mrs. Petunia?

TILLIE: [*Sizes him up.*] You're not one of these root doctors or numerologists?

DOLLY: Don't mind her, Professor. [*To* TILLIE.] He occupies the Chair of Zoology at Tuskeegee University...

TILLIE: [*Aside.*] No doubt, uncomfortably. [*Direct.*] How nice. I wonder if you get as tired of meeting trash as I do. I cannot risk introductions anywhere in Harlem. You never know whether you're meeting a deacon or a devil. Dolly's house is different, thank God.

HENNYPEST: And she is a most congenial hostess.

TILLIE: Have you been here long?

HENNYPEST: No Madame — just for the annual meeting of the American Zoological Society, at the Bronx Zoo.

DOLLY: My house guest for three days.

TILLIE: House guests are like fish.

HENNYPEST: Fish?

TILLIE: They smell after three days. But, of course, Professor Hennypest, you are a celebrity.

HENNYPEST: No, Madame, Baptist.

TILLIE: What — oh yes, related to the Kings County Hennypests?

HENNYPEST: No, Madame.

TILLIE: The North Jersey Hennypests?

HENNYPEST: No, Madame.

TILLIE: Certainly the Philadelphia, everybody is related to them.

HENNYPEST: Sorry, Madame. I am not.

TILLIE: Surely you have some relations. They are a bore, but they do give you a sort of family tree, if you get what I mean.

HENNYPEST: I guess mine was chopped down. That makes me something of a stump.

TILLIE: How *very* true. Those things do happen.

DOLLY: You are matched against a man with two Ph.D.'s, Tillie.

TILLIE: Where'd he steal them?

DOLLY: Northwestern and University of Pennsylvania. He's a little short on front —

TILLIE: I'd say he has a lot of front.

DOLLY: Don't let her frighten you, Professor.

HENNYPEST: Saepe satins fuit dissimulare quam ulicisci. [TILLIE *gawks, he translates.*] It is better not to see an insult than avenge it. [*Exiting.*]

TILLIE: Leaving?

HENNYPEST: Immediately after breakfast. I'm going up to the Bronx Zoo.

TILLIE: Visiting relatives?

HENNYPEST: No, Madame, animals.

TILLIE: Homo sapiens and animals are both living beings. [*Smiling triumphantly.*]

HENNYPEST: Then I *am* visiting relatives — our relatives. [*Pauses, then exiting.*] I suppose I'll see you at the party.

TILLIE: *Me??* I never visit zoos.

DOLLY: He means Cobina's party tonight.

TILLIE: [*To* HENNYPEST *with disbelief.*] *You'll* be at the party?

HENNYPEST: Yes, Madame, do save a dance for me.

TILLIE: I'm not good at dancing.

HENNYPEST: You'll be good with me. Just hold tight and let me lead.

TILLIE: Hold tight? I'm allergic to bay windows.

HENNYPEST: Then we'll just hold hands.

TILLIE: Holding hands with strange men makes me nervous.

HENNYPEST: I'll have my tranquilizer.

TILLIE: I have an aversion to tranquilizers.

HENNYPEST: How do you relax, Madame?

TILLIE: [*Conclusively.*] Through meditation; very private and personal! Any companionship there would provoke a saint!

HENNYPEST: [*Crossing to foyer, pauses.*] Amen, Madame. Perhaps at benediction you'll join me in prayer. [*Stumbles, smiles apologetically, turns up his nose and exits left.*]

DOLLY: I find him so amusing.

TILLIE: [*Somewhat miffed.*] More of a peasant than a professor. Unbutton his vest and the whole man will tumble out.

DOLLY: Well, he is a heavy eater—

TILLIE: And a heavyweight nuisance!

SOPHIE: [*Entering with tea on tray, tarries on stairs.*] Come and get it.

DOLLY: Right here, dear.

SOPHIE: Lord, today!

[*She reluctantly places the tray on the coffee table, then pours a cup. As* TILLIE *reaches for the cup, thinking it is for her,* SOPHIE *gobbles down a drink and exits nonchalantly as the two ladies sit dumbfounded.*]

TILLIE: Well—I never!

DOLLY: [*Readying tea.*] That girl! That girl! She's like driving a car. When I see the red in her eyes, I jam on the brakes.

TILLIE: As long as there's one ounce of vitamin "I" in your face, they will insult us.

DOLLY: Vitamin I?

TILLIE: Ink, Dolly, ink. [*Touching her face—colorwise.*]

DOLLY: Tillie, you are a scream. [*Serving tea, airishly.*]

TILLIE: By the way, Dolly. Why don't you move out to Brooklyn? Harlem has gotten to be such a cesspool of nobodies. [*Sipping, equally airishly.*]

DOLLY: Oh, I'm holding my ground on Strivers Row.

TILLIE: Why the hoi polloi has invaded and ruined Harlem.

DOLLY: [*Defensively.*] True, we all live in the same area, but we don't travel in the same circle.

TILLIE: You may, but what about Cobina?

DOLLY: My daughter never associates with anyone without my approval. [*Both sipping a la grande dames.*]

TILLIE: Then what was she doing at the benefit party at the Savoy Ballroom last week — slumming?

DOLLY: I tell you, we did not participate. I purchased tickets, but when 1 found out the affair was unrestricted, I gave my tickets to the grocery boy.

TILLIE: I could have sworn I saw that child with some moonfaced boy — looking as brown and broke as Haile Selassie.

DOLLY: And what were *you* doing there?

TILLIE: Only to cover the event for my newspaper. My social reporter was ill because she didn't want to become a mother. But her ordeal was nothing compared to those nobodies. That awful Dr. Davis swung me around doing the Atomic Flop. [*Dramatizes Atomic Flop.*]

DOLLY: Oh — you're too rigid.

TILLIE: Will he be here tonight?

DOLLY: Of course, he and his wife.

TILLIE: I'll join you for a headache when they arrive.

DOLLY: Listen, I'm having a debutante party — not a jamboree.

TILLIE: If it's all you say it will be, then I'll carry it in the front page of the *Black Dispatch* next week.

DOLLY: [*Annoyed.*] Which will be far better than this week's headline — "Three in Bed Causes Divorce."

TILLIE: People like dirt — and I believe in digging deep into it for them.

DOLLY: You should elevate their readership.

TILLIE: What else is there to print besides news about these charitable affairs! If someone is born, marries, or dies, he's given a benefit. Only other event is news about the antics of these dizzy debs.

DOLLY: Charity is for the devil's poor. Society is for God's chosen few. Debs do silly things, mixing society and charity. But they aren't half as bad as these roue widows clinging to these chippy boys.

TILLIE: [*Strangling.*] Er — er — well a modern woman must have an escort.

DOLLY: Be thankful that you still have your reputation.

TILLIE: Reputation is only what your worst enemy thinks!

[*The doorbell rings.* DOLLY *rises.*]

DOLLY: True — true — [*Calling.*] Sophie — Sophie — the door — Sophie... [*She hides her limp as she walks towards the hall door.*]

TILLIE: Down there drunk, I bet.

SOPHIE: [*Passing down the hall.*] I ain't gonna have that. [*Going towards arch door.*] I'm comin! Keep your boots laced. [*The bell rings again.*]

DOLLY: Hurry — hurry.

SOPHIE: [*Exits.*] Plague take it!

DOLLY: Hurry–hurry.

TILLIE: [*Having peeped at the pad.*] I see you've invited old Tyler Beecher, the old robust beer barrel. He squeezes so hard, it causes my stockings to run.

DOLLY: But he's gentle and nice.

TILLIE: The man isn't wood!

DOLLY: All men like to go on a little spree. But they always come back.

TILLIE: Yes, slightly soiled.

SOPHIE: [*In the door.*] A boy is heah — wanna know if you got any work he kin do.

TILLIE: [*Incredulously.*] A boy looking for work!!

DOLLY: No snow outside. The windows are cleaned. No. I guess not dear. [*Trying to think of something.*]

SOPHIE: He's a nice boy.

DOLLY: Tell him Father Divine has a Sunday School in the next block.

SOPHIE: The back parlor needs waxing.

DOLLY: Haven't you done that yet?

SOPHIE: I ain't getting down on these knees. He tole me not to git no cones on 'em.

DOLLY: All right, show him down to the kitchen —

SOPHIE: Now you talking — come on, Sonny.

TILLIE: [*Informatively.*] Dolly — is he trustworthy?

DOLLY: [*Excitedly.*] Sophie —

SOPHIE: I know — come, Sonny.

> [CHUCK *enters through arch door. A bashful boy about twenty, he walks in timidly. He fingers a crushed hat in his hands. His clothes are aged but clean.* TILLIE's *haughty manner frightens him. He steps behind the sofa.*]

SOPHIE: Meet the *dark* Daughters of the American Revolution.

DOLLY: Sophie!

CHUCK: [*Anxiously.*] I'll do anything, Miss. Fire the furnace —

DOLLY: Have you any reference?

CHUCK: Yessum! U.S. Government Conservation Agency, stocking ponds with baby fish.

TILLIE: A fish planter!

CHUCK: Then I went into the army —

DOLLY: [*To* CHUCK.] Oh a war veteran — a real hero. [*To* TILLIE.]

CHUCK: Not exactly. I was stationed on Marshall Island where the biggest battle I had was with the gallinippers.

TILLIE: I suppose you slew them.

CHUCK: Yessum — by the hundreds.

DOLLY: [*Seriously.*] Oh you are a real hero, killing hundreds of galli-nippers.

TILLIE: Ts–sk! Yes, with a spray.

DOLLY: I guess he'll do, Tillie.

SOPHIE: [*To* DOLLY.] After all who's paying him — if he gets paid.

CHUCK: I'll work for whatever you're willing to pay.

TILLIE: Unbelievably generous! Was Bellevue one pond where you planted fish?

CHUCK: Ma'am?

SOPHIE: Somebody got to wax the floors.

DOLLY: Yes — yes — [*To* CHUCK.] Do a good job now.

CHUCK: Yessum. I sure will. Thank you, ma'am.

SOPHIE: Pick up your cross and follow me.

[SOPHIE *and* CHUCK *exit through hall door.*]

DOLLY: He is safe, I hope.

TILLIE: Looked pretty anxious to get in.

DOLLY: But his face, did you notice that round and handsome face?

TILLIE: Humph! Plain as the Ethiopian moon! Where is Rowena? She said she would be here in ten minutes. [*Rising — observing her wrist watch.*] I must go.

DOLLY: [*Moving tray to table near steps.*] Now you have plenty of time — no need to whiz off.

TILLIE: I have a meeting at the YWCA. The Ad Hoc Committee for Retarded Prostitutes is meeting. First, I must pick up Rowena.

DOLLY: Where did Rowena stop?

TILLIE: At Brenda's. Just had to chat with her. Brenda married, Ben, you know.

DOLLY: [*Surprised.*] No — clever girl indeed.

TILLIE: In spite of those knock–knees, too. She snatched him right out from under Cobina, eh?

DOLLY: [*Indifferently.*] Who cares? He's too old for her anyway.

TILLIE: [*In finally, close to* DOLLY.] Will you tell me just whom are you landing for Cobina?

DOLLY: [*Laughing.*] I knew time you popped in here, that's what you were after. [TILLIE *sitting next to her.*] Well, there's Charlie —

TILLIE: [*Scoffing.*] Some deb is always on his lap.

DOLLY: Yes, but not on his mind. Then there's Roy Tomkinson.

TILLIE: [*Derisively.*] The C.P.A! He's a constant pain in the tootsie.

DOLLY: Mother doesn't like him anyway. There's Ed —

TILLIE: Judge Tucker's son?

DOLLY: [*Brightening.*] Yes — now, he —

TILLIE: But I thought — that is — oh, he is real quality.

DOLLY: Then there is —

TILLIE: Judge Tucker said —

DOLLY: What?

TILLIE: Well — I heard that Ed is out for someone else.

DOLLY: That's ridiculous. He's been here every night during Cobina's vacation from school.

TILLIE: Every night?

DOLLY: At least every other night. Harlem sees him plenty.

TILLIE: No doubt slumming! Brooklyn girls are his favorites!

DOLLY: [*Mounting indignation.*] I bet you right now, he is down there in Central Park, horseback riding with Cobina.

TILLIE: He takes Rowena to the formal dances.

DOLLY: Is that so? He never mentions her. He avoids her —

TILLIE: Only occasionally because of her bright mind.

DOLLY: [*Rising.*] Bright? That's an inflated statement! [*Walking toward the window.*]

TILLIE: Cobina is cute as a button, but Ed doesn't like buttons.

DOLLY: [*Turning.*] You'll need more than that *Black Dispatch* to make him your nephew!

TILLIE: I didn't say that. My niece will choose whom she pleases —

DOLLY: You said enough! [*Coming downstage center, thundering as* TILLIE *backs away.*] You've been running all up and down Strivers Row trying to find out who —

[COBINA *comes stamping into the room through the arch door. She is followed by* MRS. PACE *and* OSCAR VAN STRIVEN. OSCAR *stops confused at the door.* MRS. PACE *follows* COBINA *to the upper end of the sofa.* COBINA *is eighteen, wears riding habit. She is bubbling over with rage. Crossing* DOLLY *without saying a word, she stops next to the chair extreme left and flings her coat in it.*]

COBINA: Oh, let me alone!

DOLLY: [*Going to* COBINA.] Have you no manners?

COBINA: [*Boisterously.*] I checked them in the hall!

[MRS. PACE, *a very cold and stately woman of sixty, stares at* COBINA. *She is extremely correct in her costume. Her mixed gray hair gives her an air of distinction. She wears a tailored winter suit with a cape. Her mouth is a thin line of depression. The little furrow in her forehead, her black eyes piercing from underneath her brows, one usually cocked, have a disarming effect. People say her eyebrows are optical wings of social deportment.*]

MRS. PACE: Stop wobbling! Stop swagging like a bag of wet dough. The idea! [*To* TILLIE.] Hello, Petunia!

[OSCAR *is a businesslike man about forty–five years of age. Though he speaks with absolute sincerity, his mind seems to be somewhere else. Acknowledges* TILLIE's *presence by nodding.*]

OSCAR: She was slouching against a lamp post on the corner of 133rd Street and Lenox Avenue!

TILLIE: What kind of horse riding is that? [*Slyly.*] Do — tell — I never!

DOLLY: Cobina, what about the horse you phoned for?

MRS. PACE: [*Walks down left.*] The horse didn't answer the phone!

OSCAR: [*To* COBINA.] I have asked you to explain.

COBINA: [*Turning in wrath.*] Let me alone!

MRS. PACE: [*Fiercely.*] Waiting for someone on that corner.

OSCAR: A pack of noisy brats, winking at you.

COBINA: They were playground kids.

MRS. PACE: What time was the strip tease to begin?

OSCAR: [*Moves left to* COBINA.] I won't have it. You know I won't. I will pack you up and drive you back to Radcliffe, before you can bat your eye. Whom were you waiting for, I ask you?

MRS. PACE: In Washington, you would be positively disgraced.

TILLIE: [*Chirping.*] And in Brook —

MRS. PACE: Yes, Brooklyn. I know, Tillie. What are you doing here, digging up dirt before the party begins?

TILLIE: Why, Mrs. Pace.

DOLLY: [*To* COBINA.] If it weren't for your party tonight, I would —

COBINA: I told you I didn't want any party.

MRS. PACE: Stop twisting! All my efforts wasted. When will you learn poise?

COBINA: I don't give a hoot about phonies and stuffed shirts —

DOLLY: [*Shakes pad in* COBINA's *face.*] Don't speak like that about my guests, child.

COBINA: I'm not a child. I'm now eighteen.

DOLLY: Well, ex–child. Only my funeral could stop this party.

COBINA: Is it my party or your coronation? [*Waving.*]

MRS. PACE: Keep your hands still. I ought to have you in Washington.

OSCAR: We're going to settle this thing...

COBINA: [*Verging on tears.*] Daddy —

MRS. PACE: Stop taxing your face! You'll look like a hag tonight.

COBINA: [*Plaintively.*] I am unhappy. I rather spend my birthday in bed. Who needs to be stuck in a receiving line to meet a bunch of phony bolonies. Society, my foot! They've all just escaped from poverty and spend their time gossiping against being overtaken. I didn't ask to be born into society. I didn't even ask to be born!

OSCAR: [*Disgustedly.*] Radcliffe!

MRS. PACE: I told you to send her to me in Washington. Why, there —

TILLIE: [*Beaming.*] This is Harlem, Mrs. Pace.

MRS. PACE: I can smell it.

TILLIE: You can't raise a rose in a junkyard.

MRS. PACE: Is the fertilizer of Brooklyn any different?

COBINA: [*Crossing to* OSCAR.] Dad, please cancel it. You know you don't care for all this social nonsense.

OSCAR: Go to your room at once!

[COBINA *exits center a la waddling duck.*]

MRS. PACE: Stop walking like a duck! I shall put a prop behind you tonight. [*Following the exiting* COBINA]. Don't bend your knees. [*Offstage.*] Curve them in line with your body. You ought to stay off horses. Let go that balustrade! [*Offstage, a tumbling noise.*] Look out!

DOLLY: [*Exiting, followed by* OSCAR.] Oh!

COBINA: [*Offstage.*] Make her stop shouting at me!

[TILLIE *grabs pad from table, studies it religiously.*]

MRS. PACE: [*Offstage.*] Please! Please!

COBINA: [*Offstage.*] No, I'm not hurt!

DOLLY: [*Offstage.*] Thank God, she isn't hurt.

MRS. PACE: [*Offstage*] She fell with the grace of a feeble cow.

TILLIE: [*Has returned pad to table as* DOLLY *returns.*] Dear Mrs. Pace, so completely put out. [TILLIE *is leaving, but hesitates.*]

DOLLY: [*Reassuringly.*] Mother will make a lady out of her yet.

TILLIE: Perhaps through hypnosis.

DOLLY: [*Arms.* TILLIE, *nudging her exit.*] You aren't going?

TILLIE: Yes, dear, I must. And have I got a story! Tell Rowena to meet me at the YWCA. The meeting has certainly started —

OSCAR: [*Entering.*] Mrs. Petunia, wait a minute, please.

TILLIE: [*Led forward by* OSCAR.] Of course, Oscar.

DOLLY: [*Skeptically, moving up.*] What is it, Oscar?

OSCAR: [*Heavily.*] Something I must tell you. I know you will need Mrs. Petunia's advice.

DOLLY: [*Crossing, turning* TILLIE *to leave.*] Tillie has an engagement, Oscar.

TILLIE: [*Unyieldingly.*] Oh, but Dolly — Oscar looks so grave.

DOLLY: [*Softly.*] That's what I'm afraid of. What is it, Oscar?

OSCAR: You know those lots, the Jamaica lots?

DOLLY: Do I — with them on our hands for five years?

TILLIE: Your property near the city dump?

OSCAR: [*Smiling.*] Yes — that is — yes.

DOLLY: What about it?

OSCAR: I have a buyer for them.

DOLLY: [*A smile brightens her face.*] You don't say. Oscar, I —

TILLIE: [*Carelessly, disappointed.*] Do tell!

DOLLY: [*Happily.*] I told you all we had to do was wait. It is a miracle. [*Talking to* TILLIE.]

OSCAR: A lady is going to build a twelve–room house and develop a lawn, tennis courts and swimming pool —

TILLIE: [*Eagerly.*] This is news, who?

OSCAR: Miss Ruby Jackson.

TILLIE: [*Searchingly.*] Jackson . . . Jackson? Not the insurance Jacksons? They went into bankruptcy after paying me my husband's premiums on his life insurance policy.

OSCAR: This Jackson only came into money recently and —

DOLLY: Recently, of course, then we wouldn't know her.

TILLIE: Jackson — Jackson — wait, you mean the maid or the cook who won a large sum of money from the sweepstakes?

OSCAR: That's her.

DOLLY: Why Oscar, that's nothing to be so tragic about. I think she is very wise. What a break for us!

TILLIE: You hardly need my advice on that.

OSCAR: Oh! I do — there is something else.

DOLLY: [*Lightly.*] Now what could it be?

OSCAR: Sure you won't get angry?

DOLLY: Oscar, just like a child. No dear.

OSCAR: [*Mildly.*] She wants to meet society.

TILLIE: [*Sitting.*] That's nothing. Tell her to join the Elks.

OSCAR: I mean the razzle dazzle set.

DOLLY: [*Suspiciously.*] So?

OSCAR: [*In a humble manner.*] I invited her — to Cobina's debut.

DOLLY: [*Swooning against the sofa, she is caught by* OSCAR.] W–w–w–what!

TILLIE: [*Jumps up and runs to her.*] Don't let her fall! Dolly, if you faint, I'll join you. [*They get her on the sofa.*] You what?

DOLLY: Are you crazy? What do you mean to make me, the laughing stock of the season? My daughter's debut — a sideshow for some ambitious scrub woman. Her eyes flaming with social suds!

OSCAR: But, Dolly, just this once — I *must* I tell you. The woman is a first–class cook for a Forest Hills family. Her pies have won prizes —

DOLLY: A plain, common, shabby cook. How could you? That woman will not enter this house. I will not have her. Self–rising flour has inflated her brain. The woman is sick. Have her here! No! Most emphatically, NO! [*Pounds the sofa three beats.*]

OSCAR: [*Pleadingly.*] It is business. She told me she only wants to get an introduction. She knows you can do it for her. She has read about you. That is all I need to clinch the deal. It won't hurt. You will introduce her, and then it will all be over.

DOLLY: What am I, the promoter for some social striver? Tillie, tell him how silly it would be. Oh, for Pete's sake, I'm sick of this. [*Stretching out on sofa.*]

TILLIE: [*Unimpressively.*] Now, Mr. Van Striven, there must be some other way.

DOLLY: What will people say? The Smiths — the Davies — the Judge and — [*Rising quickly.*]

TILLIE: [*Clicking.*] What will people say — er — er — [*Exiting.*] Dolly, I must be going. I must.

DOLLY: I am afraid. I have planned — planned — and planned. [*Thinking.*]

OSCAR: [*Coming down to sofa.*] Miss Jackson cannot do that much harm in one night.

DOLLY: That's out. No sir! One moment of unwise benevolence can tear down a lifetime of prominence. You would dare mention this right to Tillie Petunia. That heckler, always trying to outshine me.

OSCAR: I figured both of you would agree. Who could think of laughing with you and Tillie backing up Miss Jackson.

DOLLY: [*Resentfully crossing.*] Tillie! Who do you think is the leading socialite in this neck of the woods? I need no one to help me say No! No! No! [*Punctuates* "NO" *by tapping his chest.*]

OSCAR: I have invited her. She may bring a friend. I don't know what I can tell her now.

DOLLY: Tell her it is off. Tell her *anything*. She cannot come here. That's that!

OSCAR: [*Angered.*] I will not.

DOLLY: [*Stunned.*] Oscar!

OSCAR: I was hoping I wouldn't have to tell you this. But if that deal doesn't go through, if I don't sell Miss Jackson those lots, we will lose this house.

DOLLY: [*Irritated.*] Now that wasn't very bright.

OSCAR: Doubt it, huh? Well, notes on the mortgage have been mounting. They have not been paid for months. Slipping because I have not had the money.

DOLLY: [*Casually.*] You have the money. You should have paid them. You keep reinvesting the profits.

OSCAR: You guzzle the bulk of every dollar I make.

DOLLY: Me?

OSCAR: Yes you! Who must keep up with Tillie and the rest of those greenback burners. From one resort to another, Atlantic City,

Saratoga, Martha's Vineyard, a roving band of gypsies cannot keep pace with you. Clothes, clothes, enough to supply the Ethiopian Army. Money, more money! Radcliffe itself, costing me a Scotch fortune! Where do you think it is coming from? I ain't Father Divine!

DOLLY: [*To* OSCAR.] You are exaggerating. [*Quickly.*]

OSCAR: I most certainly am. This party, almost two thousand dollars. More gowns, band — liquor for a bunch of beer drinkers. I got to pay for it. All this for you. Yet you accuse me of throwing — [*Spots the vacancy sign — blasting.*] and that sign! [DOLLY *jumps.*] I told you to keep that sign in the window. How can I rent those rooms upstairs. I have to have some money. I told you. What do you reserve them for — guests? Guests who don't pay. [DOLLY *moves toward the sofa.*] I'll show you, I will put a turnstile to the third floor, and your guests will have to drop a silver dollar in it before they go up there and pile on one of those idle beds.

DOLLY: Oscar, my friends!

OSCAR: [*His voice rises, forcefully.*] Shut up! Your vanity has run me into a hold. Your vanity is going to pull me out or it'll crack like the walls of Jericho. [MRS. PACE *enters from hall. She stares at* OSCAR *like he is a raging maniac.*] You shall pave the way for Miss Jackson or move into the Harlem River Flats — and like it — the F.H.A. is doing all the real estate business, anyway.

MRS. PACE: [*Hurting.*] What in the devil is this? [OSCAR *stares at her disgustedly.*]

DOLLY: [*Goes pleading to* MRS. PACE. *Who is now in front of the sofa.* OSCAR *moves over to the vase of flowers.*] Mother — Oscar invited a cook to the party. [*Childlike.*]

MRS. PACE: [*Adroitly.*] The caterer has already —

SOPHIE: [*Enters through arch door.*] I need some more money for — [*Freezes. Then edges to the right as* OSCAR *gives her a mean look.*]

DOLLY: [*Helplessly.*] Not to cook, but as a guest. He says it is business.

[SOPHIE, *feeling the tension. works her way around to the chair facing the sofa.*]

MRS. PACE: [*Her lips tighten. Her brow cocks. The words flow fast and tingling.*] Business! The mantle with which a man can cover his vices as well as his virtues. Business. A concealing, conniving word!

DOLLY: I will have to accept her. [*Tearfully.*]

MRS. PACE: Some silly, stupid striver!

MRS. PACE: [*Tilting her chin.*] Pray if you know how. [*Turning.*] Sophie, pack my bag! I am going to Washington!

[DOLLY *opens her mouth to speak.* SOPHIE *looks puzzled.* MRS. PACE *stands rigid and firm.* OSCAR *blasts.*]

OSCAR: Sit down!

MRS. PACE: [*Stepping up to* OSCAR.] To whom are you talking?

OSCAR: Sit down!!

[*As if he had jerked a string that held them up,* MRS. PACE *and* DOLLY *flop on the sofa.* SOPHIE *flops in the chair.* OSCAR *towers over them. They sit frightened, stiff as dummies.*]

[*Curtain.*]

SCENE 2

It is evening. The reception room is warm and cozy. The soft lights and vases of cut flowers in abundance add luster to the room. Soft music from an orchestra in the back parlor trails in. At the rise of the curtain, SOPHIE, *in a more frilly cap and apron, moves about adding another flower from her arm to the several vases, counting each placement.*

SOPHIE: One hundred and seventeen, one hundred and eighteen, one —

CHUCK: [*Appearing from left foyer, wearing a short white waiter's jacket armed with flowers and a covered bird cage.*] Sophie, who is Fred?

SOPHIE: What's that?

CHUCK: Over and over, this parrot's been saying, "Hey, Fred, drop dead."

SOPHIE: [*Continuing her placements.*] You do look a lot like Fred, but you don't have his dull disposition.

CHUCK: [*Leaving cage. He crosses and bows.*] Thank you, your Grace.

SOPHIE: [*Twirls around, freezes into a pose and curtsies.*] You are welcome, Sir Chuck.

CHUCK: See you later. [*Exiting, resuming the cage.*]

SOPHIE: Where are you going?

CHUCK: [*Stalling.*] To the garbage can.

SOPHIE: Getting into the trash can is your affair, but the flowers?

CHUCK: Mrs. Van Striven ordered me to remove them from the den and discard them.

SOPHIE: [*Stopping her chores.*] Wait a minute! No complaint's been filed with me. [*Crosses, inspecting* CHUCK's *flowers.*]

CHUCK: I must get fresh ones from the florist. I have to hurry before it closes.

SOPHIE: I see nothing wrong with these flowers.

CHUCK: The rejection comes not from sight, but from smell.

SOPHIE: [*After a whiff.*] They do have the strangest stink!

CHUCK: The parrot vomited on them.

SOPHIE: [*Lifting the cage cover.*] Why, you featherfaced bonehead!

CHUCK: She's asleep. According to Mrs. Van Striven, she'll sleep as long as her cage is covered.

SOPHIE: Asleep, my foot! She's drunk!

PARROT: [*Well, her voice, anyway.*] Hey, Fred, drop dead! QQQUUU-UAAAARRRRKKKK!

CHUCK: She's had much more than a swig of whiskey.

SOPHIE: Not whiskey! I gave her *gin*.

CHUCK: Why?

SOPHIE: She hates flowers! Whenever flowers, get more attention than her, she squawks, scratches and bites them. Gin usually calms her down. This time — with such a flower overload — instead of protesting, she just puked!

CHUCK: For the duration of the party, she is now confined to the cellar.

SOPHIE: That's too doggone much. Covering her cage is enough. Place her in my room.

CHUCK: Won't Mrs. Van Striven —

SOPHIE: In *my* room! I got the only pad in the house that's without two or three dozen roses making faces at you.

CHUCK: As you say, Madame. [*Leaving.*]

SOPHIE: And don't go buy no more flowers. We can't afford them. [CHUCK *stops.*] LORD! You should have heard Papa Van Striven this morning, blasting the budget.

CHUCK: I heard him.

SOPHIE: [*Suspiciously.*] Nothing seems to get past you. What is your story anyway?

CHUCK: [*Impulsively drops the cage.*] Can I trust you?

PARROT: [*Reacting to the drop, loudly.*] HEY, FRED, DROP DEAD! HEY, FRED, DROP DEAD!!!

SOPHIE: [*Topping him.*] Get him out of here before he wakes up the dead! [*The* PARROT *continues as* CHUCK *grabs the cage and exits foyer left as the* PARROT'S *voice trails off.*] A bird in hand is worth two in the bush. A parrot in your fist, twist and don't miss. [*Resumes placing cut flowers, pauses, trying to recall her count.*] One hundred and — one hundred and — oh, what the hell! [*Jams the remaining flowers into a vase already loaded.*] Two hundred!

HENNYPEST: [*Appears in foyer, from left, dressed in a tuxedo and focusing his camera on* SOPHIE.] Focus, please.

SOPHIE: [*With a rose, she strikes a Statue of Liberty pose.*] Cheeze. [*He snaps.*] You should be sick of taking my picture by now.

HENNYPEST: I photograph my wife every day —

SOPHIE: [*This is old hat.*] "You remind me of her."

HENNYPEST: You'll even perform like her if you'll assist me. My cummerbund is shrinking.

SOPHIE: [*Missing it.*] Your —

HENNYPEST: [*From pocket, he reveals his cummerbund.*] Here, Sophie —

SOPHIE: Oh — your vest! Looking like your wife and acting in her place is two — [*She gets it on him but not with ease.*] Different things!

HENNYPEST: [*Innocently.*] Why, Sophie —

OSCAR: [*Offstage.*] Forward, MARCH! One, two, three, four — [*In a single-file line, the family marches in, led by* COBINA. *They stop center awaiting orders from the commanding* OSCAR.] One, two, three, HALT! It may not be the grand march of the ball, but it will do. Take your positions. At ease!

[*Yes,* HENNYPEST *snaps the family, gestures approvingly and exits right. They form a receiving line at a right angle to the arch doorway so that* OSCAR *will be the first to greet the guests,* DOLLY *second, and* COBINA *third.* MRS. PACE *is opposite of them, sustaining a detachment. They are most properly dressed in evening clothes and jewelry.* COBINA *wears the traditional deb white and holds a bouquet of flowers in her hands.* DOLLY, *her feet hurting and no guests having arrived, poses uncomfortably.* OSCAR *and* MRS. PACE *exchange angry glances.* SOPHIE *gives a last–minute touch to the flowers.*]

DOLLY: If I ever get out of this alive, I shall never stop thanking God.

MRS. PACE: Nobody ever gives God a thought except for about a half–hour on Sundays and fifteen minutes prior to their demise.

OSCAR: It is nine–fifteen. Where are the people?

MRS. PACE: If anybody shows up besides this Miss Jackson, we're lucky.

[*The music grows softer.*]

DOLLY: I wish I could be calm. Mother, if you just hadn't insisted on this debut.

MRS. PACE: You should have been calm when you married that. Matchmaking is as old as the hills. My mother's husband was picked. Mine was picked. You became restless and picked that thing out of the wood pile!

OSCAR: There is nothing wrong with my family.

MRS. PACE: Just the one idiot on your father's side. [DOLLY *goes to the window.*]

COBINA: Stop worrying, Mother.

MRS. PACE: [*Crossing correcting bouquet.*] Cobina, hold that bouquet exactly sixteen inches below the chin. NOW KEEP IT THERE. [*Returning to her post.*]

SOPHIE: [*Swaying with sudden inspiration.*] Joe brought me some flowers once.

COBINA: Were they orchids?

SOPHIE: Naw — honeysuckles.

MRS. PACE: This is no time to discuss flowers with servants!

SOPHIE: Did anybody ever bring you any flowers?

MRS. PACE: Be quiet! I was showered with flowers.

SOPHIE: What, poison ivy?

COBINA: [*Seeing* CHUCK *was in the hall.*] Chu — Chu —

MRS. PACE: What's wrong with you, Cobina? It's only the boy hired to serve.

COBINA: [*Sneezing, faking.*] Awchu — awchu — was just sneezing.

DOLLY: [*Returning from the window.*] Not a single car out there. The Van Strivens entertaining and not a block of cars.

MRS. PACE: Cobina, stop twisting your neck! You are not a turtle! What are *you* limping for?

DOLLY: I'm walking all right.

MRS. PACE: You ever see a three–legged bear in a swamp?

DOLLY: My foot hurts.

MRS. PACE: Wait until the misery climbs up. You will have plenty time to complain then. [*The doorbell rings.*] Someone's coming!

DOLLY: [*Rushes up to the window.*] I bet it's a Packard. No, it's just a cut–rate cab.

[SOPHIE *goes through arch door.*]

MRS. PACE: In line, Dolly.

OSCAR: [*To* MRS. PACE.] Will you relax?

MRS. PACE: [*Whispering quickly.*] Remember Cobina, shoulders kept straight with all movements from the waist down. Swaying the hips is not permissible. So don't jiggle them like your mother. [*The* VAN STRIVENS *are ready.*]

LILY: [*Offstage.*] My dear Sophie, am I late?

SOPHIE: Naw, chile, you is first. I was gitting scared nobody was coming.

LILY: [*Sweeps into the room like a breeze. She is somewhere between twenty and thirty, exotic and glamorous in a sort of theatrical way with hair in an up-sweep. She speaks in a deep–throated voice, soft and warm.*] Cobina! My child, how perfectly sweet!

[COBINA *smiles and curtsies in her best manner.* LILY *kisses* COBINA. SO-PHIE *waits at the door.* OSCAR *bows.*]

LILY: Mr. and Mrs. Van Striven, how do you do? [*Tapping the* VAN STRIVENS' *palms lightly.*]

DOLLY: [*Raising her elbows.*] Hello, Lily—we are glad you came.

OSCAR: Indeed we are. Miss Livingston—you are more pretty than ever.

LILY: Regardless how bad we women may look in the morning, Oscar, we never wake up needing a shave. [OSCAR *laughs.*]

MRS. PACE: Hello, Lily.

LILY: [*Swaying from* DOLLY *across the floor.*] Mrs. Pace, how charming. Everything is so exquisite. Cobina, just like a bride. Aren't you happy?

MRS. PACE: [*Batting her eyes rapidly.*] Indeed, Lily — and you are on time as usual.

LILY: [*She holds a pose, exactly like a dancer from the court of King Tut.*] How could I ever miss this party! Late, no such word in the theater. Punctuality, darling, punctuality! [SOPHIE *has moved in.* LILY *locks her fingers underneath her chin and sways about the room.*] What a paradise! Mrs. Pace, the most charming flower in this whole Garden of Eden.

MRS. PACE: Oh — Lily, a Harlem garden, but a garden just the same.

LILY: Exactly like the last scene in "Gal of Charleston" — the ideal home, the perfect family, and the maid —

DOLLY: Now, Lily, you will spoil Sophie. Take her wrap, Sophie.

SOPHIE: If she ever stops fluttering like a butterfly.

LILY: My wrap — eh — yes, take it, Sophie. [LILY'*s gown is a low–back affair with two panels attached to her shoulders. They beat and fan the air.*]

SOPHIE: What a pretty frock! Where'd you git it?

LILY: Fifth Avenue.

SOPHIE: Ain't it gorgeous? Mine is like that.

DOLLY: Sophie —

LILY: Have no fear. I know Sophie. It comes from Lord and Taylor's.

SOPHIE: Mine came from Lord and Numbers.

LILY: Really? [DOLLY *nudges* SOPHIE.]

SOPHIE: I prayed to the Lord that night before I got it. He gimmie the figuh in my dream. Next day I went right down an bought that frock and —

DOLLY: [*Shoving* SOPHIE.] I know you want to powder up a bit, Lily. What would a party be without you?

LILY: [*Exiting with* DOLLY.] Me miss this! Not for the world — Dolly, you are limping!

DOLLY: [*Bracing.*] Rheumatism, darling — [*Exits with* LILY *via arch.*]

SOPHIE: [*Examining the wrap.*] Ain't this elegant?

MRS. PACE: [*Harshly.*] You get out of here!

SOPHIE: Lay it on me, Mr. Striven. Lay it on me!

OSCAR: If you persist in addressing the guests, I'll deduct a fine from your salary.

SOPHIE: [*Sincerely.*] My dough? I'm leaving.

MRS. PACE: Get down in the kitchen with the skillets where you belong! Such decorum for a maid. Why, in Washington —

OSCAR: Never mind, Mother.

MRS. PACE: Why don't you make that maid stay in her place? You addressed like that — get below!

OSCAR: Take the wrap to the ladies lounge, Sophie. And you had better stay down on the floor below.

SOPHIE: [*Going toward the arch door.*] All right. I'm leaving tomorrow. [*Exits.*]

COBINA: She means it, too.

MRS. PACE: Good riddance. [*The orchestra plays.*]

OSCAR: [*Direct.*] This party is costing me too much to have it spoiled by you. I shall do my best to stay out of your way the remainder of the evening.

MRS. PACE: Good!

OSCAR: Do me a favor?

MRS. PACE: [*Coming center.*] I make no promise, but what is it?

OSCAR: The ribbon around your neck is loose. Tighten it.

MRS. PACE: [*Reaching the back of her neck.*] It's — it's not loose.

OSCAR: Yes, yes, I know, I know. [*Exits left.*]

MRS. PACE: [*Dawning, then violently.*] Why you insulting Jackson — you — [*Exits after* OSCAR.]

COBINA: [*Laying flowers on the table.*] I'll be glad when this party is over.

CHUCK: [*Peeping in from the arch door.*] Cobina!

COBINA: [*Happily, surprised.*] Chuck!

CHUCK: [*They go toward each other.*] Honey!

SOPHIE: [*Passing in the hall, interrupts.*] Hey now! [CHUCK *and* COBINA *stand wanting but frightened.*]

CHUCK: Oh she knows, honey — she knows.

SOPHIE: Umm hmm.

COBINA: You won't tell, Sophie.

SOPHIE: Who me — gwan girl. [*Winks and exits left.*]

COBINA: Oh Chuck! Darling! You scared me nearly to death, when you passed in the hall. Why didn't you warn me?

CHUCK: [*Whispering.*] I tried to. I had to come. I couldn't take a chance.

COBINA: But Mother and Grandmother—Chuck, you shouldn't have come.

CHUCK: Oh they think I just came to do some work. Darling, I missed you on the corner, this morning I came here—I—

COBINA: Dad came along in the car, he and Granny. They brought me home. What happened?

CHUCK: I went downtown to see about a job.

COBINA: You get it?

CHUCK: No—and after making me wait an hour. I came back up to our meeting place. No sign of you. I said I was going to be right here, tonight. I made up a tale. I thought sure your mother wouldn't hire me. Sophie made her. Here I am. I am going to serve and see that none of those other guys get you, even Ed—

COBINA: Oh, him—

CHUCK: Yeah, has he come yet?

COBINA: No.

CHUCK: Well, give him your hand, but give me your kisses.

COBINA: Not one, just to be formal?

CHUCK: None. You don't want to, do you?

COBINA: [*Reluctantly.*] I have once.

CHUCK: Oh.

COBINA: But kissing him is like scratching a place that doesn't itch.

CHUCK: Try mine again. [*They kiss.*]

COBINA: Oh, Chuck—I'm afraid. [*Music swells.*]

CHUCK: But, darling, this is your debut.

COBINA: I don't want any debut. I want you.

CHUCK: May I have the first dance? [*They dance.*] Give them a chance to dance.[*The doorbell rings.*]

COBINA: The door!

CHUCK: [*Dashing about.*] Where's my tray?

COBINA: [*Excitedly.*] You didn't have any. Hurry! Hurry!

[*CHUCK exits through arch door. OSCAR enters from salon.*]

OSCAR: You seem nervous. [*She gathers her bouquet. OSCAR goes to the door. MRS. PACE enters from the salon.*]

MRS. PACE: Places! Where's Dolly? Where is — Soph — no, that boy? [*DOLLY enters from hall.*] It is about time you got here.

DOLLY: Oh — I hope it's Judge and Mrs. Tucker.

OSCAR: [*Offstage.*] Well well well — Brooklyn at her best. Come right in, Ed.

[*TILLIE enters the arch door, arm in arm with ROWENA. ED follows, talking in pantomime with OSCAR. TILLIE is well–gowned and jeweled. She wears a highpowered society smile. ROWENA is an attractive girl of nineteen or twenty, with a searching stare in her eyes. She's dressed with impeccable care. ED is a young man of about twenty–five. He wears full dress clothes and carries his top hat with a dash of urbanity. TILLIE speaks with a gloating suspicion.*]

TILLIE: Cobina — Mrs. Van Striven — and of course, Mrs. Pace.

COBINA: Hello, Rowena.

ROWENA: Hello, Cobina. I know exactly how you feel. Shift into your half squat, child. Get high like I did, bow at nine, out at ten.

ED: Cobina — what an angel you would make!

TILLIE: Ed, how could you! Cobina wouldn't think of Father Divine. [*Sitting on sofa.*]

ED: I didn't mean that — [*Shaking hands with MRS. PACE.*]

MRS. PACE: We are pleased that you came.

ED: Where there is a debut, you will always find Ed Tucker.

COBINA: What will we debs do to ever win you, Ed?

ED: Just trust in God and keep your powder dry.

TILLIE: Isn't that cute? Ed has a brand of humor all his own. Where there's life there's still hope, Cobina.

DOLLY: [*To CHUCK.*] Take their wraps, Chunk — I mean Chuck!

TILLIE: Aren't you the porter who transplants fish?

CHUCK: [*Taking her coat.*] Yes, Madame.

ED: [*Amused.*] Well, porter, trot me out some trout!

CHUCK: Right this way, please. [CHUCK *exits*.]

ROWENA: Auntie — isn't Cobina stunning?

TILLIE: White is always pretty, Rowena. It does make one look so plain, like you were when you were confirmed.

OSCAR: The bar is wide open, Ed.

ED: Bar — you say — liquor.

OSCAR: And how. [*The orchestra plays*.]

ED: Liquor does different things to different people. But it only makes me drunk. [*Teams up with* ROWENA.]

ROWENA: Whatever it does to you, it does twice as much to me. Oh sinner, lead me on. [*They tango a few steps and exit off left followed by* OSCAR.]

[DOLLY *peeps out of the window*.]

TILLIE: Looking for someone, Dolly?

DOLLY: [*Coming down center*.] I don't mind telling you, Tillie, I'm worried. The people, where are they?

TILLIE: I don't know — I thought the place was packed by now. Where's Miss Jackson?

DOLLY: Who knows — after all, you'll be rubbing elbows with her.

TILLIE: There are times when we simply must condescend. If wellbred must rub elbows with the gutterbred, where else should it be — but in Harlem.

DOLLY: [*Exiting into salon*.] Sometimes, Tillie, I wonder how you and I manage to live on the same globe. [*Exiting*.]

TILLIE: You're feeling all right, Mrs. Pace?

MRS. PACE: [*Frigidly*.] Yes, Petunia, steaming like a kettle.

OSCAR: [*Enters*.] Give your old dad the first dance, Cobina.

COBINA: Certainly, dad — [*They exit into salon*.]

MRS. PACE: [*Moves to center*.] I see you brought him.

TILLIE: Oh — Oh — and such a swell boy. Mrs. Tucker says every deb in New York is after him.

MRS. PACE: Now that's tragic.

TILLIE: Isn't it?

MRS. PACE: Where are Judge and Mrs. Tucker?

TILLIE: Ed said if they approve of a girl, they go to her debut! If not, they stay away, very cordially, of course. So far my niece's debut has been the only one they've attended. Now isn't that strange?

MRS. PACE: You think you'll take him back?

TILLIE: What do you mean?

MRS. PACE: You know what I mean.

TILLIE: That isn't a very friendly question.

MRS. PACE: [*Cuttingly.*] I can tell my friends from my enemies by their emotional vibrations.

TILLIE: Pray tell, what are mine?

MRS. PACE: Positively negative.

LILY: [*Outside.*] Come on now. [LILY *swings in from doorway left, dancing the "La Congo."* HENNYPEST, *in a tuxedo, attempts the difficult steps in following her.*] That's it! Hello, Mrs. Petunia, look what I found.

HENNYPEST: [*To* TILLIE.] How do you do — this time?

TILLIE: The same as I was this morning.

LILY: [*Dancing down center.*] We are doing the La Congo!

TILLIE: Bring him back alive!

HENNYPEST: [*Winking.*] Even otherwise, Mrs. Petunia — I must have a dance with you.

TILLIE: It will be a pleasure.

LILY: [*Stopping.*] You're cute. As D.W. said, "Gal, this is a story of savage love. Feel the heathen in the part. Let yourself go. Let loose every limb." A–a–a–a–hh! [*She and* HENNYPEST *glide off.*]

TILLIE: She took him right into her bosom.

MRS. PACE: That's New York for you. Now, Washington —

TILLIE: [*Quickly.*] And Brooklyn —

MRS. PACE: [*Lecturing like.*] In Boston, they say "Has he manners?" In Brooklyn, "How much money has he got?" And New York — they say "Let's take the sucker!"

TILLIE: That may be true about New York, but Brooklyn —

MRS. PACE: [*Quickly.*] Just a petticoat for New York's gaudy frock.

TILLIE: [*Rising.*] You don't know Brooklyn — you never came over there.

MRS. PACE: Oh, yes I do. I frequent it.

TILLIE: To visit?

MRS. PACE: Yes, my father's grave.

TILLIE: There's something else in Brooklyn besides graveyards.

MRS. PACE: Yes, churches.

TILLIE: [*Huffing.*] Humph! [*Exiting into salon.*]

ROWENA: [*Passing from hall to veranda.*] My, it's stuffy in here. How about some fresh air on the veranda, Aunt Tillie?

MRS. PACE: [*Cutting in.*] Your aunt is full of air! All hot!

[ROWENA *exits to veranda. Bell rings.*]

MRS. PACE: Where's that boy?

OSCAR: [*Entering from salon.*] I'll answer it.

DOLLY: [*Entering from hall.*] This must be something real. Where is Cobina?

MRS. PACE: She's with Ed.

DOLLY: Oh! Cobina should be right here in the line.

MRS. PACE: Never mind, she's got Ed cornered. It's you the one who's spoiling everything — with your silly manners.

OSCAR: [*Offstage.*] Go right in, Leon!

MRS. PACE: [*Quickly.*] Stop grinning. You'll scare the daylights out of them.

[LOUISE *and* LEON *enter. They are both in their thirties.* LOUISE *is the older of the two. Both wear evening clothes with taste.* LOUISE *may be a bit overdressed to compensate for her unattractiveness.* LEON'S *attraction to women is magnetic. His hands are unable to resist female contact.*]

DOLLY: [*Very pretentious.*] Dr. and Mrs. Davis, so glad you came. Louise, that coat, those lines.

LOUISE: [*In a high–pitched irritated voice.*] Good evening, Dolly.

DOLLY: [*Flattering.*] You look like a dark–souled villainess. That coat!

LOUISE: It ought to. It cost enough. [DOLLY *goes blank.*]

MRS. PACE: Dr. Davis, we were afraid you wouldn't get out of that old hospital.

LEON: [*Going over to* MRS. PACE.] Couldn't keep me from this party. I do believe you are getting younger. [MRS. PACE *actually blushes.*]

DOLLY: [*Scrutinizing* LOUISE'S *coat.*] How do you do it, Leon?

LEON: [*Glancing at* DOLLY.] What, Mrs. Van Striven?

DOLLY: [*Helplessly.*] I'm so happy you came. I don't know what to say.

LEON: [*Smiling.*] Anything you say is all right as long as it is accompanied with your lovely smile.

DOLLY: [*Befuddled.*] Isn't he simply a darling? Where does he learn such lovely things?

LOUISE: I wish I knew. The only times he says them things to me is in his sleep.

MRS. PACE: Dolly is already gitting tipsy. Now you go and try to catch up.

LEON: [*Removing his coat.*] Now you just wait for me, Van Striven. All these attractive ladies. Hmm, as I always say, women grow old from neglect and not from age, eh, Oscar?

OSCAR: Oh yes — oh yes.

LOUISE: That's why I love him so. Who else can phrase a lie so beautifully?

OSCAR: Come on, Leon. I think I have what you need.

LOUISE: [*Nervously.*] Any strange women down there?

DOLLY: No, dear —

LOUISE: He's safe then. Take my wrap. [LEON *reaches for it.*] No, wait — [*Searching her wrap.*] Where is it? Where is my — here it is all right, darling. Take it now.

[LEON *exits with* OSCAR. LOUISE *reveals the objects, her refuge powder puff and lipstick, etc.*]

DOLLY: [*Coming down center.*] Louise, I'm proud of the way your career and marriage succeeded.

LOUISE: Under the circumstances, everything is so–so, except every week our names lead off the squabble column. That *Black Dispatch* prints it even if I just pinch the man.

DOLLY: [*Sits on the sofa.*] Ignore it. One of these days I am going to sue that scandal sheet.

MRS. PACE: [*Sits in the chair facing the sofa.*] Bravo. Now Dolly, let her enjoy herself.

LOUISE: I always do at the Van Strivens'. Excuse me while I check this map I call a face. I surely have to watch out.

DOLLY: You're looking like a peach.

LOUISE: As long as there is a beauty parlor and a monthly check, I will feel well armed. I'm not giving up, though. He runs around, but after he gets through chasing Diana around the woods, he always comes back. If he should ever fail to come back—

DOLLY: Divorce?

LOUISE: Not as simple as that. [*With deep feeling.*] Dolly, be sure Cobina marries a man older than herself. It is no fun to see a man grow robust and handsome while you fight like the very devil to sugar coat the waning forties. Life begins at forty—huh! What a lie. Always there is just one affair after another. I can't make them. I just can't. They wear you down so. He never gets tired.

DOLLY: There are plenty other affairs besides these strenuous dances, Louise.

LOUISE: They're pretty much the same. Take the art exhibit night before last. A Bohemian atmosphere, they call it. All the guests piled up on Bloomstein's bargain pillows, smoking and drinking, low lights and shocking music.

MRS. PACE: [*Seconding.*] A society pledged to primitive discipline.

DOLLY: Then there are those endless ofay affairs!

LOUISE: The whole of the village—ultra modern!

DOLLY: So many of us prefer them.

LOUISE: Yes. Especially those that—pass.

MRS. PACE: [*Tactfully.*] You can't escape God and Africa.

LOUISE: Don't I know it! I will not attend another on Sugar Hill or anywheres else. Leon might as well let that soak through his plastered head. I get tired of straining my ears trying to hear what he is saying to some doll-faced model!

DOLLY: You still have the upper hand. A doll face is a handicap. It distracts from the curves.

LEON: [*Enters from the hall.*] There you are, my little sugar lump. Let's dance.

LOUISE: [*Rises.*] No more liquor for you. [*Taking his arm.*]

LEON: But I had no more than a thimble full. [*After a reproachful glare from her.*] All right, my sweet, just as you say. [LEON *and* LOUISE *exit to left.*]

MRS. PACE: She loves the ground he staggers on.

DOLLY: [*Again at the window.*] Three lousy cars! Look, mama, look! The neighbors are staring at our house, the jealous Peeping Tom.

MRS. PACE: And this is a Van Striven affair.

DOLLY: Here I was afraid too many people would come, and instead there is hardly any at all.

MRS. PACE: You sure they were received?

DOLLY: Of course they were. Because they all responded in writing. The Tuckers — they all did. I knew something would happen. I told you this debut would not go over. I knew it. Maybe they think it will be too stiff. Oh, the devil, where is Oscar?

MRS. PACE: Drowned in his martini.

ROWENA: [*Entering from veranda.*] And whom may I ask do you wish such a fate?

MRS. PACE: Oh, Rowena, why your fate will lead directly to the island, if you don't stop parading on the veranda without a coat.

ROWENA: There's such a lovely breeze sweeping up the street.

MRS. PACE: You will catch your death of cold in that thin dress.

ROWENA: [*Sitting on sofa.*] It doesn't bother me. Winter or summer, I take my dip. I'm mad about the water. I just can't resist it. [*Lights cigarette.*] Aunt Tillie knows exactly where to find me when I'm missing. Out at the beach home on the sound.

MRS. PACE: I imagine you have quite a time keeping up with her.

ROWENA: In a way. Auntie gets about more than I do. Yesterday, she was in New Rochelle, Mt. Vernon, and then down to East Orange, all in the space of two short hours.

MRS. PACE: [*Sits in chair facing her.*] She has an abundance of energy.

ROWENA: And how! When she got home this afternoon, she had been to a dozen places, then phoned an army of people —

MRS. PACE: [*Carefully.*] But weren't you with her this morning and the balance of the day?

ROWENA: To keep up with that human rocket! No, I missed her at the trade building. Mind you, there only ten minutes and was gone. She travels like a gale of wind.

MRS. PACE: [*Nodding.*] And she called a number of people?

ROWENA: Oh yes, quick calls. All of them but Mrs. Tucker. She talked for hours —

MRS. PACE: [*Smelling a rat.*] Mrs. Tucker?

ROWENA: Yes, Ed's mother. [MRS. PACE *snaps her fingers.*] Why, Mrs. Pace, you look so queer. What —

MRS. PACE: [*Rising.*] Excuse me, Rowena.

ROWENA: Must you go?

MRS. PACE: I am going to do a bit of phoning myself.

ROWENA: [*Crossing to phone.*] May I dial for you? I'd simply love to.

MRS. PACE: [*Going toward hall door.*] That phone there is a little too public. The one upstairs is much more suitable for dishing dirt.

ROWENA: See you later. [*Thinking aloud.*] I wonder what I said? [*Wanders toward hall door.*] Young man — I say, hey you — [CHUCK *enters nervously.*] Well, if you don't mind. Pardon me for interruption —

CHUCK: I — I wasn't doing anything.

ROWENA: [*Walking down center coyly.*] Oh, but you were. How can I spoil your moment of ecstasy. It was all about you like a veil.

CHUCK: Is there something I can do for you, Miss?

ROWENA: Do for me — oh yes — I would like for you to get a drink.

CHUCK: Yes, Miss, what kind?

ROWENA: Oh some of that bull shot.

CHUCK: [*Puzzled.*] Bull — I ain't — I — that is — I'm working for Mr. Van Striven. Just for the party, you know. Nice gentleman, Mr. Van Striven.

ROWENA: [*Shrewdly.*] And a nice daughter?

CHUCK: What you mean, Miss — er — Cobina is a very beautiful, that is —

ROWENA: Sweet?

CHUCK: I think so. I guess so —

ROWENA: You should know. I saw you kiss her.

CHUCK: [*Amazed.*] You hadn't come. Where were you?

ROWENA: Oh, tonight too — dear, dear. I meant last Wednesday, the actors' benefit at the Savoy.

CHUCK: [*Seizing her.*] Why — er — you — you didn't tell? You can't. You'll spoil everything. Please, Rowena, please! Please don't. Promise me? [COBINA *enters from the left.*] Promise me! You must! You must!

COBINA: [*Dumbfounded.*] Chuck! [*Doorbell rings.*]

CHUCK: [*Whirling around.*] I was just — er — er —

COBINA: [*She looks at* ROWENA *and bites her lip. The bell rings. She braces angrily.*] The doorbell is ringing!

CHUCK: [*Pleadingly.*] But Cobina, I can explain everything.

COBINA: The doorbell is ringing!

[CHUCK *rushes out into the hall.*]

ROWENA: [*Pointing.*] Aha. I thought you were coming from the weekends just a little too often.

COBINA: What are you talking about?

[OSCAR *and* DOLLY *enter from salon.*]

ROWENA: I understand, kiddo, as a servant he looks about as much at home as a bear in a penthouse. [*The orchestra plays.*]

DOLLY: [*Excitedly.*] Where is your nosegay? Where is mother? Where is Sophie? Get set!

COBINA: [*Studying.*] Were they kissing?

DOLLY: What — who — where — who's kissing?

OSCAR: [*Booms.*] Relax, for God's sakes!

CHUCK: [*Off stage*] Yes ma'am, come right in, ma'am. [COBINA *gets in line, breathlessly, after getting her nosegay.*]

[RUBY *enters from arch door, happy and smiling. She is a woman of thirty–nine, dressed in an ostentatious outfit with a feather sticking straight up in her hair. She walks with an exaggerated restraint. Her mouth is filled with gold. She speaks anxiously and hopefully.*]

RUBY: Good evening.

DOLLY: [*Opens her mouth, but is unable to speak. She is shocked. She sways slightly and catches herself again us* OSCAR *tries to smile with exasperation.*] Good heavens!

COBINA: [*Curtsying.*] How do you do?

OSCAR: Miss Jackson — my wife, Mrs. Van Striven — my daughter, Cobina.

RUBY: [*To* COBINA, *grinning.*] Hello, baby. You're cute as a chorus girl. [*Coming down center timidly.*] You all can come on in, Beulah, I guess.

[BEULAH *cuts in from the arch door, as if she has just finished the final step in the lindy hop. She is a loose swaying girl of twenty–two. She has a mass of curled hair, pigeon toes and a dissipating face. She wears a tight coat, split skirt, and a tam. She walks an arresting switch, with her hands stuck in her sides.*]

BEULAH: Hi, everybody — the stuff is heah.

DOLLY: [*Gasping.*] Pinch me, Cobina, am I breathing?

BEULAH: Bring me a pint of gin and sixteen glasses. Ouch!

COBINA: [*Curtsying.*] Glad you came.

BEULAH: [*To* COBINA.] I'm Beulah — whatcha squattin' foh? [DOLLY *starts forward.* OSCAR *restrains her.*]

COBINA: It's the vogue.

BEULAH: Thought you'd done got too tight under the belt.

DOLLY: [*Blasting.*] Oscar!

OSCAR: Yes, dear, of course. [*To* RUBY.] Miss Jackson, after all — you understand that —

RUBY: Shore, honey — I know, but Beulah and Joe fell in for a little snack an' I jus' had to bring 'em with me. It was that or I would have to stay away.

DOLLY: You should have done the latter.

OSCAR: [*With a saving grace.*] We will go right in and rest your things.

[BEULAH *moves in on* OSCAR *and squeezes his hand, flinging her fur piece in his arm.*]

BEULAH: Rest the mink, papa. You an' me is gonna have heaps of fun. [DOLLY *steps in and gets a whiff of* BEULAH*'s breath and stumbles back.*] Just gin chile. [*Laughing*] The old dame busted her kickers.

DOLLY: Miss — please!

BEULAH: [*Shifting her weight.*] I'm Beulah.

RUBY: Yes mum, Mrs. Van Striven, that's my friend Beulah. Joe's comin —

DOLLY: [*Angrily.*] So what?

BEULAH: So I'm Beulah!

OSCAR: [*Going toward hall door.*] This way, please.

BEULAH: [*Shouting.*] Wait for Joe!

[JOE *is heard entering off stage. Music fades.*]

JOE: [*Offstage.*] Scram, sam. Get lost! You nickel snatching taxi driver!

[JOE *enters archway from right. He is about twenty–five. A man about town, anyway a man about certain towns, or if you will, certain parts of all towns. His associates call him a "hepped cat." Togged out in a draped coat that pinches in shapely at the waist and then blossoms about his hips and ends with a snazzy flare. His britches stand way up about under his arm pits and are hitched even higher by his gaudy braces over the shoulders. His pants leg down to the top of his shoes, ballooning a bit at the knees. His hat of a Tyrolean version shades his features in the best tin–horn gangster manner. He speaks to* CHUCK *behind him.*]

JOE: Hi, folks, I'm Joe the Jiver. [*Freezes, posing the hep cat's stance — his arms down, his fists tight, his forefingers pointing outward from the sides.*]

OSCAR: That's er — er — Joe — Joe —

JOE: [*Bending and bracing up, he is all over the room in a show off manner.*] What a dommy from pistromy. Dig the layout. It's a solid killer from maniller. Get off that pillar.

RUBY: [*Tickled high–pitched laughter.*] Joe keeps me laffing all the time.

BEULAH: Fall in, Joe. The joint is jumping.

COBINA: [*Curtsying.*] How are you?

[DOLLY *yanks* COBINA *backward.*]

JOE: [*To* COBINA.] Lamp the chick. Mellow as a chellow. She lays that thing. Same as I was a king.

OSCAR: [*Indignantly.*] That's my daughter.

JOE: Dig pop's gait sharp as a tack, hard as a nail. Them powerful tails dangle like a whale. [OSCAR *walks away.*] Some vine, pop. Dig mine. [*Lifting the lapels of his coat.*]

DOLLY: Mr. —

JOE: Smothers, Joe Smothers!

DOLLY: As this is a formal affair —

JOE: [*Advances on* DOLLY, *she walks away, half frightened.*] Don't play cheap, I ain't no bo peep. Let me get you straight. 'Fore it is too late. I'm here to stay, so on your way. [*Turning away from her.*] That chick comes on like an Eskimo.

DOLLY: [*Hatefully.*] I would like to speak to you alone!

JOE: Come 'round any day but Thursdays. That's when sud–busters git their pay. I'll 'spect you around. So don't let me down. I'll lay some spiel that'll bust your heel!

OSCAR: [*With an effort.*] Mr. Smothers, you'll find the bar downstairs. I'm sure you are more interested in that!

JOE: [*Snappingly.*] Right, Jack Lark! That's where I park with a fine skin in the dark.

BEULAH: [*Snapping her fingers, she jumps back and wiggles. Gazing to the back parlor.*] Whoo–ie — that's Tom Wild and his Wildcats playing. Look at them broads struggling.

DOLLY: Struggling?

BEULAH: Dancing, dame, dancing!

JOE: That's nothin', they's shuffle and mug like they've been drugged. Let me light up and cut some rug. [*Music reaches crescendo.*]

BEULAH: This ball is a slight drag.

JOE: Don't whine, wait'll I put up my sign. Look out biffers' 'um coming on like the March of Time, yippee! [JOE *rushes center, bending and bracing up in rhythm with the music.* BEULAH *raises and flaps her arms as she begins the break in the lindy hop. They dance wildly. The music comes up in full. They make the place jump.* DOLLY *swoons against* OSCAR *in exasperation.* OSCAR *tries to get things under control again.* COBINA *is amused. She snaps her fingers and sways as* CHUCK *looks about helplessly.*] Ain't this a killer — hey hey! [JOE *swings around with* BEULAH *who hops back, runs toward him as he swings her around.*]

DOLLY: [*Screaming in exasperation with her hand raised high.*] Stop the wildcats! [*As she stops within* JOE's *dance range,* BEULAH's *swinging leg hits* DOLLY's *foot.* DOLLY *screams in pain.*] My foot! [*Music blasting.*]

OSCAR: [*Rushing to* DOLLY, *upsets* COBINA, *bouquet and all.*] My Wife!

COBINA: [*Excitedly.*] My flowers! [*Complete freeze of action and music.*]

BEULAH: [*Being dropped to the floor, sits rubbing her side.*] My ass! [RUBY *does not say a word.*]

[*Curtain.*]

ACT II

SCENE 1

SCENE: *The same as Act I, Scene I.*
TIME: *A few minutes later.*

SETTING: *At the rise of the curtain,* OSCAR *is sitting on the sofa. He is mopping his brow and trying very hard to get over the recent escapade. He talks to* RUBY, *who sits near him. The orchestra plays.*

RUBY: [*Pathetically.*] I know Joe would be sort of out of place, but he is so full of life, usually people beg me to bring him along. These — that is, your kind don't understand him.

OSCAR: That's all right, Miss Jackson. Forget them.

RUBY: Yes suh, but Mrs. Van Striven's foot, oh, I'm so sorry 'bout that.

OSCAR: [*Clearing his throat.*] That's nothing. She'll be all right. Now this dump — er, this piece of ground is right in the heart of the new upcoming community. Five lots and —

RUBY: Well — that is, I only want to entertain the best. Are there any high–toned folks out there?

OSCAR: Just as grand as these are here, if not better.

RUBY: Does Mrs. Van Striven know them?

OSCAR: I believe she knows some very fine Long Island families.

RUBY: Then she'll introduce me sorter formal–like to them? You know, all elegant with a lot of noise. I'll throw a house–warming out there that'll be heard from here to Krum Elbow!

OSCAR: [*Scratching his head.*] I think we'd better dance. [*Rises and offers his arm.*]

COBINA: [*Enters from hall door.*] Dad, Mother says will she have to send down here for you again?

OSCAR: Someone has to stay down here and take care of the guests. Is she any better?

COBINA: Her foot is better, but her grandiloquence still pains.

OSCAR: That will heal in due time. Tell her I will be up shortly.

COBINA: But, Dad, she won't come down until you —

OSCAR: Shortly, Cobina, shortly!

TILLIE: [*Entering from salon.*] Isn't this a lovely ball, Miss Jackson?

RUBY: As rambunctious as Park Avenue. We is class, ain't we? [OSCAR *and* RUBY *exit into salon.*]

TILLIE: [*Ironically.*] Aren't we though! [*Noticing* COBINA.] Some debut, isn't it, Cobina?

COBINA: I wish Mama thought so. Excuse me, as I have to tell her what

Dad said. [*Exits through hall door.* TILLIE *tips to salon door and calls* LOUISE.]

TILLIE: H–s–s–s–s–st!

LOUISE: [*Backing in, talking to* LEON.] I said dance, not squeeze the life out of her.

LEON: [*Entering from salon.*] I am, Louise, I am.

LOUISE: Why do you hold her so tight? You don't hold me that way.

LEON: Now, Louise —

ROWENA: [*Enters from salon and slips her hand under his arm.*] All right, Dr. Davis — we can finish now.

LEON: [*Watching* LOUISE.] Oh yes — oh yes!

LOUISE: [*To* ROWENA.] Be sure it's the dance you mean.

ROWENA: [*Chiding.*] Oh my — my —

[ROWENA *and* LEON *exit into salon.*]

LOUISE: [*Watching them.*] I hope I don't have to break his neck before twelve o'clock.

TILLIE: You don't think Leon and Rowena —

LOUISE: [*Suggestively.*] She's woman —

TILLIE: You know Rowena better than that.

LOUISE: Oh, it isn't just for her, everybody he dances with. You wait until I get him home. Tillie, you ought to be glad your husband is dead. [*Sits on the sofa powdering her face.*]

TILLIE: Safe in heaven, thank God — er — You'll have something on your hands soon as that Joe and Beulah get together again.

LOUISE: Attractive?

TILLIE: You heard of a face that would stop a clock? Well, Beulah would silence a telephone.

LOUISE: Not one iota of difference to Leon, he never looks that high. If I catch him near her — why did I come. Honestly, I should have taken your advice this afternoon.

TILLIE: You see the inner circle stayed at home . . .

LOUISE: Just why did you put in an appearance, after what you said?

TILLIE: Oh, well, I have a score to settle.

LOUISE: But I do believe you've gone too far.

ED: [*Enters from salon, he staggers a bit.*] Where's that little imp, Cobina. If she can't duck down to that bar more than anything I have ever seen.

TILLIE: Ed is so handsome when he is mad, isn't he?

LOUISE: [*Indifferently.*] A handsome lover is one thing. [ED *exits through hall door,* LOUISE *leans over to* TILLIE.] A good husband is another. I pity Cobina if she gets him.

TILLIE: [*Quickly.*] Or Rowena —

LOUISE: [*Bewildered.*] What?

TILLIE: [*Softly.*] Didn't you know —

LOUISE: But Dolly said —

TILLIE: That's what she thinks.

LOUISE: I believe in fighting in the open.

TILLIE: Maybe you'd better change your technique.

LOUISE: [*Efficiently.*] I haven't done so badly. Standing on my feet seven hours a day, singing out verbs to a bunch of dumb brats, getting by on a bowl of chili and cut–rate frock, all to put him through medical school. Now, he's all rosy and popular. Debonair, they say. Well, I'm fattening no frogs for any snakes. He knows I'm not going to keep on fighting in the dark or otherwise — he's mine and the female creature that tries to really take him from me will gaze up at the Harlem moon underneath six feet of woodlawn dirt!

TILLIE: Woodlawn?

LOUISE: Cemetery. He winks at every young thing he sees now. I'm not jealous, but —

TILLIE: Well, you take a woman like that Ruby Jackson.

LOUISE: So the Ruby Jackson came.

TILLIE: What a headline! "Pimp and Pal Wreck Society Gal."

LOUISE: Now, Tillie, that's what I have been wanting to talk to you about. That bar *Black Dispatch* is —

ED: [*Enters with* COBINA *from hall.*] I found her at the bar guzzling as usual.

COBINA: [*Halting to powder her nose.*] Wait — let me get this shine off.

TILLIE: [*Enviously.*] Cobina, you seem a bit limited in your selections tonight!

COBINA: I have what I want.

LOUISE: [*Happily.*] Is that so — oh, Ed is —

COBINA: They didn't have to give this party for me. I had him all the time.

ED: [*With self–esteem.*] Don't be too sure.

COBINA: [*Brusquely.*] What — you — what sparrow pecked that into your head?

ED: [*Abashed, he takes her arm.*] I don't got you. Lower that mirror so I can see your face.

COBINA: [*Jerking away.*] Wait — wait —

ED: [*To* TILLIE.] I get tired of these girls with their five–and–ten faces. They listen to you with one hand, touching up a string of hair, while holding a mirror with the other.

[HENNYPEST *enters from salon.*]

COBINA: A woman's prerogative.

LOUISE: And a final refuge.

[HENNYPEST *gestures to* TILLIE.]

TILLIE: [*To* HENNYPEST.] One moment, Professor. We can't miss this.

ED: [*Avoiding.*] You put your entire trust in physical manifestations. You are perfectly confident in the right shade of nail polish, the perfect number of oily cuffs, lips of a shady red ink. Don't they, Professor?

HENNYPEST: Well, now, that is —

COBINA: [*Interrupting.*] A lecture on the philosophy of woman. You are becoming serious. [*She winks at* TILLIE *and* LOUISE.] Before you go too deep, what do you expect in the fairer sex?

ED: Something pretty scarce around here, brains!

COBINA: Oh be still! Brains, that's just a camouflage for your overween-ing arrogance. Take us for what we are. Not for what you want us to be in your narrow little heart. What sort of an opinion is that?

ED: Mine! The sensible one, the one of any real man.

COBINA: Real man? You mean an impetuous youth. Surely, Professor, you do not agree with him?

HENNYPEST: [*Moves down center.*] I am not sure it would be wise for me to get into this.

COBINA: Name me just one man, one great man, who hasn't had the love of a woman to push him on — to just —

ED: Just so much dead weight.

HENNYPEST: [*To* ED.] I don't think so. The heart of a woman does more to mankind than all the gold and silver that ever has been mined. She has a smile for every joy, a tear for every sorrow, a consolation for every grief — for every fault, a tolerant forgiveness, and a prayer for every hope.

ED: It doesn't matter. I understand them perfectly.

HENNYPEST: Then go to the head of the class. Ahead of the philosophers, scientists, poets, musicians, and psychologists who have fallen in their zest to analyze woman. The fact is that woman doesn't understand herself. She has yet to be solved. The few men who have been silly enough to think that, they had either learned of their mistake before they died, or passed into eternity as congenital idiots.

COBINA: [Coy.] Idiots!

TILLIE: [Directly to HENNYPEST.] That could have been left out.

ED: [Touching his moustache lightly.] Aw — anyway, they're made to love, not to understand. Their charm, their beauty, their glory has all been reduced to a price —

HENNYPEST: Of all other attributes of vices, the personal piety born of chastened love is woman's crowning charm. Can there be love without understanding?

ED: But you said they are not understandable —

HENNYPEST: Indeed, indeed, like the stars and flowers, her presence imports warmth and life–giving energy to hearts bowed down. Her influence bends earth to heaven and heaven to earth. Do we understand the universe? [LOUISE nods with affirmation.] No. [LOUISE relaxes innocently.] We only think we do. Does the universe understand us? [LOUISE looks askingly.] I believe it does. Such is the position of woman. You give her the proper love. I am sure the understanding will come about in due time.

LOUISE: [Exuberant.] Professor Hennypest, that is beautiful. Isn't it, Mrs. Petunia?

TILLIE: [Casually.] I have heard it before. [The orchestra plays.]

COBINA: And you will forever. Truth withstands both the tide and the times.

ED: [Unaffected.] If a woman can't tell me she loves me first, then she can use the first door out. This chivalry stuff is just so much nonsense. I can get along without her very well.

TILLIE: Don't let them get the best of you, Ed.

COBINA: [*In praise.*] Oh, Professor, what an intricate mechanism we women are. Really, it's — it — Louise, aren't you glad you are a woman?

TILLIE: [*Rises and goes to* ED.] Ed, you know you can't judge us here. This is Harlem. There are women — that is, girls — well, you know. Now you take Brooklyn. We have —

CHUCK: [*Enters from hall door. He carries a drink on the tray.*] Bull shot!

TILLIE: [*Whirling to* CHUCK.] What?

[COBINA *laughs.* LOUISE *sits dreamingly on the sofa.*]

CHUCK: [*Looking about.*] Re — er, Miss Rowena called for — bull shot.

[ED *moves toward* CHUCK.]

ED: [*To* CHUCK.] You might have called for her first.

CHUCK: I'm sorry. Will you have one?

ED: I don't drink this Harlem hootch. [TILLIE *smiles at* COBINA.]

COBINA: Give it to me. [*She takes the drink before* ED *can stop her. Sits on chair at right.*]

ED: [*Both rivals on either side of* COBINA.] That's the third time I have seen you carry a glass to your lips. [COBINA *gulps the drink down.*]

LEON: [*Enters followed by* HENNYPEST. LEON *very carefully removes from his shoulder a string of hair, looks to see if* LOUISE *saw it. He throws it away quickly, then goes to her.*] Our dance, Louise.

LOUISE: [*Looking up at him with a marked dumbness.*] Oh Leon, do you know what an intricate mechanism woman is?

LEON: [*Mysteriously.*] What the Sam Hill are you talking about?

LOUISE: [*Hunching him with her elbow.*] You would! Come on.

LEON: But baby —

LOUISE: [*On her way out.*] That's nice what you say, but to hold him you have to wake up what's worse in him.

[LOUISE *and* LEON *exit into salon.*]

HENNYPEST: [*to* TILLIE.] Madame Petunia, will you —

TILLIE: [*Disgustedly.*] Good grief. I might as well get it over with. [*Exits into salon with* HENNYPEST.]

COBINA: [*Returning glass to* CHUCK.] It was swell.

ED: Who asked you?

CHUCK: No one.

ED: Well, mix them, but don't mix in.

COBINA: [*To* ED.] You are going too far. You stop bulldozing him. He's working for Dad.

CHUCK: [*Starts away.*] I must get back to the bar.

ED: [*To* CHUCK.] Come back here!

CHUCK: [*Stopping.*] Listen, pal —

ED: Pal?

CHUCK: [*With force.*] As man to man. Maybe you don't like me. Well, I don't like you either.

ED: If you were swinging that tray for ofays, you wouldn't be talking like you are.

CHUCK: That has nothing to do with it.

COBINA: Daddy will not tolerate you speaking to him in that manner.

CHUCK: [*Giving* ED *a coin.*] No, thank you — I'm paid.

COBINA: [*To* ED.] You're making me sick! Chuck is just as good as you are. He's a member of Alpha Beta Zeta, the same as you are.

ED: What?

COBINA: Yes, and —

ED: What chapter?

CHUCK: [*To* ED.] Aida Chapter — snake! [*Both do a razzle–dazzle handshake and a frat gesture.*]

ED: They're letting in anything now. [*To* COBINA.] Are you dancing or not?

COBINA: I've changed my mind. They're dying for you in there. [ED *exits into salon.*]

CHUCK: And that's what they want to put off on you.

COBINA: Darling — I gave him a look that hasn't been washed in years. You know I wouldn't have him with a down payment on a radio.

JOE: [*Swings in from salon with* BEULAH, *both slightly drunk.*] Old Jim Pool from Liverpool. Cut that powerful muggin' and gruggin'.

BEULAH: [*Clapping her hands.*] Come on, you dicties. Swing out. Di–di–di–dum–dum.

JOE: [*Snapping his fingers. — Jumping back*, LILY *appears just inside the room.*] What's your story, Morning Glory? Git off the shelf. Swing yourself.

LILY: [*Moves in nearer.*] Aha! [LILY *swings a couple of times.*]

JOE: Come on, Garbo, blow your top. [*She stops dead still.*]

LILY: I beg your pardon.

JOE: Don't start puffin'. You ain't done nothin'.

TILLIE: [*Peeps in from the hall.*] What is this?

JOE: If you can't fall, stick to the wall. Joe is takin' charge. [TILLIE *emerges.*] Git back, granny—hep—hep. You're too large. [TILLIE *recedes.*]

BEULAH: Here I come, Papa. On your mark.

JOE: [*To* CHUCK.] Stack some ham on that platter. Tray away, what's the matter?

CHUCK: Food is served on the floor below.

JOE: [*Stopping the strutting.*] I ain't no square from Delaware, nor bloke from Idaho. Grab that platter. Take some air. Who's gwine eat on any flooh?

COBINA: [*To* CHUCK *quickly.*] Wait on the veranda for me, Chuck. [CHUCK *exits through French doors.*]

JOE: Say chick, you're crumpy as a Uneeda biscuit.

LILY: Cobina, who is this man?

COBINA: Mr. Smothers, Joe Smothers.

LILY: Delighted, I'm sure.

JOE: Send my brown body to the morgue.

BEULAH: You kill me with that drawl. Where's Professor Chickenbreast? [*Exits into salon.*]

LILY: I'm not the slightest bit amused.

JOE: You let me down to the ground. Let me show you the town. [LILY *smiles.*]

COBINA: I believe you can take care of yourself. [*Exits through French doors.*]

JOE: [*Getting, close to* LILY.] Them big black eyebrows. Them long lashes. They flop a breeze that causes me to squeeze. A fine feeling shakes my frame. Gosh, ain't this a shame!

LILY: [*Crossing.*] Ha–ha–ha–ha–ha–ha —

JOE: [*Right on* LILY.] Getcha! Hoi! Hoi! There's plenty squares who can slave. But a hard–cuttin' lover is in the rave.

LILY: With whom did you come?

JOE: [*Sing–song.*] Ruby — Ruby Tutti–fruity.

LILY: Now I understand.

JOE: Don't jump in the amen row. Ruby's jus' lousy with dough.

LILY: [*A new interest.*] From the sweepstakes?

JOE: A hundred and fifty grand. Old slick Joe is the man. Swing out with me a while. I'll tog you out in style.

LILY: Listen, big boy. Don't jive me now.

JOE: Believe me if I sing you in praise — a half a hundred tender ways. Believe me if I still repeat that you are glamorous and sweet. But if you see my glances stray, just shrug and look the other way. And don't believe, dear, nor weep if I tell my secrets in my sleep.

[COBINA *and* CHUCK *enter from veranda.* CHUCK *exits down hall.* COBINA *watches* JOE *and* LILY.]

LILY: I'm a woman of the stage, you know.

COBINA: Lily, do you know what you are doing?

LILY: Aw, does anyone?

JOE: [*Elated.*] Lily, your wit, your repartee, good God, you knock a hole in me. They are like your face and neck, overwhelm me. Dazzle me! Send me! Leave me a perfect wreck!

SOPHIE: [*Dashes in from foyer left.*] Joe, Joe, I —

JOE: [*Whirls around startled.*] Sophie Slow, ready as a radio!

SOPHIE: [*Leaps into his arms.* LILY *is indignant.*] Bust me, Joe. Bust me! My Joe. Good ole Joe. Sharp as a tack. Ain't them the togs I brought cha?

LILY: [*Looking around helplessly, tosses her head back.*] That took the starch out of him.

COBINA: Sophie, is that your he?

SOPHIE: In the flesh. My Joe, ain't he cute?

JOE: I thought you pulled your slave act in the Bronx.

SOPHIE: Naw, babe, I cut out. No more of that fifteen cents an hour for me. Up there they nelly starved me to death with that cheese and pumpinicker bread. I like here better. I kin fuss all I wants. Boy, that drape hugs you tight as your skin. You been jiving Lily? [*Crosses to* LILY.]

LILY: No, he amused me.

SOPHIE: I know. Different name but same feelin'! Come on up to my room, Joe. [LILY *hustles into parlor.*]

JOE: Naw, honey, don't be funny. I got to stash down here.

SOPHIE: I nevah knowed you hung out with the swanks, you and your pranks.

COBINA: Sophie, if Mother sees you —

SOPHIE: That's right. Say, Joe, I got to git below.

JOE: You fall on down. I got to kill some wine an' be right down in a half of chime. [SOPHIE *exits foyer left.*]

COBINA: Mr. Smothers, you seem completely put out.

JOE: [*Sitting on sofa.*] Listen chile, out, out awhile. None of your jinks, I got to think.

RUBY: [*Enters from back parlor.*] Miss Cobina, kin you tell me where your ma is?

COBINA: Up in her room, I think. I'll try to find her.

RUBY: Never mind, maybe she's busy.

COBINA: I don't mind. [*Exits through foyer left.*]

RUBY: Joe, has you been smokin' any marianna weeds? [*Sits beside* JOE.]

JOE: Cut out that innocent act. I'm gittin' outah this shack? [RUBY *takes his arm.*]

RUBY: But babe, I'm having a ball. You must be, too. You wanted to come so bad.

JOE: I just wanna leave. Let go my sleeve!

RUBY: What done happen? 'Course you should nah come on so hard.

JOE: That ain't it at all. I'm leaving, that's all. One thing I don't do. Cross my chicks, they git me blue.

RUBY: I ain't crossed you. I let you jive them biggies.

[TILLIE *enters from parlor.*]

JOE: I ain't callin' no name. [*Sees* TILLIE.] Cut out. I gotta spiel to this dame. [RUBY *rises and exits slowly foyer left.* JOE *urges her on. He shouts at her.*] Beat it stuff. I don't wanna git rough. [*Sits on sofa.*]

TILLIE: Mr. Smothers—

JOE: Can it!!

TILLIE: S–s–s–sh.

JOE: [*Boisterously.*] None of that high–falutin' junk. What the hell you take me for, a chump?

TILLIE: What, Joe — what's the matter?

JOE: You got me on the run, woman, She knocked me for my fun.

TILLIE: Who, Mrs. Van Striven? You do just what I told you—

JOE: When I fell in through the door. I didn't 'spect to see Sophie Slow.

TILLIE: Will you stop that silly rhyme and tell me just what is—

JOE: Just this. You done run me into a chick of mine who's worse than a nest of starving monkeys when she's riled. How can I wreck this joint with her—

TILLIE: You mean that awful maid?

JOE: Better say that when she's out of sight. She swings a mean fist when she fights.

TILLIE: Is she one of—

JOE: Yeah, what of it?

TILLIE: I gave you credit for having better use of your talents. [*Sits close to* JOE.] But listen, don't let me down now. Make everybody miserable. Start a fight or something. Ruin them. Give them a pain in the neck. That dancing was great stuff. Raise the tin roof off this stable. [*Marked bitterness.*] These Van Strivens and their uppish ways!

JOE: I don't know. They seem sorter nice.

TILLIE: Nice — they're mean little people who'll shrink up and die from one good scandal.

JOE: But Ruby wants to be a muckitymuck. I have to—

TILLIE: You do your job. When Ruby wants to meet society, I'll give her a sendoff. These jittery quacks do nothing but try to impress their neighbors and live in constant agitation and comparison with me. [*Walks down center.*] Me, Tillie Petunia!

JOE: What about the old dame with the ramrod up her back? She passed me like greased lightning.

TILLIE: [*Turns, coming center.*] That imitation of a Victorian. She's the sharpest–tongued one of these strivers. Don't let her scare you. She'll fidget and squirm if you blow your nose hard. Rip all the sham off all of them. [LILY *enters from parlor* TILLIE *rises quickly.*] Oh, Lily — we were just talking about you.

LILY: That shows importance. Importance is quite essential, you know.

[LILY *relaxes on sofa.* TILLIE *snaps the wall lights off, darkening the room with the exception of a beam light.* TILLIE *exits left.*]

JOE: [*Easing up behind* LILY.] Do you dig, do you dig? Let this pig fit your jig.

LILY: No, thank you!

JOE: [*Easing around edge of sofa, creeping closer to* LILY.] Light up and grow limp, Lily.

LILY: I want to enjoy a moment of solitude. Miss Livingston to you.

JOE: [*Beside* LILY.] Lemme stash my frame on that freakish lounge, while that glimmer beats down on my woolly–kong and tickle out the Romeo in me.

LILY: The Smothers technique is back.

JOE: Never got out from my chest, just a short recess.

LILY: I'm a wicked woman.[*The orchestra plays.*]

JOE: Wickedness is for a lady, goodness for a hag. The first sends me. The last one is a drag.

LILY: What do you want me to do?

JOE: Bust me with your beauty. You're such a cutie.

LILY: I'm not that beautiful.

JOE: Enough for me, babe, you seem so true. I gotta lay this hard love on you.

LILY: If you love like you lie, you're good.

JOE: I'm better than that. I'm a hepped cat. [JOE *leans over* LILY, *who squires and squirms.*] Easy — easy, don't start wringling. Watch your skin start tingling. [LILY *kisses* JOE *quickly.* JOE *kicks and jumps up in delight.*] Whooie! Bo–peep, come and git your sheep!

OSCAR: [*Rushes in from parlor.*] Miss Livingston, what are you doing?

LILY: [*Jumping up quickly.*] Just — just a scene, Mr. Van Striven!

OSCAR: [*Turning up lights.*] A scene — a scene — these lights.

JOE: [*All over the room.*] Yeah, Jack, the mad scene from Gimbels' basement.

BEULAH: [*Enters from parlor.*] Say, Papa, let's finish our dance.

OSCAR: Sorry — I must see my wife. [*Exits through arch door left.*]

BEULAH: [*Scornfully.*] The guy has to git permission from his dame.

CHUCK: [*Rushes in from foyer left.*] Where is Miss — Cobina?

LILY: I — I don't know.

   [ED *enters from parlor.*]

ED: Oh — pardon me! [*Turns.*]

JOE: [*To* ED *with a purpose.*] Say, Jim — Cobina — you seen her?

ED: [*Reproachfully.*] What — and you too?

JOE: What's that?

ED: [*Points to* CHUCK.] Him — and now you?

CHUCK: I don't get you, pal.

ED: I thought you weren't playing that role for nothing. What a damn cheap trick!

JOE: [*Raising his fist.*] Don't bite off too much.

LILY: Ed Tucker, you'd better —

JOE: [CHUCK *and* ED *face to face.*] Easy, honey, this is funny. The well–bred and the gutter–bred gonna bust heads.

CHUCK: [*To* ED.] I ain't looking for no trouble.

ED: Plenty nerve. Who do you think you are fooling, anyway?

   [JOE *encircles* CHUCK *and* ED.]

BEULAH: Look out — let me git a ringside special. [*Stands up in a chair.*]

ED: So you took Cobina to the actors' benefit.

   [JOE *edges them out.*]

LILY: Is that the fellow she was with?

ED: [*Swearing at him.*] You're the guy who's been taking up all her time, the reason why she breaks all her dates with me. You upstart. Why don't you stay in the alley with the rest of —

COBINA: [*Dashes in from parlor.*] What is this?

ED: What's the idea going around with him pretending you like me?

COBINA: What are you talking about?

CHUCK: [*Quickly.*] Rowena just told him. He knows, Cobina.

COBINA: [*To* ED.] Well — well, it's my business. You might as well know now —

ED: I'll see what Mrs. Van Striven has to say.

COBINA: Well, go ahead!

JOE: He's gonna run and tell Mama.

CHUCK: Now listen —

ED: Take your filthy hands off me —

[JOE *pushes* CHUCK.]

BEULAH: [*Slugging the air.*] Pile drive him. Break down his bridge work!

ED: You —

[JOE *steps in to push* CHUCK *into* ED. *At this moment,* ED *ducks.* COBINA *screams. The blow catches* JOE *in the face.* JOE *knocks* ED *down near the sofa.* BEULAH *leaps up and down in the chair up left.*]

BEULAH: Plaster him in the kisser. This is a killer, just like a Saturday night at the Hole–In–The–Wall.

COBINA: [*Screaming.*] Stop it — stop it!

CHUCK: [*To* JOE.] What did you do that for? This is my affair.

LILY: Mrs. Van Striven —

JOE: [*Tapping his thumb with his tongue.*] Come one — come all.

[DOLLY *enters at arch door.*]

CHUCK: [*Lets loose a lightning blow.* JOE *spins around — staggers blindly — stumbles and falls at* BEULAH'S *feet.*] You started it.

COBINA: Chuck — Chuck — don't! Papa — Mama — somebody!

TILLIE: [*Rushes in from the parlor. She sees* ED *knocked out on the floor. She runs over to him, screaming hysterically.* ROWENA *stops in the door.*] Ed, darling — oh, his face is bruised. [*She kisses him tenderly.*] Ed — oh, Ed —[*Shouting at* CHUCK.] You dare strike — you —

CHUCK: I didn't do it.

COBINA: Joe did it. Joe, it was he.

[BEULAH *lifts* JOE *to his feet.*]

TILLIE: [*Screaming at* JOE.] You Lennox Avenue lizard. I'll have you put in jail.

JOE: You said wreck it, start a fight —

TILLIE: [*Holding* ED's *head in her arms.*] Not him — [ED *is coming to.*] Ed, darling — [*To* JOE.] You fool — you backdoor pimp!

DOLLY: [*Confused with anger.*] Wreck it — wreck what?

[TILLIE *rises slowly.* DOLLY *is right in back of her.* TILLIE's *eyes blink.*]

TILLIE: [*Trembling.*] Nothing, I —

JOE: [*Angrily.*] What the hell, she told me to wreck your party. Make it a scandal.

DOLLY: Scandal — my party — my greatest party — [DOLLY *swings* TILLIE *around, facing her.*]

JOE: Sure she did. Ask her. Told me to come along with Ruby. Get some hoodlums, like Beulah, and make the ball a flop.

TILLIE: That's a lie.

BEULAH: [*To* TILLIE.] You beefy hussy!

TILLIE: [*Pleading.*] He's lying, Dolly. I never saw him before in my —

JOE: Ask Ruby. She knows I begged her to bring me. [*To* TILLIE.] Pimp, am I?

[ROWENA *turns tearfully in the door.*]

MRS. PACE: [*Rushes in from the arch door.*] The police are coming!

[JOE *makes a dash to exit. He stumbles, but dashes out wildly.*]

BEULAH: Me and cops don't mix! [*Makes a dash for the door, knocking* TILLIE *off balance.* TILLIE *tumbles into* DOLLY, *who lands on the sofa. All the guests converge around the sofa.*]

SOPHIE: [*Dashing in with a trail of policy slips following.*] The cops coming. Git them policy slips out!

MRS. PACE: Dolly, what are you doing?

DOLLY: [*Holding fast to sprawling* TILLIE, *she takes off her shoe.*] I'm going to put some misery where it belongs.

TILLIE: Don't you put your hands on me!

HENNYPEST: [*Dashing in with his camera, focusing from a downstage vantage point.*] Focus, please.

[*All freeze just as* DOLLY *raises her slipper above* TILLIE's *posterior.*]

[*Curtain.*]

SCENE 2

TIME:*Later that evening.*
PLACE: *The same*
   At the rise of the curtain, ROWENA *paces the floor, excited over the recent happenings.* ED *is sitting in the chair at left, nursing his right eye.*

ROWENA: You ought to be ashamed of yourself!

ED: I, ashamed? What about your aunt and her rummies spoiling the party? Just like her, always messing up — [*Gestures, exposing a black eye, a real mouser.*]

ROWENA: Get my wrap, I'm going home.

ED: Don't shout at me! I only dance to my own music. I'm sick and tired of both of you trying to make small of other people and end up stuck with the dummy cap yourselves.

ROWENA: Stop talking about her!

ED: [*Rising.*] Stop the world! Her majesty, party–nuisance number one. Same thing at Small's last night, got high and pushed me off a stool, splashing rum all over —

ROWENA: Aunt Tillie was in Corona last night.

ED: Maybe her spirit was, but her body was with me at Small's Paradise and as high as a kite.

ROWENA: You took her there?

ED: [*Crossing to right.*] Let us say she took me there.

ROWENA: [*Crossing to* ED.] You're a conceited liar!

ED: And for a grand finale, we shacked up at the Hotel Theresa.

ROWENA: What are you saying? [*Her eyes glued on him.*]

DOLLY: [*Enters the foyer in a huff.*] You assassins still here? Get going!

ROWENA: [*To* ED, *undistracted.*] You are lying!

DOLLY: [*Missing the point.*] Lying? You're as welcome here as a bastard at a family reunion. [*Crosses, snatches wrap from sofa, flings it at her.*]

MRS. PACE: [*Enters from left, steaming.*] Where is Tillie? Where is that horrible creature?

DOLLY: Denture hunting. She lost her partials during the melee.

MRS. PACE: I have been on the phone and —

ROWENA: [*Finally with realization to* ED.] You — you — drip! You dripping drip! [*Crosses, slaps him and picks up her wrap and flees thru foyer and off right.* ED *instinctively pursues her, but pauses and calmly picks up his hat, faces* MRS. PACE *and* DOLLY.]

ED: [*Scornfully, conclusively.*] So long, social coolies!

DOLLY: [*Crossing to him, gracefully, bowing regally and joined by* MRS. PACE.] Adios ameba! [*Both arm and oust him before he knows what is happening. After a pause,* DOLLY *collapses on the sofa.*] Oh, Mother, I feel like the last drip from a faucet!

MRS. PACE: [*Crossing behind sofa.*] I found out that —

RUBY: [*Enters from left with* LOUISE, *both in their wraps.*] Mrs. Van Striven, I can't tell you how sorry I is.

MRS. PACE: My daughter wants to be alone.

RUBY: Yessum, I was just leaving and —

MRS. PACE: Leave by the lower floor then.

[RUBY *exits from the foyer after a sad glance at* DOLLY.]

LOUISE: Dolly, I had a perfectly delightful time.

MRS. PACE: This is one time that a lie is not in order!

LOUISE: I did. Didn't we, Leon? [*Looking back.*] Where is that man? Leon?

LEON: [*Entering from left.*] Coming, honey.

LOUISE: You're not going to take her home with you, are you?

LEON: [*Now pretty high, he makes a production out of getting on his scarf and coat.*] Who — who — who?

LOUISE: Look at him — who — who? Wait until I get you home.

LEON: I have to speak before the Medical Association tomorrow. [*His scarf is now like a lasso around his neck.*] You're not going to scratch my face up tonight.

LOUISE: [*Jerking* LEON's *scarf.*] It won't be your face!

MRS. PACE: Louise!!!

LOUISE: I'm sorry, Mrs. Pace. [*Sits next to* DOLLY.]

MRS. PACE: We saw you come up from that 134th Street railroad flat up on Sugar Hill. Dolly sponsored you in and made you what you are to-day.

LOUISE: She did, and I would cut off my right arm for her.

MRS. PACE: [LEON *still entangling the scarf.*] You had better save your arm for him. [*Referring to* LEON.] Tillie told you not to come to our party, didn't she?

LOUISE: Yes, Mrs. Pace —

DOLLY: What's this?

LEON: [*Crossing to* DOLLY, *his hand tracing her spine.*] I told Louise that she should have phoned you — hic — hic — [DOLLY *disassociates his hand.*]

LOUISE: I didn't mean to hide it. You and Tillie both have been nice to me.

DOLLY: I am convinced that you wouldn't want to hurt me.

LOUISE: Never! Never! Never! It's that man's womanizing escapades. He keeps my mind boggled up! If it just weren't for this man, I would be a full–time lady instead of a part time hag!

MRS. PACE: Leon! [*He crosses to her, pinching her cheek affectionately. She distances herself.*] When are you going to stop playing cupid to every young creature you see?

LEON: [*Staggers.*] I guess it's the African in me, a woman for every mood.

LOUISE: Get going! I'm going to start *demooding* you tonight! [*Pushing him out.*]

LEON: Now, honey. It's you I love. I don't mismeasure your treasure. What are you going to do to your pappa–wappa?

LOUISE: I'm putting you on a diet.

LEON: [*At the foyer exit.*] Oh, I don't mind my weight going down.

LOUISE: It won't be your weight. The diet is saltpeter!

[LEON *swoons as* LOUISE *waves goodbye and shoves him off right, following him.*]

CHUCK: [*Entering from left.*] Mrs. Van Striven, I apologize for striking that —

MRS. PACE: Get your pay and leave by the lower floor.

CHUCK: There is something else —

MRS. PACE: Please take it up with Mr. Van Striven!

[CHUCK *moves down right.*]

LILY: [*Enters from left foyer, posing dramatically with her wrap draped around her left shoulder, acting out a scene with* HENNYPEST, *who follows her. She projects a Jamaican accent.*] Ha–ha–ha, then I say, "The quality of mercy is not strained, it droppeth, as the gentle rain from heaven."

HENNYPEST: [*Throwing kisses.*] Bravo — bravo. Yum — um.

LILY: It is an attribute to God Himself; and earthly power doth show likest God's, when mercy seasons justice. Therefore, Jew —

HENNYPEST: That's I.

MRS. PACE: Stop it! The masquerade is over!

LILY: [*Descending into room.*] I simply had to do that scene. I'm rehearsing *The Merchant of Venice* — to be laid in Jamaica. [MRS. PACE *gawks.*] I mean the setting of the play is laid in Jamaica. Instead of Portia, I'm called Portiaette.

MRS. PACE: You have 'et too much already. You are drunk!

DOLLY: Good night, Lily.

HENNYPEST: [*Glowing.*] I'm escorting her home.

DOLLY: Don't lose your way back, Professor.

[*Backing out,* HENNYPEST *collides with* LILY, *posturing another flight.*]

LILY: Goodnight reminds me of last season's African version of *Romeo and Juliet*. [*Crossing down center.*] "Good night, Good night. Parting is such sweet sorrow. Good night 'til it be morrow." [*Flings her wrap over her right shoulder, whirls and exits via foyer to the right. Two beats behind her,* HENNYPEST *waves a cuppish farewell and pursues* LILY.]

CHUCK: [*Impatiently.*] Mrs. Van Striven, I must talk to you.

MRS. PACE: [*Quickly.*] You still here! [*Crossing to left entrance.*] Oscar! Oscar! Come and show this person out!

OSCAR: [*Enters from parlor with* RUBY.] One minute. I must pay the orchestra.

MRS. PACE: This boy is annoying Dolly.

CHUCK: Honest, sir, it's about —

MRS. PACE: Pay him and get rid of him!

OSCAR: [*Exploding.*] This is a union band. Every minute counts. Come, young man, I will give you your money. Wait here, Miss Jackson. No doubt, tomorrow I shall be applying for welfare.

[CHUCK *follows* OSCAR *off left.*]

RUBY: [*Crossing to chair left.*] I'll just sit right here. [*Sits.*]

MRS. PACE: [*After a long pause that discomforts* RUBY, *she stiffens.*] For the past half–hour, I have been trying to converse with my daughter.

RUBY: Please don't let me stop you.

MRS. PACE: I am not encouraging conversation with you, but you do figure prominently in what concerns me.

DOLLY: [*Coldly, turning away.*] Her presence is part of a total design to embarrass me.

MRS. PACE: Why did you bring this rowdy Mr. Smothers into this house?

RUBY: Because he asked me to.

MRS. PACE: What if you had refused his request?

RUBY: He'd probably come on, on his own. Men like Joe is heaps of fun and heaps of risk. You don't refuse them anything.

MRS. PACE: How did he come to know Petunia so well?

RUBY: He hangs out at the Blue Ball Poolroom. Her paper business is just next door. I didn't know she told him to funk up your party. 'Course, I don't know the tricks of you high–toned folks. Bringing him here was surely a miscarriage.

MRS. PACE: You have met our upper class. I hope you are satisfied.

RUBY: I am, but —

MRS. PACE: But what?

RUBY: I'm going to buy that big mansion on Long Island. 'Course you all will be my house guests and — [DOLLY *crosses stage.*]

MRS. PACE: [*Tensely.*] Don't lose your dignity, Dolly!

DOLLY: [*Exploding with laughter above couch.*] Ha — ha — ha — ha —

[RUBY *rises, goes toward hall.*]

RUBY: It's just that I want to be in society.

DOLLY: The world swims before my eyes.

MRS. PACE: Keep your dignity —

DOLLY: Come here, Miss Jackson. [RUBY *picks up stool at right and down center, sits hopefully center.*] What a blind and silly woman you are.

RUBY: [*Disappointedly.*] My Madame, the one I use to work for, says I have the makings of a lady.

[MRS. PACE *sits on sofa.*]

DOLLY: [*Severely.*] A lady! Such a superficial term. Is your life position one of distinct advantage? Do you dress correctly? That rooster feather in your hair, positively nauseating. This being a lady is a complicated thing! It requires development, step by step. You are not even in the kindergarten. What do you possess that might make you worthy?

RUBY: Goodness.

DOLLY: [*She almost whispers.*] And what do you think I possess?

RUBY: [*Firm but kind.*] Snobbishness! Vanity! Pride!

MRS. PACE: And I?

RUBY: Meanness! Stiffness! It all amounts to just being snobbish.

MRS. PACE: [*With modest condescension.*] She's a snob. I am a snob. Well, who isn't? Snobbery is a universal failing — or maybe it's a virtue. It is the art of rubbing it in the other person. And it isn't peculiar to our smart set either.

RUBY: I wouldn't be one for —

MRS. PACE: But you are. You are a snob of humility and modesty. Now, are you not sorry for what you have said?

RUBY: No'm.

DOLLY: If you think so lightly of us, why have you selected us?

RUBY: I know every rich cultured woman ain't a lady. Still, every ten–dollar scrub woman ain't a saint. God is funny. He mixed them up. When you work all your days, suddenly you git powerfully rich, ain't much else to do but show off and git talked about.

DOLLY: [*As an equal.*] Money can buy you all the publicity you need, but not breeding. Now, Grandfather was an original settler in Rockland County and an Episcopalian minister. Dad became president of Skidwell College —

MRS. PACE: Where I was dean of women until I retired and moved to Washington.

DOLLY: Oscar's background is equally outstanding.

MRS. PACE: Though a far lesser eclipse of Anglo–Saxon sunshine with the African moon. We overlook one Dutch ancestor who went to the debtor's jail —

DOLLY: But a good name. Van Striven! Does that mean anything to you?

RUBY: Yessum.

DOLLY: Indeed, what?

RUBY: That the line between you and me is very thin.

DOLLY: [*Indignantly.*] I am trying to rationalize this thing with you. If you are capable of speaking with sense.

MRS. PACE: What was your father?

RUBY: A dog ketcher.

DOLLY: You couldn't be satirizing?

RUBY: Who?

DOLLY: Skip it. What did your grandfather do?

RUBY: He ran aroun' lak a blind mule in a hailstorm because Culnal Cheatum tricked him outah his farm. Five little devils use to break loose in his brain, he said, so he'd go aroun' buttin' his head against pine trees. I was a little mite of a gal when he used to say, "Dad–bob-bit, naow I'se too pooh to gie you the up–bringing you deserve."

DOLLY: Then you admit you lack breeding?

RUBY: Maybe I does, but the hoss that won me this money shore had plenty.

DOLLY: What I can't understand is why are you struggling to get into my social set and away from your own, such as Joe or Beulah.

RUBY: I like you better.

DOLLY: Is there any difference between you and Beulah?

RUBY: Yessum, in a way.

DOLLY: Then everybody isn't the same breed?

RUBY: Well, er —

DOLLY: Are they, Miss Jackson? [RUBY *is confused*.] Are they, Miss Jackson?

RUBY: I mean — the difference between me and Beulah is just like the dif-ference between you and Miss Petunia.

MRS. PACE: A matter of attitude?

RUBY: Yessum, that's it, that's just what I mean — a attitude is what I got that they don't have and don't want.

DOLLY: [*Resigning*.] I see. Is that all you have to offer for your social am-bitions?

RUBY: Skersely much more, Mrs. Van Striven.

DOLLY: [*Conclusively, rising*.] I am afraid the price you are willing to pay will not purchase you a ticket into the inner circle. [*Strolls left, looking off*.]

RUBY: [*Meditatively*.] I — get — you. My mistake.

[MRS. PACE *rises. Exiting right*. RUBY, *thoroughly dejected, comes to put chair back to table — pauses*. DOLLY *crosses as* MRS. PACE *stands rigidly*. RUBY *comes down center*.]

RUBY: I have stood over a hot greasy stove, rolling out biscuits, peeling onions 'til my eyes turned red. I never want to see another roasting pot! Have you ever had hot grease pop on you on a sizzling morning in August? And home to sit out on a stinking stoop — with a pile of cussing sickly men, lousing around like lizards in a pile of rotten logs! Aw, what's the use — [*Exits to parlor.*]

DOLLY: That's over — thank heaven. [*Sits on sofa.*]

MRS. PACE: May it never be repeated. [*Hears voices in the hall.*]

COBINA: [*Offstage.*] And I think I ought to know!

OSCAR: [*Offstage.*] Go on inside!

MRS. PACE: [*As* COBINA *enters from foyer left followed by* CHUCK *and* OSCAR.] You want Dolly to explode? Speak up!

COBINA: No, I'm not ashamed! And I don't care!

OSCAR: I just learned why Cobina can't stay at college over the weekends. [*He comes down center.* CHUCK *stands nearby.*]

MRS. PACE: Running down here for those stupid swing sessions. Swing! That horrible noise called music.

OSCAR: No! [*Indicates* CHUCK.] He's the reason.

DOLLY: [*With a toss of her head.*] Him? That person. That boy! This — Cobina —

MRS. PACE: W–w–w–what?

DOLLY: [*Going over to her.*] What's been going on? What do you mean? Cobina, where do you know this person from?

COBINA: The Village.

MRS. PACE: [*Cocking her brows.*] Dolly, you permit Cobina to be seen with such people! How long have you known this this — nobody? [OSCAR *sits on sofa rubbing his hands.*]

COBINA: About a year.

DOLLY: [*To* COBINA.] Where have you been seeing him?

OSCAR: She said they have been going to the park.

DOLLY: [*Wincing.*] My daughter in a public park. Cobina, I don't understand! Jeepers creepers! Did he make love to you?

COBINA: Aw, Mother!

MRS. PACE: Hold yourself together, Dolly! Keep your dignity! [*Steps on* DOLLY's *foot.*]

DOLLY: Ouch! Get off my foot! [*Flops on sofa.*] What have I done to deserve this? Och, it's too much, much too much. My poor aching feet.

MRS. PACE: [*To* CHUCK.] Do you realize what an uncouth thing you've done?

CHUCK: I tried to tell all of you. I didn't mean to be sly or —

OSCAR: [*Interrupting.*] They have been out evenings together.

MRS. PACE: [*Incensed.*] Evening. A sheltering veil for promiscuity. Black evil night! And why have you seen her at night?

CHUCK: I worked during the day.

MRS. PACE: Then I suppose you have something in your pocket besides a pair of dice.

OSCAR: He is not working now. He was discharged.

MRS. PACE: If you think Cobina is endowed to support you —

CHUCK: I love Cobina. I love her with all my soul.

DOLLY: But what could you offer her?

CHUCK: My youth — my —

MRS. PACE: What can she do with that?

OSCAR: I have explained to Chuck. Such a thing is utterly impossible, completely out of the question — [*Rises, crosses to* CHUCK.]

COBINA: [*Defiantly.*] I'm sick of being led around by the nose.

OSCAR: Cobina, I seldom interfere in your affairs. I allow you to your own judgment. You are eighteen. This is a big thing. Too big for you to decide alone.

MRS. PACE: This is most unhealthy or — something.

COBINA: I don't care. I love him.

DOLLY: What do you see in this boy?

COBINA: See — see — probably no more than you, but I feel different.

MRS. PACE: Keep your remarks out of the gutter.

COBINA: What difference does it make? Mother ran away to marry Dad and —

MRS. PACE: And she has been regretting it ever since.

COBINA: Nobody is going to pick out my boyfriend. I'm sick of these jaded jerks. With their swell heads, they're on the painful side of the absurd. They love only themselves.

OSCAR: We know what's good for you.

COBINA: I don't want what's good!

DOLLY: [*Going over to* CHUCK.] You have been listening to Sophie. And you, young man — you know what you've done? You have pulled a sneaking, unmanly trick! The idea of seeing my daughter in the park — in the Village — with those kooks.

CHUCK: We went other places — shows, bus riding, fights —

MRS. PACE: Fights?

CHUCK: Yessum, prize fights at Madison Square Garden.

COBINA: Chuck can fight, too.

OSCAR: [*Gladly — drawn to* CHUCK.] Oh, he can?

DOLLY: [*Interrupting.*] A prize fighter! What is your name?

CHUCK: Chuck Reynolds.

DOLLY: Mrs. Chuck Reynolds — How lacking in lyricism!

OSCAR: I've always wanted to manage a boxer —

CHUCK: Boxing ain't my calling.

DOLLY: Why did you decide to come here?

CHUCK: I didn't want you all to engage Cobina to anyone else.

DOLLY: And if we had?

CHUCK: I am not ready to marry, but we would have eloped.

OSCAR: [*Crossing to* CHUCK.] And I would have had it annulled.

CHUCK: We would have kept it a secret.

MRS. PACE: Her mother hid her elopement. But she did not hide the results.

DOLLY: Mother! [*Truly embarrassed.*]

OSCAR: As you see, Chuck, your way of life is different. Though you say you have been to college.

MRS. PACE: [*To* OSCAR.] College, where?

OSCAR: [*Explodes.*] Aw, Bugalu College or something —

MRS. PACE: You mean institution!

OSCAR: There are plenty of Harlem businessmen who would have gladly given you a job.

CHUCK: They must be hiding somewhere.

OSCAR: Jobs just don't fall out of the tree of hope.

CHUCK: I came here with a letter of introduction from college to the Reverend Cooke. He was glad to see me. He invited me to hear him preach the following Sunday.

OSCAR: The Reverend Cooke gave you no assistance?

CHUCK: He was kind. He gave me a copy of the New Testament. Next I went to Gotsby Employment Agency.

OSCAR: I know, recently opened.

CHUCK: I told Mr. Gotsby I needed a job. He said he couldn't find one himself. That's why he opened his agency.

OSCAR: There is a wide gap between you and my daughter. What I mean is, there is a lot of difference between you and me, and —

CHUCK: We do belong to the same sex.

COBINA: Score one for Chuck. Hooray!

OSCAR: Putting it as politely as I can, permission to see my daughter is denied.

CHUCK: I didn't ask your permission, sir.

OSCAR: You didn't, but —

DOLLY: Did you come here to win our friendship or extract it?

CHUCK: I have Cobina's consent. She's eighteen now.

COBINA: Both of you may have been kidding me when you told me that a girl at eighteen can make her own decisions, but I believed you. So please shut up!

OSCAR: [Crossing to COBINA.] What will it be? Shell steaks or chopped chuck?

COBINA: Chopped chuck with CHUCK!

DOLLY: Name the first offspring Groundmeat!

RUBY: [Stepping up to CHUCK.] Sonny, I sure like the way you talk.

OSCAR: Oh, Miss Jackson, I'll be with you in a minute.

RUBY: What would you do if you had my money?

CHUCK: Madame, education isn't a bad investment. A sharp mind deters chiselers and —

OSCAR: [Blustering.] Now just a minute —

MRS. PACE: Keep your dignity.

OSCAR: [*Evenly.*] A few minutes ago, before my daughter's declaration of chop meat independence, I was about to offer you a job —

CHUCK: As a panic peddler?

OSCAR: Come again.

CHUCK: Panic peddlers, blockbusting goons — hired by real estate dealers to funk up neighborhoods.

[DOLLY *looks askance at* MRS. PACE *and mimes* "Language?" MRS. PACE *mimes* "Funk is proper."]

CHUCK: Johnny Whiteface flees the neighborhood, taking everything except his cemetery.

OSCAR: [*Not with pride.*] Business is business.

CHUCK: That's what's wrong with it.

OSCAR: No, you certainly won't fit into my stable.

CHUCK: Thank you for including me out.

OSCAR: There are times when the end justifies the means. If the end is a good one, you bend the moral code a little —

CHUCK: Or bust it.

OSCAR: Show me a business strictly on the up and up, and I'll show you where it is coasting on eggs. Such is the fashion and pattern of our time. Anybody in this business who doesn't earn fifty thousand a year is loafing. Sure, I trigger the whole busting sequence. Blockbusting is an odious name for my craft. Real estate speculator, yes. But as long as we have the average American with his average prejudice, we blockbusting bastards will be in business. And nothing you can say will release any ants in my conscience!

DOLLY: [*She's had it.*] Enough! Absolutely enough! This talk of business — flavored with nasty words — does not belong in our home!

CHUCK: I think —

DOLLY: Enough, damnit, enough. [*Tearfully regretting.*]

COBINA: Chuck isn't as impractical as you think. He has already taken the civil service exam for recreation director.

DOLLY: [*With new interest.*] Did he pass?

CHUCK: I made the second highest mark. [*The* VAN STRIVEN'*s glaciers melt. All are drawn to* CHUCK.]

OSCAR: [*Putting his arm around* CHUCK.] Well, tell me something. You will be appointed?

CHUCK: I guess I will unless something better turns up.

MRS. PACE: Civil service is civil service.

CHUCK: It can be a dead end.

DOLLY: Mother, what about his background?

MRS. PACE: Some people have backgrounds. Others have backbone.

OSCAR: [*To* MRS. PACE.] Do you mean you accept him?

MRS. PACE: When I objected to you twenty years ago, I did so in vain.

COBINA: Thank you, Granny. [*Kisses her.*]

[*Commotion off upper left stage: dog barking, tumbling footsteps on the stairs, and* TILLIE's *frantic voice.*]

TILLIE: Let go! Let go! Do you hear me? [*Dog growls, cries and whines.* TILLIE, *in her wrap, enters from left foyer all shaky and disheveled.*] That damn dog of yours had my bridge work down there in his kennel.

COBINA: [*Alarmed, dashes out, followed by* CHUCK, OSCAR, MRS. PACE, *and* RUBY.] Oh, is he hurt?

TILLIE: He wouldn't let go until I stuck him with a hair pin.

DOLLY: Now, will you get the hell out of here?

TILLIE: I can't get out of here fast enough. Where's my niece? Where's Ed?

DOLLY: They left long ago.

TILLIE: [*Recapturing her composure.*] How dare they leave me.

DOLLY: When ordered out, they obeyed!

TILLIE: You'll have to explain to my lawyer how that mutt got my partial!

DOLLY: Get out! Let the doorknob bang your backside! [*Steps toward her.*]

TILLIE: Don't you touch me again!

MRS. PACE: [*Enters from left, stops center.*] Touch you! Why, you deceiving, calculating wench! I knew when you came flying by here this morning that you were up to nothing good. You should have been spanked in Macy's window!

DOLLY: She has been ding–donging with Ed Tucker.

MRS. PACE: [*With asperity.*] That's it! That's why this old bag was sinking us and at the same time securing Ed Tucker tightly to her monstrous bosom! Thanks gossip–monger for telling our guests not to come.

DOLLY: What's this?

MRS. PACE: I have been trying to tell you for the last half–hour that I phoned our guests. Some tried to lie out of it. Others admitted that Petunia warned them that the party was going to be a disaster. That this scrub–woman Jackson was coming and others who are more at home in jail.

TILLIE: What if I did! Who do you think you are? Van Strivens — VAN SKUNKS! You dare lay your filthy hands on me. I'm not afraid of you. I'll show you. I'm going to sue you. I will make you the biggest goats of the season. I shall smear your names in the biggest and bold-est letters on the front page of the *Black Dispatch*. You little upstarts. You scheming, broke climbers. As long as you give parties, I don't need any comic section in my newspaper!

DOLLY: So you will, eh?

TILLIE: B–e–l–i–e–v–e me!

DOLLY: [*Fiercely.*] You back–biting, two–faced hussy!

MRS. PACE: Don't spare the rod, but keep your dignity.

DOLLY: Nothing that you can print can scandalize me more than I can dis-credit you! The mud you fling on me will splatter back into the map you call a face!

TILLIE: [*Most gratified.*] Seeing you socially dead is worth any price. I'm glad I fouled up your party.

DOLLY: Rejoice, evil child! But exactly what poison did you sprinkle among my friends?

TILLIE: I told them that the creeps and floozies crashing the party were bound to cause a riot.

MRS. PACE: That would deter God Himself. [*Sits chair down left.*]

TILLIE: They realized something that you don't.

DOLLY: And that is?

TILLIE: That without the press, all of you are papier mâché.

DOLLY: The press be damned. *I know who I am.* I've been middle–class for three generations.

TILLIE: You're still just another face in the Harlem coalbin.

MRS. PACE: Rumors persist that your grandmother was a slut!

TILLIE: That's a lie!

MRS. PACE: And that your membership in every committee for fallen girls is an act of repentance.

TILLIE: Grandma was the *owner* of the best whorehouse in downtown Brooklyn, regardless of race, creed, or need. Slut herself, she was not.

MRS. PACE: Your credentials for the underclass are excellent. You are vulgar and gauche. Your disgraceful ancestors and unrefined instincts add up to zero. Why my daughter tolerates you is —

TILLIE: [*Angrily.*] Tolerate me! People fear me. Had your guests come here tonight, my press would have blackballed their names. Their fear of me outweighed their loyalty to you. With that kind of clout, I need no ancestor. I am my own ancestor.

DOLLY: Fear is a weapon that can work for you or against you. [*Takes photo film from desk drawer, crosses, showing it to* TILLIE.] Won't your butt look swell on the front pages of the *Amsterdam News*?

TILLIE: [*Stunned, grabs at it.* MRS. PACE *grabs it first and clears.*] You're . . . you're lying —

DOLLY: After it's developed, I'm giving it to the *Amsterdam News*. Hennypest snapped it just as I was spanking you. Oh, what a front–page feature that will make!

TILLIE: [*Painfully.*] They would print it — with monstrous glee.

DOLLY: No doubt at all. And with a little retouch that would expose your nude bottom. Remember, Mother, the picture of the Baptist minister with his leading soprano, both nude?

MRS. PACE: [*Claps her hands, unnerving* TILLIE.] Hallelujah! Hallelujah!

TILLIE: That picture will scandalize us both. Please give me that film.

DOLLY: I will give you nothing.

TILLIE: How much do you want for it?

DOLLY: It is not for sale.

TILLIE: You'll ruin my reputation. You'll ruin our reputation.

DOLLY: It's too late for salvation.

TILLIE: I promise not to print anything about you and what has happened.

DOLLY: And what about that disaster zone you call a mouth?

TILLIE: In my mouth your name will no longer find comfort.

DOLLY: Bless you. Now, get out!

MRS. PACE: She said get out! [TILLIE *crosses to arch.*]

DOLLY: Just a minute. [*Tears up negative and gives it to* TILLIE.]

TILLIE: You did this because you think you are the better person.

DOLLY: [*Firmly.*] Good night, Tillie.

TILLIE: At best, we were stepfriends. I'm going to miss that.

DOLLY: Now we're close enemies.

TILLIE: Sometimes your worst enemy is your best friend.

[*She has gone.* DOLLY *sits on sofa.* MRS. PACE *crosses behind sofa and presses* DOLLY's *shoulders reassuringly.*]

DOLLY: [*Soul searching.*] I should have destroyed her.

MRS. PACE: You stayed within the bounds of decency.

DOLLY: She will destroy herself.

RUBY: [*Entering with* OSCAR.] So, you just expect me in your office at nine tomorrow morning.

MRS. PACE: You mean you will buy anyway?

RUBY: Why, surely, I ain't changed my mind.

DOLLY: [*Stunned.*] Why, Miss Jackson!

RUBY: Never you mind, honey. Forget the sendoff. I need a good place to live. The razzle dazzle can come later.

MRS. PACE: [*Coaxing.*] Having such a nice home, you will want to have nice friends.

DOLLY: [*Crossing to* MRS. PACE.] Mother, are we to accept her?

MRS. PACE: [*Whispering to* DOLLY.] How much did you say that sweepstake was?

DOLLY: Two hundred and fifty thousand dollars.

MRS. PACE: Well then —

DOLLY: Of course.

RUBY: Don't you bother, child. You all seem to do 'bout the same thing I do.

MRS. PACE: Now, Miss Jackson, it ain't what you do. It's the way how you do it. [*Braces herself.*]

RUBY: Well, all right then.

DOLLY: Miss Jackson, please forgive me. If I have made you unhappy, then let me show you how happy I can make you. You must, for there is something that you can teach me.

RUBY: But what can I teach you? 'Doubt it's how to pick a lucky horse?

DOLLY: You can teach me to have a heart as big as yours. I am beginning to think my way of doing things is somewhat phony.

RUBY: Why, Mrs. Van Striven.

DOLLY: Will you?

RUBY: Sakes alive . . . I sure will.

DOLLY: [*Crossing embracing her.*] Thank you, my dear. Why don't you stay overnight?

OSCAR: Yes, do. I might change my mind about putting a turnstile to that third floor. Unhem — we can get right down to business the first thing in the morning.

RUBY: That's right nice of you all.

DOLLY: Mother, show Miss Jackson to the Booker T. Washington bedroom.

MRS. PACE: Come, Miss Jackson. [*Crosses to arch and waits.*]

RUBY: Ain't she sweet. [*Struts toward archway, totally lacking in grace.*]

MRS. PACE: [*Stopping her.*] Miss Jackson, please. The first lesson in social deportment is not to walk like a duck. Walk this way. [*Braces and strolls through archway, pauses, looks back and exits.*]

RUBY: She walks like she's leading me to Jesus at the second coming. [*Assuming an exact carbon copy of* MRS. PACE *she exits after pausing and winking.*]

[DOLLY *quickly closes the window, takes* "ROOM FOR RENT" *sign and tucks it neatly in the window as* OSCAR *embraces her agreeably.*]

[*Curtain.*]

Langston Hughes

SIMPLY HEAVENLY

LANGSTON HUGHES (James)

The author, poet, playwright and editor was born in Joplin, Missouri and grew up in Lawrence, Kansas and Cleveland, Ohio. He attended Columbia College and Lincoln University in Pennsylvania. He was resident playwright at Karamu Theatre in Cleveland, and columnist for the *Chicago Defender*.

Hughes, the best-known personality of the Harlem Renaissance, remains one of America's most prolific black writers and has been called "the poet laureate of the Black race." Hughes authored and edited more than 35 volumes including poetry, novels, short stories, plays, biography, history, and anthologies. Volumes of poetry include *The Weary Blues, The Dream Keeper, Shakespeare in Harlem* and *Ask you Moma*. Novels include *Not Without Laughter*. Autobiographies include *The Big Sea*, and books on black history include *A Pictorial History of the Negro in America* (with Milton Meltzer). His "Simple" books include *Simple Speaks His Mind, Simple Takes a Wife, Simple Stakes a Claim*, and *Simple's Uncle Sam* (1965). His children's books include *Famous American Negroes*, and *The First Book of Jazz*. His edited anthologies include *The Poetry of the Negro* (with Arna Bontemps), *The Book of Negro Humor*, and *The Best Short Stories by Negro Writers*.

Other plays and dramatic works include: *Mulatto, The Barrier, Litle Ham, The Emperor of Haiti, Mule Bone* (co-author Zora Neale Hurston), *Simple Takes a Wife, Simply Heavenly, Black Nativity, Tamborines to Glory, Jerico–Jim Crow, The Prodigal Son, Don't You Want to be Free, Soul Gone Home, St. Louis Woman*, and *Limitations of Life*.

Awards: Recipient of *Opportunity Magazine* Poetry Prize (1925); Harmon Gold Medal for Literature (1931); Guggenheim Fellowship (1935); Rosenwald Fellowship (1942); American Academy of Arts and Letters Grant (1947); Springarn Medal (1960).

CHARACTERS

JESSE B. SEMPLE	Harlemite
MADAM BUTLER	Simple's landlady
ANANIAS BOYD	Simple's neighbor
MRS. CADDY	Joyce's landlady
JOYCE LANE	Simple's girl
HOPKINS	A genial bartender
PIANIST	A bar fly
MISS MAMIE	A plump domestic
BODIDDLY	A dock worker
CHARACTER	A snob
MELON	A fruit vendor
GITFIDDLE	A guitar player
ZARITA	A glamorous goodtimer
ARCIE	Bodiddly's wife
JOHN JASPER	Her son
ALI BABA	A root doctor
A POLICEMAN	
A NURSE	

TIME: *The present*
PLACE: *Harlem, U.S.A.*
MOOD: *Of the moment*

SCENES

CHARACTER NOTES

GENERAL: The characters in *Simply Heavenly* are, on the whole, ordinary, hard-working lower-income bracket Harlemites. Paddy's Bar is like a neighborhood club, and most of its patrons are not drunkards or bums. Their small kitchenette rooms or overcrowded apartments cause them to seek the space and company of the bar. Just as others seek the church as a social center, or the pool hall, or dance hall, these talkative ones seek the bar.

SIMPLE: Simple is a Chaplinesque Character, slight of build, awkwardly graceful, given to flights of fancy, and positive statements of opinion — stemming from a not so positive soul. He is dark with a likable smile, ordinarily dressed, except for rather flamboyant summer sport shirts. Simple tries hard to succeed, but the chips seldom fall just right. Yet he bounces like a rubber ball. He may go down, but he always bounds back up.

JOYCE: Joyce is a quiet girl more inclined toward club work than bars, toward "culture" rather than good-timing. But she is not snobbish or cold. She is tall, brown skin, given to longish ear-rings, beads, scarves, and dangling things, very feminine, and cries easily. Her charm is her sincerity.

BOYD: Boyd has probably been half-way through college before his army service in Europe. Serious-minded, pleasant-looking, trying to be a writer, perhaps taking English courses at New York University on the last of his G.I. money. Almost every Harlem bar has such a fellow among its regular customers, who acts sometimes as a kind of arbiter when "intellectual" discussions come up.

ZARITA: Zarita is a lively bar-stool girl wearing life like a loose garment, but she is not a prostitute. Brassy-voiced, good-hearted, good-looking, playing the field for fun and drinks, she lives a come-day-go-day existence, generous in accepting or giving love, money, or drinks. A good dancer.

MISS MAMIE: Mamie is a hard-working domestic, using biting words to protect a soft heart and a need for love too often betrayed.

GITFIDDLE: Gitfiddle is a folk artist going to seed, unable to compete with the juke box, TV, and the radio, having only his guitar and his undisciplined talents. He furnishes all the music, with the Barfly pianist, for the songs and interludes.

MADAM BUTLER: Madame Butler has a bark that is worse than her bite — but her bark is bad enough. Large, fat, comical and terrible, she runs her rooming house as Hitler ran Germany.

MUSICAL NUMBERS

[Music by David Martin]

ACT ONE

Scene Two:	*Simply Heavenly*	*Joyce and Simple*
Scene Five:	*Did You Ever Hear the Blues?*	*Mamie and Melon*
Scene Six:	*Deep in Love With You*	*Simple*
Scene Seven:	*I'm Gonna Be John Henry*	*Simple*

ACT TWO

Scene One:	*When I'm in a Quiet Mood*	*Mamie and Melon*
	Look for the Morning Star	*Pianist and Joyce*
Scene Two:	*Look for the Morning Star*	*Joyce and Simple*
	I Want Somebody To Come Home To	*Joyce*
Scene Three:	*Let's Ball Awhile*	*Zarita and Guests*
Scene Nine:	*A Good Old Girl*	*Mamie*
Scene Eleven:	*Look for the Morning Star*	*Ensemble*

ACT ONE

SCENE ONE

A lonely guitar is playing in the darkness — it's the Blues...

SIMPLE's *room. Early spring evening.* SIMPLE, *just coming home from work, removes his jacket as he enters, but before he can hang it up, the voice of* MADAM BUTLER, *his landlady, is heard calling up the stairs, through the half–open door.*

LANDLADY: Mr. Semple! Oh, Mr. Semple!

SIMPLE: Yes'm?

LANDLADY: I heard you come in! Mr. Semple, would you mind taking Trixie out for a walk? My arthritis is bothering me.

SIMPLE: Madam Butler, please! I've got no time to walk no dog tonight. Joyce is waiting for me.

LANDLADY: From all I've heard, that girl's been waiting for you to marry her for years! A few minutes of waiting for you to show up tonight won't hurt.

SIMPLE: Madam, my private affairs ain't none of your business.

LANDLADY: Um–hum! Well, you don't need to take Trixie to no tree — just the nearest fireplug. [BOYD, *a fellow–roomer, peers in.*]

SIMPLE: Aw, I ain't hardly got home from work good, yet... Hello, Boyd. Come on in. Landladies is a bodiddling! How come she never make none of the other roomers — or you — to walk her dog?

BOYD: She knows I won't do it, that's why.

SIMPLE: Don't you ever get behind in your rent?

BOYD: Not to the point of walking dogs. But you seem to walk Trixie pretty often.

SIMPLE: Mostly always.

LANDLADY: Did you say you would take the dog?

SIMPLE: Oh, hell, lemme go walk the bitch.

LANDLADY: No profanity in my house.

SIMPLE: Madam, that's a perfectly good word meaning a fine girl dog — bitch — for female dog.

LANDLADY: There'll be no bitches in my house — and that goes for your girl friend, Zarita, too.

SIMPLE: I'll thank you to leave my friends out of this.

LANDLADY: I'll thank you to keep your profanity to yourself. This is a decent house. Now, come on and walk my dog — else pay me my rent.

SIMPLE: I'll walk your dog — because I love Trixie, though, that's what! If I had a dog, I wouldn't keep it penned up in the house all day neither. Poor old thing, airless as she is.

LANDLADY: She's not hairless.

SIMPLE: I said airless, Madam! Shut up airtight, wonder Trixie don't get arthritis, too. Dog and womens, dogs and womens! Damn! What am I gonna do?

BOYD: Good luck, pal. [SIMPLE *and* BOYD *exit. Blackout. In the darkness, Trixie's bark is heard. Auto horns, street noises.* SIMPLE's *voice addresses the barking dog.*]

SIMPLE: Now, Trixie, come on now. Come on, Trixie, do your duty. Leave that other dog alone, Trixie! Hound, get away from here! O.K., O.K., let's head on in the house. [*Bark.*] Now, go on to your madam. I guess you love her. Well, I love somebody, too! My choice, Joyce! She's the one I found — and that's where I'm bound. Trixie, that's where I am bound. [*The music of "Simply Heavenly" rises happily as the lights come up to reveal* JOYCE's *room.*]

SCENE TWO

JOYCE's *room a bit later.* JOYCE *is singing as, in a frilly dressing gown, she is putting her clothes away.*

JOYCE: Love is simply heavenly!
　　What else could it be?
　　When love's made in heaven
　　And you are made for me.
　　Love is simply heavenly!
　　What else can I say?
　　When love sends an angel
　　To hold me close this way.
　　Love is like a dream
　　That's too good to be true,
　　But when your lips kiss mine

The dream turns into you.
Yes, it's simply heavenly!
Our love's just divine —
For love is made in heaven
And you, my love, are mine!
Love is simply heavenly —

[*Voice of her* LANDLADY *calls from below stairs.*]

MRS. CADDY: Oo–oo–oo–oo! Miss Lane!

JOYCE: Yes ?

MRS. CADDY: I'm letting Mr. Semple come up. O.K?

JOYCE: Yes, indeed, Mrs. Caddy, I'm expecting him. [SIMPLE *knocks slightly and enters grinning.*]

SIMPLE: Hey, Baby! [*He closes the door, to which* JOYCE *objects.*]

JOYCE: Jess! No! Just a crack...

SIMPLE: Aw, your old landlady's worse than mine. At least I can shut my door when I got company.

JOYCE: You're a man. I'm a — [SIMPLE *bugs* JOYCE.]

SIMPLE: Lady! Which is what I like about you. Joyce, morals is your middle name. But you can still be a lady behind closed doors.

JOYCE: I know, Jess, those are the landlady's rules. Besides, I respect Mrs. Caddy.

SIMPLE: She don't respect you if she thinks soon as the door is shut...

JOYCE: Sshhss! Come on, rest your jacket, honey. It's warm.

SIMPLE: I knowed there was something! I forgot to bring your ice cream! I passed right by the place, too!

JOYCE: We can walk out for a soda.

SIMPLE: Or a beer?

JOYCE: Tomorrow's communion Sunday, and I do not drink beer before communion.

SIMPLE: You just don't drink beer, period! Gimme a little sugar and skip the beer.

JOYCE: Don't think I'll skip the ice cream.

SIMPLE: Let's set on the — [*He dances toward the studio bed.*]

JOYCE: There's a chair.

SIMPLE: Baby, what's the matter? Don't you trust me yet?

JOYCE: I don't mind you being close to me. But when you get close to a bed, too —

SIMPLE: Then you don't trust yourself.

JOYCE: Have you ever known me to —

SIMPLE: That's the trouble . . .

JOYCE: That goes with marriage, not courtship. And if you don't move on from courtship to engagement soon, Jess Semple, and do something about that woman in Baltimore.

SIMPLE: My wife! Isabel — she run me out — but she could claim I left her. She could find some grounds to get a divorce.

JOYCE: Since you're not together, why don't you get one?

SIMPLE: Joyce, I don't want to pay for no woman's divorce I don't love. And I do not love Isabel. Also, I ain't got the money.

JOYCE: I would help you pay for it.

SIMPLE: One thing I would not let you do, Joyce, is pay for no other woman's divorce. No!

JOYCE: Well, if you and I just paid for half of it, you'd only be paying for your part of the divorce.

SIMPLE: That woman wants me to pay for it all! And, Joyce, I don't love her. I love you. Joyce, do you want me to commit bigamy?

JOYCE: Five years you've been away from your wife — three years since you met me! In all that time you haven't reached a point yet where you can ask for my hand without committing bigamy. I don't know how my love holds out so long on promises. But now my friends are all asking when I'm going to get married. Even my landlady's saying it's a mighty long time for a man to just be "coming around calling," just sitting doing nothing.

SIMPLE: I agree, baby — when there ain't no action, I get kinder drowsy.

JOYCE: Well, to me, a nice conversation is action.

SIMPLE: Conversationing makes me sleepy.

JOYCE: Then you ought to go to bed early instead of hanging over Paddy's Bar until all hours. You have got to go to work just like I do.

SIMPLE: When I sleep, I sleep fast. Anyhow, I can't go to bed early just because you do, Joyce, until — unless —

JOYCE: Until what?

SIMPLE: Until we're married.

JOYCE: Simple!

SIMPLE: But, listen! It's Saturday night, fine outside. Spring in Harlem! Come on, let's us get some ice cream.

JOYCE: O.K., but, Jess, are you coming to church in the morning to see me take communion?

SIMPLE: You know I'll be there. We'll just take a little stroll down Seventh Avenue now and catch some air, heh?

JOYCE: And you'll bring me home early, so we can both get our rest.

SIMPLE: In a jiffy, then I'll turn in, too.

JOYCE: You don't mean into a bar?

SIMPLE: Baby, one thing I *bar* is *bars*.

JOYCE: Turn your back so I can dress.

SIMPLE: Don't stand over there. Anybody could be looking in.

JOYCE: There are no peeping–toms in this house. [SIMPLE *turns his back as she dresses, but drops his pack of cigarettes on the floor, bends down to get it, then remains that way, looking at* JOYCE *from between his legs.*]

JOYCE: Baby, is your back turned?

SIMPLE: Yes'm. [JOYCE *glances his way, clutches her dress to her bosom and screams.*]

JOYCE: Oh, Simple!

SIMPLE: I love it when you call me Simple.

> [*Head still down, he proceeds to turn a somersault, coming up seated on the floor with his back toward her.*]

SIMPLE: Now say my back ain't turned.

JOYCE: I didn't mean you had to turn inside out.

SIMPLE: That's the way you've got my heart — turned in ... [*He turns his eyes to look at her.*]

JOYCE: Then turn your head so I can dress.

SIMPLE: O.K., Joyce. Now, is everything all right?

JOYCE: Everything is all right.

SIMPLE: So you feel O.K.?

JOYCE: Simply heavenly! Oh, Jess, it's wonderful to be in love.

SIMPLE: Just wonderful — wonderful — wonderful —

[As JOYCE dresses, they sing.]

BOTH: Love is simply heavenly!
    What else could it be?
    When love's made in heaven
    And you are made for me.
    Love is simply heavenly!
    What else can I say?
    When love sends an angel
    To hold me close this way.
    Love is like a dream
    That's too good to be true,
    But when your lips kiss mine
    The dream turns into you.
    Yes, it's simply heavenly!
    Our love's just divine —
    For love is made in heaven
    And you, my love, are mine!

SIMPLE: Love is simply heavenly!
    What else could it be?
    When love is made in heaven
    And you are made for me.

JOYCE: Love is simply heavenly!
    What else can I say?
    When love sends me an angel
    To hold me close this way.

SIMPLE: Love is like a dream
    That's too good to be true,

[Dressed now, JOYCE emerges and SIMPLE rises to embrace her.]

JOYCE: But when your lips kiss mine
    The dream turns into you.

BOTH: Yes, it's simply heavenly!
    Our love's just divine —
    For love is made in heaven
    And you, my love, are mine!

[Blackout.]

SCENE THREE

Paddy's Bar. Midnight.

At a battered old piano in the corner a roustabout PIANIST *is playing a syncopated melody while* HOPKINS, *the bartender, beats lightly on the bar with a couple of stirrers as if playing drums. The music ceases as* MISS MAMIE, *a large but shapely domestic servant, enters and sits at her usual table.*

HOPKINS: Good evening, Miss Mamie. How's tricks?

MAMIE: Hopkins, them white folks over in Long Island done like to worked me to death. I'm just getting back to town.

PIANIST: You ought to have a good man to take care of you, Miss Mamie — like me.

MAMIE: Huh! Bill, from what I see of you, you can hardly take care of yourself. I got a mighty lot of flesh here to nourish.

PIANIST: Big woman, big appetite.

MAMIE: Right — which is why I like to work for rich folks. Poor folks ain't got enough to feed me.

PIANIST: I never eat much. But I sure am thirsty.

MAMIE: Stay that way! Hopkins, gimme a gin. [BODIDDLY, *a dock worker, leaps in shouting.*]

BODIDDLY: Hey, now, anyhow!

MAMIE: Anyhow, what?

BODIDDLY: Anyhow, we's here! Who's setting up tonight? [*Dead silence. No one answers.*] Well, Hop, I'll take a short beer.

MAMIE: It ain't nobody's payday in the middle of the week, Bodiddly. And the only man in this bar who manages to keep a little change in his pocket is Mr. Boyd here, drawing his G.I. pension.

BODIDDLY: [*Points at* BOYD *proudly.*] My boy!

BOYD: Hi, Bo!

MAMIE: Huh! There's as much difference between you and Ananias Boyd as between night and day.

BODIDDLY: Yeah, I know! His predilect's toward intellect — and mine's toward womens.

HOPKINS: And beer.

BODIDDLY: Boyd's the only man around here who's colleged.

BOYD: For all the good it does me. You dockworkers make more a week than I ever see writing these stories.

BODIDDLY: But none of us gets pensions.

MAMIE: None of you all in the war and got wounded neither. But if I was a man, I would have gone to war so I could get me a pension.

PIANIST: They had lady soldiers.

BODIDDLY: Whacks and Wavers.

MAMIE: By that time I were too big. [A LITTLE MAN *in nose glasses, carrying an umbrella, enters with an armful of highbrow papers and magazines. Noticing no one, he takes a table and begins to remove his gloves.*] There comes that character trying to make people think he's educated. One thing I like about Boyd here, even if he is a writer, he ain't always trying to impress folks. Also he speaks when he comes in a public place. [*The* LITTLE MAN *sits at an empty table.*]

CHARACTER: A thimble of Scotch, please.

BODIDDLY: A thimble of Scotch! [*All laugh but* BOYD.]

CHARACTER: And a tumbler of plain water, no ice.

HOPKINS: Right, sir! Like the English. [*As if to show her derision* MAMIE *orders loudly.*]

MAMIE: Hopkins, gimme some more gin.

HOPKINS: Coming up, Miss Mamie! [*A* VENDOR's *cry is heard outside. Carrying a watermelon, a jovial fellow,* WATERMELON JOE, *enters.*]

MELON: Watermelons! Juicy sweet!
Watermelons! Good to eat!
Ripe and red —
That's what I said —
Watermelons!

MAMIE: Joe, you better shut up all that catterwalling! You ain't working this time o' night?

MELON: Yes I is. I done sold all but one watermelon. Who wants it? Sweet as pie! No lie! My, my, my!

MAMIE: [*Inspects the melon.*] Hmmm! It do look good. Thumps good, too. Leave it for me behind the bar. I'll take it.

MELON: Thank you, Miss Mamie.

BODIDDLY: Better tie your pushcart to the curb 'fore somebody steals it.

MELON: I'm ahead of you, Diddly — got it locked to the lamp post. Boy, when I cry "Watermelons!" do you all know what happens to wom-ens ?

BODIDDLY: What?

MELON: Their blood turns to water and their knees start to shake 'cause they know I'm a man, and no mistake! Why, I sold a woman a water-melon one day and moved in and stayed three years.

BODIDDLY: That's nothing, I just spoke to a strange lady once setting on a stoop — and went upstairs and ain't come down yet. That was in 1936.

MELON: Diddly, you lying. Your wife done run you out twice with a kitchen knife.

BODIDDLY: I mean, excusing temporary exits.

MAMIE: Well, I been buying watermelons, Joe, for two summers, and I finds your fruits sweeter than you.

MELON: That's because you don't know me well, baby. Besides, I do not use my professional voice in your personal presence:

W–a–ter — melons!
Melons! Melons! Melons!
Sweet as they can be!
Sweet, good Lord!
But they ain't as sweet as me!
Watermelon Joe has got your
Wa–ter — melons!
[*He eases up to her cheek.*]
Me–lawns!...Me–loans!...Me–loons!

MAMIE: Man, you better get away from me! You know I got a husband, Watermelon Joe.

MELON: Where's he at?

MAMIE: I don't know where he's at, but I got one. And if I ain't, I don't want you.

MELON: [*Croons in her ear.*] Watermelons. Wa–ter–mel–ons

MAMIE: I sure do like your watermelons, though.

MELON: Nice red melons...

CHARACTER: [*Rises indignantly.*] Stereotypes! That's all both of you are. Disgraceful stereotypes!

MAMIE: [*Turns on him furiously.*] Mister, you better remove yourself from

my presence before I stereo your type! I like watermelons, and I don't
care who knows it. That's nothing to be ashamed of, like some other
colored folks are. Why, I knowed a woman once was so ashamed of
liking watermelons that she'd make the clerk wrap the melon up before she'd carry it out of the store. I ain't no pretender, myself, neither no passer.

BODIDDLY: What do you mean, passer?

MAMIE: Chitterling passer—passing up chitterlings and pretending I
don't like 'em when I do. I like watermelon and chitterlings both, and
I don't care who knows it.

CHARACTER: Just stereotypes, that's all. [*He shakes his head.*]

MAMIE: Man, get out of my face!

CHARACTER: Stereotypes...stereotypes . . . stereo... [*He retreats muttering.*]

MAMIE: Why, it's getting so colored folks can't do nothing no more without some other Negro calling you a stereotype. Stereotype, hah! If
you like a little gin, you're a stereotype. You got to drink Scotch. If
you wear a red dress, you're a stereotype. You got to wear beige or
chartreuse. Lord have mercy, honey, do—don't like no blackeyed
peas and rice! Then you're a down–home Negro for true—which I
is—and proud of it! [MAMIE *glares around as if daring somebody to dispute her. Nobody does.*] I didn't come here to Harlem to get away from
my people. I come here because there's more of 'em. I loves my race.
I loves my people. Stereotype!

CHARACTER: That's what I said, stereotypes!

MAMIE: You better remove yourself from my presence, calling me a
stereotype.

CHARACTER: Tch–tch–tch! [*Clicking his tongue in disgust, the* LITTLE MAN
leaves the bar as MAMIE *rises and threatens him with her purse. The* PI-
ANIST *rushes over to congratulate her.*]

PIANIST: Gimme five, Miss Mamie, gimme five! [*They shake hands.*]

MAMIE: Solid!

PIANIST: You and me agreed! I could drink on that.

MAMIE: You go right back where you was and set down.

BODIDDLY: Who agrees is me! Bartender, set up the bar—this far—from
Mamie to me. What'll you have, Cleopatra, a beer?

MAMIE: You know I drinks gin, Bodiddly. And I needs another one. That character done got me all upset. Where's all the decent peoples tonight? Where's Jess Simple?

BODIDDLY: I seen old Simp a couple of hours ago walking down Lenox Avenue with his girl. But Joyce turns in early. And when she turns in, she turns him out.

MAMIE: That's what I call a decent woman.

MELON: Damn if I do.

MAMIE: And that Simple is a good man. He needs himself a decent woman — instead of gallivanting around with chippies like Zarita that keeps a bar door flapping all night long. I never seen a woman could run in and out of a bar so much and so fast.

BODIDDLY: Ah, but that Zarita, she's sure a fine looking chick.

MAMIE: She wears her morals like a loose garment. Ain't no woman's man safe with her around.

MELON: She sure will drink a body up. Zarita damn near drunk me out of a whole car load of melons one night.

MAMIE: You sure is weak for young womens.

MELON: Miss Mamie, I could be weak for you.

MAMIE: Melon, scat! I done told you, get from over me! Scat! [*The door flies open and a seedy looking fellow rushes in calling to the bartender.*]

GITFIDDLE: Hey, Hop! Hey, Hop! Lend me my guitar from behind the bar there, please. Hurry up, man! I'll bring it back.

HOPKINS: What's the hurry?

GITFIDDLE: There's a big party of folks in the Wonder Bar down the street spending money like water.

HOPKINS: Here you are, Git.

GITFIDDLE: Thank you, man! [*He takes guitar and exits.*]

HOPKINS: I sure hope he can play up a few dollars — that man has been broke so long, it just ain't fair.

MAMIE: A good musicianer — doing nothing but playing for quarters folks throw him!

MELON: They say a woman brought old Gitfiddle low.

MAMIE: Getting high brought him low! Womens helps more mens than they don't.

MELON: I sure wish you'd help me.

MAMIE: Wish again, honey, because I ain't coming. I likes a man who works in one place, with one job, not all up and down the streets where he's subject to temptation. And as for me, I don't need nobody to help me.

MELON: [*Shrugs.*] Well, so that's that!

SIMPLE: [*Entering.*] Good evening!

MAMIE: We been missing you. Excusing Boyd there, this bar's full of nothing but characters.

BOYD: Thank you, Miss Mamie.

MAMIE: Where you been, Simple?

SIMPLE: Eating ice cream.

CROWD: What?

SIMPLE: And I had my picture took.

BODIDDLY: With your lady fair.

SIMPLE: For my lady fair. All posed like this. [*He assumes an attitude.*]

HOPKINS: She must've fell out laughing at that pose.

SIMPLE: She did not. That's one thing about Joyce. She never laughs at nothing about me, never does, which is why I loves that girl.

BOYD: You can find more reasons for liking a woman, Jess. Every time, a different woman, it's a different reason.

HOPKINS: Pay him no mind, Mr. Boyd. Zarita laughs with him and at him.

SIMPLE: Zarita's different. I do not, never will, can't—won't, and don't love no jumping jack of a Zarita. A man can't hardly keep Zarita in his arms, let alone in his heart.

HOPKINS: So we know, Jess Simple!

SIMPLE: But I have kept Joyce in my heart ever since I met her—and she is there to stay. Dog–gone it, I wish I had my divorce from Isabel. But at last, it looks like I am making some headway. They say a man's life changes every seven years. I sure hope I am going through the change.

HOPKINS: Mr. Change, what are you drinking?

SIMPLE: [*Takes an envelope from his pocket.*] Give me and Boyd a couple of beers. Then I want you to read something. Didn't even show it to Joyce yet—not to get her hopes up too high. It's from my wife.

BOYD: I don't want to read your personal letters, Jess.

SIMPLE: Here, pal, read it — because I can't believe my eyes.

BOYD: Um–mmmm! Well, here goes: "Dear Mr. Semple: Jess, at last I have found a man who loves me enough to pay for my divorce. This new man is a mail clerk, his first wife being dead, so he wants me for his second."

SIMPLE: Thank you, Father!

BOYD: "He knows I been married and am still married in name only to you, as you have not been willing to pay for the legal paper which grants freedom from our entanglement. This man is willing to pay for it. He says he will get a lawyer to furnish me grounds unless you want to contest. I do not want no contest, you hear me! All I want is my divorce. I am writing to find out if you will please not make no contest out of this. Let me hear from you tonight as my husband–to–be has already passed the point where he could wait. Once sincerely yours, but not now, Isabel."

SIMPLE: Sounds just like my wife!

HOPKINS: I suppose you've no intention of cross–filing.

SIMPLE: I would not cross that wife of mine no kind of way. My last contest with that woman was such that the police had to protect me. So that man can have her. I do not even want a copy of the diploma. I told Isabel when we busted up that she had shared my bed, my board, my licker, and my hair oil, but that I did not want to share another thing with her from that day to this, not even a divorce. Let that other man pay for it — they can share it together. Me, I'll be married again before the gold seal's hardly out from under the stamper.

HOPKINS: Good! Perhaps you'll settle down, stop running around, and stay home nights with Joyce.

SIMPLE: Married, I'll get somewhere in the world, too. Let's drink to it. And that man in Baltimore better pay for my wife's divorce! If he don't, I'll fix him. Here's my toast. [*He lifts his glass of beer.*]

In a horserace, Daddy–o,
One thing you will find —
There ain't NO way to be out in front.
Without showing your tail
To the horse behind . . .

[ZARITA *enters glittering.*]

ZARITA: Hey now! Hi, all and sundry!

SIMPLE: Zarita!

ZARITA: Excuse me, folks, for being in a hurry.

MAMIE: I told you so!

ZARITA: Jess, I'm going to Jersey! Come on! Coleman and his girl've got their car outside.

SIMPLE: The one with the top down?

ZARITA: That's the chariot — and I got nobody to ride back there with me.

MAMIE: Don't that child just bring you to tears?

SIMPLE: Is Coleman sober?

ZARITA: Just feeling a little groovy that's all! Come on!

BODIDDLY: Woman, shut that outside door! It's chilly. You know it ain't official summer yet.

ZARITA: Your blood's thin. My, it's hot in here! Come on, Jess. The motor's running.

SIMPLE: The motor might be running, but I ain't. Come here, girl. I got somethings to say to you. Zarita, you know I'm almost engaged to be married. I can't be running around with you.

ZARITA: You really got yourself tangled up. Well, anyhow, we'll just ride over the bridge to a little after–hours spot in Jersey for a few drinks, and come right back. There's no harm in that.

SIMPLE: You sure you coming right back? And Coleman is gonna drive me right to my door?

ZARITA: Or mine! Your room is kinder little and small and cold. Sugar, is you is, or is you ain't? [*She moves toward the door.*]

SIMPLE: Zarita, it's chilly out there and I ain't got my top coat.

ZARITA: Oh, Knuckle–Nose, we got a fifth of licker in the car to keep us warm. And there's some fine bars just across the George Washington bridge. You does or you don't?

SIMPLE: Aw, Zarita!

ZARITA: Old Simple Square, do I have to beg and plead with you? Listen! I've got my own money. I'll even treat you to a couple of drinks. Come on! Aw, come on! [*She entices him with a caress and they exit.*]

MAMIE: There goes a lamb to slaughter again. Ain't it a shame the kind of a deal a good woman gets when she goes to bed early!

BODIDDLY: Huh?

MAMIE: I ain't talking about a man like you with 17 children. I'm talking about Joyce.

BODIDDLY: Oh!

MAMIE: She goes to bed early, leaving Simple to yield to temptation.

MELON: I'd never yield, Miss Mamie. But if I did, I'd yield with you.

MAMIE: Melon, I say, get out of my face. It's mighty near midnight. Lemme go home.

MELON: If I didn't have my pushcart to wheel, I would 'scort you, Miss Mamie.

MAMIE: Watermelon Joe, with you at the handle, I might have to jump out and walk — or roll out, one — wild as you is with womens. Hopkins, hand me my watermelon and let me go to my virtuous couch. Good night, all, good night! [*She exits with her watermelon under her arm.*]

MELON: Huh, so she don't trust me to 'scort her home. Anyhow, I think I'll truck along after her and see can't I tote her melon to a taxi. Watermelons! Nice red ones! [*He exits.*]

BODIDDLY: Gimme a sherry, man. What'll you have, Boyd?

BOYD: Nothing, thanks.

[ARCIE *enters bustling.*]

BODIDDLY: Arcie, my love, what you doing out this time of night?

ARCIE: I come out looking for you — and done looked in seven bars.

[HOPKINS *automatically pours* ARCIE *some sherry.*]

BODIDDLY: And had a drink in each and every one!

ARCIE: Naturally! A lady don't go in a bar and not buy nothing. Diddly, lover, listen, there ain't but five of our children home — which means an even dozen is still out in the streets.

BODIDDLY: The children's big enough to take care of themselves.

ARCIE: If you was any kind of a father — If you was any kind of . . .

BODIDDLY: Woman, hush! And put that sherry wine down — before you be walking sidewise to keep from flying. Let's be getting upstairs — before some more of our children don't get home. Be seeing you, folks!

ARCIE: That man!

[ARCIE *and* BODIDDLY *go out. The bar is empty except for* BOYD *who rises to leave.*]

HOPKINS: Say, Boyd, as a writer, would you say them folks are stereo-types?

BOYD: In the book I'm writing they're just folks. Good night, Hop.

GITFIDDLE: [*Comes reeling into the bar as* BOYD *exits.*] Got–dog it! I done broke another string!

HOPKINS: Well, did you make any money?

GITFIDDLE: They paid me off in drinks. I had nothing to eat all day. Here, Hop, lend me another half for a sandwich — and keep this for secu-rity. [*He offers his guitar to* HOPKINS.]

HOPKINS: You must think Paddy's Bar is a bank. I lent you two dollars and a quarter already this week. Here's fifty cents more.

GITFIDDLE: Thanks, Hop! But wait a minute, Hop — lemme play you just one more blues. [*The woebegone* GITFIDDLE *strums a lonesome blues on his guitar as the lights lade to darkness*]

[*Blackout.*]

SCENE FOUR

> *Hospital room. Next day. During Blackout a bed backed by a white screen already attached is wheeled downstage center with* SIMPLE *already propped up in bed, very quiet. Both his legs are up in traction. Near the head of his bed is a single white chair. A* NURSE *all in white tiptoes in and calls softly. He answers with a groan.*

NURSE: Mr. Semple.

SIMPLE: Aw–um–mmm–mm–m!

NURSE: Such groaning! You aren't that bad off.

SIMPLE: When I suffers, Nurse, I like to suffer loud.

NURSE: There's a gentleman to see you. [*She beckons the caller.*] Here he is, sir.

MELON: Thank you, Nurse. [MELON *enters.* NURSE *exits*] Oh, man! You're all packed for shipping!

SIMPLE: Strung, hung and slung's what I am. Melon, this is the most! Um–mmm–mm–m!

MELON: All I heard was, you was in an accident.

SIMPLE: It were an accident, all right. Got–dog that Zarita! My mind told me —

MELON: Never mind what your mind told you, Daddy–o, just gimme the details. Here.

SIMPLE: What's that?

MELON: I brought you some books.

SIMPLE: I wish you'd of brought me a quart of beer and some pigs feet. I ain't much on books.

MELON: Comic books, man.

SIMPLE: Oh, *Horror in Hackensack. Terror in Trenton.*

MELON: Man, that's the crazy history of New Jersey.

SIMPLE: This makes me feel better already. Thanks, Melon.

MELON: Now, tell me what happened.

SIMPLE: The car tried to climb the George Washington Bridge, instead of going *across* it — turned half over — Coleman, his girl, and Zarita and me. But I was the *only* one that got throwed out, and on my — bo-hunkus. Melon, I'm all bruised up on my sit–downer.

MELON: I told you, you should stop balling, and take care of yourself.

SIMPLE: If I had took care of myself, I would not have these pretty nurses taking care of me now.

MELON: But look at the big hospital bill when you get out.

SIMPLE: Lemme hit one number, I'll settle it. But what worries me is when I'm going to get out.

MELON: You will never get out if you don't observe the rules and stop telling folks to bring you beer and pigs feet and things you are not supposed to have.

SIMPLE: But alcohol had nothing to do with it.

MELON: Oh, no?

SIMPLE: Womens aggravate a man, drunk or sober. Melon, I hope Joyce knows Zarita ain't nothing to me, even if I do accidentally go riding with her. But I don't want to discuss how come I'm in this hospital. You know, no matter what a man does, sick or well, something is always liable to happen — especially if he's colored. In this world, Melon, it's hard for a man to live until he dies.

[NURSE *enters.*]

MELON: I think you'll make it.

NURSE: There's a Miss Joyce Lane to see you. [*A look of great helplessness comes over* SIMPLE. *He appeals to his friend.*]

SIMPLE: Melon . . .

MELON: It's Joyce.

SIMPLE: Just like a man has to face his Maker alone, the same goes for facing a woman.

MELON: You want to see her, don't you?

SIMPLE: Worse than anything, I want to see Joyce, Melon. Also, I — I — I —

MELON: Also, you don't want to see her. I know. Good luck, old man. [*The* NURSE *shows* MELON *out. As they exit,* JOYCE *enters.*]

JOYCE: Jess! [*Tears come, and she takes out her handkerchief.*]

SIMPLE:: Baby, please don't cry. I'm all right.

JOYCE: But your legs! Are they broken?

SIMPLE: Doc says they ain't. But they sure are bent.

JOYCE: Then why are they all trussed up that way?

SIMPLE: Because I can't lay on my hine, that's why.

JOYCE: Your what?

SIMPLE: My hindparts is all skint up, Joyce. I hope that's a polite word for saying it.

JOYCE: But aren't you hurt badly?

SIMPLE: NO.

JOYCE: I am.

SIMPLE: Baby, don't you want to set down? Here on the bed. Then pull your chair up close, please.

JOYCE: Oh, Jess!

SIMPLE: I know, Joyce, I know. I hadn't ought to done it.

JOYCE: With a drunken driver, too — and Zarita.

SIMPLE: You know I love you.

JOYCE: And that's the way you show it? With your legs tied up in the air — on account of a —

SIMPLE: Auto wreck —

JOYCE: Woman.

SIMPLE: Just a little old innocent joy ride.

JOYCE: Oh, stop it!

SIMPLE: Baby, did you take communion this morning?

JOYCE: Yes, Jess, I did. I was almost late. I waited for you to go with me.

SIMPLE: Did they sing, "Jesus Knows Just How Much I Can Bear"?

JOYCE: Not today.

SIMPLE: I used to like that song. You know how I feel now? Just like I felt the last time Aunt Lucy whipped me. Did I ever tell you about that, Joyce?

JOYCE: No.

SIMPLE: It were a girl caused that whipping.

JOYCE: I'm not surprised, Jess.

SIMPLE: Aunt Lucy is dead and gone to glory, Joyce. But it were Aunt Lucy taught me right from wrong. When I were a little young child, I didn't have much raising. I knocked around every–which–where, pillar to post. But when Aunt Lucy took me, she did her best to whip me and raise me, too — 'cause Aunt Lucy really believed in her Bible. "Spare the rod and spoil the child." I were not spoiled. But that last whipping is what did it — made me the man I am today . . . I could see that whipping coming, Joyce, when I sneaked out of the henhouse one of Aunt Lucy's best hens and give it to that girl to roast for her Sunday School picnic, because that old girl said she was aiming to picnic *me* — except that she didn't have nothing much to put in her basket. I was trying to jive that girl, you know. Anyhow, Aunt Lucy found out about it and woke me up the next morning with a switch in her hand . . . But I got all mannish that morning, Joyce. I said, "Aunt Lucy, you ain't gonna whip me no more, I'se a man now — and you ain't gonna whip me." Aunt Lucy said, "You know you had no business snatching my best laying hen right off her nest." Aunt Lucy was angry. And big as I was, I was scared . . . Yet I was meaning not to let her whip me, Joyce. But, just when I was aiming to snatch that switch out of her hand, I seed Aunt Lucy was crying. I said, "What you crying for?" She said, "I'm crying 'cause here you is a man and don't know how to act right yet, and I done did my best to raise you so you'll grow up to be a good man. I wore out so many switches on your back — still you tries my soul. But it ain't my soul I'm thinking of, son, it's you. Jess, I wants you to carry yourself right. You understand

me? I'm getting too old to be using my strength up like this. Here!"
Aunt Lucy hollered, "Bend over and lemme whip you one more
time!"...Big as I was, Joyce, you know I bended. When I seen her
crying, I would have let Aunt Lucy kill me before I raised a hand.
When she got through, I said, "Aunt Lucy, you ain't gonna have to
whip me no more — I'm going to do my best to do right from now
on, and not try your soul. And I am sorry about that hen..." Joyce,
from that day to this, I have tried to behave myself. Aunt Lucy is gone
to Glory, now, but if she's looking down, she knows that's true. That
was my last whipping. But it wasn't the whipping that taught me what
I needed to know. It was because she cried and cried. When peoples
care for you and cry for you — and love you — Joyce, they can
straighten out your soul. [SIMPLE, *lost in his story, had not been looking
at* JOYCE. *Instead, as he finishes, he is looking at the ceiling. Suddenly* JOYCE
turns to bury her head on the back of her chair, sobbing aloud. SIMPLE, *forgetting that his legs are tied and that he cannot get out of bed, tries to rise.*]
Joyce!...Joyce!...Joyce! [*If he could, he would go to her and take her in
his arms.*] Joyce you're crying for me!

JOYCE: I'm not! I'm crying for your grandmother.

SIMPLE: It wasn't my grandmother I was telling you about, Joyce, it were
my Aunt Lucy.

JOYCE: Well, whoever it was, she had her hands full with you.

SIMPLE: She loved me, Joyce, just like I love you...Come here, feel my
heart — it's beating just for you...Joyce, please come here. [*He
reaches out his hand and* JOYCE *comes. She takes it, and he pulls her toward
him.*] Feel my heart. [*He puts her hand on his heart. But suddenly* JOYCE
buries her head on his chest and sobs violently. SIMPLE *puts an arm about
her and smiles, quietly happy.*]

[*Blackout.*]

SCENE FIVE

Paddy's bar. Saturday night. The joint is jumping. GITFIDDLE *is plunking his guitar.* BODIDDLY *is at the bar,* HOPKINS *behind it.* MAMIE *and
MELON sit at a table.* ARCIE *is in the middle of the floor, cutting up as if
she were a young woman.* JOHN JASPER, *one of her teenage jitterbug sons,
comes in, hits a few steps himself, whirls around, then taps her on the
shoulder.*

JOHN JASPER: Mama! Hey, Mama!

ARCIE: [*Stops dancing.*] Get away from me, son! Can't you see your mama is having a good time and don't want to be bothered with no children? Stop that dancing! Where's all my children? Arcilee and Melinda and Mabel and Johnny and Little Bits and Cora? Also Lilac? Huh?

JOHN JASPER: They all in the street, gone to Saturday night parties and things. Mama, lend me a quarter. I want to take the bus down to 96th Street to the Swords and Sabres dance.

ARCIE: Ask your daddy. He ain't paid me off yet. [*She again continues dancing as the boy approaches* BODIDDLY *at the bar.*]

JOHN JASPER: Hey, Daddy, gimme a quarter.

BODIDDLY: Scram! You too young to be in this bar, John Jasper. Here take this quarter, boy, and scram! Children all under a man's feet!

JOHN JASPER: Thanks, Dad! [*He skips off.* MISS MAMIE *and* MELON *do a slow Lindy hop to that music.*]

BODIDDLY: Woman, you better stop spending my money before you get it. Is you done your Saturday night shopping yet?

ARCIE: Can I do it on credit? Hand it over, Diddly, lover!

BODIDDLY: Many mouths as you got to feed, you better get to the stores before they close.

ARCIE: Them's your children, too. Ain't you gonna help me carry the grits?

BODIDDLY: Woman, you know I'm tired. Go do your shopping.

ARCIE: Treat me first.

BODIDDLY: Hop, give this woman a glass of Domesticated Sherry. [HOPKINS *laughs and pours her another glass of sherry before she exits.* ZARITA *enters.* MELON *and* MAMIE *stop dancing.*]

ZARITA: Simple hasn't been in yet tonight, has he, Hop?

HOPKINS: Not yet.

BODIDDLY: But if he's able to walk, he'll be here before it's over.

ZARITA: He's been back at work three or four days, and I haven't seen him. You know, Hop, when I went by Harlem Hospital, he acted like he was mad at me.

HOPKINS: No wonder — you took him riding and got him all banged up.

ZARITA: He didn't have to go. Nobody forced him. I just said, "Come on." Say, Hop, what you doing this morning when you get off from work?

HOPKINS: I'm going home, Zarita.

ZARITA: There's a nice new after–hours spot opened down on Seventh Avenue.

HOPKINS: I said, I am going home.

ZARITA: You didn't always go home so early after work, Mr. Hopkins.

HOPKINS: Do you call three o'clock in the morning early?

ZARITA: Real early! Don't you remember that night you drove me over to Newark?

HOPKINS: I remember.

ZARITA: And we didn't get back early either.

HOPKINS: Zarita, this is one morning I'm turning in. Maybe Simple'll take you to this new Bottle Club.

ZARITA: Maybe he will — if he ain't still mad. Anyhow, if you see him, tell him I'll be back. I will be back.

HOPKINS: Cool, Zarita, cool. [ZARITA *exits in rhythm to* GITFIDDLE'*s guitar.*]

MELON: Hey, Git, you sounds mighty good plunking over there in the corner. C'mon, Miss Mamie, let's dance some more.

MAMIE: Yes, you ought to be on the juke box.

GITFIDDLE: Juke boxes is the trouble now, Miss Mamie. Used to be, folks liked to hear a sure–enough live guitar player. Now, I start playing, somebody puts a nickel in the piccolo, drowns me out. No good for musicianers any more, but I got to make the rounds, try to hustle. See you later, Miss Mamie.

MAMIE: Git, I'd rather hear you than records any day. When you come back, I'm gonna throw you a dollar just to pick a blues for me.

GITFIDDLE: I won't be long, Miss Mamie, won't be long. [*He exits as* JOHN JASPER *runs in. At the piano the* BARFLY *continues to jazz.*]

JOHN JASPER: Papa!

BODIDDLY: John Jasper, now what you want? A man can't . . .

JOHN JASPER: Ronnie Belle . . .

BODIDDLY: A man can't enjoy his self . . .

JOHN JASPER: Ronnie Belle . . .

BODIDDLY: . . . without some child stuck up in his face.

JOHN JASPER: [*Dances as he talks.*] Ronnie Belle says she won't stay home and mind the babies, and it's my turn to go out this Saturday night. She says if I go, she's going.

BODIDDLY: You tell Ronnie Belle I'll come up there and fan her good, if she don't do what she's supposed to. I declare to goodness, these young folks nowadays! You get upstairs, John Jasper, and tell your sister what I said.

JOHN JASPER: Yes, sir, Papa! [*He exits.*]

MAMIE: Diddly, you sure got some fine children.

BODIDDLY: And every one of them born in New York City, Harlem. When I left the South, I never did go back. [JOHN JASPER *returns, dancing to the piano.*]

BODIDDLY: Lord, that boy's back again. John Jasper, now what do you want?

JOHN JASPER: Mama says for you to come on upstairs and bring her a pint of cooking sherry.

BODIDDLY: You know your mama ain't gonna do no cooking this time of the night! Tell Arcie to come down here and get her own wine. Scat, boy, scat! [JOHN JASPER *dances out.*]

MAMIE: Diddly, that's the cutest one of your children. I'll give him a dime myself.

BODIDDLY: Lemme get way back in the corner so's no more of my kinfolks can find me — not even my wife. [*He goes into a corner as* SIMPLE *enters.*]

MAMIE: Look who's coming there!

PIANIST: Hey, Jess!

MELON: Jess Semple!

HOPKINS: [*Lifting a bottle of beer.*] It's on the home!

MAMIE: Welcome home!

BODIDDLY: To the land of the living!

MAMIE: Amen! Bless Jess!

HOPKINS: Zarita was just looking for you. [*Happily the customers retire to tables with the drinks as* SIMPLE *remains leaning stiffly on the bar.*]

SIMPLE: Don't mention Zarita, please, Hop! She's near about ruint me. Joyce is treating me cool, cool, cool, since I come out the hospital and I explained to her over and over I was just out riding. Hop, oh, Hop! Oh, man, have I got a worried mind! You know when I reached home my old landlady come handing me a Special Delivery from my wife which stated that the Negro in Baltimore has only made one payment on our divorce, leaving two payments to go. Hop, you're educated! How much is one payment on $400, leaving two payments to go?

HOPKINS: $133.33 and one–third cents.

SIMPLE: Now I could just about pay one–third cents.

HOPKINS: I thought you said that man in Baltimore loved your wife so much he was willing to pay for the whole divorce.

SIMPLE: Inflation's got him — so he just made one down payment. Isabel writ that if I would make one payment now, she would make one, then everybody could marry right away. But I cannot meet a payment now — with the hospital bill, rent up, food up, phones up, cigarettes up — everything up — but my salary. Divorces are liable to go up, too, if I don't hurry up and pay up. Lord! Women, women, women! [*He paces the floor.*]

MELON: Don't let women get you excited, man! Set down and take it easy.

[*Offered a seat,* SIMPLE *protects his haunches with his palms.*]

SIMPLE: The last thing I want to do is set down!

MAMIE: Then stand up to it like a man! You made your own bed hard. What you drinking?

SIMPLE: Whiskey.

VOICES: Whiskey?

MELON: And you're usually a beer man!

SIMPLE: Tonight I want whiskey. Hop, I said, whiskey! I'm broke, busted, and disgusted. And just spent mighty near my last nickel for a paper — and there ain't no news in it about colored folks. Unless we commit murder, robbery or rape, or are being chased by a mob, do we get on the front page, or hardly on the back. Take flying saucers. For instance according to the *Daily News*, everybody has seen flying saucers in the sky. Everybody but a Negro. They probably won't even let flying saucers fly over Harlem, just to keep us from seeing one. Not long ago, I read where some Karl Krubelowski had seen a flying saucer, also Giovanni Battini saw one. And way out in Pennsylvania mountains some Dutchman named Heinrich Armpriester seen one. But did you read about Roosevelt Johnson or Ralph Butler or Henry Washington or anybody that sounded like a Negro seeing one? I did not. Has a flying saucer ever passed over Lenox Avenue yet? Nary one! Not even Daddy Grace has glimpsed one, nor Ralph Bunche.

Negroes can't even get into the front page news no kind of way. I can't even see a flying saucer. When I do, that will be a great day.

HOPKINS: It would probably scare you to death — so you wouldn't live to see your name in the papers.

SIMPLE: Well, then — I could read about it in the other world then — and be just as proud — me, Jess Semple, kilt by a flying saucer.

ARCIE: [*Enters yelling tipsily.*] Bodiddly! Bodiddly! Why don't you come on upstairs?

BODIDDLY: Aw, woman, hush! Every time I turn around there's families under my feet. Set down and leave me be.

ARCIE: I did not come to set down. It's past midnight. I come to get you to go to bed.

BODIDDLY: I know when to go to bed my own self.

ARCIE: Then come on, you great big no–good old bull–necked son–of–a–biscuit eater!

BODIDDLY: Sit down, I'll buy you a sherry wine. Hop!

[ZARITA *enters with* ALI BABA, *an enormous well–dressed fellow in a turban.*]

ZARITA: Hello, you all! Hey, Jess Semple! Folks, dig this champion roots–herbs–and–numbers–seller from south of the border. I just come by to show you my new man I met at the Baby Grand. Don't he look like a sultan? But we got business. Come on! We're gonna do the town, ain't we, Ali Baba?

MAMIE: Ali Baba?

ZARITA: Sugar Hill, Smalls, and every place! Come on, Texas Tarzan, come on! Jess, I'm glad you came out of that little accident O.K. 'Bye, all!

[ZARITA *kisses* ALI BABA. *He sneezes.* MELON *ducks. As* ZARITA *and her new man exit,* SIMPLE *looks sheepish.*]

BODIDDLY: She don't need us tonight.

HOPKINS: She's got her a two–ton Sugar Daddy.

MELON: She's got her a human shower.

MAMIE: Paddy's Bar is small–time to Zarita this evening. She'll be in here Monday all beat out, though — and looking for Jess Semple.

SIMPLE: Or somebody else simple — but it won't be me.

MELON: Where have I heard that before?

SIMPLE: Where have I heard that before? [*They glare at each other.*]

MELON: Where have I heard that before? [SIMPLE's *feelings are hurt.*]

SIMPLE: I'm going and see Joyce. I need to see somebody that loves me.

[*A* POLICEMAN'S VOICE *is heard in the street.*]

POLICEMAN: Hey, you! Stay off the street with that noise box. Don't you know it's against the law, out here hustling for dimes? Next time I hear that racket, I'll run you in.

GITFIDDLE: Yes, sir, Officer! [GITFIDDLE *enters crestfallen.*] A man can't play music nowhere no more. Juke box drowns him out in the bars, cops run him off the streets, landlady won't let you play in your own room. I might as well break this damn box up!

MAMIE: Gitfiddle, I told you, you can play for me.

BODIDDLY: Me too.

ARCIE: Sure, Git.

MELON: And me, Git.

MAMIE: Come on, now! Let's have some music like you feels it, Gitfiddle.

MELON: Did you ever hear the Blues
    On a battered old guitar?
    Did you ever hear the Blues
    Over yonder, Lord, how far?
    Did you ever hear the Blues
    On a Saturday night?
    Did you ever hear the Blues
    About some chick ain't done you right?
    Baby, did you ever hear the Blues?

MAMIE: Did you ever hear the Blues
    On an old house–rent piano?
    Did you ever hear the Blues
    Like they play 'em in Savannah?
    Did you ever hear the Blues
    In the early, early morn?
    Wondering, wondering, wondering
    Why you was ever born?
    Baby, did you ever hear the Blues?

MELON: When the bar is quiet
    And the night is almost done,

Them old Blues overtake you
At the bottom of your fun.
Oh, Lord, them Blues!
Echo . . . echo . . . echo . . . of the Blues!

MAMIE: Good morning, Blues! Good morning!
Good morning, Blues, I say!
Good morning, Blues, good morning!
You done come back to stay?
You come back to bug me
Like you drug me yesterday?

MELON: Blues, I heard you knock last night,
But I would not let you in.
Knock, knock, knock, last night
But I would not let you in.
I tried to make believe
It weren't nothing but the wind.

ALL: Blues, Blues, Blues!
It were the Blues!
Maybe to some people
What the Blueses say is news
But to me it's an old, old story

MAMIE: Did you ever hear the Blues
On a battered old guitar?
Did you ever hear the Blues
Over yonder, Lord, how far?
Did you ever hear the Blues
On a Saturday night?

BOTH: Did you ever hear the Blues
About some chick ain't done you right?

ALL: Baby, did you ever hear the Blues?

[*Blackout.*]

SCENE SIX

JOYCE's *room. Sunday evening.*
JOYCE *is sewing. The bell rings seven times. The* LANDLADY *calls from offstage.*

MRS. CADDY: I'll answer it, Miss Lane. I'm right here in the hall.

JOYCE: Oh, thank you, Mrs. Caddy. You're about the nicest landlady I know.

MRS. CADDY: Are you decent? Do you want to see Mr. Semple? He's kinda cripple — so down here or up there?

JOYCE: I'm sewing, so let him come up here, please — if he can make it.

SIMPLE: [*Enters and closes the door.*] I've made it. Well, I'm back on my feet, up, out, and almost at it.

JOYCE: I see. You may come in. Remember the door — Mrs. Caddy's rules.

SIMPLE: [*Opens the door a crack.*] Dog–gone old landlady! Joyce, I know I'm a black sheep. But I explained it all to you the last time you come by the hospital.

JOYCE: I accepted your explanation.

SIMPLE: But you don't seem like you're glad to see me, now I'm out — the way you didn't say almost nothing when I come by Friday.

JOYCE: I'm glad to see you.

SIMPLE: Then lemme kiss you. Ouch! My back! [*He yells in pain as he bends over.*]

JOYCE: Oh!

SIMPLE: I think my veterbrays is disconnected.

JOYCE: What did the X–rays show?

SIMPLE: Nothing but a black mark. The doctor says I'm O.K. Just can't set down too suddenly for a while.

JOYCE: Then have a slow seat.

SIMPLE: Joyce, is you my enemy? You sound so cool. Am I intruding?

JOYCE: Oh, no. I'm just having a nice peaceful Sunday evening at home — which I must say, I haven't had too often since I've been knowing you.

SIMPLE: Baby darling, I'm sorry if I'm disturbing you, but I hope you're glad to see me. What you making?

JOYCE: Just lingerie for a girl friend who's getting married.

SIMPLE: Step–ins or step–outs?

JOYCE: Slips, Jess, slips. Jess Semple, stop breathing down my neck. The way you say things sometimes, you think I'm going to melt again, don't you! Well, instead you might get stuck with this needle. Listen, hand me that pattern book over there. Let me see how I should insert this lace.

SIMPLE: What're you doing with all those timetables and travel books, baby?

JOYCE: Just in case we ever should get married, maybe I'm picking out a place to spend our honeymoon — Niagara Falls, the Grand Canyon, Plymouth Rock...

SIMPLE: I don't want to spend no honeymoon on no rock. These books is pretty, but, baby, we ain't ready to travel yet.

JOYCE: We can dream, can't we?

SIMPLE: Niagara Falls makes a mighty lot of noise falling down. I likes to sleep on holidays.

JOYCE: Oh, Jess! Then how about the far West? Were you ever at the Grand Canyon?

SIMPLE: I were. Fact is, I was also at Niagara Falls, after I were at the Grand Canyon.

JOYCE: I do not wish to criticize your grammar, Mr. Semple, but as long as you have been around New York, I wonder why you continue to say, I were, and at other times, I was?

SIMPLE: Because sometimes I were, and sometimes I was, baby. I was at Niagara Falls and I were at the Grand Canyon — since that were in the far distant past when I were a coachboy on the Santa Fe. I was more recently at Niagara Falls.

JOYCE: I see. But you never were "I were"! There is no "I were." In the past tense, there is only "I was." The verb *to be* is declined, "I am, I was, I have been."

SIMPLE: Joyce, baby, don't be so touchous about it. Do you want me to talk like Edward R. Murrow?

JOYCE: No! But when we go to formals I hate to hear you saying, for example, "I taken" instead of "I took." Why do colored people say, "I taken," so much?

SIMPLE: Because we are taken — taken until we are undertaken, and, Joyce baby, funerals is high!

JOYCE: Funerals are high.

SIMPLE: Joyce, what difference do it make?

JOYCE: Jess! What difference does it make? Does is correct English.

SIMPLE: And 'do' ain't?

JOYCE: Isn't — not ain't.

SIMPLE: Woman, don't tell me *ain't* ain't in the dictionary.

JOYCE: But it ain't — I mean — it isn't correct.

SIMPLE: Joyce, I gives less than a small damn! What if it aren't? [*In his excitement he attempts to sit down, but leaps up as soon as his seat touches the chair.*]

JOYCE: You say what if things aren't. You give less than a damn. Well, I'm tired of a man who gives less than a damn about "What if things aren't." I'm tired! Tired! You hear me? Tired! I have never known any one man so long without having some kind of action out of him. You have not even formally proposed to me, let alone writing my father for my hand.

SIMPLE: I did not know I had to write your old man for your hand.

JOYCE: My father, Jess, not my old man. And don't let it be too long. After all, I might meet some other man.

SIMPLE: You better not meet no other man. You better not! Do and I will marry you right now this June in spite of my first wife, bigamy, your old man — I mean your father. Joyce, don't you know I am not to be trifled with? I'm Jesse B. Semple.

JOYCE: I know who you are. Now, just sit down and let's spend a nice Sunday evening conversing, heh?

SIMPLE: [*Sits down, but it hurts him.*] Ouch!

JOYCE: Oh, Sweety! Let me make you a nice cool drink. Lemonade?

SIMPLE: Yes, Joyce, lemonade. [JOYCE *exits. Suddenly* SIMPLE *realizes what he has agreed to drink and cries in despair.*] Lemonade! [*He sits dejected until* JOYCE *returns.*] Baby, you ain't mad with me, is you? [JOYCE *smiles and shakes her head, no.*] Because I know you know what I mean when I say, "I is" — or "I are" or "was" or whatever it be. Listen, Joyce, honey, please. [*He sings.*]

When I say "I were" believe me.
When I say "I was" believe me, too —
Because I were, and was, and I *am*
Deep in love with you.

If I say "You took" or "taken"
Just believe I have been taken, too,

Because I were, and am, and I *is*
Taken in by you

If it *is* or it *ain't* well stated,
And it *ain't* or it *aren't* said right,
My love still must be rated
A love that don't fade over night.

When I say "I am" believe me.
When I say "I is" believe me, too —
Because I were, and was, and I *is*,
Deep in love with you.

Damn if I ain't!

JOYCE: A small damn? [*He grabs her.* JOYCE *screams.*]

[*Blackout.*]

SCENE SEVEN

SIMPLE*'s room.*

   A month later. MR. BOYD *comes down the hall and sees* SIMPLE*'s door ajar. He looks in.*

BOYD: Hey, fellow, what you doing home on Saturday night?

SIMPLE: Boyd, man, come on in. Joyce is gone to some gal's wedding shower — and damn if I'm going out to any bar. Still and yet, Boyd, I'm in a good mind to take that money I been saving and blow it all in, every damn penny, because man, it looks hopeless. Push done come to shove on that divorce, I got to pay for my part of it. So last month I started saving. But, damn, I got so far to go!

BOYD: How much do you have to save in all?

SIMPLE: One hundred thirty–three dollars and thirty–three cents. I'm as far as Leviticus.

BOYD: What do you mean, Leviticus?

SIMPLE: Aunt Lucy always said, "The Bible is the Rock: Put your trust therein." So that's where I'm putting my money. I got to save $133.33. If I put a ten dollar bill in each chapter every week from Genesis on, in eighteen and a half weeks I will have it — and I'll only have to go as far as Nahum.

BOYD: Nahum?

SIMPLE: That's a book in the Bible, somewhere down behind Ezekiel. If I ever get to Nahum that's it. I done put ten in Genesis, ten in Exodus, and five in Levi.

BOYD: I thought you said *ten* every week.

SIMPLE: I were a little short this past week. Anyhow, I got twenty–five.

BOYD: Come on, let's go around to Paddy's.

SIMPLE: Thanks, Daddy–o! I will not yield to temptation! No! Not especially since I done got another letter from that used–to–be wife of mine, Isabel. Sit down, Boyd. Listen. "Jesse B. Semple, you are less than a man. You marry a girl, neglect her, ignore her, and won't help her divorce herself, not even when your part ain't only but one–third of the payment. You can go to hell! You do not deserve no gold seal on your decree, because you have not put a cent into it. Therefore, since I am going to pay for this divorce myself, your paper may not be legal. From now on, you kiss my foot! Isabel Estherlee Jones. P.S. I have taken back my maiden name, as I wants no parts of you attached to me any longer. MISS JONES."

BOYD: She's angry.

SIMPLE: Seems like it. Boyd, I will not let Isabel get the last word on me. I'll send that lawyer my part of the money next week, even if I have to put my whole paycheck in to do it. Right now I got twenty–five in the Bible. When I add my old check, that won't leave but about ah — er — a sixty to go. I can pawn a suit, one overcoat, and my radio — which might still leave about fifty. Boyd, can you lend me fifty?

BOYD: Fellow, are you out of your mind?

SIMPLE: This is an emergency. I need a gold seal on my divorce, too — so I got to pay for it. I got to have that gold seal, Boyd! I got to have it! It's got to be legal for Joyce. But then it's up to me to get that money, ain't it, Boyd? It ain't up to you nor nobody else — it's just up to me.

BOYD: Yes, Simple, I'm afraid it is. Get hold of yourself, make a man of yourself. You got to live up to your obligations.

SIMPLE: You done said a big word, Boyd.

BOYD: And it's a big thing you've got to do, fellow, facing up to yourself. You're not the first man in the world to have problems. You've got to learn how to swim, Jess, in this great big ocean called the world.

SIMPLE: This great big old white ocean — and me a colored swimmer.

BOYD: Aw, stop feeling sorry for yourself just because you're colored. You can't use race as an excuse forever. All men have problems. And even if you are colored, you've got to swim beyond color, and get to that island that is you — the human you, the man you. You've got to face your obligations, and stand up on that island of you, and be a man.

SIMPLE: Obligations! That's a word for you, Boyd! Seems like to me obligations is just a big old rock standing in a man's way.

BOYD: Then you've got to break that rock, fellow. Or, maybe I should say rocks.

SIMPLE: I know what you mean — like the beer rock, huh, Boyd?

BOYD: Um–hum!

SIMPLE: And the licker–rock — only I don't drink much whiskey.

BOYD: Well, say the bar–rock in general.

SIMPLE: That night–owl rock.

BOYD: Out until four A.M.

SIMPLE: Yes, the chick–chasing rock.

BOYD: Zarita!

SIMPLE: Not mentioning no names! But, man, I done shook that chick. But then there's always that old trying–to–save–money rock.

BOYD: You mean putting–it–off–until tomorrow rock.

SIMPLE: Which has really been my stumbling rock.

BOYD: You got to bust it, man. You know about John Henry, don't you?

SIMPLE: Sure I do.

BOYD: He was the champion rock–buster of them all.

SIMPLE: My Uncle Tige used to sing about him. Boyd, I been making up my mind to break through my rocks, too. [BOYD *smiles.*] Yes, I is, Boyd, I is.

BOYD: You just got to bust 'em, fellow, that's all. [BOYD *exits.*]

SIMPLE: [*Takes off his shirt and changes into a ragged pajama top.*] Bust 'em! I got to bust 'em. Like that song of Uncle Tige's. That old man sure could sing — made up songs, too. [SIMPLE *sits on bed to take off his shoes.*] Made his own about John Henry which went — lemme see. [*He tries to remember.*] How did it go? Something about —

They say John Henry was a man.
And they say he took a hammer in his hand —
[*He uses one shoe as a hammer.*]

That's it!
And busted a rock
So hard he gave the world a shock!
Yes, they say John Henry was a man.
They say John Henry won a prize,
And they say he gave his life to win that prize.
[*He comes forward.*]
Yes, they say he hammered on
Until his breath was gone!
[*As if speaking to himself.*]
They say John Henry won a prize.
[*He reaches toward his back pocket*]
Well, there's a prize I'm gonna win,
And the time's long gone I should begin.
[*From his wallet he shakes his last five dollar bill, opens the Bible, and puts it in between the pages.*]
But it's better late than never,
And no time ain't forever.
[*He clasps the Bible to his chest.*]
So right now, I'm gonna start to win.
[*He turns forward resolutely, putting Bible down.*]
It takes a long haul to get there, so they say,
And there's great big mountains in the way.
But I'm gonna make it through
If it's the last damn thing I do.
[*He bangs his hand on the Bible.*]
I'm gonna be John Henry, be John Henry,
I'm gonna be John Henry, too.

[*Curtain.*]

ACT TWO

SCENE ONE

The music of the Blues on the guitar, slow, haunting, syncopated, precedes the rise of the curtain. Paddy's Bar. A week later. Evening.

ARCIE *is sitting alone at a table drinking sherry wine and working a crossword puzzle in the paper.* BOYD *is writing in a notebook at another table. The* PIANIST *lazily runs his fingers over the keys as* HOPKINS, *behind the bar, stifles a yawn.*

HOPKINS: Blue Monday night, no money, and I feel like hell. What you writing, Boyd?

BOYD: Just making some notes for a story I might write — after observing life in Harlem over the weekend.

HOPKINS: You didn't go to Philly Sunday to see that young lady?

BOYD: She's vacationing in Paris, which is O.K. by me, because when we get ready to honeymoon, I won't have to take her to Europe.

HOPKINS: Far as I could take a chick on a honeymoon would be the Theresa Hotel.

BOYD: That's about as far as I could take one, unless I sell some of this stuff I've been writing.

[MAMIE *enters, panting.*]

HOPKINS: Hey, Mamie! What's the matter?

MAMIE: I'm seeking escape — that Melon — [MELON *enters with a hangdog air.*] Man, if you would just stop following me! Now that you're so bold as to call at my house every night, at least let me have a little peace when I take a walk, without you at my heels.

MELON: Aw, Miss Mamie, you know I'm drawn to you.

MAMIE: When I get home from work, man, *I am tired.* I just want to set down, and rest, and read my paper. But Tang–a–lang–lang! You ring the bell! It looks like here lately, at home, in the bar, anywhere, every time —

When I'm in a quiet mood, here you come.
When I'm deep in solitude, here you come.
When I feel like settling down —

MELON: There I are!

MAMIE: When I'm gazing at the moon —

MELON: In falls your star!

MAMIE: My dial is set, the tone is low,
There's nice sweet music on my radio
I take a book, the story's fun
But when you ring my bell, I never get my reading done.
When I'm in a quiet mood, up you pop.
When I'm playing solitaire, in you drop.

MELON: The way you upset me makes my heartstrings hum —

MAMIE: When I'm in a quiet mood

BOTH: Here you [I] come!

MAMIE: It's raining outside. It's nice in the house.
Everything is cool — quiet as a mouse.
The doorbell rings. Who can it be?
My solitude is ended, Lord, you're looking for me!
Slippers on my feet, in my boudoir chair,
F–M on the dial, "The Londonderry Air."

The telephone rings, you say you're coming by.
When you get to my door —

BOTH: My, Oh, my!

[MAMIE *walks away*, MELON *follows*.]

MELON: Oh, you act so cute and you switch so coy —
Mamie, I was meant to be your playboy.
I dial your phone, hear you yell, "Damn Sam!"
Which means that you know I'm your honey lamb.
With hankering heart, I just follow you.
Your kisses are as sweet as sweet mountain dew.
I ring your bell, it's just old me —
I come around to try to keep you company.
I've sampled lots of melons whose flavor's fine,
But you are the sweetest melon on my vine.
I know that you love me by the look in your eye.
When I knock at your door —

BOTH: My! Oh, my!

MAMIE: When I'm in a quiet mood, up you pop.
When I'm playing solitaire, in you drop.

MELON: The way you upset me makes my heartstrings hum.

MAMIE: When I'm in a quiet mood —

BOTH: Here you [I] come!

MAMIE: When the night is free to get my beauty sleep,
I cannot sleep, so I'm counting sheep.
The doorbell rings — I shoot the sheep — Bam! Bam!
'Cause there in the door stands some old moth–eaten lamb.
I could scream! It's not a dream —
Here you come — to upset me! . . . And, honey, I'm leaving.
Here I go! . . . And I mean it!

MELON: Well, I guess this time she really means it.

MAMIE: Well, if you're coming, come on!

MELON: I'm going to follow — here I come!

[MAMIE *and* MELON *exeunt.* SIMPLE *bursts in exuberantly.*]

SIMPLE: Hey, now, moo–cow! Gimme a little milk. Barman, untap your key. Suds us up! Let's drink to it, even if it is my last dollar.

HOPKINS: Your last dollar, didn't you get paid this week?

SIMPLE: I did, but I took that money — all of it — and added it to what was in the Bible and sent it off to Baltimore — $133.34. Being last on payments, I had to pay that extra penny to change Divorce Pending to Divorce Ending!

HOPKINS: Congratulations!

SIMPLE: Joyce knows I love her. But to get a woman to make his bed down, a man has to make his mind up. Joyce is sweet, I mean! My queen — my desire, my fire, my honey — the only woman who ever made me save my money!

ARCIE: Simple.

SIMPLE: Yes, ma'am?

ARCIE: What's a four–letter word for damn?

SIMPLE: Arcie, do you see that sign? [*He points to:* "NO PROFANITY IN HERE."] Well, I do not repeat no four–letter words in public.

ARCIE: Damn! [ZARITA *enters briskly switching.*]

ZARITA: Hi, folks! I thought I'd stop by and have a quick one. Mr. Semple, how do you do? Set me up, Hop. [*She approaches* SIMPLE.] How are you, Sugar?

SIMPLE: Zarita, could I have a word with you, private?

ZARITA: Of course! It won't be the first time.

ARCIE: Hummmmmm–mm–m! I thought so. That girl is like a magnet to that man.

[HOPKINS *pours* ARCIE *a drink as* SIMPLE *and* ZARITA *go aside.*]

HOPKINS: Stay out of other people's business, Arcie.

ARCIE: O.K! O.K!

ZARITA: So you're not even going to speak to me again?

SIMPLE: What I do say is, I ain't gonna talk to you. Good evening — and Good–bye! Excuse me.

ZARITA: Aw, not like that, Jess, listen . . . [ZARITA *puts an arm around* SIM-PLE.]

ARCIE: Hey there, you writer, Boyd. What is the path in the field which a plow makes called?

BOYD: Furrow.

ARCIE: Six letters, just right. Now, wait a minute. Tell me, what is a hole with just one opening?

BOYD: How may letters?

ARCIE: Six, starts with D.

HOPKINS: Dugout?

ARCIE: Just fits. A dead general. A God–damn dead general!

[SIMPLE *pulls away from* ZARITA.]

ZARITA: But, Jess, you know you and me together always has fun.

SIMPLE: Zarita, I'm the same as about to get married. I got responsibili-ties.

ZARITA: I am a lady, Jess Semple. Don't worry, I'll stay out of your life. I'm tired of paying you a sometime call when I'm feeling lonely. Anyhow, I always did bring my own licker. You never had none.

SIMPLE: But I always treat you when I meet you — when I can. Zarita, you know I'd give you the shirt off my back.

ZARITA: And I'd gladly give you mine. Go on and get your rest, Jess. You never turned in this early before.

SIMPLE: I still got to make a week's work before that lay–off comes.

ZARITA: I guess you'll say good night, even if you wouldn't say hello.

SIMPLE: Good night.

ZARITA: Good night.

[SIMPLE *expects* ZARITA *to leave. Instead she stands there and smiles at him her sweetest smile.* SIMPLE *looks at the bar as if he wants to sit down on the stool again, then looks at* ZARITA. *Finally he decides to leave.*]

SIMPLE: Going my way, Boyd?

BOYD: I might as well, it's getting late. So long, folks.

ARCIE: And I ain't finished this puzzle.

BOYD: Hop'll help you. Good night. [SIMPLE *and* BOYD *exeunt, as the* PI-ANIST *ripples the keys.*]

ARCIE: It ain't but a quarter to twelve. What's happening to Simple?

ZARITA: He's getting domesticated. You know, Arcie, I wish someone would feel about me the way Simple feels about Joyce, and she about him, even if they do have their ups and downs. I guess a little trouble now and then just helps to draw people together. But you got to have somebody to come together with. [*The notes on the piano rise hauntingly.*] Gee, Bill, you play pretty sometimes.

PIANIST: I studied to be a concert pianist, but the concert never did come off.

ZARITA: What's that you're playing now? Sounds familiar. [*She leans on the piano.*]

PIANIST: Some new piece a colored boy wrote, I heard it on the radio. Let me croon it to you:

Just a little shade and shadow
Mixed in with the light
Helps to make the sunshine brighter
When things turn out right

ZARITA: Just a little pain and trouble
Mixed in with the fair
Helps to make your joys seem double
When clouds are not there.
Look for the morning star
Shining in the dawn!
Look for the rainbow's arch
When the rain is gone!
Don't forget there're bluebirds
Somewhere in the blue.
Love will send a little bluebird
Flying straight to you.

[*The light fades as* JOYCE *is heard singing.*]

Look for the morning star
Shine, shine, shining in the dawn!
Rainbow, rainbow, rainbow's arch
When the rain is gone.
Don't forget you'll find bluebirds
Somewhere in the blue.
Love will send a little bluebird
Flying straight to you . . .

[*Blackout as the melody continues into the next scene.*]

SCENE TWO

JOYCE's *room. Two weeks later.*
   JOYCE *is serving* SIMPLE *some sandwiches as she continues to sing.* SIMPLE *looks very serious.*

JOYCE: ... Love will send a little bluebird
   Flying straight to you ...
   Just a little shade and shadow ...

SIMPLE: ... Shades and shadows, just like the song says. Listen, Joyce, you know when I first met you on that boatride, I said to myself, "That girl's too good for me. I can't make no headway with that kind of woman." Yes, I did! To tell the truth, Joyce, you have me a kinder hard road to go — you know, with your morals and —

JOYCE: And you already married.

SIMPLE: Yes, but not wedlocked ...

JOYCE: Still and yet there was a shadow between us ...

SIMPLE: Of bigamy,

JOYCE: And gossip,

SIMPLE: Old landladies,

JOYCE: Friends,

SIMPLE: And I run around a lot in them days, too ...

JOYCE: In shady places — speakeasies, and things, so you said ...

SIMPLE: Shady nothing! Them places was really dark — after–hours spots, Joyce. Now I know better. I'm older! And when I look at you, oh I can see the sun, Joyce! It was dark, but now the clouds are rolling by.

JOYCE: Just a little shade and shadow
   Mixed in with the light
   Helps to make the sunshine brighter
   When things turn out right.

SIMPLE: True, so true!

JOYCE: Just a little pain and trouble
   Mixed in with the fair
   Helps to make your joys double
   When clouds are not there.

SIMPLE: Wonderful the morning star
   Shining in the dawn!

JOYCE: Wonderful the rainbow's arch

BOTH: When the rain is gone!

JOYCE: Don't forget you'll find bluebirds
Somewhere in the blue.
Love will send a little bluebird
Flying straight to you.

SIMPLE: Sing about the morning star
Shine–shine–shining in the dawn!
Rainbow, rainbow, rainbow's arch

BOTH: When the rain is gone

JOYCE: I am sure we'll find bluebirds
Right here in the blue

BOTH: Love has sent a singing bluebird
Straight to me and you.

[*They kiss as the music rises lyrically.*]

JOYCE: Oh, Jess! Life is really wonderful!

SIMPLE: I wouldn't be caught dead without it. But — er — a —

JOYCE: But what, Jess?

SIMPLE: It's wonderful. But, Joyce, baby, something is always happening to a Negro — just when everything is going right. Listen — I'm sorry, but there's something I got to tell you, much as I don't want to.

JOYCE: About your divorce?

SIMPLE: No, sugar, that's all filed, paid for, ought to be ready for the seal soon. Something else has come up. It's that — it's that — well, the notice come last week that it was coming. I just didn't tell you — I'm being laid off my job.

JOYCE: Oh, Jess! Not fired!

SIMPLE: No, not fired, just temporary, three or four months till after New Year's while they converts. Converting! And us planning to get married. Every time a Negro plans something —

JOYCE: Aw, come now! We'll get married, Jess.

SIMPLE: I can't even get my laundry out — let alone put my dirty shirts in.

JOYCE: Jess, I'll do your laundry. Bring me a bundle tomorrow and I'll bring them back to you — rub–a–dub–dub — white as snow.

SIMPLE: You're a doll, Joyce, you almost never come to my room.

JOYCE: Well, this'll give me a chance to see the curtains I made for you.

SIMPLE: Come see.

JOYCE: I will—when I bring this laundry, and if you need it, Jess, I can let you have a little money.

SIMPLE: I couldn't take no money from you.

JOYCE: But you can have it.

SIMPLE: I'd be embarrassed.

JOYCE: Have you got enough to eat?

SIMPLE: Oh, sure, I'll make out.

JOYCE: Well, on the weekend, Mr. Semple, you're going to dine with me. Make up your mind to that. And don't say one word about being embarrassed. Everything is going to be all right, I know. I talk to the Lord every night on my knees and I know.

SIMPLE: How long exactly it'll be before that job opens up again, to tell the truth, I don't know. Joyce, what are we going to do? We wants to get married, and all these years I have not saved a thing. Baby, have you figured up how much our wedding is going to cost?

JOYCE: There's no need to worry about that now. You've got enough on your mind tonight, darling. I just want you to know that I'm behind you.

SIMPLE: But, Joyce, baby, look! I ain't got nothing put away. I don't know if our plans are gonna go through or not.

JOYCE: Look, Jess, don't worry. If you ain't got the money to buy no license, well, when we get ready to get married we gonna get that license.

SIMPLE: But, Joyce, honey, I don't want you to be building no castles in the sand.

JOYCE: Jess, I have built my castles in my heart. They're not in no sand. No waves is gonna beat them down. No wind is gonna blow them apart. Nothing can scatter my castles. I tell you, nothing! Their bricks are made out of love and their foundations are strong. And you, Jess Semple, you are the gate–keeper of my castle—which is in my heart. You are the gate–keeper of my castle. [JOYCE *sits on the floor at* SIMPLE's *feet and lays her head in his lap.*] Oh, Jess, we'll have our own little place, our own little house, and at night we'll both be there after jobs are done. Oh, Jess, baby, you don't know how much—

I want somebody to come home to

When I come home at night.
I want someone to depend upon
I know will do right.

I want somebody to come home to
I'm sure will be at home.
I want someone who is sweet and kind
I know will not roam.

I'm a homebody — and this homebody
Wants somebody to share my share
For each homebody needs somebody
Who will always be right there.

I want somebody to come home to
Who'll make my dreams come true
A nice someone who'll be the one
I know will be you.
[*Repeating from release closing with this.*]
A nice homebody who's just somebody
Lovely to come home to.

[*Blackout.*]

SCENE THREE

SIMPLE*'s room. Early evening.*
       SIMPLE *is lying on his bed, shoes off and shirt tail out, dozing. A doorbell is heard ringing madly. Commotion downstairs and in the hallway.* ZARITA *bursts in on a startled* SIMPLE. *A large red pocketbook swings from one of her arms.*

ZARITA: It's my birthday, Jess! And I brought my friends around to celebrate — since you're broke these days and don't come out no more.

[SIMPLE *leaps up and begins to tuck his shirt in and put on a shoe. Voices are heard on the stairs.*]

BODIDDLY: What floor is it on?

HOPKINS: You're sure he's expecting us?

MAMIE: We rung the bell.

MELON: I been here before.

ARCIE: I'm having trouble with these steps.

[BOYD *is seen outside* SIMPLE*'s door.*]

BOYD: Shsss–ss–sss! Be quiet. What the hell is going on? You want to get us in trouble with the landlady? [*By now the crowd — which includes all the bar customers and as many strangers as desired to make the staging lively — has pushed* BOYD *into the room.*]

ZARITA: I tell you, it's my birthday, Jess! Come on in, everybody.

MELON: Happy birthday!

PIANIST: Happy birthday, Zarita!

[GITFIDDLE *begins to play.*]

SIMPLE: Zarita, your birthday ain't mine. And I don't want —

ZARITA: But I want to share it with you, Daddy! We brought our own liquor. When it runs out, we'll send and get some more. Won't we, Melon?

MELON: Liquor's about gone now, Whoopee–ee–ee!

ARCIE: Have some o' my sherry, Simple. I got my own bottle.

ZARITA: Jess, honey, I forgot to tell you I'd be twenty–some odd years old today. We started celebrating this morning and we're still going strong.

BODIDDLY: The ball is on!

ZARITA: Let the good times roll in "D"!

MELON: Whoopee!

[ZARITA *begins to sing.*]

ZARITA: If you ain't got nothing
And there's nothing to get,
Who cares long as you're doing it?
If you ain't got anything
Better to do,
Why not do what's good to do?

MELON: What's that?

ZARITA: Ball, ball, let's ball awhile!
Ball, ball, honey chile!
Sing! Shout! Beat it out!

ALL: Dance! Prance! Take a chance!
Grab the blues and get them told —
When you're happy in your soul.

ZARITA: Start the music playing
Let the good times roll.

ALL: Whail! Sail! Let it fly!

ZARITA: Cool fool: we're riding high!

ALL: Ball, ball, let's ball awhile!

[*Everybody dances wildly with a dazed* SIMPLE *in their midst, one shoe still off.*]

ZARITA: Ball, ball, let's ball awhile!
Ball, ball, honey chile!
Sing! Shout! Beat it out!
Dance! Prance! Take a chance!
Grab the blues and get them told —
When you're happy in your soul.

Start the music playing,
Let the good times roll.
Whail! Sail! Let it fly!
Cool Fool: We're riding high!
Ball, ball, let's ball awhile!

ALL: Ball, ball, let's ball awhile!
Ball, ball, honey chile!
Sing! Shout! Beat it out!
Dance! Prance! Take a chance!
Grab the blues and get them told —
When you're happy in your soul.

ZARITA: Start the music playing
Let the good times roll!

[*The whole room starts rocking.*]

ALL: Wail! Sail! Let it fly!
Cool fool! We're riding high!
Ball! Ball! Let's ball awhile!

BODIDDLY: Hey now!

ZARITA: Ow! It's my birthday! We're balling!

HOPKINS: Happy birthday, Zarita!

MELON: Dog-gone it! This bottle is empty.

ARCIE: Mine, too. Diddly, go get some more.

BODIDDLY: Send Melon. Here's fifty cents. [*He tosses* MELON *a coin.*]

ZARITA: Play that again, Git, "Let's Ball Awhile."

MAMIE: Ball! Ball! Honey chile!
Ball! Ball! Let's ball awhile!

ARCIE: Yippeee–ee–ee–e! Diddly, shake yourself! [ZARITA's *big red pocketbook is swinging wildly on her arms as the crowd stops dancing and moves back to let her and* SIMPLE *cavort madly together in a fast and furious jitterbug, each trying to outdo the other in cutting capers.*] Aw, do it, Zarita! [ZARITA *spins around and around with her purse in her hand swirling high above her head. Suddenly the clasp comes open — the innumerable and varied contents of her enormous pocketbook fly all over the room, cascading everywhere: compact, lipstick, handkerchief, pocket mirror, key ring with seven keys, scattered deck of cards, black lace gloves, bottle opener, cigarette case, chewing gum, bromo quinine box, small change, fountain pen, sunglasses, address books, fingernail file, blue poker chips, matches, flask and a shoe horn.*]

ZARITA: Oh, ooo–oo–o! My bag! Stop the music! Stop, Git, stop!

ARCIE: Girl, your perfume done broke!

ZARITA: My *Night in Egypt*!

BODIDDLY: If you broke your mirror, it's seven years bad luck

PIANIST: Help her pick her thing up, man.

BODIDDLY: I'm helping. But what's this! [*Holding up a red brassiere.*]

BOYD: Lord, women sure can have a lot of stuff in their pocketbooks!

MAMIE: She's even got poker chips!

ZARITA: Jess, you help me, baby. The rest of you all stay where you are. I don't know some of you folks, and I don't want to lose nothing valuable.

ARCIE: You ain't got nothing I want, child.

ZARITA: Where's my *China Girl* lipstick in the jade–studded holder? I don't want to lose that lipstick! Jess, you reckon it rolled outside?

SIMPLE: Might could be. Lemme look. [*Just then the doorbell rings nine times.*] My ring!

ZARITA: My lipstick! Where's my lipstick? Help me, sugar. [ZARITA *pulls* SIMPLE *down with her on the floor to search for the lipstick in the doorway as the bell continues to ring.*].

ARCIE: Somebody let Melon in with that licker.

BODIDDLY: Let that man in.

HOPKINS: The door's still open. He ought to have sense enough to come in.

BODIDDLY: I say to hell with the bell, and help Zarita find her stuff. Whee! Smell that *Night in Egypt!*

[SIMPLE *finds the lipstick and* ZARITA *kisses him.*]

SIMPLE: Here it is!

ZARITA: Aw, goody! [GITFIDDLE *starts the music again and all dance.*] Aw, Simple, just because we're dancing, you don't have to keep on kissing me.

SIMPLE: Who's kissing who, Zarita? *You're* kissing me.

BODIDDLY: Come up for air, you two! Come up for air! Aw, play it, Git.

[*The music soars. But suddenly the room becomes dead silent as everyone stops still, except* SIMPLE *and* ZARITA *who are embracing.* JOYCE *is standing in the doorway. Drunkenly* ARCIE *speaks.*]

ARCIE: Come on in girl, and join the fun!

PIANIST: Slappy Slirthday!

JOYCE: [*Hardly believing her eyes.*] This is Mr. Semple's room, isn't it?

PIANIST: Sure is. We're having a ball.

ZARITA: [*Back to the door, hollers.*] Play it again, Git! Come on — "Let's Ball a While!" Where's Melon with the licker? . . . Oh! [*Suddenly both she and* SIMPLE *see* JOYCE. SIMPLE *is astounded.*]

SIMPLE: Joyce!

JOYCE: Jess, I brought your laundry I washed for you. I thought you might want to wear one of the shirts Sunday.

ZARITA: Tip on in, Joyce, and enjoin my birthday. We don't mind. I'm Zarita. Just excuse my stuff all over the place. We been having a ball, Simp and me and —

JOYCE: I did not know you had company, Jess.

[WATERMELON JOE *arrives with his arms full of bottles and pushes past* JOYCE.]

MELON: Gangway! The stuff is here and it's mellowed! Get out of the door, woman! Make room for Watermelon Joe — and the juice with the flow.

JOYCE: [*Hands* SIMPLE *his bundle as* MELON *distributes bottles.*] Excuse me for being in your guests' way. Here, please take your laundry.

[*The loud voice of* SIMPLE'S LANDLADY *is heard calling angrily as she enters in kimono and curlers.*]

LANDLADY: Wait a minute! I'm the landlady here, and what I want to know is, who is this strange man walking in my house with his arms full of bottles! And *who* left my front door open? Who? I want to know who? Did you, Jess Semple? This is a respectable house. What's going on here? Do you hear me, Mr. Semple?

SIMPLE: [*Meekly.*] Yes'm. These is just some guests, that's all.

LANDLADY: Well, get 'em out of here — raising sand in my house! Get 'em out I say! [*She exits in a huff.*]

JOYCE: I'm going — as quick as I can. [*She starts to pass* SIMPLE.]

SIMPLE: Joyce!...Joyce! You know she don't mean you. I wants a word with you, Joyce.

JOYCE: [*Turns on him furiously, fighting back her tears.*] With me? You don't need to explain to me, Jess Semple. Now I have seen that Zarita woman with my own eyes in your bedroom. No wonder you're giving a birthday party to which I am not invited. I won't be in your way tonight, Jess — nor ever — any more. [*She looks back into the room as she leaves.*] Enjoy yourselves. Good night! [JOYCE *rushes down the hall and out of the house.*]

SIMPLE: Joyce!...Joyce!...Joyce!...

ZARITA: Huh! Who does that old landlady think she is? You pay your rent, don't you, Simple? Come on, folks, let's ball awhile.

PIANIST: Happy slirthday!

SIMPLE: [*Stands holding his parcel of laundry.*] I'm sorry, Miss Arcie, Boyd, Diddly!...*To hell with your birthday*, Zarita!...Folks, I'm sorry. Will you all go?

[ARCIE *scurries out. The others follow.* MELON *retrieves several of the bottles and takes them with him.* ZARITA *picks up her red bag and swaggers out with* MAMIE *behind her.*]

ZARITA: I know where we can ball, folks — at my house! Come on!

MAMIE: I been throwed out of better places than this.

[GITFIDDLE *turns at the door and looks at* SIMPLE *as if to say he's sorry, but* SIMPLE *does not look up.* BOYD, *the last to go, closes the door. All exit down the stairs, leaving* SIMPLE *in the middle of the floor. He feels his cheek, looks in the mirror, then takes his handkerchief and violently tries*] *to wipe* ZARITA's *lipstick from his jaw. He throws the handkerchief on the dresser and sinks down on the bed, his head in his hands.*]

SIMPLE: Oh, my God! [GITFIDDLE's *guitar is heard going down the stairs.*] Oh, my God!...My God!...Oh, God! [THE LIGHTS DIM TO A SINGLE SPOT *on the forlorn figure. There is the snapping of a broken sting on the distant guitar.*]

[*Blackout.*]

SCENE FOUR

Paddy's Bar. A quiet Sunday evening.
    SIMPLE *enters and gloomily begins taking articles from his pockets and putting them on the bar.*

SIMPLE: Hop, is you seen Zarita?

HOPKINS: Nope. Guess she's still recovering from her birthday.

SIMPLE: If you do see her, give her this junk.

HOPKINS: Looks like to me you've snatched her purse.

SIMPLE: I'd snatch her head if I could! That woman has ruint me now — Joyce is out of my life.

HOPKINS: Have a drink fellow, on me.

SIMPLE: This is one time I do not want a drink, Hop. I feel too bad. I have phoned her seventeen times, and Joyce will not answer the phone. I rung her bell four nights straight. Nobody would let me in. I sent Joyce eight telegrams, which she do not answer.

HOPKINS: And Zarita?

SIMPLE: I don't never want to see Zarita no more. The smell of that *Night in Egypt* is still in my room.

HOPKINS: A man should not fool around with a bad woman when he's got a good woman to love.

SIMPLE: Don't I know that now!

HOPKINS: Have you tried to see Joyce today? Sunday, she might be home.

SIMPLE: Tried? Are you kidding? That's all I've done. These is my bitter days! Hop, what shall I do?

HOPKINS: I don't know, Jess.

SIMPLE: Negroes never know anything important when they need to. I'm going to walk by her house again now. I just want to know if Joyce got home safe from church.

HOPKINS: She's been getting home safe all these years.

SIMPLE: Hop, I'm nearly out of my head. I got to talk to her. I'll stand in front of her house all night if I have to.

[ZARITA *enters, cool, frisky, and pretty as ever.*]

HOPKINS: Uh–oh!

ZARITA: Hel–lo! Jess, I'm glad I caught you. I was a little shy about coming around to your place for my things.

SIMPLE: I brought your things here, Zarita. [HOPKINS *puts them on the bar.*]

ZARITA: I thought you might, you're so sweet, sugar. Lemme treat you to a drink, and you, too, Hop.

SIMPLE: No, thank you.

ZARITA: Don't be that way. Set us up, here, Hopkins.

SIMPLE: I'm not drinking no more myself.

ZARITA: What? Just because you're out of work, you don't have to put down all the pleasures. Say, listen, Jess, if you're broke, I can let you have a little money.

HOPKINS: Zarita!

ZARITA: But no jive, Jess. Because you're wifeless and workless, a nice little old guy like you don't have to go hungry, never. I cook string–beans and ham almost every day.

SIMPLE: I don't like stringbeans.

ZARITA: I'll fry you some chicken, then.

SIMPLE: Forget it, please!

ZARITA: O.K. If you're that proud. [*She opens her purse.*] Anyhow, here honey–boy, take this ten — in case you need it.

SIMPLE: Um–um! NO! Thanks, Zarita, no! [*He backs away.*]

ZARITA: I meant no harm. I'm just trying to cheer you up. Like that party which I brought around to your house. Knowing you wasn't working, thinking maybe you'd be kinder embarrassed to come to my place for my birthday and not bring a present, I brought the party to you. Meant no harm — just to cheer you up.

SIMPLE: Please don't try to cheer me up no more, Zarita. Hop, I'm cutting out. I'm going by — you know where I told you, one more time. [SIMPLE *starts out.*]

HOPKINS: Don't try to break her door down.

SIMPLE: I'm just gonna stand on the sidewalk and look up at her window.

HOPKINS: I hope you see a light, pal.

[SIMPLE *exits as the* PIANIST *begins to play softly,* "Look for the Morning Star." *He sings, starting with the release.*]

PIANIST: Look for the morning star
Shining in the dawn
Look for the rainbow's arch
When the rain is gone.

[*The remainder of the song he hums.* ZARITA, *lonely, looks around at the quiet bar, then cries in desperation.*]

ZARITA: I'm lonesome, Hop! I'm lonesome! I'm lonesome! [*She buries her head on the bar and weeps as the piano continues.*] I'm lonesome...

[*Blackout.*]

SCENE FIVE

SIMPLE'*s room. Late evening.*
    SIMPLE *is lighting a cone of incense in a saucer on his dresser as* BOYD *pokes his head in the door, sniff, and enters.*

BOYD: Hy, fellow! What's that burning on the dresser?

SIMPLE: Incense. I lit it to keep warm. I really hates winter.

BOYD: Oh, man, cold weather makes you get up and go, gives you vim, vigor, vitality!

SIMPLE: It does not give me anything but a cold — and all that snow outside!

BOYD: Perhaps you are just not the right color for winter, being dark. In nature you know, animals have protective coloration to go with their environment. Desert toads are sand–colored. Tree lizards are green. Ermine, for example, is the color of the snow country in which it originates.

SIMPLE: Which accounts for me not having no business wading around in snow, then. It and my color do not match. But, please, let's stop talking about snow, Boyd.

BOYD: Agreed — as cold as it is in this icebox!

SIMPLE: Landladies has no respect for roomers a–tall, Boyd. In fact, ours cares less for her roomers than she does for her dog. She will put a roomer out — dead out in the street — when he does not pay his rent, but she does not put out that dog. Trixie is her heart! She keeps Trixie warm. But me, I has nothing to keep warm by, but incense. I'm sick of this kind of living, Boyd. Maybe if I just had a little something, a place to live, some money, I could win Joyce back. If I don't get her back, Boyd, I don't know! I just don't know!

BOYD: I can lend you a small amount, Jess, if you need it — you know, five or ten.

SIMPLE: But I borrows only when I *hope* I can pay back, Boyd. [*A creaking sound is heard on the steps. The* LANDLADY'S VOICE *is heard outside.*]

LANDLADY: I do believes somebody's smoking marijuana in my house.

SIMPLE: Listen! Don't I hear a elephant walking? [*She knocks loudly on* SIMPLE's *door.*] Come in!

LANDLADY: Mr. Semple, I am forced to inform you that I allows no reefer smoking in my home.

SIMPLE: I allows none in my room, neither.

LANDLADY: Then what do I smell?

SIMPLE: Chinese incense from Japan.

LANDLADY: Is you running a fast house?

SIMPLE: Madam, you have give me a idea!

LANDLADY: I am not joking, Jess Semple. Tell me, how come you burning that stuff in my house? Is it for bad luck or good?

SIMPLE: I don't believe in no lucky scents. I am just burning this for fun. It also gives out heat. Here, I will give you a stick to perfume up your part of the house.

LANDLADY: Thank you, I'll take it even if it do smell like a goodtime house to me. And that nude naked calendar you got hanging on your wall ain't exactly what I'd call decent. Don't you licker store give out no respectable girls on their calendars?

SIMPLE: They do, but they got clothes on.

LANDLADY: Naturally! Never would I pose in a meadow without my clothes on.

SIMPLE: I hope not, Madam.

LANDLADY: Meaning by that...

SIMPLE: Meaning you have such a beautiful character you do not have to show your figure. There is sweetness in your face.

LANDLADY: I appreciates that, Mr. Semple. [*She shivers.*] Whee! It is right chilly up here.

SIMPLE: It's a deep freeze.

LANDLADY: If you roomers would go to bed on time — and your guests would go home — including Mr Boyd — I would not have to keep heat up until all hours of the night.

SIMPLE: Has the heat been up tonight?

LANDLADY: You know it were warm as toast in this house at seven p.m. Funny where your heat disappears to. Downstairs I fails to notice any change myself.

SIMPLE: Madam, science states that heat is tied in with fat.

LANDLADY: Meaning...?

SIMPLE: You're protected.

LANDLADY: I don't study ways of insulting roomers, Jess Semple, and that is the second sly remark you made about me tonight. I'll thank you to regret it.

SIMPLE: Madam, I does regret it!

LANDLADY: To my face — fat! Huh! You heard him, Mr. Boyd. [*She exits muttering.*] Elephant, huh? Behind in your rent, huh!

BOYD: Now our landlady's angry.

SIMPLE: I tell you, something's always happening to a colored man! Stormy weather! Boyd, I been caught in some kind of riffle ever since I been black. All my life, if it ain't raining it's blowing. If it ain't sleeting, it's snowing. Man, you try to be good, an what happens? You just don't be good. You try to live right. What happens? You look back and find out you didn't live right. Even when you're working, and you try to save money, what happens? Can't do it. Your shoes is wore out. Or the dentist has got you. You try to save again. What happens? You drunk it up. Try to save another time. Some relative gets sick and needs it. What happens to money, Boyd? What happens?

BOYD: Come on, man, snap out of it! Let's go down to Paddy's and have a drink. At least we can sit up in the bar and get warm — and not think about what happens.

SIMPLE: You go, Boyd. What happens has done already happened to me

[*Slowly* BOYD *leaves. Half through the door suddenly a bright thought comes to him. He smiles and snaps his fingers, then exits closing the door, leaving* SIMPLE *alone as the* LIGHT FADES SLOWLY TO DARKNESS.]

[*Blackout.*]

SCENE SIX

Sidewalk on Lenox Avenue, downstage apron, with a sign LENOX AV-ENUE, *a let–down flap at left. Early evening.* BOYD *walks briskly down the street as if on a mission, entering right. Exits left. Following him,* JOHN JASPER *comes dancing along the sidewalk right, selling papers and stopping to hit a step now and then.*

JOHN JASPER: Paper!...*Amsterdam News*!...Read all about it! Get your paper! [*He dances off left.* BODIDDLY *enters right followed by* ARCIE *hobbling along behind him.* BODIDDLY *turns, stops.*]

BODIDDLY: Woman, you better stop tagging *behind* me on the street, and walk *beside* me, like a wife should — before I lose my impatience.

ARCIE: Diddly, these new shoes hurt my feet.

BODIDDLY: I paid $20 for them shoes for you! Arcie, ain't you read in the Bible where Moses walked for forty years in the wilderness bare-footed? Now, here you can't a block without complaining!

ARCIE: But Diddly, lover, I ain't Moses.

BODIDDLY: Aw, come, woman! [*Exeunt. Enter* MAMIE, *trailed by* MELON *right.*]

MAMIE: Melon, you got more nerve that Liberace's got sequins. You ain't gonna get nowhere, so there's no need of you trailing me through the streets like this.

MELON: I can't help it, Miss Mamie. I'm marked by a liking for you! [*He addresses her in rhymed jive, spoken.*]

You're my sugar,
You're my spice,
You're my everything
That's nice.

MAMIE: Melon, I done told you —
You *ain't* my sugar
You *ain't* my spice.

If you was a piece of cheese
I'd throw you to the mice.

[*She moves on with* MELON *in pursuit.*]

MELON: Miss Mamie —
Your words are bitter
But your lips are sweet.
Lemme kiss you, baby —
And give you a treat.

MAMIE: Melon —
When cows start playing numbers
And canary birds sing bass,
That is when you'll stick your
Big mouth in my face.

[MAMIE *exits indignantly with* MELON *pleading as he follows.*]

MELON: Aw, Miss Mamie, listen!
Wait a minute now!
I ain't no canary bird,
And you sure ain't no cow.
But...

[*Exit* MELON.]

[*Blackout.*]

SCENE SEVEN

JOYCE's *room. Same evening.*
    BOYD *stands at the door as* JOYCE *opens it.*

BOYD: I hope you'll pardon me, Miss Lane — and maybe it's none of my
business at all — but I was just walking down Lenox Avenue when the
idea came to me and I felt like I ought to come and talk to you. [*He
stands awkwardly.*]

JOYCE: You may sit, Mr. Boyd. [*She takes his hat.*]

BOYD: Thank you. I — I —

JOYCE: Yes?

BOYD: Well, it's about Simple. You know, I mean Jess Semple. He didn't
ask me to come to see you. In fact, he doesn't know I'm here at all.
But he's been rooming right next to me quite a while now, and I —
well — well, I never saw him like he is before.

JOYCE: [*Begins to freeze.*] You know him well?

BOYD: Very well.

JOYCE: Are you one of his drinking buddies of the Paddy's Bar set?

BOYD: I'm not much of a drinking man, Miss Lane. I'm a writer.

JOYCE: A writer! What do you write?

BOYD: Books.

JOYCE: Books!

BOYD: About Harlem.

JOYCE: Harlem! I wish I could get away from Harlem.

BOYD: Miss Lane, I'm worried about Simple.

JOYCE: You're worried about Simple. He never seems to worry about himself.

BOYD: I think maybe you really don't know about that birthday party.

JOYCE: There's really nothing I want to learn.

BOYD: Except that it wasn't Simple's party. He didn't plan it, and didn't know anything about it until it descended on him.

JOYCE: Huh! Just like that — from above.

BOYD: They came to surprise us.

JOYCE: You too? You don't look like the type of man to attract that conglomeration of assorted humans. If you're going to tell me something, Mr. Boyd, tell me the truth.

BOYD: Well, everybody just likes Simple. That's his trouble. He likes people, so they like him. But he's not going with all those women. He wasn't even going with Zarita.

JOYCE: [*Does not believe him.*] You can have your hat, Mr. Boyd, if you will.

BOYD: [*Takes his hat and continues talking.*] I mean, not lately, not for two or three years, since he's met you — why, he doesn't talk about anybody but you, hasn't for a long time — Joyce, Joyce, Joyce! Now, he's even talking to himself in the night, trying to explain to you. I room next door, and sometimes I can hear him crying late in the night. Nobody likes to hear a grown man crying, Miss Lane.

JOYCE: [*Sternly dismissing him.*] Thank you very much, Mr. Boyd.

BOYD: Miss Lane!

[*She closes the door as he backs out.* JOYCE *comes toward the center of the room, stops, thinks, then rushes to the closet and begins to put on her coat.*]

[*Blackout.*]

SCENE EIGHT

SIMPLE*'s room. Same evening.*
        SIMPLE *is alone, standing beside his dresser turning the pages of the Bible.*

SIMPLE: My old Aunt Lucy always said, "The Bible is the Rock, and the Rock is the Truth, and the Truth is the Light." Lemme see. [*He reads from Job.*] It says here, "Let thy day be darkness. Let no God regard it from above, neither let the light shine upon it . . . Man is born unto trouble." Lemme turn over! [*He tries the next page.*] Uh–huh! This is just as bad. "They meet with darkness in the daytime and grope in the noonday like as in the night." Great Gordon Gin! What part of the Bible am I reading out of? Job! No wonder! He's the one what suffered everything from boils to blindness. But it says here the Lord answered Job. Looks like don't nobody answer me. Nobody! [*He shuts the Bible and goes to the window.* JOYCE *comes up the stairs and down the hall. Outside his door she calls.*]

JOYCE: Jess! [*His body stiffens.*]

SIMPLE: Am I hearing things?

JOYCE: Jess!

SIMPLE: I must be going crazy! Can't be that voice.

JOYCE: [*Knocks softly and enters.*] Jess!

SIMPLE: Joyce! Why are you here?

JOYCE: To see you, Jess. There's something maybe I ought to tell you.

SIMPLE: There's nothing for you to tell me, Joyce.

JOYCE: But, Jess — [*After a long silence he speaks.*]

SIMPLE: You've come to *me*, Joyce.

JOYCE: Yes, Jess.

SIMPLE: Every time something's happened between us, in the end you come to me. It's my turn to come to you now.

JOYCE: You tried. I wouldn't let you in. I got those messages. I heard you ringing my bell. It's my fault, Jess.

SIMPLE: It's not your fault, Joyce. I had no business trying to see you then. But I wasn't man enough not to try.

JOYCE: Jess, you were at my door and I wouldn't let you in.

SIMPLE: All my life I been looking for *your* door. But sometimes you let the wrong me in, not the me I want to be. This time, when I come through your door again, it's gonna be the me I ought to be.

JOYCE: I know, Jess — we've had problems to solve. But —

SIMPLE: The problem to solve is me, Joyce — and can't no one solve that problem but me. Until I get out of this mud and muck and mire I been dancing in half my life, don't you open your door to the wrong me no more. *Don't open your door.* And don't say nothing good to me, Joyce. Don't tell me nothing a–tall. [*He has already risen. Now she rises, embracing him, but he pushes her away.*] Joyce, baby, darling, no . . . . [*He wants to call her all the sweet names he knows, to take her in his arms, to keep her then and there and always. But instead he speaks almost harshly.*] No! Don't say nothing — to me — Joyce. [*He opens the door. As* JOYCE *turns to go, she looks at* JESS, *lifts her head, and smiles the most beautiful smile a man has ever seen — a smile serene and calm and full of faith.* THE LIGHTS DIM TO A SPOT *on her face as she turns and leaves without a word. Suddenly there is a great burst of music, wild, triumphant, wonderful, and happy.*]

[*Blackout.*]

SCENE NINE

Paddy's Bar on a winter night.
   BODIDDLY, BOYD, GITFIDDLE, *and the* PIANIST *are scattered about.*
MELON *leans over* MISS MAMIE'S *table and emits a playful howl.*

MELON: Ow–ooo–oo–o! Miss Mamie, you're a killer, that you is! Sweet my lands! You–oo–O!

MAMIE: Melon, I don't want no wolf–howling compliments. I just come here to set in peace. I don't want to be bothered with you drunken Negroes.

MELON: Who is drunk?

MAMIE: You!

BODIDDLY: She's right, you is.

MELON: Listen here! Diddly and Mamie, both you all belong to my church — the Upstairs Baptist — yet you go around talking about me like a dirty dog.

MAMIE: Well, you do drink — guzzle, guzzle, guzzle!

MELON: I don't get drunk!

MAMIE: I say you do!

MELON: Woman, listen! Miss Mamie, I respects you too much to dispute your word. If you say I do, I does.

MAMIE: Now that that's settled, come and have a drink on me. A little eye–opener in the morning, a bracer at noon, and a nightcap at night, never hurt nobody.

MELON: Mamie, you got money?

MAMIE: I always got me some money, been had money, and always will have money. And one reason I do is, I'm a lone wolf, I runs with no pack.

MELON: I would pack you on my back if you would let me.

MAMIE: I don't intend to let you. To tell the truth, I doubt our intentions. And, Melon I wants you to know: [*She sings.*]

I been making my way for a long, long time,
I been making my way through this world.
I keep on trying to be good
'Cause I'm a good old girl.
I been making my way with a boot and a shoe.
In no oyster have I found a pearl.
I trust myself — so I've got luck
'Cause I'm a good old girl.
Sometimes the devil beckons
I look at the devil and say,
[MELON *touches her hand.*]
Stop that!
Devil, devil, devil —
Devil, be on your way!
I been making my way through thick and thin
'Spite o' devilish men in this world.
There ain't no man can get me down
Not even Harry Belafonte,
'Cause I'm a good old girl.
[MAMIE *rises and addresses the entire bar.*]
I make five or ten dollars, sometimes more a day.
You men what ain't working know that that ain't hay.

Don't let no strange man get his hand on you —
There's no telling, baby, what a strange cat will do.
It takes all kinds of folks to spin this globe around,
But one bad actor tears your playhouse down.
Don't ever let no bad actor come around —
There's no telling, Baby, what that cat's trying to lay down!
Sometimes the devil beckons.
I look at the devil and say, [MELON *approaches*.]
Devil, devil, devil —
Ain't you got enough trouble?
Devil, be on your way!
I been making my way through thick and thin'
'Spite o' devilish men in this world.
There's no man can get me down
'Cause I'm a good old girl.
My name is Mamie —
I'm a good old girl!
Like Mamie Eisenhower,
I'm a good old gal!
[*To shouts of approval from the bar crowd, she continues.*]
I been making my way for a long, long time!
Now listen, Punchy: I've been making my way:
I've been making my very own way for a long, long time.
I don't need you, Melon.
I've been making my way through this world.
Who needs that face?
I keep on trying to be good.
You think I'm a doll?
I'm a good old girl —
Might be a human doll! Anyhow —
I been making my way through thick and thin
'Spite o' devilish men in this world,
[MELON *grins*.]
You always been this ugly, Melon?
There ain't no man can get me down
'Cause I'm a good old girl!
I keep repeating — I'm a good old girl!

Now, what's the sense of going on with this?

BODIDDLY: Melon, I guess you realize there's nothing more independent
than an independent woman. You's better stop worrying Miss Mamie
or she'll floor you and stomp on your carcass.

MELON: Diddly, if you don't have some respect for my personal conversation, I'm going to bust a watermelon over your head.

BODIDDLY: Take it easy, man. See you later. Hi, Simp! [SIMPLE *enters shivering, passing* BODIDDLY *as he exits.*]

SIMPLE: Hi, Bo! Hop! Man, this bar is the warmest place I know in winter. At least you keep steam up here.

HOPKINS: Cold as it is, do you mean to tell me you haven't got any steam in your room?

SIMPLE: I done beated on my radiator pipe six times today to let my old landlady know I was home — freezing.

HOPKINS: And what happened?

SIMPLE: Nothing — she just beat back on the pipes at me. Which is why I come down here, to get warm just like Boyd.

HOPKINS: Want a drink?

SIMPLE: I sure could use one.

HOPKINS: Coming up.

SIMPLE: Hey Boyd? I got something to tell you. I'm working part–time, back down at the plant as a helper — helping reconvert.

BOYD: That's wonderful!

SIMPLE: With a good job and a good wife, man, it'll be like Joyce used to say when I kissed her — "Simply Heavenly." And when we get married, Boyd, you're gonna be standing there beside me at my wedding. You're gonna hand me the ring. Ain't that what the best man does?

MAMIE: Yeah, that's right. [MELON *approaches.*] Melon, ain't you got no home?

BOYD: Hey, this is the first time you've sprung this on me, about being your best man. After all we've only known each other for a few years. A best man is usually somebody you grew up with, or something.

SIMPLE: I didn't grow up with nobody, Boyd. So I don't know anybody very well. So, will you please be my best man?

BOYD: Best man, eh? Then I'll have to start buying me a brand new suit. And a best man is due to give a bachelor's party for the groom a night or two before the ceremony. Your wedding's going to cost me a lot of dough, Jess.

SIMPLE: Just a keg of beer. I mean a private one — with my name on it.

BOYD: You got it, lad. I live to see the day! [*He rises.*]

SIMPLE: Where you going, Boyd?

BOYD: Listen, Jess! Hot or cold. I've got to bust that book–writing rock and I've got to get home to my typewriter. Good night, all.

SIMPLE: Well, that's settled. Thank God, I don't have to worry about Zarita. I ain't seen her for months.

HOPKINS: Zarita's getting ready to fly to Arizona for Christmas. That Big Boy, Ali Baba, sent her a ticket. She's all set to go. I think they're going to get married.

SIMPLE: I wishes her all the luck in the world. But I sure wish I could understand a woman.

HOPKINS: Socrates tried, he couldn't. What makes you hold such hopes?

SIMPLE: Long as I live, Hop, I lives in hopes. [*Loud weeping is heard outside.*] Damn, there's some woman hollering now.

HOPKINS: I wonder what's wrong. [ARCIE *enters crying and sinks at a table.*] What's wrong, Arcie?

ARCIE: Gimme a sherry, Hopkins, quick! Gimme a sherry.

HOPKINS: What's the matter, Arcie?

ARCIE: Abe Lincoln is going to the army

SIMPLE: The army?

ARCIE: My oldest son, Abraham Lincoln Jones.

SIMPLE: Well, why didn't you say so?

ARCIE: I'm trying to! Abe got his draft call.

SIMPLE: Don't cry, Arcie. The army'll do the boy no harm. He'll get to travel, see the world.

ARCIE: The first one of my children to leave home!

SIMPLE: As many as you got, you shouldn't mind *one* going somewhere.

ARCIE: I does mind. Abe is my oldest, and I does mind. Fill it up again, Hop.

SIMPLE: That boy Abe is smart, Arcie. You'll be proud of him. He's liable to get to be an officer.

HOPKINS: At least a sergeant — and come back here with stripes on his sleeve.

SIMPLE: Else medals on his chest. Now, me, if I was to go in the army today — now that we's integrated — I would come back a general.

HOPKINS: Quit your kidding.

SIMPLE: I would rise right to the top today and be a general — and be in charge of white troops.

MELON: Colored generals never command white troops.

SIMPLE: The next war will be integrated. In fact, I'd like to command a regiment from Mississippi.

HOPKINS: Are you drunk?

SIMPLE: No, sir.

MELON: Then why on earth would you want to be in charge of a white regiment from Mississippi?

SIMPLE: In the last war, they had white officers in charge of Negroes. So why shouldn't I be in charge of whites? Huh? General Simple! I would really make 'em toe the line. I know some of them Dixiecrates would rather die than left face for a colored man, but they would left face for me.

MELON: Man, you got a great imagination.

SIMPLE: I can see myself now, in World War III, leading white Mississippi troupes into action. Hop, I would do like all the other generals do, and stand way back on a hill somewhere and look through my spy–glasses and say, "Charge on! Mens, charge on!" Then I would watch them Dixiecrats boys go — like true sons of throwing down the enemy. When my young white lieutenants from Vicksburg jeeped back to headquarters to deliver their reports in person to me, they would say, "Captain General, sir, we have taken two more enemy positions." I would say, "Mens, return to your companies — and tell 'em to keep on charging on!" Next day, when I caught up to 'em, I would pin medals on their chests for bravery. Then I would have my picture taken in front of all my fine white troops — me — the first *black* American general to pin medals on white soldiers from Mississippi. Then, Hop — man, oh, man — then when the war be's over, I would line my companies up for the last time and I would say, "Mens, at ease. Gentlemen of the Old South, relax. Put down your fighting arms and lend me your ears — because I am one of you, too, borned an bred in Dixie. [GITFIDDLE *begins to play a syncopated march — a blend of "Dixie," "Swanee River," and "Yankee Doodle."*] And I'm willing to let bygones be bygones, and forget how you failed to obey my orders in the old days and right faced–ted when I said "Left," because you thought I was colored. Well, I is colored. I'll forget that. You are me — and I am you — and we are one. And now that our fighting is done,

let's be Americans for once, for fun. Colonels, captains, majors, lieutenants, sergeants, and, Hopkins, open up a keg of nails for the mens,
drink! And when we all stagger back to peace together, let there be
peace—between you, Mississippi, and me! Company—'tention!
Right shoulder arms!...Forward, march!...Come on, boys, I'm
leading you! Come on! By the left flank march!" [SIMPLE *proudly inspects his troops as they pass in review. Others in the bar, except* MISS MAMIE,
applaud and cheer.]

HOPKINS: March, fellows, march!

SIMPLE: By the right flank, march!

HOPKINS: March, fellows, march!

ARCIE: Ain't that fine!

HOPKINS: March, march, march!

SIMPLE: Forward! March!

HOPKINS: March! March! March! [SIMPLE *exits as if leading an army with
banners. The music rises to a climax, then suddenly ends. In the silence* MISS
MAMIE *speaks.*]

MAMIE: You know something—that boy is sick.

[*Blackout.*]

SCENE TEN

A phone booth. Christmas Eve.
   Chimes are softly tolling "Jingle Bells" as SIMPLE *speaks excitedly into
the phone.*

SIMPLE: Joyce?...Joyce?...Is this Joyce?...Yes, it's Jesse B...It's
Simple, honey!...What? You say I sound like a new man? I am a new
man! And I got something for you, Joyce. It's Christmas Eve and, you
know, well—like it says in the Bible, "Wise men came bringing
gifts."...Joyce, I got a few little gifts for you on my Christmas
tree...Sure, I got a tree! What's on it for you?...I don't want to
tell you, Joyce. I want to show you. You say you're coming right
over?...Oh, baby! [*With the receiver still in his hand, he rises excitedly and starts out, but is jerked back by the cord. Quickly he hangs up and
leaves as the music of "Jingle Bells" fills the air.*]

[*Blackout.*]

SCENE ELEVEN

SCENE: SIMPLE's *room*
TIME: *Christmas Eve*
AT RISE: *A star shines in the darkness. The lights come up revealing* SIMPLE *and* JOYCE *standing before a tiny Christmas tree. The star glows atop his tree hung with tinsel and little balls of colored glass. On the tree there are four gifts tied with ribbons: one is a letter, one a roll of paper, one a long parchment, and one is a tiny box.* JOYCE *has just entered the room.*

JOYCE: Jess!

SIMPLE: Look. [*He shows her the tree.*]

JOYCE: Oh! It's beautiful!

SIMPLE: May I take your coat? Won't you sit down? [*He hands her the parchment as* JOYCE *perches on the edge of a chair.*]

JOYCE: Jess, what is it? A picture of some kind? Maybe a map? Why, it's all in Roman letters. It's a divorce!

SIMPLE: With a gold seal on it, too.

JOYCE: Free! Jess, you're free! Like in *Uncle Tom's Cabin*!

SIMPLE: Yes, baby, I'm free. That's the paper.

JOYCE: It's dated a whole month ago. Jess, why didn't you tell me you had your divorce?

SIMPLE: I was waiting for something else to go with it. Here, this is for you, to. [*He hands her an envelope.*]

JOYCE: My father's writing!

SIMPLE: Read it. You see, your ole — your father — gimme your hand. [*While she reads the letter,* SIMPLE *opens the little box on the tree and polishes a ring on his coat lapel.*] Now, can I take your hand? [*He slips the ring on her finger.*] For you — if you'll wear it?

JOYCE: Forever! [*She starts to rise, but gently he pushes her down and returns to the tree.*]

SIMPLE: This is something only married people can have. And it's not ready, yet, either. They just about now digging the first hole in the ground — busting that first rock. We both got to sign our names — if you're willing.

JOYCE: An apartment! Oh, Jess! A place to live! An apartment!

SIMPLE: Can we both sign our names, Joyce?

JOYCE: Yes, Jess! [JOYCE *rises, scattering papers, and flings her arms about him.*]

SIMPLE: Now we can get ready for that wedding in June.

JOYCE: Oh, Jess! Jess, baby! Jess! [*Singing, they embrace.*]

SIMPLE: Just for you these Christmas tokens
On our Christmas tree —

JOYCE: Help to make me know that you are
Santa Claus to me.

SIMPLE: Just a little pain and trouble
Mixed in with the past

BOTH: Help to make our joys double
When we're sure they'll last

JOYCE: Wonderful the morning star
Shining in the dawn!

BOTH: Wonderful the rainbow's arch
When the rain is gone.

[*The bar is revealed as the entire company enters singing and form tableaux, some around the piano,* MAMIE *at her table with* MELON, BODIDDLY, ARCIE, *and* JOHN JASPER *making a family group at another table. The entire chorus of "Look for the Morning Star" is repeated as all come forward for bows.*]

ALL: Don't forget there's bluebirds
Somewhere in the blue.
Love will send a little bluebird
Flying straight to you.

[*Repeat chorus and bows.*]

[*Curtain.*]

Douglas Turner Ward

DAY OF ABSENCE

DOUGLAS TURNER WARD (also known as Douglas Turner)

Grew up in New Orleans, LA, attended Wilberforce University, and the University of Michigan before coming to New York City in 1948. He began a successful acting career as Douglas Turner in the Off-Broadway Circle-In-The-Square Production of *The Iceman Cometh*. Other credits include *Lost in the Stars*, New York City Center; *A Raisin in the Sun*, as Sidney Poitier's understudy on Broadway and afterwards taking over the lead during its ten-month national tour; *A Land Beyond the River*, opposite Diana Sands; *One Flew Over the Cuckoo's Nest* on Broadway; Off-Broadway in *The Blacks* and *Blood Knot*; on TV in *East Side, West Side* and *The Edge Of Night*; and on the screen in *Women of Brewster Place*.

After an unsuccessful attempt in 1960 to get his first two plays *Happy Ending* and *Day of Absence* (written under his family name Douglas Turner Ward) produced, actor Robert Hooks opened the one–act comedies at St. Marks Playhouse in1965. The double bill ran Off–Broadway for 504 performances. Ward joined with Robert Hooks in founding the Negro Ensemble Company (NEC), which produced all of his plays. Ward, in addition to his writing and duties as artistic director of the company, directed and acted in many of the NEC productions, including his own work.

Other plays by Ward include *Brotherhood, The Reckoning*, and *The Redeemer*.

Awards: Vernon Rice/Drama Desk Award for play writing and Obie for *Happy Ending* and *Day of Absence*; Obie Award in 1973 for performance in *The River Niger*; an AUDELCO Board of Directors Award (1974); Adolph Caesar Performing Arts Award (1987). Douglas Turner Ward was inducted into the Theatre Hall Of Fame in 1996.

CHARACTERS

The play is conceived for performance by a Black cast, a reverse minstrel show done in white face.

CLEM	a country cracker
LUKE	another
MARY	young white mother
JOHN	young white father
FIRST OPERATOR	
SECOND OPERATOR	
THIRD OPERATOR	
SUPERVISOR	
MAYOR	a small town official
JACKSON	his assistant
MEN FROM THE TOWN	
BUSINESSMAN	
CLUB WOMAN	
COURIER	
CLAN	as in KKK
ANNOUNCER	
AIDE	
RASTUS	the missing man

SCENE: *Street*
TIME: *Early morning.*

CLEM: [*Sitting under a sign suspended by invisible wires and bold-printed with the lettering:* "STORE."] 'Morning, Luke . . .

LUKE: [*Sitting a few paces away under an identical sign.*] 'Morning, Clem . . .

CLEM: Go'n' be a hot day.

LUKE: Looks that way . . .

CLEM: Might rain though . . .

LUKE: Might.

CLEM: Hope it does . . .

LUKE: Me, too . . .

CLEM: Farmers could use a little wet spell for a change...How's the Missis?

LUKE: Same.

CLEM: 'N' the kids?

LUKE: Them, too...How's yourns?

CLEM: Fine, thank you...[*They both lapse into drowsy silence, waving lethargically from time to time at imaginary passersby.*] Hi, Joe!

LUKE: Joe...

CLEM: ...How'd it go yesterday, Luke?

LUKE: Fair.

CLEM: Same wit' me...Business don't seem to git no better or no worse. Guess we in a rut, Luke, don't it 'pear that way to you?—Morning, ma'am.

LUKE: Morning...

CLEM: Tried display, sales, advertisement stamps — everything, yet merchandising stumbles 'round in the same old groove...But — that's better than plunging downwards I reckon.

LUKE: Guess it is.

CLEM: Morning, Bret. How's the family? That's good.

LUKE: Bret —

CLEM: Morning, Sue.

LUKE: How do, Sue.

CLEM: [*Staring after her.*]...Fine hunk of woman.

LUKE: Sure is.

CLEM: Wonder if it's any good?

LUKE: Bet it is.

CLEM: Sure like to find out!

LUKE: So would I.

CLEM: You ever try?

LUKE: Never did...

CLEM: Morning, Gus...

LUKE: Howdy, Gus.

CLEM: Fine, thank you.

[*They lapse into silence again.* CLEM *rouses himself slowly, begins to look around quizzically.*]

CLEM: Luke...?

LUKE: Huh?

CLEM: Do you...er, er, feel anything—funny...?

LUKE: Like what?

CLEM: Like...er—something—strange.

LUKE: I dunno...haven't thought about it.

CLEM: I mean...like something's wrong—outta place, unusual?

LUKE: I don't know...What you got in mind?

CLEM: Nothing...just that—just that—like somp'ums outta kilter. I got a funny feeling somp'ums not up to snuff. Can't figger out what it is...

LUKE: Maybe it's in your haid?

CLEM: No, not like that...Like somp'ums happened—or happening— gone haywire, loony.

LUKE: Well, don't worry 'bout it, it'll pass.

CLEM: Guess you right. [*Attempts return to somnolence but doesn't succeed.*] ...I'm sorry, but you sure you don't feel nothing peculiar...?

LUKE: [*Slightly irked.*] Toss it out your mind, Clem! We got a long day ahead of us. If something's wrong, you'll know 'bout it in due time. No use worrying about it 'till it comes and if it's coming, it will. Now, relax!

CLEM: All right, you right...Hi, Margie...

LUKE: Marge.

CLEM: [*Unable to control himself.*] Luke, I don't give a damn what you say. Somp'ums topsy-turvy, I just know it!

LUKE: [*Increasingly irritated.*] Now look here, Clem—it's a bright day, it looks like it's go'n' git hotter. You say the wife and kids are fine and business is no better or no worse? Well, what else could be wrong?.. . If somp'ums go'n' happen, it's go'n' happen anyway and there ain't a damn fool thing you kin do to stop it! So you ain't helping me, your-self or nobody else by thinking 'bout it. It's not go'n' be no better or no worse when it gits here. It'll come to you when it gits ready to come and it's go'n' be the same whether you worry about it or not. So stop letting it upset you! [LUKE *settles back in his chair.* CLEM *does like-*

wise. LUKE *shuts his eyes. After a few moments, they reopen. He forces them shut again. They reopen in greater curiosity. Finally, he rises slowly to an upright position in the chair, looks around frowningly. Turns slowly to* CLEM.] ... Clem? ... You know something ? .... Somp'um is peculiar ...

CLEM: [*Vindicated.*] I knew it, Luke! I just knew it! Ever since we been sitting here, I been having that feeling!

[*Scene is blacked out abruptly. Lights rise on another section of the stage where a young couple lie in bed under an invisible-wire-suspension-sign lettered:* "HOME." *Loud insistent sounds of baby yells are heard.* JOHN, *the husband, turns over trying to ignore the cries,* MARY, *the wife, is undisturbed.* JOHN's *efforts are futile, the cries continue until they cannot be denied. He bolts upright, jumps out of bed and disappears offstage. Returns quickly and tries to rouse* MARY.]

JOHN: Mary ... [*Nudges her, pushes her, yells into her ear, but she .fails to respond.*] Mary, get up ... Get up!

MARY: Ummm ... [*Shrugs away, still sleeping.*]

JOHN: GET UP!

MARY: UMMMMMMMMM!

JOHN: Don't you hear the baby bawling! ... NOW GET UP!

MARY: [*Mumbling drowsily.*] ... What baby ... whose baby ... ?

JOHN: Yours!

MARY: Mine? That's ridiculous ... what'd you say ... ? Somebody's baby bawling ? ... How could that be so? [*Hearing screams.*] Who's crying? Somebody's crying! ... What's crying ... WHERE'S LULA?!

JOHN: I don't know. You better get up.

MARY: That's outrageous! ... What time is it?

JOHN: Late 'nuff! Now rise up!

MARY: You must be joking ... I'm sure I still have four or five hours sleep in store — even more after that head-splittin' blow-out last night ... [*Tumbles back under covers.*]

JOHN: Nobody told you to gulp those last six bourbons —

MARY: Don't tell me how many bourbons to swallow, not after you guzzled the whole stinking bar! ... Get up? ... You must be cracked ... Where's Lula? She must be here, she always is ...

JOHN: Well, she ain't here yet, so get up and muzzle that brat before she does drive me cuckoo!

MARY: [*Springing upright, finally realizing gravity of situation.*] Whaddaya mean Lula's not here ? She's always here, she must be here . . . Where else kin she be? She supposed to be . . . She just can't *not* be here— CALL HER!

[*Blackout as* JOHN *rushes offstage. Scene shifts to a trio of* TELEPHONE OPERATORS *perched on stools before imaginary switchboards. Chaos and bedlam are taking place to the sound of buzzes. Effect of following dialogue should simulate rising pandemonium.*]

FIRST OPERATOR: The line is busy—

SECOND OPERATOR: Line is busy

FIRST OPERATOR: Is busy—

FIRST OPERATOR: Doing best we can—

SECOND OPERATOR: Having difficulty—

THIRD OPERATOR: Soon as possible—

FIRST OPERATOR: Just one moment—

SECOND OPERATOR: Would you hold on—

THIRD OPERATOR: Awful sorry, madam—

FIRST OPERATOR: Would you hold on, please—

SECOND OPERATOR: Just a second, please—

THIRD OPERATOR: Please hold on, please—

FIRST OPERATOR: The line is busy—

SECOND OPERATOR: The line is busy—

THIRD OPERATOR: The line is busy—

FIRST OPERATOR: Doing best we can—

SECOND OPERATOR: Hold on please—

THIRD OPERATOR: —Can't make connections—

FIRST OPERATOR: Won't plug through—

THIRD OPERATOR: Sorry madam—

FIRST OPERATOR: If you'd wait a moment—

SECOND OPERATOR: Doing best we can—

THIRD OPERATOR: Sorry—

FIRST OPERATOR: One moment—

SECOND OPERATOR: Just a second—

THIRD OPERATOR: Hold on —

FIRST OPERATOR: YES —

SECOND OPERATOR: STOP IT! —

THIRD OPERATOR: HOW DO I KNOW —

FIRST OPERATOR: YOU ANOTHER ONE!

SECOND OPERATOR: HOLD ON DAMMIT!

THIRD OPERATOR: UP YOURS, TOO!

FIRST OPERATOR: THE LINE IS BUSY

SECOND OPERATOR: THE LINE IS BUSY —

THIRD OPERATOR: THE LINE IS BUSY — [*The switchboard clamors a cacophony of buzzes as* OPERATORS *plug connections with the frenzy of a Chaplin movie. Their replies degenerate into a babble of gibberish. At the height of frenzy, the* SUPERVISOR *appears.*]

SUPERVISOR: WHAT'S THE SNARL UP???!!!

FIRST OPERATOR: Everybody calling at the same time, ma'am!

SECOND OPERATOR: Board can't handle it!

THIRD OPERATOR: Like everybody in big New York City is trying to squeeze a call through to li'l ole us!

SUPERVISOR: God!...Somp'un terrible musta happened!...Buzz the emergency frequency hookup to the Mayor's office and find out what the hells going on! [*Scene blacks out quickly to* CLEM *and* LUKE.]

CLEM: [*Something slowly dawning on him.*] Luke...?

LUKE: Yes, Clem?

CLEM: [*Eyes roving around in puzzlement.*] Luke...?

LUKE: [*Irked.*] I said what, Clem?

CLEM: Luke...? Where — where is — the — the — ?

LUKE: THE WHAT?!

CLEM: Nigras...?

LUKE: ????What...?

CLEM: Nigras...Where is the Nigras, where is they, Luke...? ALL THE NIGRAS!...I don't see no Nigras...

LUKE: Whatcha mean...?

CLEM: [*Agitatedly.*] Luke, there ain't a darkey in sight...And if you remember, we ain't spied a nappy hair all morning... The Nigras, Luke! We ain't laid eyes on nary a coon this whole morning!!!

LUKE: You must be crazy or something, Clem!

CLEM: Think about it, Luke, we been sitting here for an hour or more— try and recollect if you remember seeing jist *one* go by?!!!

LUKE: [*Confused.*] ... I don't recall ... But ... but there musta been some... The heat musta got you, Clem! How in hell could that be so?!!!

CLEM: [*Triumphantly.*] Just think, Luke! ... Look around ya ... Now, every morning mosta people walkin' 'long this street is colored. They's strolling by going to work, they's waiting for the buses, they's sweeping sidewalks, cleaning stores, starting to shine shoes and wetting the mops—right?! ... Well, look around you, Luke—where is they? [LUKE *paces up and down, checking.*] I told you, Luke, they ain't nowheres to be seen.

LUKE: ???? ... This ... this ... some kind of holiday for 'em — or something ?

CLEM: I don't know, Luke ... but ... but what I do know is they ain't here 'n' we haven't seen a solitary one ... It's scaryfying, Luke ...!

LUKE: Well ... maybe they's jist standing 'n' walking and shining on other streets —Let's go look!

[*Scene blacks out to* JOHN *and* MARY. *Baby cries are as insistent as ever.*]

MARY: [*At end of patience.*] SMOTHER IT!

JOHN: [*Beyond his.*] That's a hell of a thing to say 'bout your own child! You should know what to do to hush her up!

MARY: Why don't you try?!

JOHN: You had her!

MARY: You shared in borning her!!

JOHN: Possibly not!

MARY: Why, you lousy—!

JOHN: What good is a mother who can't shut up her own daughter?!

MARY: I told you she yells louder every time I try to lay hands on her — Where's Lula? Didn't you call her?!

JOHN: I told you I can't get the call through!

MARY: Try ag'in —

JOHN: It's no use! I tried numerous times and can't even git through to the switchboard. You've got to quiet her down yourself. [*Firmly.*] Now, go in there and clam her up 'fore I lose my patience! [MARY *exits. Soon, we hear the yells increase. She rushes back in.*]

MARY: She won't let me touch her, just screams louder!

JOHN: Probably wet 'n' soppy!

MARY: Yes!! Stinks something awful! Phooooey! I can't stand that filth and odor!

JOHN: That's why she's screaming! Needs her didee changed—Go change it!

MARY: How you 'spect me to when I don't know how?! Suppose I faint?!

JOHN: Well let her blast away. I'm getting outta here.

MARY: You can't leave me here like this!

JOHN: Just watch me!...See this nice split-level cottage, peachy furniture, multi-colored teevee, hi-fi set 'n' the rest?...Well, how you think I scraped 'em together while you curled up on your fat li'l fanny?...By gitting outta here—not only *on time*...but EARLIER!—Beating a frantic crew of nice young executives to the punch—gitting there fustest with the mostest brown-nosing you ever saw! Now if I goof one day—just ONE DAY! —You reckon I'd stay ahead? NO!...There'd be a wolf-pack trampling over my prostrate body, racing to replace my smiling face against the boss' left rump!... NO, MAM! I'm zooming outta here on time, just as I always have and what's more—you go'n' fix me some breakfast, I'M HUNGRY!

MARY: But—

JOHN: No buts about it! [*Flash blackout as he gags on a mouthfull of coffee.*] What you trying to do, STRANGLE ME!!!! [*Jumps up and starts putting on jacket.*]

MARY: [*Sarcastically.*] What did you expect?

JOHN: [*In biting fury.*] That you could possibly boil a pot of water, toast a few slices of bread and fry a coupler eggs!...It was a mistaken assumption!

MARY: So they aren't as good as Lula's!

JOHN: That is an overstatement. Your efforts don't result in anything that could possibly be digested by man, mammal, or insect!...When I married you, I thought I was fairly acquainted with your faults and weaknesses—I chalked 'em up to human imperfection...But now I know I was being extremely generous, over-optimistic and phenomenally deluded!—You have no idea how useless you really are!

MARY: Then why'd you marry me?!

JOHN: Decoration!

MARY: You shoulda married Lula!

JOHN: I might've if it wasn't 'gainst the segregation law!... But for the sake of my home, my child and my sanity, I will even take a chance on sacrificing my slippery grip on the status pole and drive by her shanty to find out whether she or someone like her kin come over here and prevent some ultimate disaster. [*Storms toward door, stopping abruptly at exit.*] Are you sure you kin make it to the bathroom wit'out Lula backing you up?!!!

[*Blackout. Scene shifts to* MAYOR'*s office where a cluttered desk stands center amid papered debris.*]

MAYOR: [*Striding determinedly toward desk, stopping midways, bellowing.*] WOODFENCE!... WOODFENCE!... WOODFENCE! [*Receiving no reply, completes distance to desk.*] Jackson!...Jackson!

JACKSON: [*Entering worriedly.*] Yes, sir...?

MAYOR: Where's Vice-Mayor Woodfence, that no-good brother-in-law of mine?!

JACKSON: Hasn't come in yet, sir.

MAYOR: HASN'T COME IN!!!... Damn bastard! Knows we have a crucial conference. Soon as he staggers through that door, tell him to shoot in here! [*Angrily focusing on his disorderly desk and littered surroundings.*] And git Mandy here to straighten up this mess—Rufus too! You know he shoulda been waiting to knock dust off my shoes soon as I step in. Get 'em in here!... What's the matter wit' them lazy Nigras?... Already had to dress myself because of JC, fix my own coffee without MayBelle, drive myself to work 'counta Bubber, feel my old Hag's tits after Sapphi—NEVER MIND!—Git 'em in here— QUICK!

JACKSON: [*Meekly.*] They aren't...they aren't here, sir...

MAYOR: Whaddaya mean they aren't here? Find out where they at. We got important business, man! You can't run a town wit' laxity like this. Can't allow things to git snafued jist because a bunch of lazy Nigras been out gitting drunk and living it up all night! Discipline, man, discipline!

JACKSON: That's what I'm trying to tell you, sir . . . they didn't come in, can't be found . . . none of 'em.

MAYOR: Ridiculous, boy! Scare 'em up and tell 'em scoot here in a hurry befo' I git mad and fire the whole goddamn lot of 'em!

JACKSON: But we can't find 'em, sir.

MAYOR: Hogwash! Can't nobody in this office do anything right?! Do I hafta handle every piddling little matter myself?! Git me their numbers, I'll have 'em here befo' you kin shout to — [*Three men burst into room in various states of undress.*]

ONE: Henry — they vanished!

TWO: Disappeared into thin air!

THREE: Gone wit'out a trace!

TWO: Not a one on the street!

THREE: In the house!

ONE: On the job!

MAYOR: Wait a minute!! . . . Hold your water! Calm down—!

ONE: But they've gone, Henry—GONE! All of 'em!

MAYOR: What the hell you talking 'bout? Gone? Who's gone— ?

ONE: The Nigras, Henry! They gone!

MAYOR: Gone? . . . Gone where?

TWO: That's what we trying to tell ya — they just disappeared! The Nigras have disappeared, swallowed up, vanished! All of 'em! Every last one!

MAYOR: Have everybody 'round here gone batty? . . . That's impossible, how could the Nigras vanish?

THREE: Beats me, but it's happened!

MAYOR: You mean a whole town of Nigras just evaporate like this— poof!—Overnight?

ONE: Right!

MAYOR: Y'all must be drunk! Why, half this town is colored. How could they just sneak out!

TWO: Don't ask me, but there ain't one in sight!

MAYOR: Simmer down 'n' put it to me easy-like.

ONE: Well . . . I first suspected somp'um smelly when Sarah Jo didn't show up this morning and I couldn't reach her—

TWO: Dorothy Jane didn't 'rive at my house—

THREE: Georgia Mae wasn't at mine neither — and SHE sleeps in!

ONE: When I reached the office, I realized I hadn't seen nary one Nigra all morning! Nobody else had either — wait a minute — Henry, have you?!

MAYOR: ???Now that you mention it . . . no, I haven't . . .

ONE: They gone, Henry . . . Not a one on the street, not a one in our homes, not a single, last living one to be found nowheres in town. What we gon' do?!

MAYOR: [*Thinking.*] Keep heads on your shoulders 'n' put clothes on your back . . . They can't be far . . . Must be 'round somewheres . . . Probably playing hide 'n' seek, that's it! . . . JACKSON!

JACKSON: Yessir?

MAYOR: Immediately mobilize our Citizens Emergency Distress Committee!—Order a fleet of sound trucks to patrol streets urging the population to remain calm — situation's not as bad as it looks— everything's under control! Then, have another squadron of squawk buggies drive slowly through all Nigra alleys, ordering them to come out wherever they are. If that don't git 'em, organize a vigilante search-squad to flush 'em outta hiding! But most important of all, track down that lazy goldbricker, Woodfence and tell him to git on top of the situation! By God, we'll find 'em even if we hafta dig 'em outta the ground!

[*Blackout. Scene shifts back to* JOHN *and* MARY *a few hours later. A funereal solemnity pervades their mood.* JOHN *stands behind* MARY *who sits, in a scene duplicating the famous "American Gothic" painting.*]

JOHN: . . . Walked up to the shack, knocked on door, didn't git no answer. Hollered: "LULA? LULA . . . ?"—Not a thing. Went 'round the side, peeped in window—nobody stirred. Next door—nobody there. Crossed other side of street and banged on five or six other doors— not a colored person could be found! Not a man, neither woman or child—not even a little black dog could be seen, smelt or heard for blocks around . . . They've gone, Mary.

MARY: What does it all mean, John?

JOHN: I don't know, Mary . . .

MARY: I always had Lula, John. She never missed a day at my side... That's why I couldn't accept your wedding proposal until I was sure you'd welcome me and her together as a package. How am I gonna git through the day? My baby don't know *me*, I ain't acquainted wit' *it*. I've never lifted cover off pot, swung a mop or broom, dunked a dish or even pushed a dustrag. I'm lost wit'out Lula, I need her, John, I need her. [*Begins to weep softly.* JOHN *pats her consolingly.*]

JOHN: Courage, honey... Everybody in town is facing the same dilemma. We mustn't crack up...

[*Blackout. Scene shifts back to* MAYOR's *office later in day. Atmosphere and tone resembles a wartime headquarters at the front.* MAYOR *is poring over huge map.*]

INDUSTRIALIST: Half the day is gone already, Henry. On behalf of the factory owners of this town, you've got to bail us out! Seventy-five per cent of all production is paralyzed. With the Nigra absent, men are waiting for machines to be cleaned, floors to be swept, crates lifted, equipment delivered and bathrooms to be deodorized. Why, restrooms and toilets are so filthy until they not only cannot be sat in, but it's virtually impossible to get within hailing distance because of the stench!

MAYOR: Keep your shirt on, Jeb —

BUSINESSMAN: Business is even in worse condition, Henry. The volume of goods moving 'cross counters has slowed down to a trickle — almost negligible. Customers are not only not purchasing—but the absence of handymen, porters, sweepers, stock-movers, deliverers and miscellaneous dirty-work doers is disrupting the smooth harmony of marketing!

CLUB WOMAN: Food poisoning, severe digestitis, chronic diarrhea, advanced diaper chafings and a plethora of unsanitary household disasters dangerous to life, limb and property!... As a representative of the Federation of Ladies' Clubs, I must sadly report that unless the trend is reversed, a complete breakdown in family unity is imminent... Just as homo-sexuality and debauchery signalled the fall of Greece and Rome, the downgrading Southern Bellesdom might very well prophesy the collapse of our indigenous institutions... Remember—it has always been pure, delicate, lily–white images of Dixie femininity which provided backbone, inspiration and ideology for our male warriors in their defense against the on-rushing black horde. If our gallant men are drained of this worship and idolatry — God knows! The cause won't be worth a Confederate nickel!

MAYOR: Stop this panicky defeatism, y'all hear me! All machinery at my disposal is being utilized. I assure you wit' great confidence the damage will soon repair itself.—Cheerful progress reports are expected any moment no—Wait! See, here's Jackson. Well, Jackson?

JACKSON: [*Entering.*] As of now, sir, all efforts are fruitless. Neither hide nor hair of them has been located. We have not unearthed a single one in our shack-to-shack search. Not a single one has heeded our appeal. Scoured every crick and cranny inside their hovels, turning furniture upside down and inside out, breaking down walls and tearing through ceilings. We made determined efforts to discover where 'bouts of our faithful uncle Toms and informers—but even they have vanished without a trace... Searching squads are on the verge of panic and hysteria, sir, wit' hotheads among 'em campaigning for scorched earth policies. Nigras on a whole lack cellars, but there's rising sentiment favoring burning to find out whether they're underground—DUG IN!

MAYOR: Absolutely counter such foolhardy suggestions! Suppose they are tombed in? We'd only accelerate the gravity of the situation using incendiary tactics! Besides, when they're rounded up where will we put 'em if we've already burned up their shacks — IN OUR OWN BEDROOMS?!!!

JACKSON: I agree, sir, but the mood of the crowd is becoming irrational. In anger and frustration, they's forgetting their original purpose was to FIND the Nigras!

MAYOR: At all costs! Stamp out all burning proposals! Must prevent extremist notions from gaining ascendancy. Git wit' it... Wait—'n' for Jehovah's sake, find out where the hell is that trifling slacker, WOODFENCE!

COURIER: [*Rushing in.*] Mr. Mayor! Mr. Mayor!... We've found some! We've found some!

MAYOR: [*Excitedly.*] Where?

COURIER: In the — in the — [*Can't catch breath.*]

MAYOR: [*Impatiently.*] Where, man? Where?!

COURIER: In the colored wing of the city hospital!

MAYOR: The hos— ? The hospital! I shoulda known! How could those helpless, crippled, cut and shot Nigras disappear from a hospital! Shoulda thought of that!... Tell me more, man!

COURIER: I—I didn't wait, sir... I—I ran in to report soon as I heard—

MAYOR: WELL GIT BACK ON THE PHONE, YOU IDIOT, DON'T YOU KNOW WHAT THIS MEANS?

COURIER: Yes, sir. [*Races out.*]

MAYOR: Now we gitting somewhere!...Gentlemen, if one sole Nigra is among us, we're well on the road to rehabilitation! Those Nigras in the hospital must know somp'um 'bout the others where'bouts... Scat back to your colleagues, boost up their morale and inform 'em that things will zip back to normal in a jiffy! [*They start to file out, then pause to observe the* COURIER *reentering dazedly.*] Well...? Well, man...? WHAT'S THE MATTER WIT' YOU, NINNY, TELL ME WHAT ELSE WAS SAID?!

COURIER: They all...they all...they all in a—in a—a coma, sir...

MAYOR: They all in a what...?

COURIER: In a coma, sir...

MAYOR: Talk sense, man?...Whaddaya mean, they all in a coma?

COURIER: Doctor says every last one of the Nigras are jist laying in bed ...STILL...not moving...neither live or dead...laying up there in a coma...every last one of 'em...

MAYOR: [*Splutters, then grabs phone.*] Get me Confederate Memorial... Put me through to the Staff Chief...YES, this is the Mayor...Sam? ...What's this I hear?...But how could they be in a coma, Sam?... You don't know! Well, what the hell you think the city's paying you for!...You've got 'nuff damn hacks and quacks there to find out!... How could it be somp'um unknown? You mean Nigras know somp'um 'bout drugs your damn butchers don't!...Well, what the crap good are they!...All right, all right, I'll be calm...Now, tell me... Uh huh, uh huh...Well, can't you give 'em some injections or somp'um...?—You did...uh huh...DID YOU TRY A LI'L ROUGH TREATMENT? That too, huh...All right, Sam, keep trying... [*Puts phone down delicately, continuing absently.*] Can't wake em' up. Just lay there. Them that's sick won't git no sicker, them that's half-well won't git no better, babies that's due won't be born and them that's come won't show no life. Nigras wit' cuts won't bleed and them which needs blood won't be transfused...He say dying Nigras is even refusing to pass away! [*Is silently perpexed for a moment, then suddenly breaks into action.*] Jackson!...Call up the police—THE JAIL! Find out what's going on there! Them Nigras are captives! If there's one place we got darkies under control, it's there! Them sonsabitches too onery to act right either for colored or white! [JACKSON *exits. The*

COURIER *follows.*] Keep your fingers crossed, citizens, them Nigras in jail are the most important Nigras we got! [*All hands are raised conspicuously aloft, fingers prominently ex-ed. Seconds tick by. Soon* JACKSON *returns crestfallen.*]

JACKSON: Sheriff Bull says they don't know whether they still on premises or not. When they went to rouse Nigra jailbirds this morning, cell-block doors refused to swing open. Tried everything—even exploded dynamite charges—but it just wouldn't budge... Then they hoisted guards up to peep through barred windows, but couldn't see good 'nuff to tell whether Nigras was inside or not. Finally, gitting desperate, they power-hosed the cells wit' water but had to cease 'cause Sheriff Bull said he didn't wanta jeopardize drowning the Nigras since it might spoil his chance of shipping a record load of cotton pickers to the State Penitentiary for cotton-snatching jubilee... Anyway—they ain't heard a Nigra-squeak all day.

MAYOR: ???That so...? WHAT TRAINS 'N' BUSSES PASSING THROUGH? There must be some dinges riding through?

JACKSON: We checked... not a one on board.

MAYOR: Did you hear whether any other towns lost their Nigras ?

JACKSON: Things are status-quo everywhere else.

MAYOR: [*Angrily.*] Then what the hell they picking on us for!

COURIER: [*Rushing in.*] MR. MAYOR! Your sister jist called—HYSTERICAL! She says Vice-Mayor Woodfence went to bed wit' her last night, but when she woke up this morning he was gone! Been missing all day!

MAYOR: ???Could Nigras be holding brother-in-law Woodfence hostage?!

COURIER: No, sir. Besides him—investigations reveal that dozens or more prominent citizens—two City Council members, the chairman of the Junior Chamber of Commerce, our City College All-Southern half-back, the chairlady of the Daughters of the Confederate Rebellion, Miss Cotton-Sack Festival of the Year and numerous other miscellaneous nobodies—are all absent wit'out leave. Dangerous evidence points to the conclusion that they have been infiltrating!

MAYOR: Infiltrating???

COURIER: Passing all along!

MAYOR: ???PASSING ALL ALONG???

COURIER: Secret Nigras all the while!

MAYOR: NAW! [CLUB WOMAN *keels over in faint.* JACKSON, BUSINESSMAN *and* INDUSTRIALIST *begin to eye each other suspiciously.*]

COURIER: Yessir!

MAYOR: PASSING???

COURIER: Yessir!

MAYOR: SECRET NIG—!???

COURIER: Yessir!

MAYOR: [*Momentarily stunned to silence.*] The dirty mongrelizers!... Gentlemen, this is a grave predicament indeed...It pains me to sur- render priority of our states' right credo, but it is my solemn task and frightening duty to inform you that we have no other recourse but to seek outside help for deliverance.

[*Blackout. Lights re-rise on Huntley–Brinkley–Murrow–Sevareid– Cronkite–Reasoner-type* ANNOUNCER *grasping a hand-held microphone (imaginary) a few hours later. He is vigorously, excitedly mouthing his commentary, but no sound escapes his lips...During this dumb wordless section of his broadcast, a bedraggled assortment of figures marching with picket signs occupy his attention. On their picket signs are inscribed vari- ous appeals and slogans.* "CINDY LOU UNFAIR TO BABY JOE"..."CAP'N SAM MISS BIG BOY"..."RETURN LI'L BLUE TO MARSE JIM"..."INFOR- MATION REQUESTED 'BOUT MAMMY GAIL"..."BOSS NATHAN PROTEST TO FAST LEROY." *Trailing behind the marchers, forcibly iso- lated, is a woman dressed in widow-black holding a placard which reads:* "WHY DIDN'T YOU TELL US — YOUR DEFILED WIFE AND TWO AB- SENT MONGRELS."]

ANNOUNCER: [*Who has been silently mouthing his delivery during the picket- ing procession, is suddenly heard as if caught in the midst of commentary.*] Factories standing idle from the loss of non-essential workers. Stores shuttered from the absconding of uncrucial personnel. Uncollected garbage threatening pestilence and pollution...Also, each second somewhere in this forrmer utopia below the Mason and Dixon, dozens of decrepit old men and women usually tended by faithful nurses and servants are popping off like flies—abandoned by sons, daughters and grandchildren whose refusal to provide their dodder- ing relatives with bedpans and other soothing necessities result in their hasty, nasty, messy corpus delicties...But most critically af- fected of all by this complete drought of Afro-American resources are policemen and other public safety guardians denied their daily quota of Negro arrests. One officer known affectionately as "TWO-A-

DAY-PETE" because of his unblemished record of TWO Negro headwhippings per day has already been carted off to the County Insane Asylum straight-jacketed, screaming and biting, unable to withstand the shock of having his spotless slate sullied by interruption ... It is feared that similar attacks are soon expected among municipal judges prevented for the first time in years of distinguished bench-sitting from sentencing one single Negro to a hoosegow or pokey....Ladies and gentlemen, as you trudge in from the joys and headaches of workday chores and dusk begins to descend on this sleepy Southern hamlet, we REPEAT — today — before early morning dew had dried upon magnolia blossoms, your comrade citizens of this lovely Dixie village awoke to the realization that some — pardon me! Not some — but ALL OF THEIR NEGROES were missing...Absent, vamoosed, departed, at bay, fugitive, away, gone and so-far unretrieved...In order to dispel your incredulity, gauge the temper of your suffering compatriots and just possibly prepare you for the likelihood of an equally nightmarish eventuality, we have gathered a cross-section of this city's most distinguished leaders for exclusive interviews...First, Mr. Council Clan, grand-dragoon of this area's most active civic organizations and staunch bell-wether of the political opposition...Mr. Clan, how do you ACCOUNT for this incredible disappearance?

CLAN: A PLOT, plain and simple, that's what it is, as plain as the corns on your feet!

ANNOUNCER: Whom would you consider responsible?

CLAN: I could go on all night.

ANNOUNCER: Cite a few?

CLAN: Too numerous.

ANNOUNCER: Just one?

CLAN: Name names when time comes.

ANNOUNCER: Could you be referring to native Negroes?

CLAN: Ever try quaranteening lepers from their spots?

ANNOUNCER: Their organizations?

CLAN: Could you slice a nose off a mouth and still keep a face?

ANNOUNCER: Commies?

CLAN: Would you lop off a titty from a chest and still have a breast?

ANNOUNCER: Your city government?

CLAN: Now you talkin'!

ANNOUNCER: State administration?

CLAN: Warming up!

ANNOUNCER: Federal?

CLAN: Kin a blind man see?!

ANNOUNCER: The Court?

CLAN: Is a pig clean?!

ANNOUNCER: Clergy?

CLAN: Do a polecat stink?!

ANNOUNCER: Well, Mr. Clan, with this massive complicity, how do you think the plot could've been prevented from succeeding?

CLAN: If I'da been in office, it never woulda happened.

ANNOUNCER: Then you're laying major blame at the doorstep of the present administration?

CLAN: Damn tooting!

ANNOUNCER: But from your oft-expressed views, Mr. Clan, shouldn't you and your followers be delighted at the turn of events? After all—isn't it one of the main policies of your society to *drive* the Negroes away? *Drive* 'em back where they came from?

CLAN: DRIVVVE, BOY! DRIIIIVVVE! That's right!... When we say so and not befo'. Ain't supposed to do nothing 'til we tell 'em. Got to stay put until we exercise our God-given right to tell 'em when to git!

ANNOUNCER: But why argue if they've merely jumped the gun? Why not rejoice at this premature purging of undesirables?

CLAN: The time ain't ripe yet, boy... The time ain't ripe yet.

ANNOUNCER: Thank you for being so informative, Mr. Clan—Mrs. Aide? Mrs. Aide? Over here, Mrs. Aide... Ladies and gentle-men, this city's Social Welfare Commissioner, Mrs. Handy Anna Aide... Mrs. Aide, with all your Negroes *AWOL*, haven't developments alleviated the staggering demands made upon your Welfare Department? Reduction of relief requests, elimination of case loads, removal of chronic welfare dependents, et cetera?

AIDE: Quite the contrary. Disruption of our pilot projects among Nigras saddles our white community with extreme hardship... You see, historically, our agencies have always been foremost contributors to the Nigra Git-A-Job movement. We pioneered in enforcing social welfare theories which oppose coddling the fakers. We strenuously believe in helping Nigras help themselves by participating in meaning-ful labor. "Relief is Out, Work is In," is our motto. We place them as maids, cooks, butlers, and breast-feeders, cesspool-diggers, wash-basin maintainers, shoe-shine boys, and so on—mostly on a volun-teer self-work basis.

ANNOUNCER: Hired at prevailing salaried rates, of course?

AIDE: God forbid! Money is unimportant. Would only make 'em worse. Our main goal is to improve their ethical behavior. "Rehabilitation Through Positive Participation" is another motto of ours. All unwed mothers, loose-living malingering fathers, bastard children and shift-less grandparents are kept occupied through constructive muscle-therapy. This provides the Nigra with less opportunity to indulge in his pleasure-loving amoral inclinations.

ANNOUNCER: They volunteer to participate in these pilot projects?

AIDE: Heavens no! They're notorious shirkers. When I said the program is voluntary, I meant white citizens in overwhelming majorities do the volunteering. Placing their homes, offices, appliances and persons at our disposal for use in "Operation Uplift"...We would never dare place such a decision in the hands of the Nigra. It would never get off the ground!...No, they have no choice in the matter. "Work or Starve" is the slogan we use to stimulate Nigra awareness of what's good for survival.

ANNOUNCER: Thank you, Mrs. Aide, and good luck...Rev?...Rev?... Ladies and gentlemen, this city's foremost spiritual guidance coun-selor, Reverend Reb Pious...How does it look to you, Reb Pious?

PIOUS: [Continuing to gaze skyward.] It's in His hands, son, it's in His hands.

ANNOUNCER: How would you assess the disappearance, from a moral standpoint?

PIOUS: An immoral act, son, morally wrong and ethically indefensible. A perversion of Christian principles to be condemned from every pul-pit of this nation.

ANNOUNCER: Can you account for its occurrence after the many decades of the Church's missionary activity among them?

PIOUS: It's basically a reversion of the Nigra to his deep-rooted primi-tivism...Now, at last, you can understand the difficulties of the Church in attempting to anchor God's kingdom among ungratefuls. It's a constant, unrelenting, no-holds-barred struggle against Satan to wrestle away souls locked in his possession for countless centuries! Despite all our aid, guidance, solace and protection, Old BeezleBub still retains tenacious grips upon the Nigras' childish loyalty — comparable to the lure of bright flames to an infant.

ANNOUNCER: But actual physical departure, Reb Pious? How do you explain that?

PIOUS: Voodoo, my son, voodoo . . . With Satan's assist, they have probably employed some heathen magic which we cultivated, sophisticated Christians know absolutely nothing about. However, before long we are confident about counteracting this evil witchdoctory and triumphing in our Holy Savior's name. At this perilous juncture, true believers of all denominations are participating in joint, 'round-the-clock observances, offering prayers for our Master's swiftest intercession. I'm optimistic about the outcome of his intervention . . . Which prompts me—if I may, sir—to offer these words of counsel to our delinquent Nigras . . . I say to you without rancor or vengeance, quoting a phrase of one of your greatest prophets, Booker T. Washington: "Return your buckets to where they lay and all will be forgiven."

ANNOUNCER: A very inspirational appeal, Reb Pious. I'm certain they will find the tug of its magnetic sincerity irresistible. Thank you, Reb Pious . . . All in all—as you have witnessed, ladies and gentlemen— this town symbolizes the face of disaster. Suffering as severe a prostration as any city wrecked, ravaged and devastated by the holocaust of war. A vital, lively, throbbing organism brought to a screeching halt by the strange enigma of the missing Negroes . . . We take you now to the offices of the one man into whose hands has been thrust the final responsibility of rescuing this shuddering metropolis from the precipice of destruction . . . We give you the honorable Mayor, Henry R. E. Lee . . . Hello, Mayor Lee.

MAYOR: [*Jovial.*] Hello, Jack.

ANNOUNCER: Mayor Lee, we have just concluded interviews with some of your city's leading spokesmen. If I may say so, sir, they don't sound too encouraging about the situation.

MAYOR: Nonsense, Jack! The situation's well-in-hand as it could be under the circumstances. Couldn't be better in hand. Underneath every dark cloud, Jack, there's always a ray of sunlight, ha, ha, ha.

ANNOUNCER: Have you discovered one, sir?

MAYOR: Well, Jack, I'll tell you . . . Of course we've been faced wit' a little crisis, but look at it like this—we've faced 'em befo': Sherman marched through Georgia — ONCE! Lincoln freed the slaves — MOMENTARILY! Carpetbaggers even put Nigras in the Governor's mansion, state legislature, Congress and the Senate of the United States. But what happened?—-Ole Dixie bounced right on back up . . . At this moment the Supreme Court's trying to put Nigras in our schools and the Nigra has got it in his haid to put hisself everywhere . . . But what you 'spect go'n' happen?—Ole Dixie will kangaroo back even higher. Southern courage, fortitude, chivalry and superiority always wins out . . . SHUCKS! We'll have us some Nigras befo' daylight is gone!

ANNOUNCER: Mr. Mayor, I hate to introduce this note, but in an earlier interview, one of your chief opponents, Mr. Clan, hinted at your own complicity in the affair—

MAYOR: A LOT OF POPPYCOCK! Clan is politicking! I've beaten him four times outta four and I'll beat him four more times outta four! This is not time for partisan politics! What we need now is level-headedness and across-the-board unity. This typical, rash, mealy-mouth, shooting-off-at-the-lip of Clan and his ilk proves their insincerity and voters will remember that in the next election! Won't you, voters?! [*Has risen to the height of campaign orator.*]

ANNOUNCER: Mr. Mayor! . . . Mr. Mayor! . . . Please—

MAYOR: . . . I tell you, I promise you —

ANNOUNCER: PLEASE, MR. MAYOR!

MAYOR: Huh? . . . Oh—yes, carry on.

ANNOUNCER: Mr. Mayor, your cheerfulness and infectious good spirits lead me to conclude that startling new developments warrant fresh-found optimism. What concrete, declassified information do you have to support your claim that Negroes will reappear before nightfall?

MAYOR: Because we are presently awaiting the pay-off of a masterful five-point supra-recovery program which can't help but reap us a bonanza of Nigras 'fore sundown! . . . First: Exhaustive efforts to pinpoint the where'bouts of our own missing darkies continue to zero in on the bullseye . . . Second: The President of the United States, following an emergency cabinet meeting, has designated us the prime disaster area of the century—National Guard is already on the way . . . Third: In an unusual, but bold maneuver, we have appealed to the NAACP 'n' all other Nigra conspirators to help us git to the bottom of the vanishing act . . . Fourth: We have exercised our non-reciprocal option and requested that all fraternal Southern states express their solidarity by lending us some of their Nigras temporarily on credit . . . Fifth and foremost: We have already gotten consent of the Governor to round up all stray, excess, and incorrigible Nigras to be shipped to us under escort of the State Militia...That's why we've stifled pessimism and are brimming wit' confidence that this fullscale concerted mobilization will ring down a jackpot of jigaboos 'fore light vanishes from sky!—

ANNOUNCER: Congratulations! What happens if it fails?

MAYOR: Don't even think THAT! Absolutely no reason to suspect it will ...[*Peers over shoulder, then whispers confidentially while placing hand over mouth by* ANNOUNCER's *imaginary mike.*]...But speculating on the dark side of your question—if we don't turn up some by nightfall, it may be all over. The harm has already been done. You see the South has always been glued together by the uninterrupted presence of its darkies. No telling how unstuck we might git if things keep on like they have—Wait a minute, it musta paid off already! Mission accomplished 'cause here's Jackson head a time wit' the word...Well, Jackson, what's new?

JACKSON: Situation on the home front remains static, sir—can't uncover scent or shadow. The NAACP and all other Nigra front groups 'n' plotters deny any knowledge or connection wit' the missing Nigras. Maintained this even after appearing befo' a Senate Emergency Investigating Committee which subpoenaed 'em to Washington post haste and threw 'em in jail for contempt. A handful of Nigras who agreed to make spectacular appeals for ours to come back to us, have themselves mysteriously disappeared. But, worst news of all, sir, is our sister cities and counties, inside and outside the state, have changed their minds, fallen back on their promises and refused to lend us any Nigras, claiming they don't have 'nuff for themselves.

MAYOR: What 'bout Nigras promised by the Governor?!

JACKSON: Jailbirds and vagrants escorted here from chain-gangs and other reservations either revolted and escaped enroute or else vanished mysteriously on approaching our city limits...Deterioration rapidly escalates, sir. Estimates predict we kin hold out only one more hour before overtaken by anarchistic turmoil...Some citizens seeking haven elsewheres have already fled, but on last report were being forcibly turned back by armed sentinels in other cities who wanted no parts of 'em—claiming they carried a jinx.

MAYOR: That bad, huh?

JACKSON: Worse, sir...we've received at least five reports of plots on your life.

MAYOR: What?!—We've gotta act quickly then!

JACKSON: Run out of ideas, sir.

MAYOR: Think harder, boy!

JACKSON: Don't have much time, sir. One measly hour, then all hell go'n' break loose.

MAYOR: Gotta think of something drastic, Jackson!

JACKSON: I'm dry, sir.

MAYOR: Jackson! Is there any planes outta here in the next hour?

JACKSON: All transportation's been knocked out, sir.

MAYOR: I thought so!

JACKSON: What were you contemplating, sir?

MAYOR: Don't ask me what I was contemplating! I'm still boss 'round here! Don't forgit it!

JACKSON: Sorry, sir.

MAYOR: ...Hold the wire!...Wait a minute...! Waaaaait a minute—GODAMIT! All this time crapping 'round, diddling and footsing wit' puny li'l' solutions—all the while neglecting our ace in the hole, our trump card! Most potent weapon for digging Nigras outta the wood-pile!!! All the while right befo' our eyes!...Ass! Why didn't you re-mind me?!!!

JACKSON: What is it, sir?

MAYOR: ...ME—THAT'S WHAT! ME! A personal appeal from ME! *Directly to them!*...Although we wouldn't let 'em march to the polls and express their affection for me through the ballot box, we've al-ways known I'm held highest in their esteem. A direct address from their beloved Mayor!...If they's anywheres close within the sound of my voice, they'll shape up! Or let us know by a sign they's ready to!

JACKSON: You sure *that'll* turn the trick, sir?

MAYOR: As sure as my ancestors befo' me who knew that when they puck-ered their lips to whistle, ole Sambo was gonna come a-lickety-splitting to answer the call!...That same chips-down blood courses through these Confederate gray veins of Henry R. E. Lee!!!

ANNOUNCER: I'm delighted to offer our network's facilities for such a cru-cial public interest address, sir. We'll arrange immediately for your appearance on an international hookup, placing you in the widest proximity to contact them wherever they may be.

MAYOR: Thank you, I'm very grateful... Jackson, re-grease the machinery and set wheels in motion. Inform townspeople what's being done. Tell 'em we're all in this together. The next hour is countdown. I demand absolute cooperation, city–wide silence and inactivity. I don't want the Nigras frightened if they's nearby. This is the most important hour in town's history. Tell 'em if one single Nigra shows up during hour of decision, victory is within sight. I'm gonna git 'em that one — maybe all! Hurry and crack to it! [ANNOUNCER *rushes out, followed by* JACKSON. *Blackout. Scene re-opens, with* MAYOR *seated, eyes front, spotlight illuminating him in semi-darkness. Shadowy figures stand in the background, prepared to answer phones or aid in any other manner.* MAYOR *waits patiently until "GO!" signal is given. Then begins, his voice combining elements of confidence, tremolo and gravity.*] Good evening... Despite the fact that millions of you wonderful people throughout the nation are viewing and listening to this momentous broadcast— and I thank you for your concern and sympathy in this hour of our peril—I primarily want to concentrate my attention and address these remarks solely for the benefit of our departed Nigra friends who may be listening somewheres in our farflung land to the sound of my voice ... If you are — it is with heart-felt emotion and fond memories of our happy association that I ask— "Where are you...?" Your absence has left a void in the bosom of every single man, woman and child of our great city. I tell you— you don't know what it means for us to wake up in the morning and discover that your cheerful, grinning, happy-go-lucky faces are missing!... From the depths of my heart, I can truly meekly, humbly suggest what it means to me personally. You see—the one face I will never be able to erase from my memory is the face—not of my Ma, not of Pa, neither wife or child — but the image of the first woman I came to love so well when just a wee lad — the vision of the first human I laid clear sight on at childbirth — the profile—better yet, the full face of my dear old... Jemimah—God rest her soul... Yes! My dear ole mammy, wit' her round ebony moonbeam gleaming down upon me in the crib, teeth shining, blood-red bandanna standing starched, peaked and proud, gazing down upon me affectionately as she crooned me a Southern lullaby... OH! It's a memorable picture I will eternally cherish in permanent treasure chambers of my heart, now and forever always... Well, if this radiant image can remain so infinitely vivid to me all these many years after her unfortunate demise in the Po' folks home—THINK of the misery the rest of us must be suffering after being *freshly* denied your soothing presence?! We need ya. If you kin hear me, just contact this station 'n' I will welcome you back personally. Let me just tell you that since you eloped, nothing has been the same. How could it? You're part of us, you belong to us. Just give us a sign and we'll be contented that all is well... Now if you've skipped away on a little fun-rest, we understand, ha, ha. We know you like a good time and we don't begrudge it to ya. Hell—er, er, we like a good time ourselves—who doesn't?... In fact, think of all the good times we've had together, huh? We've had some real fun, you and us, yesiree!... Nobody knows better than you and I what fun we've had together. You singing us those old Southern coon songs and dancing those Nigra jigs and us clapping, prodding 'n' spurring you on! Lots of fun, huh?!... OH BOY! The times we've had together— If you've snucked away for a bit of fun by yourself, we'll go 'long wit' ya— long as you let us know where you at so we won't be worried about you... We'll go 'long wit' you long as you don't take the joke too far. I'll admit a joke is a joke and you've played a LULU!... I'm warning you, we can't stand much more horsing 'round from you! Business is business 'n' fun is fun! You've had your fun so now let's get down to business! Come on back, YOU HEAR ME!!!... If you been hoodwinked by agents of some foreign government, I've been authorized by the President of these United States to inform you that this liberty-loving Republic is prepared to rescue you from their clutches. Don't pay no 'tention to their siren songs and atheistic promises! You better off under our control and you know it!... If you been bamboozled by rabblerousing nonsense of your own so-called leaders, we prepared to offer same protection. Just call us up! Just give us a sign!... Come on, give us a sign... give us a sign—even a teeny-weeny one...??!! [*Glances around checking on possible communications. A bevy of headshakes indicate no success.* MAYOR *returns to address with desperate fervor.*] Now look— you don't know what you doing! If you persist in this disobedience, you know all too well the consequences! We'll track you to the end of the earth, beyond the galaxy, across the stars! We'll capture you and chastise you with all the vengeance we command! 'N' you know only too well how stern we kin be when double-crossed! The city, the state and the entire nation will crucify you for this unpardonable defiance! [*Checks again.*] No call...? No sign...? Time is running out! Deadline slipping past! They gotta respond! They gotta! [*Resuming.*] Listen to me! I'm begging ya'all, you've gotta come back...! LOOK, GEORGE! [*Waves dirty rag aloft.*] I brought the rag you wax the car wit'. Don't this bring back memories, George, of all the days you spent shining that automobile to shimmering perfection...? And you, Rufus?!... Here's the shoe polisher and the brush!... 'Member, Rufus?... Remember the happy mornings you spent popping this rag and whisking this brush so furiously 'till it created music that was sympho-nee to the ear...? And you — MANDY?...Here's the wastebasket you didn't dump this morning. I saved it just for you?...LOOK, all ya'll out there...? [*Signals and a three-person procession parades one after the other before the imaginary camera.*]

DOLL WOMAN: [*Brandishing a crying baby doll as she strolls past and exits.*] She's been crying ever since you left, Caldonia...

MOP MAN: [*Flashing mop.*] It's been waiting in the same corner, Buster...

BRUSH MAN: [*Flagging toilet brush in one hand and toilet plunger in other.*] It's been dry ever since you left, Washington...

MAYOR: [*Jumping in on the heels of the last exit.*] Don't these things mean anything to y'all? By God! Are your memories so short?! Is there nothing sacred to ya?...Please come back, for my sake, please! All of you — even you questionable ones! I promise no harm will be done to you! Revenge is disallowed! We'll forgive everything! Just come on back and I'll git down on my knees — [*Immediately drops to knees.*] I'll be kneeling in the middle of Dixie Avenue to kiss the first shoe of the first one 'a you to show up...I'll smooch any other spot you request ...Erase this nightmare 'n' we'll concede any demand you make, just come on back—please???!!...PLEEEEEEZE?!!!

VOICE: [*Shouting.*] TIME!!!

MAYOR: [*Remaining on knees, frozen in a pose of supplication. After a brief, deadly silence, he whispers almost inaudibly.*] They wouldn't answer... they wouldn't answer...

[*Blackout as bedlam erupts offstage. Total blackness holds during a sufficient interval where offstage sound–effects create the illusion of complete pandemonium, followed by a diminution which trails off into an expressionistic simulation of a city coming to a strickened standstill: industrial machinery clanks to halt, traffic blares to silence, etc.... The stage remains dark and silent for a long moment, then lights re-arise on the ANNOUNCER.*]

ANNOUNCER: A pitiful sight, ladies and gentlemen. Soon after his unsuccessful appeal, Mayor Lee suffered a vicious pummeling from the mob and barely escaped with his life. National Guardsmen and State Militia were impotent in quelling the fury of a town venting its frustration in an orgy of destruction—a frenzy of rioting, looting and all other aberrations of a town gone berserk...Then—suddenly—as if a magic wand had been waved, madness evaporated and something more frightening replaced it: Submission . . . Even whimperings ceased. The city: exhausted, benumbed — Slowly its occupants slinked off into shadows, and by midnight, the town was occupied exclusively by zombies. The fight and life had been drained out . . . Pooped . . . Hope ebbed away as completely as the beloved, absent Negroes . . . As our crew packed gear and crept away silently, we treaded softly — as if we were stealing away from a mausoleum . . . The Face Of A Defeated City.

[*Blackout. Lights rise slowly at the sound of rooster-crowing, signalling the approach of a new day, the next morning. Scene is same as opening of play.* CLEM *and* LUKE *are huddled over dazedly, trancelike. They remain so for a long count. Finally, a figure drifts on stage, shuffling slowly.*]

LUKE: [*Gazing in silent fascination at the approaching figure.*] . . . Clem . . . ? Do you see what I see or am I dreaming . . . ?

CLEM: It's a . . . a Nigra, ain't it, Luke . . . ?

LUKE: Sure looks like one, Clem — but we better make sure — eyes could be playing tricks on us . . . Does he still look like one to you, Clem?

CLEM: He still does, Luke — but I'm scared to believe —

LUKE: . . . Why . . . ? It looks like Rastus, Clem!

CLEM: Sure does, Luke . . . but we better not jump to no hasty conclusion . . .

LUKE: [*In timid softness.*] That you, Rastus . . . ?

RASTUS: [*Stepin Fetchit, Willie Best, Nicodemus, B. McQueen and all the rest rolled into one.*] Why . . . howdy . . . Mr. Luke . . . Mr. Clem . . .

CLEM: It is him, Luke! It is him!

LUKE: Rastus?

RASTUS: Yeas . . . sah?

LUKE: Where was you yesterday?

RASTUS: [*Very, very puzzled.*] Yes . . . ter . . . day? . . . Yester . . . day . . . ? Why . . . .right . . . here . . . Mr. Luke . . .

LUKE: No you warn't, Rastus, don't lie to me! Where was you yestiddy?

RASTUS: Why . . . I'm sure I was . . . Mr. Luke . . . Remember . . . I made . . . that . . . delivery for you . . .

LUKE: That was MONDAY, Rastus, yestiddy was TUESDAY.

RASTUS: Tues . . . day . . . ? You don't say . . . Well . . . well . . . well . . .

LUKE: Where was you 'n' all the other Nigras yesterday, Rastus?

RASTUS: I . . . thought . . . yestiddy . . . was . . . Monday, Mr. Luke — I coulda swore it . . . I . . . See how . . . things . . . kin git all mixed up? . . . I coulda swore it . . .

LUKE: TODAY is WEDNESDAY, Rastus. Where was you TUESDAY?

RASTUS: Tuesday . . . huh? That's somp'um . . . I don't . . . remember . . . missing . . . a day . . . Mr. Luke . . . but I guess you right . . .

LUKE: Then were was you!!!???

RASTUS: Don't rightly know, Mr. Luke. I didn't know I had skipped a day —But that jist goes to show you how time kin fly, don't it, Mr. Luke . . . Uuh, uuh, uuh . . . [*He starts shuffling off, scratching head, a flicker of a smile playing across his lips.* CLEM *and* LUKE *gaze dumbfound-edly as he disappears.*]

LUKE: [*Eyes sweeping around in all directions.*] Well . . . There's the others, Clem . . . Back jist like they useta be . . . Everything's same as always . . .

CLEM: ??? . . . . Is it . . . Luke . . . !

[*Slow fade. Curtain.*]

Charlie Russell

FIVE ON THE BLACK HAND SIDE

CHARLIE L. RUSSELL

Born in Monroe, LA, attended high school in Oakland CA, received B.S. degree in English from University of San Francisco and M.S.W. (Master of Social Work) from NYU, M.F.A. in Playwriting from University of California in San Diego. Russell studied acting in New York with the Actors Studio, The National Black Theatre (NBT), and privately under Clarice Taylor. He studied directing with Gilbert Moses and the New Dramatists Guild Workshop. He was adjunct associate professor at Livingston College of Rutgers University in New Brunswick, NJ; adjunct associate professor in film script writing in the Visual Arts Dept, NYU; writer-in-residence at American Place Theatre; and drama instructor, Contra Costa College in San Pablo, California.

Russell's first Off-Broadway play, *Five on the Black Hand Side* (originally titled *Gladys*) produced by American Place Theatre was directed by Barbara Ann Teer at St. Clement's Church, New York City in 1969 and ran for 62 performances. A film of the same name was released by United Artists, 1973, directed by Oscar Williams and starring Clarice Taylor, Leonard Jackson and Virginia Capers. Sonny Jim (J. E. Gaines) and Ja'Net DuBois were also in the cast. The screenplay garnered him the NAACP Image Award (1975) for Best Film Script; he received a grant from the Institute of International Education to study African rituals and ceremonies in Nigeria for three months (1973), as well as a Rockefeller Playwright's Grant (1975). Russell was the fiction editor for *Liberator* magazine. His articles have appeared in *Essence, Encore, Black World, Onyx*, the *Manhattan Tribune*, and the *New York Amsterdam News*. His short stories have been anthologized in *The Best Short Stories by Negro Writers* (Hughes, 1967), *Afro-American Literature: Fiction* (Adams, Con, & Slepian, 1979); and he published a novella entitled *A Birthday Present for Kathryn Kenyatta*.

Other Plays and Dramatic Works: *The Black Church*, CBS-TV; *A Man Is Not Made Of Steel*, WGBH-TV (Boston), *What You Gonna Do On Monday?, Blackman?, Four No Trump!, The Incident At Terminal Ecstasy Acres, (The) Revival!*

Russell is currently working on a novel entitled, *Tales from the African American Diaspora*, a historical love story that deals with black immigration from the South to California during the early 40s.

ACT ONE

SCENE 1

TIME: *Present.*

SCENE: *Morning. An apartment located in Harlem. There is a living room, kitchen.* MRS. BROOKS, *who has a scarf on her head, is already on stage. She is humming and singing snatches from a mournful spiritual as she prepares the morning breakfast. She also prepares* MR. BROOKS' *lunch which she puts into his attaché case.*

MR. BROOKS: [*Enters excitedly with a piece of paper in his hand. He is fully dressed in a suit and a tie.*] Good morning, Mrs. Brooks. I've got it! I've got it! [*Sits down.* MRS. BROOKS *immediately gives him a cup of coffee.*]

MRS. BROOKS. Good morning, Mr. Brooks.

MR. BROOKS: Booker T. gave me an idea and I wrote it last night. Ha! Brilliant idea! I'm telling you that Booker T. is all right. [*Starts reading.*]

MRS. BROOKS. Yes, Mr. Brooks.

MR. BROOKS: This will fix his wagon. Defying his own father. Ha, ha. Yes! I don't see why I didn't think of this myself. Hmmmmm. Yes. This will fix that dad-blasted Gideon. You've got to know how to handle these college boys, Mrs. Brooks. I'm appealing to his sense of logic. [*He finishes reading the letter, much pleased with himself.*] There! Yes! I really laid it on him, Mrs. Brooks. Oh, dad blast it! Oh, thank you, Mrs. Brooks. You can give this to your youngest son. It's a list of my demands. Oh, and by the way. You can tell him that my demands are nonnegotiable.

MRS. BROOKS. Yes, Mr. Brooks. [*Takes letter and puts it away. Places* MR. BROOKS' *breakfast before him.*]

MR. BROOKS: [*Starts reading his newspaper.*] A hum. Thank you, Mrs. Brooks. Hmmmmmm. I see here that the Plessey Company has made a 648 million dollar tender offer to the Zanzibar Steel Company. Seems it's a move to strengthen their position against international competition. Brilliant idea! Sound business move! Yes! [*Checks his watch which hangs across his vest.*] Mrs. Brooks, your book, please.

MRS. BROOKS: Yes, Mr. Brooks. [*Gives* MR. BROOKS *her appointment book and waits patiently as he studies it.*]

MR. BROOKS: Hmmmmmm. I see here that you have some free time around noon. After you return from the hairdresser, I think you should take a walk. Hmmmmm. Yes, you have a good schedule today, Mrs. Brooks. A very good schedule. Yes. By the way, I strongly suggest that you make sure your blue dress is in good shape. I've decided that you can wear it to Gail's wedding.

MRS. BROOKS: But you said I could buy a new one.

MR. BROOKS: Well, I've thought about it and with all the money we're spending on Gail's wedding we simply can't afford it.

MRS. BROOKS: Yes, Mr. Brooks. [*Sits down at the table, drinking a cup of coffee. Starts crying.*]

MR. BROOKS: [*He is puzzled by his wife's tears, and he gets up to comfort her. He stands behind her, assuming the stance of the great white hunter.*] There, there, Mrs. Brooks, it's all right. I'm not mad anymore because Gail is getting married, although she knew that I had my heart set on her going to college. There, there. You did the best you could. I'm not blaming you anymore. Although I must admit that you did seem to be on her side a few times, there. Now, now, Mrs. Brooks, you know I'm not the kind of man who carries a grudge for more than a week. [*Pats* MRS. BROOKS *on the shoulders, and gives her his handkerchief.*]

MRS. BROOKS: Thank you, Mr. Brooks.

MR. BROOKS: You know, maybe it's just as well that Gail is getting married. Who knows, she might have gone to college, and turned out to be one of them college rebels like Gideon. Always talking about the white power structure this and the white power structure that. If I ever get my hands on him I'll show him something about a black power structure. [*Starts pacing the floor.*] Got the nerve to go on a strike against his own father. Have you ever heard of such a thing, your own flesh and blood? You know, Mrs. Brooks, sometimes I think it's a blessing that all of our children are grown. Maybe now you and I can sort of grow old together graceful like.

MRS. BROOKS: Oh, Mr. Brooks.

MR. BROOKS: Don't worry, Mrs. Brooks. Things are going to work out. Why, look at the way Booker T. has turned out. But he's working steady now, trying to get ahead in life. Why, he can even hold a decent conversation with you now without screaming. Yes, yes, that boy is really maturing, really growing up. [*An alarm clock goes off offstage.*] What's Gail getting up so early for?

MRS. BROOKS: They're rehearsing at the church this morning.

MR. BROOKS: That dad-blasted Gideon. Oh, if I could get just one hand on him, Mrs. Brooks. Just one.

MRS. BROOKS: Oh, I wish you two could get along.

MR. BROOKS: But you know I've tried, Mrs. Brooks, I've really tried, but what can you do when the other fellow is stubborn, pig-headed, and ungrateful? I mean even a good man has his limits, Mrs. Brooks.

MRS. BROOKS: Yes, Mr. Brooks, Gail. Gailll! It's time for you to get up. I knew she'd have a hard time getting up this morning. I told her not to stay at that party so late. Gaillll! She'll be mad if I don't wake her up. Gaillllll!

GAIL: [*From offstage.*] All right, Momma, I'm getting up. [*A* RADIO *is turned on offstage, playing rhythm and blues music.*]

MR. BROOKS: And cut off that dad-blasted radio. Booker T. is trying to sleep. [*The* SOUND *is lowered.*] That's one noisy girl. Well, in two days she'll be Martin's problem.

MRS. BROOKS: Marvin. His name is Marvin, Mr. Brooks.

MR. BROOKS: Yes, of course.

GAIL: [*Enters happily, dancing into the room.*] Hi, Mom. Hi, Pop. [*Does a few dance steps.*] Hello, world. HellOOO! Wow, I'm so happy!

MR. BROOKS: It seems to me that happiness don't have to be so frisky. Especially so early in the morning.

GAIL: Oh, Daddy, don't be so square. [*Sits down at the table.*] You should be singing with me. It's not every day your only daughter gets married. And you didn't even have to get a shotgun.

MR. BROOKS: HmPH!

MRS. BROOKS: Gail!

GAIL: Well, it's true. Marvin and I are marrying for love. Thanks, Mom. [MRS. BROOKS *gives her a cup of coffee.*]

MR. BROOKS: Don't forget that letter Mrs. Brooks. [*Stands, preparing to go to work.*]

GAIL: Oh, Daddy! You're not going to work today, are you?

MR. BROOKS: And why not? Fridays and Saturdays are my volume days. And you know that's where the profits are.

GAIL: I'll bet you'd be much nicer about the whole thing if I was marrying somebody besides Marvin.

MRS. BROOKS: Gail, that's your father you're talking to.

GAIL: Well, it's true, Momma. Daddy doesn't like Marvin.

MR. BROOKS: Ah, that's not true. I like that boy.

GAIL: Then how come you never talk to him?

MR. BROOKS: I just don't have much to say.

GAIL: You have a lot to say to everybody else.

MRS. BROOKS: Gail, you shouldn't talk like that.

GAIL: I'm sorry, Dad. [*Kisses her father.*] It's just that Marvin is so wonderful, and I want you to like him. I want everybody to be happy. Come on, Daddy, dance with me. [GAIL *does a few steps around him.*]

MR. BROOKS: I'm saving all my dancing for the wedding. I might as well warn you all that I'm going to be a tough cookie on the dance floor. [*Looks at his watch.*] Say, it's getting late. I've got to get to work.

GAIL: You really going to dance at the wedding, Daddy?

MR. BROOKS: And I'm going to be a toughie. [*He stands, and* MRS. BROOKS *gives him his attaché case in a ritual perfected over the years.*] Hmmmmmm. Yes. Thank you, Mrs. Brooks. Yes, and don't forget that little walk.

MRS. BROOKS: Yes, Mr. Brooks.

MR. BROOKS: I'll see you all. [*Walks toward the front door.*]

GAIL: Goodbye, Dad. [MR. BROOKS *stops just as he is about to exit, and returns to give* MRS. BROOKS, *who has not moved away from her spot, a light peck of a kiss on the cheek.*]

MR. BROOKS: There! [*Exits.*]

GAIL: That's why I love Marvin so much. He knows how to touch people, and he lets people touch him. Oh, Momma, he is so beautiful. Not just outside, but inside. In a lot of ways he's tough and hard like Gideon, but he has a softness about him, a warmness . . . He just radiates something, Momma, it makes me want to grab him, to hold him, to protect him against the world. [MRS. BROOKS *starts crying but* GAIL *does not notice it.* GAIL *starts reading the newspaper.*]

GAIL: Hey, Momma, remember when I was a little girl how I used to worry you to death because I didn't think anyone would marry me when I grew up? Remember? I used to ask you a thousand questions about how I could get the boys to like me? Wow, I almost pushed the panic button when I didn't have a boyfriend by the time I was eleven. I just knew I'd be an old maid. And now the moon has her sun.

MRS. BROOKS: Oh, Gail. I'm so happy for you. You don't know how many years I've prayed for this day to come. You see, I'm not just happy for you. I'm also happy because when you get married that means that I can keep a promise I made to myself many years ago. You see, I promised myself that as soon as you . . . [*The* PHONE *rings.*]

GAIL: I'll get it. Hello? Oh, hi, love. Oh, it was okay—just a bunch of girls and you know where I wanted to be. Marvin! Jive! Blow my mind. Scatter it into a thousand pieces.

BOOKER T: [*Enters.*] Jesus Christ, this is a crazy house. Alarm clocks going off all around you. Radios blasting away. And now the phone. Getting my own pad sure was a hip move. A very hip move. Now all we need is for Gideon to come sliding from that roof with all his counter-revolutionary nonsense.

MRS. BROOKS: Good morning, son. Juice and coffee?

BOOKER T: Thanks, Moms. Did Dad leave already?

MRS. BROOKS: You just missed him. Did you want something?

BOOKER T: No, not really. Just checking. Hmmmm. [*Starts reading the newspaper.*]

GAIL: Bye, love. [*Kisses the phone a few times.*] See you at the rehearsal. [*Hangs up phone and joins* BOOKER T. *at the table.*] Hi, Booker T.

BOOKER T: Don't call me by that slave name. You know everybody calls me Sharrief.

GAIL: Sorry about that, I forgot. That was Marvin, Momma. See what I mean? See how wonderful he is? Oh, Momma, we're going to be so happy!!

BOOKER T: Oh, Momma, we're going to be so happy. Girl, why don't you get out of that Doris Day bag? Walking around in them jive miniskirts.

GAIL: Daddy is so quick to judge people, and to turn them off. I'm sure he'd like Marvin, but he won't even talk to him.

BOOKER T: Oh, girl, you know Dad ain't never gonna dig no jailbird.

GAIL: Marvin was a political prisoner. Refusing to fight in that war is not a real crime. At least he stood up for his convictions. You know, sometimes I don't understand you, Booker T., excuse me, Sharrief. I wish you'd get yourself together. I'm tired of your criticisms, I want to see some of your activism.

BOOKER T: You're beginning to sound just like that creep Gideon.

MRS. BROOKS: Booker T.! Gideon is your baby brother.

BOOKER T: Ah, Momma, Gideon is incorrect. The solution to the black problem is so simple. Power comes from the barrel of a gun. Chairman Mao has already given the word, and anyone not doing the deed is jiving.

MRS. BROOKS: Gail — You can listen to this too, if you want to, Booker T. I was just telling your sister how happy I am that she's getting married because now I'm going to keep a promise I made to myself a long, long time ago. You see, I promised myself that as soon as Gail — that is . . .

GIDEON: [*Entering.*] Have no fear, the kid is here. Hey, sis, how you doing? [*Kisses his sister.*] Sure is sweet. Marvin sure is a lucky dude. We should be living in Africa. He'd have to give the family five hundred cattle, a thousand sheep, might even have to throw in a couple of lions, hey, Booker T.

BOOKER T: Hey, man, you know my real name.

GIDEON: Sorry. I'll remember next time, Booker T.

GAIL: Gideon, did you remember to tell some of the gang to come by here this morning?

GIDEON: Everything is everything, love. [*Looks at his watch.*] They ought to be here any minute now. Booker T. Washington Brooks, wow! The old man really hung a name on you, didn't he.

BOOKER T: Look, man, rather than messing with me this morning you'd be better off going on a lion hunt with a toothpick.

GIDEON: Whoa, boy. You'd better practice a little revolutionary discipline.

BOOKER T: You'd better dig yourself. I'm buying all the wolf tickets you're selling this morning. [*Pushes himself away from the table.*] I keep trying to tell you that you don't have a sense of humor. If you did, you'd realize that some things are not funny.

MRS. BROOKS: Booker T.! Gideon! We raised you two to love and respect one another.

BOOKER T: Hey, man, we'd better listen to Momma and cool it.

GIDEON: Yea. But if you want a fair one just come up on the roof, and we can work a light show.

BOOKER T: Ah, man, be serious sometimes. Hey listen, I've got to talk to you sometime today about something.

GIDEON: What?

BOOKER T: In private, man.

GIDEON: Hmmm, O.K. I've got to go to the church, then stop by the art supply store . . . Yea. All right, I'll meet you on the roof in an hour.

BOOKER T: Cool.

MRS. BROOKS: There . . . Well, Gideon, before you came in, I was telling Gail, and your brother, Booker T, how happy I was that Gail was getting married because . . .

[*Doorbell rings.*]

GIDEON: I'll get it. That must be the troops.

[GIDEON *exits then re-enters with* SAMPSON, NIA *and* STEPHANIE. SAMPSON *is carrying a portable tape recorder which is playing rhythm and blues music.*]

GAIL: Sampson, I want you to meet my older brother, Sharrief; Sharrief, Sampson.

BOOKER T: I see you carrying your music with you.

SAMPSON: Yea, it helps us swing while we do our thing, baby. If everyone started their day by listening to some boss sides, they wouldn't have to be taking all kinds of pills and things.

STEPHANIE: Right on. Music is the way we keep in touch with our ancestors. Where we get our spiritual sustenance from.

SAMPSON: Yea, it's like our life force.

GAIL: Oh, and this is Sampson's sister, Stephanie. Stephanie, this is my brother, Sharrief.

STEPHANIE: I've sure heard a lot of things about you.

BOOKER T: I don't know if that's good or bad.

STEPHANIE: Good or bad, it wouldn't matter. I make my own decisions.

GIDEON: Nia, my brother, Sharrief.

BOOKER T: Nice meeting you.

SAMPSON: Hey, Gail, I know you want to be down for the wedding reception, let me lay this step on you. I picked it up from some brothers in Philly.

[SAMPSON *and* GAIL *begin to dance,* SAMPSON *reluctantly teaching her the step.* GIDEON *and* NIA *join the party, as do* STEPHANIE *and* BOOKER T. *Rhythm and blues music.*]

GAIL: Wow! That's dynamite! Whoa. It's getting late. Gideon, show them where the stuff is. I don't want to be late. Marvin is meeting me at the church. [GIDEON *exits with* NIA, SAMPSON, *and* STEPHANIE.] Hey, Momma, you want to come with us?

MRS. BROOKS: No, baby, you all go on. I got my work to do. You know I wash every Friday.

BOOKER T: Hey, sis, I'll walk to the corner with you. And give you a break. People will see you with me, and they'll think you're into something. [*All exit except* MRS. BROOKS.]

MRS. BROOKS: [*Remembers* MR. BROOKS' *letter, and runs to the door.*] Gideon!

GIDEON: Yeah, Momma. I'll catch you in a minute. Hold the last elevator for me. Yea, Momma?

MRS. BROOKS: Mr. Brooks left this for you.

[GIDEON *starts reading the letter to himself.*]

MRS. BROOKS: What does he say?

GIDEON: [*Reads aloud.*] "Dear son Gideon. Since time is making its noble presence felt upon me, I shall be brief, and not attempt to list all of your numerous sins at this time. But I must point out that it is you who is on strike against your own father because he wants you to be a business major when you know that a degree in anthropology does not prepare one to earn money. It is you who is involved in various political activities on the campus, and thereby jeopardizing your entire college career. And finally, it is you who refuses to speak to your loving father. My demands are that you cool it, that all of these various transgressions be rectified immediately. If not sooner. I have tried to be understanding. I realize how difficult it must be for you, in fact for all of my children, to follow in such large illustrious footsteps as mine are. However, in fairness I must admit that your brother, Booker T., does show some promise. Gideon, you disappoint me. Why, this very morning I asked myself if this failure, if this rebel-rouser was really you. You whose test showed an I.Q. of 157. If we were Jewish, I'd have "shivah" set on you. However, I shall be kind, forgiving, and loving as soon as you meet my demands. Gideon, I stand ready to forgive. Gideon, repent so that you can make a mark in the business world like your loving father. Your humble father, Mr. Brooks." He's full of stuff.

MRS. BROOKS: Gideon!

SAMPSON: Hey, come on, man!

GIDEON: Well, he is full of stuff, Momma. Talking about somebody making a mark in the business world like him. You'd think he was running General Motors instead of that little old barbershop.

MRS. BROOKS: Being a barber is honest work.

GIDEON: Ah, Momma. I'm not trying to sound on Dad. It's just that I know where he's coming from. We have to start looking at the whole idea of education differently. A college education is not something you get so you can get a better job. It's a tool you get to help your people.

MRS. BROOKS: Oh, I'm telling you it's all so confusing. When I hear your father tell his side, it sounds right. And when I hear you tell yours, yours sounds right.

SAMPSON: [*From offstage.*] Hey, Gideon! Come on, man!

GIDEON: All right! I'm coming! You see, Momma, Dad wants me to play it safe, and be a good upstanding citizen. That's his way not mine. If I did that I would be turning my back on all the things I believe in.

MRS. BROOKS: Gideon.

GIDEON: Yea, Momma?

SAMPSON: Hey, man, you coming!?

GIDEON: Ah, man, be cool! I'm coming! Yea, Momma.

MRS. BROOKS: Oh, nothing. You'd better go now, they're waiting for you. What I have to say can wait until another time.

GIDEON: Well . . . O.K., Momma. I'll be back in a little while. [*Kisses his mother on the cheek.*] See you, Moms. [*Exits.*]

MRS. BROOKS: See you, son. [*Finishes getting her wash together, starts singing, and humming again, putting clothes, washing powder, bleach into a shopping cart, and exits.*]

[*Curtain.*]

SCENE 2

TIME: *One hour later.*
SCENE: *The roof. In one corner there are a rolled-up blanket, some books, and an African spear.* BOOKER T. *is already on stage.*

BOOKER T: Hey, man, what happened to you?

GIDEON: [*Enters out of breath. He carries a small package and a piece of poster paper.*] Sorry I'm late. I got hung up at the store. How is it going?

BOOKER T: I'm just here by being careful, man. Just sneaking by.

GIDEON: Yea. [*Starts making a "Just Married" sign.*]

BOOKER T: Man, I was checking this place out, I haven't been up here in a long time. Remember when I used to have my pigeons, remember that? I used to have my coop right over there. Boy, the hours I used to spend up here.

GIDEON: Yea, I remember. You wouldn't let anyone play with you. You didn't even allow me up here.

BOOKER T: Yea, man, that sure seems like a long time ago. It's funny how the time just slips away from you. [*Goes and looks down on the street below.*] Yea. Hey, remember that chick from across the street? That old big-legged girl you brought up here, and got your first piece from? What was her name? Remember how upset you were because during the whole Johnson she never stopped popping her gum? What was her name? Gloria, Gloria Cook, that was her name.

GIDEON: Man, didn't you say you wanted to talk to me about something?

BOOKER T.: Yea, man. Well, it's about Dad. We sat up talking a long time last night, and he's really getting upset.

GIDEON: Ah. That dude is always upset about something.

BOOKER T: You could at least listen to what I have to say.

GIDEON: Sure, big brother, sure.

BOOKER T: We had a long talk last night, and it just seems to me that you two ought to compromise.

GIDEON: Compromise? What are you talking about, man? Daddy is wrong as two left shoes.

BOOKER T: Hey, Dad is really not that bad when you get to know him. He just talks bad. Look, Gideon, I'm just asking you to meet the old man halfway, that's all.

GIDEON: This is incredible. This is some incredible shit, man. Dad is living in the nineteen thirties, and you're asking me to meet him halfway. Dad is the one who's got to change. Listen, man, the next time you've got some advice just keep it for yourself. And before you start trying to tell other people what to do, you ought to get your own house in order.

BOOKER T: What do you mean by that, man?

GIDEON: I said what I had to say. People who live in glass houses oughta be cool.

BOOKER T: Look, man, what's bugging you? I've been getting negative vibes from you all morning. If you've got something to say to me, why don't you just come out and say it?

GIDEON: O.K. I will — I don't know — Hey, do you have anything against sisters?

BOOKER T: Do I have anything against sisters? No, I don't have anything against sisters. Why?

GIDEON: I just want to know where you're coming from, that's all. I never see you uptown with any chicks.

BOOKER T: So.

GIDEON: There's a whole lot of boss sisters out here, can't you find one?

BOOKER T: You writing a book, or something?

GIDEON: If I were, I'd leave that chapter out.

BOOKER T: What are you talking about, what's the matter with you?

GIDEON: I just want to know if you've got anything against sisters, man. That's all!

BOOKER T: Well, I don't have anything against sisters, I already told you that.

GIDEON: Un hun. You know what, I think, I think you've probably got some gray chick right now. What do you think about that?

BOOKER T: I think you're a crazy Nigger. That's what I think. You run into some dynamite smokes or something? If you did, turn me on so I can be crazy like you.

GIDEON: Do you, man?

BOOKER T: Do I what?

GIDEON: Do you have a white girlfriend?

BOOKER T: Ah, man, what are you talking about?

GIDEON: Stop playing games, man. Be honest. You were seen going into Terry's with a blonde. You've been seen eating at the Boondock with a blonde. What's happening with you, man?

BOOKER T: So I see a white chick every now and then. Why are you getting so excited?

GIDEON: Why am I getting so excited?

BOOKER T: Yea, who I hang out with is a personal matter.

BOOKER T: I've been through a whole lot of sisters, and I haven't found any that I can really groove with, one that really understands me.

GIDEON: That's because you don't understand yourself. Hey, man, sisters are some beautiful people. Man, we can't afford to get into a negative thing with the sisters. How are we going to survive without strong families?

BOOKER T: Tell me anything, boy. Pee on my back and tell me it's raining. The next thing you'll be trying to tell me that you're up here on this roof because you're trying to keep the family together.

GIDEON: Yea, man, that's why I'm up here; otherwise I would have moved out. I want to keep the family together. The family is the basic unit in a society.

BOOKER T: The family is the basic unit in a society. Ha, that sounds like something you read in one of your books. If you kept your head out of them books sometimes you'd probably have some sense.

GIDEON: Ah, you're really phony, man, you really are. You're so full of contradictions.

BOOKER T: Well, I don't have a monopoly on that. Everybody has contradictions. Who I sleep with is my own private affair.

GIDEON: Hey, man, do you realize the political significance involved in that statement you just made? Who you sleep with, the first face you see in the morning is very important. That's your reflection, where you get your energy from. That's your mirror, can you dig that, your mirror. Instead of putting down the sisters, you ought to be dealing with your ownself. Going around sleeping with the enemy.

BOOKER T: Aw, what are you trying to run down on somebody? That chick is nobody's enemy. She's an individual, and a beautiful one at that. Different strokes for different folks, that's what I say. You do your thing, and I'll damn sure do mine.

GIDEON: Hey, what can I do to make you understand, you've got to get out of that I, I bag, man? We can't have everybody running off doing their own thing. Talking black, and sleeping white is like being a part-time soldier. And we can't win with part-time soldiers, man. We've got to be on the case twenty-five hours a day.

BOOKER T: Man, I don't care what you say.

GIDEON: You're really on an ego trip. You're worse than Dad. Running around, talking, and criticizing all the time. Why don't you check yourself out before it's too late?

BOOKER T: You'd better check your ownself out, baby brother. Why are you really getting so excited and upset about some white girl you don't even know?

GIDEON: Because I don't want to see my brother running around being a hypocrite and a jive ass phony, that's why. I want to see you get yourself together, that's why. If you're into a white thing, stop talking black. You confuse people. Don't try to hide where you're really at. Don't sneak around. Be a man. Do it out in the open. Just declare yourself a part-time member of the struggle.

BOOKER T: Ah, later for you, man. I don't have to stand here and listen to a whole lot of bullshit. [*Starts to leave.*]

GIDEON: And why don't you dig yourself, super-spade. When are you telling the folks about her? I understand she went to Vassar. I'm sure that they will be highly impressed.

BOOKER T: All right, Einstein. I know what you want. I haven't dusted you off in a long time.

GIDEON: Why you want to get into a physical thing, when all I'm asking you to do is be a man? You've got to choose, man. Fence straddling is a dangerous game.

BOOKER T: Ah, what do you know?

GIDEON: I know that you're a zero. I'll bet I know that.

BOOKER T: All right, come on, Mr. Know-It-All. I'm going to rock your skies. [*Approaches* GIDEON, *ready to do much battle.*]

GIDEON: [*Grabs spear and crouches slightly in a position of defense.*] You can rock anything you want to. I just want my cut, that's all.

BOOKER T: Put down that spear, turkey.

GIDEON: I'll put it down all right.

BOOKER T: Just put it down, I dare you. All that talk about being a man. Where is your heart?

GIDEON: In my head, where it suppose to be. See?

BOOKER T: Ah, your heart pumps lemonade. What's the matter with you, chump? You chickenshit? Why don't you drop that spear? You afraid of a fair one?

GIDEON: Can't you do anything besides talk, phony?

BOOKER T: Yea. [*Feints at* GIDEON, *testing him.*]

GIDEON: Ha! [*Flicks spear expertly in defense of himself.*] What's the matter, John Wayne?

BOOKER T: Put down the spear and I'll teach you a lesson, knock some sense into your head.

GIDEON: I'm already teaching you son, you're just not getting it. You see, it's not about a lot of talk, it's about action. Dig it?

BOOKER T: Ah, later for you. You're crazy, phony. [*Turns to leave.*] You're not worth the bother.

GIDEON: What's the matter, baby? Where is your heart?

BOOKER T: Put down that spear, and I'll show you.

GIDEON: Talk is cheap chump. The only good ideas are the ones that you put into practice.

BOOKER T: You going to put down that spear?

GIDEON: Can a buffalo skate?

BOOKER T: All right, all right, Che, I'll be seeing you. [*Exits.*]

GIDEON: Yea, maybe I'll drop by Terry's one night.

    [*Curtain.*]

SCENE 3

RUBY: [RUBY *and* MRS. BROOKS *enter through the front door.*] Girl, I sure wish I could get my hands on whoever that is keeps pushing every one of them buttons on the elevator before they get off. The old elevator door banging shut on every floor just about drove me out of my mind. I don't see how you can be so good-natured about it, Gladys.

MRS. BROOKS: Sometimes I think that's my trouble, I'm too good-natured about everything.

RUBY: Ah, girl.

MRS. BROOKS: It's true, and you know it. I just let everybody push me around.

RUBY: Don't be so hard on yourself, Gladys.

MRS. BROOKS: But, girl, this morning I made up my mind, I'm leaving Mr. Brooks.

RUBY: Gladys, it's not that bad, is it? Remember it ain't the easiest thing in the world to leave a man after all these years.

MRS. BROOKS: Humph. Telling me I couldn't buy a new dress for Gail's wedding; that was the last straw.

RUBY: You know, Gladys, there is such a thing as going from the refrigerator into the frying pan.

MRS. BROOKS: Oh, Ruby, be serious.

RUBY: I am just as serious as cancer. I mean, it's not as though the man won't work. Everybody knows that he ain't known to mess up a piece of money.

MRS. BROOKS: A lot of good it does me. Everything in the house is in his name. My name don't appear on nothing except the income tax deductions.

RUBY: Oh, girl.

MRS. BROOKS: Oh, and the way that man courted me before we got married! Such sweet names he called me. And the day after we got married he started calling me Mrs. Brooks. And now he's got me keeping that old appointment book so he'll know what I'm doing every minute of the day. The only thing I don't have to put in it is when I cough or go to the bathroom.

RUBY: Ah, child.

MRS. BROOKS: And don't let me even look like I want to disagree with him. He rants and raves up a storm, acting like he's going to thunder and lightning for forty days and forty nights.

RUBY: If ever there was a man who knows how to get mad, it's Mr. Brooks.

MRS. BROOKS: Last week I overspent buying groceries, and talking about a man carrying on! You'd have thought that seventeen cents was going to cause a panic down on Wall Street.

RUBY: Now, Gladys, you know sometimes he does have good intentions.

MRS. BROOKS: My granny always said that the road to hell is paved with good intentions.

RUBY: My granny always said that there's some good in everybody.

MRS. BROOKS: If there's some good in Mr. Brooks he's done done a Houdini with it, and made it disappear. 'Cause you sure can't see it.

MRS. BROOKS: And don't let me ask him to take me somewhere. He starts telling me about his mother. What a good woman she was, and how easy us modern women have it, how she worked from sunup to sundown. Listening to him talk about that woman you'd think she was Joan of Arc, the Virgin Mary, and Aretha Franklin all rolled up into one. And don't let me get started on how he had us raise those children. Or the fact that I'm not even getting a new dress for Gail's wedding Sunday.

RUBY: Well, do what you feel you have to, child.

MRS. BROOKS: I can't take it no more. I just can't. They all act like I don't have no feelings — like I'm an invisible woman. Nobody, absolutely nobody pays any attention to me. They act like I'm part of the scenery, like an old couch or something,. [*Starts crying.*]

RUBY: Oh, Gladys. [*The* DOORBELL *rings.*] I'll bet that's Stormy Monday.

MRS. BROOKS: Oh Lord, I don't want her to catch me crying. Coming! [*Moves toward the door, wipes away her tears.*] Coming! Come on in, Stormy, how are you doing?

STORMY MONDAY: I'm doing it to death. Gladys, you got any baking powder? Well, look who's here. How are you doing this morning, Ruby?

RUBY: Fine.

STORMY MONDAY: And how is Breck, and Gillette, and Jean Nate, and Ajax, and Wildroot?

RUBY: Fine, just fine. Everybody is fine.

STORMY MONDAY: Hey, Gladys I was reading in the papers this morning about this outfit called Weight Watchers. It seems that this lady lost fifty pounds in two months. Have you ever heard of the Weight Watchers, Ruby?

RUBY: You ever heard of S.I.J.?

STORMY MONDAY: Naw, what's that?

RUBY: S.I.J. means sock in the jaw. It's good for people who have diarrhea of the mouth. You keep messing with me, and I'm gonna give you a chance to try it.

STORMY MONDAY: Un huh. I heard that the welfare people were by your apartment last night, and almost caught Wilbur. Got to admit the man's got a whole lot of heart. Hanging out of the window, fifteen stories up. I wish I'd been there, I'd of poured lye on his hands!

MRS. BROOKS: Stormy, be nice to Ruby. You shouldn't be so hard on men.

RUBY: Yea.

STORMY MONDAY: Shoot, after all you two been through with men I don't see why you want to argue with me. Neither one of you can name me one good man. Not one.

RUBY: Shoot, ain't nothing wrong with my Wilbur!

STORMY MONDAY: Listen, all you two do is sit around and complain, talking about what you're going to do. You're scared to death of men. If a man came in right now, and said boo, you'd probably fall out flat on the floor. How either one of you can even fix your mouth to say something good about a man is a mystery to me.

MRS. BROOKS: Oh, Stormy, just because you've been burnt once you act like you've got a patent on being evil.

STORMY MONDAY: Oh, Gladys, you're always saying that, when you know it's not true. The fact is, you two have been through more changes with men than I have.

MRS. BROOKS: Humph! made up my mind this morning. I'm leaving.

STORMY MONDAY: Uh, huh. Hey, Ruby, you think Gladys is really going to leave this time?

RUBY: My name is hess, I'm not in this mess. Yall know I've been against Gladys leaving all along. Gladys ought to be used to it by now.

MRS. BROOKS: Oh, Ruby! How can you say such a thing when you know what I've had to put up with all these years? You know the only reason I stayed this long is because of the children. But it's different now Gail is getting married. When that preacher says I pronounce you man and wife, I'm starting me a new life.

RUBY: I'm sorry I said that, Gladys.

STORMY MONDAY: What's there to be sorry about? Gladys ain't going anywhere. She's just talking. Gladys, I'll bet you don't even have any money. Sitting around talking about what you're going to do. Hey, Ruby, you think Gladys got any money?

RUBY: My name is Bennet, I'm not in it!

MRS. BROOKS: I do have some money. I've got twenty-seven dollars and thirty-one cents.

STORMY MONDAY: Twenty-seven dollars and thirty-one cents! Where you planning to go, Times Square?

MRS. BROOKS: Oh, Stormy. [*Starts crying.*]

STORMY MONDAY: Oh, come on, Gladys, you know I'm your friend. I'm not trying to hurt you. I'm just trying to make a point. Let me put it to you another way. After getting the money end straight, what's the next thing you'd do?

MRS. BROOKS: Oh, I don't know.

STORMY MONDAY: How about it, Ruby? Wilbur is always talking about doing it.

RUBY: Pack your bags?

STORMY MONDAY: Ruby, sometimes you amaze me, give me five on the black hand side. [*Gives* RUBY *five.*] That's what I'm talking about! If you was leaving, wouldn't you be packing your bags, instead of sitting around folding clothes? I'll bet you haven't even thought of getting your clothes together, have you, Gladys?

MRS. BROOKS: Well, I was going to take my walk first...

STORMY MONDAY: See, that's what I'm talking about, Gladys. See? Mr. Brooks has kept you in the dark so long, honey, it's hard for you to think for yourself. Truthfully, I don't think you're ready to leave Mr. Brooks.

RUBY: Stormy Monday, I guess I had you wrong all these years. You do have some sense.

STORMY MONDAY: Yea, it's a lousy idea for you to leave Mr. Brooks, Gladys. But I think you should do something. Hmmm, let me think. Say, I'm dry as a potato chip. Gladys, you got anything to drink?

MRS. BROOKS: I think there's some Scotch left. It's down here under the sink.

RUBY: Speaking of potato chips, you got anything to nibble on?

MRS. BROOKS: Potato chips in the cabinet.

STORMY MONDAY: Ruby, you'll have to take care of your own weakness. I'll have no part of it. [*Looks beneath the sink and gets a bottle.*] Yea, this ought to do it. How about you all? You want a drink? Ruby, Gladys?

RUBY: I might have a little taste. For medicinal purposes.

STORMY MONDAY: Oh! that's my girl.

MRS. BROOKS: You know Mr. Brooks doesn't like for me to drink.

STORMY MONDAY: See, Gladys. See what I'm talking about?

MRS. BROOKS: Well, O.K. But not too much.

STORMY MONDAY: There!

RUBY: Here's looking at you, and going down me.

STORMY MONDAY: [*They all drink.*] Cheers. This is good for what ails you. Helps you relax. Hmmmmm. What was I saying?

RUBY: Come on, Stormy Monday, quit stalling. Run down your commercial.

STORMY MONDAY: Right, right. Gladys, you have to change yourself.

MRS. BROOKS: Change myself?

STORMY MONDAY: You see, the thing is, why should you leave a home you've helped to build all these years with your toil and sweat? If anybody should leave, it should be you know who. But we know that'll never happen. So what we have to do is change things so that you can live in peace in this house.

MRS. BROOKS: I see. But that's not going to be easy.

STORMY MONDAY: Gladys, you've got to become more aggressive, more assertive in this house. Yeah! We've got to figure out a way to change your image.

MRS. BROOKS: Change my image?

RUBY: How are you going to change somebody's image, and if you do, what good would it do? We know Mr. Brooks treated the old Gladys bad. He's subject to treat a new one worse than that.

STORMY MONDAY: Cool it, Ruby, just cool it. Your mouth is going forty miles an hour in a fifteen mile an hour zone. Gladys can change herself. It's like Gideon said. When they took over that building: in a people's struggle for liberation you have to change everything about yourselves? The way you think, the way you look, the way you walk. Well, the way I figure it that's the kind of change that Gladys has to go through.

MRS. BROOKS: Stormy, I got an appointment at the hairdresser.

STORMY MONDAY: [*Pours* GLADYS *another drink.*] Gladys, instead of getting your hair straightened, why don't you let me fix your hair in a natural?

RUBY: Gladys, I told you not to listen to Stormy Monday. She ain't got a lick of sense. If they put her brains in a bird it would fly backwards. Everybody uptown knows that Mr. Brooks hates naturals worse than God hates sin.

STORMY MONDAY: But that's the whole point. Gladys, if you got your hair done in a natural, Mr. Brooks would have to sit up and take notice. He'd see that he was dealing with a new person. Gladys, that's it, you've got to let me do your hair in a natural. That's the only solution.

MRS. BROOKS: Oh, I don't know about all this, Stormy. Ruby is right. Mr. Brooks wouldn't like it.

RUBY: Yea, Stormy Monday, you acting like you don't know Mr. Brooks. Besides, I doubt if Gladys' hair would do like that.

MRS. BROOKS: Yeah, it's so thin maybe it's too curly.

STORMY MONDAY: Oh, you two make me sick. You don't have any spin. Letting the man push you around all the time. Well, it's none of my business, it's no skin off my nose. But from now on I don't want to hear you two sitting around complaining all the time. The trouble is, neither of you like yourselves or have any respect for yourselves, taking all this crap from men, and that's why your men don't respect you. And you know what? I don't blame them. I've lost respect for both of you myself. [*Starts to leave.*]

MRS. BROOKS: Stormy?

STORMY MONDAY: Yea.

MRS. BROOKS: Do you think it will work? Are you sure?

STORMY MONDAY: No, Gladys, I'm not sure. But I'll tell you this. We are responsible for fifty percent of what happens to us. All I'm asking you to do is to take care of your fifty percent.

MRS. BROOKS: Oh, I, don't know. Stormy, maybe you're right, but you've gotta understand I never had someone to love me before. I liked him taking care of me, telling me what to do. I liked staying home taking care of the children, while he went out working, making the money. But you know what? For years now I've wanted to help him. I've wanted to go to school and learn how to be a manicurist. I could have done it, but he wouldn't hear it. He just patted me on my head. Well, he stopped me then, but he won't stop me now. All right, Stormy, you got a deal. I'll do it!

STORMY MONDAY: Good! Oh, Gladys, I'm so proud of you. You're beginning to change already. Come on, we have to wash your hair, so let's go into the bathroom and get started. Oh, wait. [*They all drink.*] You coming, Ruby?

RUBY: Honey, I wouldn't miss this for nothing in God's whole world.

MRS. BROOKS: Let's go change Gladys' image. [*The lights dim to black as they exit. A moment later they dim back on.* STORMY MONDAY, RUBY, *and* GLADYS *enter talking.*]

STORMY MONDAY: Come on out here where we have some room, Gladys. [STORMY MONDAY *seats* GLADYS *in a chair and removes a towel from around her head, and begins combing out* GLADYS' *natural.*] Oh, Gladys, there is one other thing I thought of that you have to do.

MRS. BROOKS: What's that, Stormy?

STORMY MONDAY: It's really a dynamite idea. You know sometimes I think I border on genius. I was just thinking. Gladys, you've got to go to that barbershop. Hold your head still, Gladys.

MRS. BROOKS: I don't know about going to that barbershop, Stormy.

RUBY: Yea, getting your hair cut is one thing, but going to that barbershop is something else again.

STORMY MONDAY: Say, Gladys, where is that material I gave you?

MRS. BROOKS: Out in the hall closet.

STORMY MONDAY: Get it for me, Ruby. I want to try something later on. Go on now, Ruby.

RUBY: Well, don't do nothing while I'm gone.

STORMY MONDAY: See, Gladys, we've got to change everything. Wearing your hair in a natural takes care of your image, but you've also got to change the way you think. That's why you've got to go to that barbershop. Oh, wait, you need some earrings. You see, you ought to demand to work in there, Gladys. They need some women in there. Give the place some style, and class. I hear it's nothing but a den of iniquity anyway. What you ought to do is make up a list of demands and present them to Mr. Brooks at his barbershop.

RUBY: [*Who has entered during the last sentences.*] Do what?!

STORMY MONDAY: Make up a list of demands and give them to Mr. Brooks at his shop. Just like Gideon and them kids did up to the college.

RUBY: You're crazy, Stormy Monday.

STORMY MONDAY: What do you say, Gladys? It's like the topping on the cake.

MRS. BROOKS: I don't know, Stormy.

STORMY MONDAY: Gladys, you've come this far.

MRS. BROOKS: Well, if you say so.

STORMY MONDAY: Now let me cut just a little more off the top.

RUBY: Not too much. Gladys'll look like a man.

STORMY MONDAY: Y'all so backwards. Do I look like a man?

RUBY: Touch it up on the sides a little, Stormy Monday.

STORMY MONDAY: Who's doing this, chick? Yes, we've almost got it. Ruby, get my mirror out of my purse, please. All right, Gladys, stand up.

MRS. BROOKS: Let me see, Ruby, let me see. Is this me?

STORMY MONDAY: Just one more second, Gladys, and then you can check it out.

RUBY: You do look sort of different . . .

MRS. BROOKS: So this is the new me.

STORMY MONDAY: Not the new you, Gladys, the real you.

RUBY: . . . . sort of like — sort of African. That's-it, Gladys, that's what you look like. One of them African queens.

MRS. BROOKS: An African queen.

STORMY MONDAY: And another thing, Gladys. If you're going to be an African queen, you've got to carry yourself like one. Hold your chin up. Stop stooping your shoulders. You've got to walk proud. Beautiful. Yea! O.K. Let's go.

MRS. BROOKS: O.K., but I've got to do something else first. [*Picks up her appointment book and tears the pages from it, throwing the pieces all over the floor.*]

STORMY MONDAY: The Queen is going to pay a visit to the King.

[*Curtain.*]

ACT TWO

SCENE 1

TIME: *Early afternoon*

SCENE: *Typical Harlem barbershop. There are two barber chairs, a jukebox, and several chairs for customers to sit in while they wait. There is a dryer, and a chair and a sink in the rear where facials are performed. There is also a closet in the rear of the shop. Pictures of famous theater and sports personalities hang on the walls.* SLIM, SWEETMEAT, *and* MR. BROOKS *are on stage.* SLIM *and* MR. BROOKS *are cleaning and rearrang-*

ing their barber's tools. SWEETMEAT *is sweeping the floor. Well-known jazz classic from the early 1950's is playing.*

VOICE: Shell steaks, shell steaks, anybody inside want some shell steaks?

MR. BROOKS AND SLIM: No, thanks.

SWEETMEAT: Come tomorrow, man.

VOICE: You must be outta your damn mind.

SWEETMEAT: So how's the wedding coming, John Henry?

MR. BROOKS: I'm handling all of the important details.

SWEETMEAT: That's good. Now I know we won't have to worry about a thing. [FUN LOVING *enters.*] Hey, here's my man. My main–man. What's happening, Fun Loving?

FUN LOVING: What you want to happen, baby?

SWEETMEAT: You got it.

FUN LOVING: Oh, yeah? Well, it's green lights all the way, baby. Nothing but green lights all the way. You got time to do my face, my man?

MR. BROOKS: Sure thing, Fun Loving. Right this way. [*Leads him to the rear.*]

FUN LOVING: [*Plays a record on the jukebox — rhythm and blues music.*] This is my man. [*Hums along with the record for a few bars.*] You ready? I've got a lot of business to take care of today, and these streets are mean. Not that that worries me. I'm not giving up nothing. I wouldn't give a cripple crab a crutch if I owned a lumber yard. [*Sits in chair.*]

SWEETMEAT: Deep in the heart of the kingdom sticks, the animals had a poolroom but the baboon was slick. 'Til up jumped the monkey from Cocoa-not Grove. He said let me get me some of this money before this joint close. The baboon said: Man, you want to shoot some pool? The monkey said, I can't shoot no pool, but if you'll pull up a stump to fit your rump, I'll play you some Coon-can 'til your rear end jumps. How about it, Slim, you want to play a couple of hands of Coon-can before another customer comes in?

SLIM: I don't have time right now, but I don't see why you want to play me, Sweetmeat. You know what happened the last time we played. The score was three to three. You lost three and I won three.

SWEETMEAT: Ah, everybody gets unlucky now and then. You quit just when I was getting the feeling of the cards. Hey, John Henry, Gideon, he still up on the roof?

MR. BROOKS: Sweetmeat, I've asked you not to mention that name to me.

SLIM: Gideon sure is one out-of-sight youngster.

MR. BROOKS: I fixed his wagon this morning. He'll come around. Mark my word.

SWEETMEAT: You really laid it on him, huh?

MR. BROOKS: Put my foot down.

SLIM: He's still on that strike, ain't he?

MR. BROOKS: That mess is coming to a squeaking halt, today. Oh, sometimes... If I could just get my hands around his neck.

SWEETMEAT: Easy now, John Henry, easy now.

MR. BROOKS: You're right, Sweetmeat. I shouldn't be wasting my time on that boy. Yes, soon all the children will be gone, and Mrs. Brooks and I will be left alone to grow old gracefully together.

SLIM: I still don't know how come you were lucky enough to get a good woman like Mrs. Brooks.

MR. BROOKS: What do you mean luck? Mrs. Brooks is no accident. I created her with these very hands. You see, the trouble with you, Slim, is that you don't understand women.

SLIM: Jesus Christ, John Henry, one of these days Mrs. Brooks is gonna get sick and tired of your crap and turn you around.

MR. BROOKS: The possibility of Mrs. Brooks being able to, as you say, turn me around is about as likely as our going skiing in Purgatory.

BLACK MILITANT: [*Enters carrying a poster under his arm. The poster is about a rally that is to be held.*] Seize the time. All power to the people. I'd like to speak to the brother who's in charge here.

MR. BROOKS: You're speaking to him.

BLACK MILITANT: Do you own this place, brother?

MR. BROOKS: Lock, stock and barrel.

BLACK MILITANT: Right on. Right on. Since you are a brother, I know that you'll put up this poster in your window. See. It's for the legal defense of Brother Ali Hassan. The fascist pig power structure is daily becoming more and more sadistic. We are oppressed because we are black and we've got to unite on the basis of our color. The pigs are not jiving, they are ready to move on us all. Thank you. [*Gives* MR. BROOKS *the poster.*] All power to the people. Blood to the horse's brow, and woe to those who can't swim, Jim. [*Exits.*]

MR. BROOKS: Calling people animals. [*Throws poster in the trash.*] Filthy mouth rascal.

SLIM: Ah, what are you talking about, John Henry? Don't get hung up on the man's words, just deal with where he was coming from.

SWEETMEAT: I know where they're coming from, running around talking about "Say it loud, I'm black and I'm proud." I'll start listening to them when they change their tune. Yes, say it soft, I'm black and I'm boss.

SLIM: You two belong in a museum. You're museum Negroes. Talk about Uncle Toms, you two are Uncle Remuses. You should have given that boy a play, John Henry.

MR. BROOKS: I'm not looking for controversities, I'm looking for business.

SLIM: You're always talking about free enterprise. If you really believe in it, you would give that brother a play. And you're supposed to be a man of principles, too.

MR. BROOKS: I am! But sometimes you have to forget about principles and do what's right.

SLIM: Well I'll say one thing for you, you're consistent. You're wrong about women and politics.

SWEETMEAT: Hey, here comes Rolls Royce. [ROLLS ROYCE *enters.*] How are you doing, Rolls Royce?

ROLLS ROYCE: As the rooster crowded, those who stood before the bar shouted: Open the door! You know what a little time we have to stay. And once departed, we return no more. What number are you investing in today, Mr. John Henry Brooks?

MR. BROOKS: 333.

ROLLS ROYCE: Thank you, sir. [*Does not write any numbers down.*] Waste not your time in vain pursuit of this and that endeavor. Groove with the Grape! For 'tis better to be happy with the fruitful grape than sadden after none or bitter fruit. Mr. Sweetmeat.

SWEETMEAT: 505. And give me a three-way combination on that, please, sir.

ROLLS ROYCE: Bless you, sir. [*Addresses* SLIM *who does not play the numbers.*] Ah, make the most of the time that you have. Before you, too, into dust descend. Dust to dust and under dust to lie. Without songs. Without singers. Without wine. Without end! Yes, when I was young

I did eagerly visit philosophers and saints. And I heard great argument about this and that. But every time I came out of the same door that I went in. [*Proceeds to* FUN LOVING.] And if the wine you drink, if the lips you press, end just the way they started, 'tis a small matter. Then think. You are today what you were yesterday. Tomorrow you shall not be less. Yes, Fun Loving?

FUN LOVING: 456. And an extra five dollars on the four to lead.

ROLLS ROYCE: [*Takes a wine bottle from his hip pocket.*] We are no other than a moving row of magic shadow shapes that come and go around and around a sun-shaped lantern held in the night by the master of the show. [*He emerges from the closet, walking fast. He points a finger at each person he passes.*] Fun Loving. 456. With an extra five dollars on the four to lead, right?

FUN LOVING: Right!

ROLLS ROYCE: [*Stops in front of* SLIM.] My man! Come fill the cup, and in the fire of spring your winter garment of repentance fling. The bird of time has but a little while to flutter, and the bird is on his flight. [*Moves on to* SWEETMEAT.] Mr. Sweetmeat. 505. And give me a three-way combination, please, sir. Right?

SWEETMEAT: Right!

ROLLS ROYCE: And Mr. John Henry Brooks. 333, right?

MR. BROOKS: Right!

ROLLS ROYCE: And lately, by the open door came shining through the dusk an angel shape bearing a huge vessel on her shoulder. And she offered me a taste from it. And it was the Grape! [*Exits.*]

SWEETMEAT: I see him do it every day, but I still don't believe it. How in the world a man can remember all those numbers without writing them down is a real deep, dark mystery to me. Man!

MR. BROOKS: Why, it's simple enough. Rolls Royce has what they call a photogenic memory.

SWEETMEAT: Oh, I see . . .

MR. BROOKS: He doesn't have to write anything down. People with a memory like his can remember whole books at a time.

A CUSTOMER: Mmmmm! My, my, my. A mind like that, and he's only a numbers man. Now to me that seems like an awful waste of talent. He ought to be downtown on Wall Street somewhere.

SWEETMEAT: I don't know what's wrong with you guys today. You know as well as I do that Rolls Royce worked down on Wall Street for years. As an elevator operator. I sure hope I hit today. I can use the dust. I got to do some mean chippie chasing. And to do that, you need some heavy greens in your pockets.

SLIM: You sure talk bad for a married man.

SWEETMEAT: My wife is the one married, not me. And another thing, Slim.

MR. BROOKS: Sweetmeat, man your post!

SWEETMEAT: [*Rushes to the door, preventing the* LADY *from entering.*] Hey, lady! You can't come in here.

EVANGELIST: The Kingdom of God is not a matter of talk, but of power. [*Attempts to push her way past* SWEETMEAT.] Choose then: Am I to come to you with a rod in my hand or in a sweet and gentle spirit?

SWEETMEAT: Shoot your best shot, lady.

EVANGELIST: Oh, be proud of yourselves! For His part, though He is absent in body, He is present in spirit. And His judgment upon the sinner is already given. Yes, Jesus! Given as if He were indeed present. [*Tries to catch* SWEETMEAT *off guard.*]

SWEETMEAT: I'm sorry, lady. We loves the word just like everybody else, but you've got to work your show from the outside. I ain't let no woman in here in fifteen years, and there ain't no sense in my breaking a record like that, now is there?

SLIM: Preach, brother, preach!

MR. BROOKS: Steady there, Sweetmeat. Steady there!

EVANGELIST: The man who sins is to be consigned to Satan for the destruction of his body. So that his spirit may be saved on the day of our Lord. In the name of the Lord Jesus Jehovah; Amen!

SWEETMEAT: Sure, lady, sure. [*Gives* EVANGELIST *money and she exits.* SWEETMEAT *starts walking down the stairs.*]

MR. BROOKS: Stop right there, sir. Stop dead in your tracks. Let's have the treatment.

SWEETMEAT: Ah, John Henry. [*Gets bottle of disinfectant and starts spraying.*]

MR. BROOKS: You missed the doorknob, Sweetmeat.

SWEETMEAT: Oh, all right. There, that ought to do it.

MR. BROOKS: That's the closest call we've had in years. I do believe you're getting old there, Sweetmeat.

SWEETMEAT: John Henry Brooks! Watch your tongue. Nobody's getting old. I played it like that. It's just like my father used to say, a heap see and a few know. You don't realize the complications of a job like mine. It requires a dab of delicacy. 'Tis true, I had to keep that good woman out, but at the same time, I had to let the word of the good Lord in. You see?

MR. BROOKS: Hmmmmmph!

SLIM: Boy, them little old ladies sure tickles me. They're all over Harlem. Don't they know Blackie's already got enough religion? It's Whitey who needs to be turned on to God.

SWEETMEAT: I heard that God is a black woman.

MR. BROOKS: Oh, my God!

SWEETMEAT: And if that's true, we're all going to have to pay some mighty steep dues. Can't nobody tell me about black women, man. They're evil! Of course, you can get around them if you're smooth. You've got to have style. Am I telling him right, Fun Loving? You got to be smooth with black women, right?

SLIM: Ah, man. [*Enter* FIRST *and* SECOND JUNKIES.]

SWEETMEAT: Hey, shine, fellows?

FIRST JUNKIE: Naw baby we're here on business. [*Passes out business card.*] Yeah. That's right. Aikens and Poole Enterprises, Unlimited. We gives the best deals in town. Hey, man! [*Whispers to his partner, who has dropped into a nod.*] Yeah, bay-bee, you can do business with us.

SWEETMEAT: Say, let me see that camera. Hmmmm. Hey, John Henry, I can use this to take pictures at the wedding. Hmmmm. How much?

FIRST JUNKIE: Fifteen.

SWEETMEAT: Fifteen dollars sure seems like an awful lot of money to me...

FIRST JUNKIE: It's made by the Japanese, my–man. Some of that Eastern Soul. Check it out. My competitors downtown are selling it for five times as much. But we can sell ours cheaper because we've got a boss connection, dig?

SWEETMEAT: Yeah, I see. I'll give you ten for it.

FIRST JUNKIE: Ah, man, you bad as them white cats up on one-two-five street. [*Drops into a nod.*] O.K., baby, you got a deal. [*Nods on this line.*] Everything is everything. Everybody is everybody. [SWEETMEAT *pays him.*] Thank you, my-man. Thank you for doing business with Aikens and Poole Enterprises, Unlimited. And remember, you can always do business with us. Even if you don't have a friend at Chase Manhattan. [*They exit.* SAMPSON *gets his coat.*]

SLIM: Man, when we get control of our community, that's the first thing we should deal with.

SAMPSON: Right on.

SWEETMEAT: Man, things sure are changing. I remember the time when I coulda got a camera like this for eight dollars.

MR. BROOKS: It's true that things are going up. But actually we're all better off with prices being higher, since that means the economy has excess capital for investing.

SWEETMEAT: That makes sense. [*He is involved with his camera.*]

MR. BROOKS: Oh, I'm telling you, America is the world's richest country. And all because of free enterprise. Yes, that's what it's all about. Free enterprise. Equal competition! ...

SLIM: How are you gonna talk about equal competition when white people control everything?

MR. BROOKS: That's the black man's trouble. He doesn't understand the various concepts of Big Business. And it's so simple. Goods and services! Free enterprise!

SLIM: John Henry, how you can still talk all that nonsense is beyond me. The man talks all that free enterprise to keep you down. Brothers ain't free nowhere else, so how they get to be free in business all of a sudden?

MR. BROOKS: You'll understand these things when you get older, Slim.

SLIM: Ah, why don't you wake up, John Henry? The man makes the goods, and as long as we're hung up on material things, we'll always be in a trick. I keep telling you that things have changed. People are skipping off to the moon, and you're still talking that talk. Like I said, you're consistent. You were wrong about women, and politics, and now you're wrong about business.

SWEETMEAT: Speaking of business. Somebody better come in here soon and get a shoeshine. I need some M-O-N-E-Y.

SLIM: You give up every little bit you get.

SWEETMEAT: Don't you worry about it. You see John Henry I've studied black women. And I know if you want to get to them you need some cash.

MR. BROOKS: Hmmmmmmph!

SWEETMEAT: Now I agree with you, John Henry, on everything but the subject of women. Black women like to be entertained. They don't want to go out with you if you can't go first class. I've studied them. I know what I'm talking about. I know 'em.

MR. BROOKS: How's that, Fun Loving? [*Gives* FUN LOVING *a mirror.*]

FUN LOVING: That looks boss, my-man. Real boss.

SWEETMEAT: Let me dust your shoes off there, Fun Loving. Then you'll be cleaner than the board of health.

FUN LOVING: Why not? I'm free as the breeze, and I do what I please. Besides, everything else about me is neat and clean. And it don't take nothing but money. Here you go, baby. [*Pays* MR. BROOKS, *giving him a liberal tip from his huge bankroll.*]

MR. BROOKS: Thank you, Fun Loving, you're a gentleman and a scholar.

SLIM: Hey, Sweetmeat.

SWEETMEAT: What's that? [*Shining* FUN LOVING'*s shoes.*]

SLIM: Women understand us better than we understand them. That's why we have so much trouble with them. 'Cause guys are so busy running down their game that they don't really listen to what their chicks are saying. We should study them more.

FUN LOVING: Hmmmmmmmph!

SWEETMEAT: What's the matter there, Fun Loving?

FUN LOVING: In my alley if you're hip to yourself that makes you hip to everybody else. I don't mean to be dipping into your business. Now I've been checking out you dudes talking about women, I'm going to let you peep a little of my game. All you need to get a woman is a strong rap. Hey! What'd I say? Every woman in the streets wants a piece of me. You dig it. They call me sweet Peter Jeter, the womb beater, the baby maker, the cradle shaker. The deer slayer, the buck binder and woman finder. I'm known from the gold coast to the rocky shores of Maine. Dig? Fun Loving is my name, and love is my game. I'm the bed tucker, the cock plucker, the mother fucker. The milk shaker, the record breaker, the population maker. The gun slinger, the baby bringer, the hum dinger, the pussy ringer, the man with the terrible middle finger. I'm Fun Loving the hard hitter, the bull-shitter, the poly-nuci gitter, the beast from the east. The judge, the sludge, the wimmen's pet, the men's fret, the faggot's pin-up boy. Fun Loving the dicker, the ass kicker, the cherry picker, the city slicker, the tiddy licker. I ain't giving up nothing but bubbly gum, and hard times. And I'm fresh out of bubble gum. I'm the man who walked the water and tied a whale's tail in a knot. I taught the fish how to swim, crossed the burning sand, and shook the devil's hand. I rode around the world on a snail, carrying a sack that said airmail. I walked forty-nine miles of barbed wire and used a cobra snake for a necktie. I took a hammer and a nail and built the world. Yes! I'm hemp the demp, the woman's pimp. I'm a bad dude. Women fight for my delights. Johnny Rip-Saw, the devil's son-in-law. I gave a highway patrolman a speeding ticket, and sold a blind man a flashlight. Oh yes! I roam the world, God knows I wander. Smoking stuff is where I get my thunder. I'm the only man in the world who knows why white milk makes yellow butter... I even know where the lights go when you cut the switch off. Now I might not be the baddest man in the whole world, but I'm in the top two. And my father is getting old.

SWEETMEAT: Work your show, Fun Loving. Work your show.

FUN LOVING: What can I tell you? With women you either got it or you don't. Here you go. [*Gives* SWEETMEAT *money plus tip and plays jukebox — rhythm and blues music — romantic.*]

MRS. BROOKS: [*Enters with* RUBY *and* STORMY MONDAY. *She has a scroll in her hand.*] John Henry!

MR. BROOKS: Sweetmeat! Sweetmeat! We're being invaded. Invaded. Get the door.

SWEETMEAT: Oh, Lordy. Hey, ladies, you can't come in here. [*Slips and falls.*]

MRS. BROOKS: John Henry Brooks, Jr. This is a new day!

MR. BROOKS: What! Mrs. Brooks!

SLIM: Mrs. Brooks!

SWEETMEAT: Mrs. Brooks! [*Gets up, but falls down again.*]

MRS. BROOKS: Mrs. Brooks! And in the name of peace, self-determination, and liberation, I demand that you sign this list of demands.

MR. BROOKS: A list of demands...

FUN LOVING, SWEETMEAT, AND SLIM: A list of demands?

RUBY, STORMY MONDAY: A list of demands!

MRS. BROOKS: A list of demands. And they're not negotiable.

[*Curtain.*]

ACT THREE

SCENE 1

TIME: *The next day, early morning.*
SCENE: *The roof. Dressed in Army fatigues,* MRS. BROOKS *is up on the roof. Army eating utensils, a first aid kit, and a helmet have been added.* MRS. BROOKS, *who has a pair of binoculars, is looking out onto the street below.]*

GAIL: [*Offstage, calls.*] Mommo, momma!...

MRS. BROOKS: Hmmmmm. Gail, are you down there?

GAIL: Did you sleep well, Momma?

MRS. BROOKS: Just like a top...And how is that father of yours this morning? Is he having his French toast?

GAIL: I guess so, he was cooking when I left. He told me to tell you that you can come home, without any penalties.

MRS. BROOKS: Did he say anything about my demands? Uh...uh... uh ...

GAIL: No, he didn't even mention them.

MRS. BROOKS: Oh, that man is impossible. Now I can come back home, eh? Oh, well, that's mighty big of him. Mighty big. But I'm not going for it. Gail, you go back down there and tell your father that I'm not taking one step until he signs my demands. All of them. Do you hear me? All of them. Oh, what's the matter, Gail?

GAIL: Oh, Momma. I'm so worried. My wedding is tomorrow, and you and Daddy are still fighting. I know I'm being selfish, but I can't help it. Why did you have to choose now to stand up to Dad?

MRS. BROOKS: Baby, I'm sorry, but I didn't choose now. I didn't choose the time. It's more like the times chose me. It just happened. It was time, that's all. Time for me to stand up for my rights.

GAIL: I'm really proud of you, Momma. I know I should be happy for you because I think you're right, but I've waited so long for Marvin and I want everything to be right with you and Dad and Gideon.

MRS. BROOKS: Don't worry, everything is going to be fine, Gail, I promise you that. Now where is Stormy?

GAIL: Does Stormy Monday have very much to do with this?

MRS. BROOKS: I'm telling you that everything is under control. Your father will come to his senses. And he is going to learn a lesson. We've got right on our side, so don't worry, you'll have a lovely wedding.

GAIL: All right, if you say so, Momma.

MRS. BROOKS: Good. Now you run along and take this list to Mr. — your father. And tell him that I want him to sign every single one of the items.

GIDEON: Hey, sis.

MRS. BROOKS: Hi, son. How is it going at the barbershop?

GIDEON: It's going great, Momma. Would you believe everyone showed up on time? Everything went like clockwork. How is it going, sis?

GAIL: A family squabble in the middle of your wedding. What can I tell you?

GIDEON: Yea, well, like I'm sorry about the timing. But I'm glad to see Momma trying to get herself together.

GAIL: Oh, Gideon, what's going on, what's going to happen?

GIDEON: I guess it all depends on Dad. He's been a good winner all these years, now we'll see if he can be a good loser.

GAIL: Well, what are you two up to anyway?

GIDEON: Just a little organizing, that's all.

GAIL: Well, it looks to me like you're trying to organize a war or something. What are you all doing?

MRS. BROOKS: Don't ask so many questions, Gail. Just take that list down to your father. And tell him it's his last chance.

GAIL: Well, I'll see you all later. [*Exits.*]

GIDEON: O.K., sis, keep the faith.

MRS. BROOKS: Stormy should have been here by now!

GIDEON: See if you can get her on that set!

GIDEON: Right, Moms. Hmmmmm, HI to H5, do you read me, H5?

[*Lights fade on roof. Come up in the* BROOKS' *apartment downstairs.*]

MR. BROOKS: [*Enters with several ties in his hand.*] Oh, I'm late. I'm late. Which one of these do you think looks the best?

BOOKER T: [*Gets up from the table where he has been having a cup of coffee.*] Let me see, Dad.

MR. BROOKS: Leaving me at a time like this. She could have put out my clothes before she left. I'll tell you, son, there is a whole lot of inconsideration going on in the world today.

BOOKER T: I like this one. Say, Dad, what if Momma decides not to come back until you've signed that list of demands that you haven't even read yet?

MR. BROOKS: Son, you're dipping in my business.

BOOKER T: Dad. I'm telling you, you should be making some plans of your own, just in case Momma is not jiving.

MR. BROOKS: I'm not, as you say, jiving either. I can put my foot down too, you know. [GAIL *enters*.] Gail, what did Mrs. Brooks say?

GAIL: She wants you to sign this, she said it's your last chance.

MR. BROOKS: I wouldn't touch that piece of paper with a pair of gloves. What is wrong with that woman anyway? The very idea. [*Goes off stage*.]

GAIL: But you could at least read it, Daddy.

MR. BROOKS: Never.

GAIL: Oh, he's so pig-headed! What am I going to do?

[*Chanting, then a commotion is heard down stairs. "Take that chain off your brain, John Henry Brooks."*]

BOOKER T: Hey, what's going on? [*Goes over to the window, and looks down.*] Say, what's this? Dig this.

[*"Women want Equality" "Equal rights like you and me."*]

GAIL: What's happening? [PHONE *rings*.] Oh, it would ring at a time like this. Hello, Marvin! Am I glad you called!

BOOKER T: Hey, it's Ruby and Gideon's friends, they've got picket signs. Hey, they're trying to stop somebody from coming in the building.

GAIL: What! Oh, I'm not excited. Momma has just got pickets around the front door, that's all. I don't know. Hey, Booker, what do the picket signs say?

BOOKER T: Hey, that's Sweetmeat they're trying to keep out.

MR. BROOKS: What's all that racket out there?

GAIL: Sweetmeat! Oh, he's one of the men who works in Daddy's barbershop, Marvin.

BOOKER T: Look at them go at it.

GAIL: Look at who go? Hold on, Marvin, I'll be right back. Let me see.

MR. BROOKS: I said what's all that commotion?

BOOKER T: You missed him, he just ran up the stairs.

MR. BROOKS: What's going on?

GAIL: Hey, look at the signs they're carrying. "Male chauvinism must go. What's good for the gander is good for the goose." Wow! "Women want to be free, give them equality."

MR. BROOKS: [*From offstage.*] Why, the nerve! Just wait 'til I get my hands on that woman.

BOOKER T: [*Opens front door to* SWEETMEAT.] Come on in, Sweetmeat.

SWEETMEAT: Where's John Henry, where's John Henry? It's a matter of life and death. [*He is out of breath.*] Where's John Henry?

MR. BROOKS: Sweetmeat! I'm right here. [*Enters, dressed to go to work.*]

SWEETMEAT: John Henry, you've got to do something. They've taken over our barbershop!

MR. BROOKS: What!

GAIL AND BOOKER T: Taken over the barbershop??!! Who?

SWEETMEAT: A bunch of kids with a lot of hair on their heads. When I got to work they was sitting in them chairs just as big as life. They even had the nerve to ask me if I had a pass from Gideon to get in. John Henry, we've got to do something... We've got all of our equipment in there.

MR. BROOKS: They can't do that to me.

[*Chanting starts again from the streets.*]

SWEETMEAT: John Henry, everything is crazy. Some fat lady and her kids carrying picket signs tried to stop me from coming in here.

MR. BROOKS: Fat lady? What are you saying? Ruby? [*Goes to look out of the window.*]

SWEETMEAT: Say, John Henry, you in some kind of trouble?

MR. BROOKS: No, of course not. Get away from there! Get away from that door! [*Turns away from the window.*] You're right, son, we've got to do something. [*Closes the window, shutting out the noise.*]

BOOKER T: Right on, Dad. Right on. That's what I've been trying to tell you all along.

MR. BROOKS: Come on, Sweetmeat, let's go clear the front door first and then we'll mop up the barbershop.

BOOKER T: Wait, Dad. Use your head, that's not the way. How would it look if people in the neighborhood saw you fighting with Ruby in the streets?

MR. BROOKS: I don't have to stand for this. They're trying my patience.

BOOKER T: I know. But we've got to use our heads. The smart thing to do is try and deal with Momma. Maybe we can get her to call off the pickets, and let you open the barbershop. Then you can talk about the demands. How about it, Dad? Let's make a deal with Momma, if we still can. Let's see if we can work out something before the whole neighborhood gets involved in this thing. What do you say?

MR. BROOKS: Hmmmmm. Well, I'll think about it.

GAIL: Oh, Daddy!

MR. BROOKS: All right, I'll think hard about it.

BOOKER T: O.K. O.K. First I'll go talk to Momma and see what she's got to say. Gail, why don't you read those demands to Dad while I'm gone? That way we'll know what we're dealing with. [*Starts to leave.*]

MR. BROOKS: Hey, son. [*Walks* BOOKER T. *to the door.*] See if you can get Gideon to talk some sense into your mother's head. Before I have to come up there and drag her down here.

GAIL: Here we go, Daddy. [*Starts reading from the list of demands.*] Hmmmmmmm. I, John Henry Brooks, Jr., being of sound mind and limb, do hereby agree to all of my wrongdoings over the past twenty-some odd years. And I do solemnly swear that I will stop all such further wrongdoings. Therefore, be it known that I agree to the following: I will call my wife Gladys. I will no longer slurp my coffee. I will start putting the top back on the tooth paste. I will not pass gas in the bedroom. I will go to church at least once a month. I will give my wife a weekly allowance and money to buy a new dress. I will no longer require my wife to keep an appointment book.

MR. BROOKS: What? No appointment book?

GAIL: I will no longer require my wife to save the trays from the T.V. dinners.

SWEETMEAT: Trays from the T.V. dinners.

GAIL: I will start cutting naturals in my barbershop. I will send my wife to school so that she can learn how to be a manicurist and work in the barbershop.

MR. BROOKS: Over my dead body! Enough!

GAIL: I will no longer . . .

MR. BROOKS: Enough! I've heard enough!

GAIL: . . . No longer lose my temper, but maintain control of myself at all times.

MR. BROOKS: [Shouts.] I said that's enough. [Lowers his voice.] I absolutely, positively, resolutely refuse to so much as look at that piece of paper any longer.

GAIL: But, Daddy, I'm not even half through yet. You could at least listen to them.

MR. BROOKS: I said that's enough. And what's more, what is that phone doing off the hook?

GAIL: Oh, God! Marvin! He hung up. Oh, no. I give up. I'm going to my room.

MR. BROOKS: This is a madhouse, Sweetmeat.

SWEETMEAT: Well, it does look like you've got your elbows in the sand.

MR. BROOKS: Ah, things are not that bad. [DOORBELL rings.] Booker T. back already? Why would Booker T. ring the doorbell? Oh, come in, son. What can we do for you?

MARVIN: Is Gail all right? What's going on? Is Gail all right?

MR. BROOKS: Of course she's all right. We're having a little misunderstanding, that's all. Oh, Sweetmeat, this is Martin. Martin is marrying . . .

GAIL: Who's that at the door, Daddy? Marvin! Oh, Marvin, I'm so glad you came. I tried to call you back. You're not mad, are you?

MARVIN: No, I'm not mad. I was just worried. What's going on, anyway? Why the pickets?

[BOOKER T. starts whistling on the roof.]

GAIL: I don't know where to start. Booker T. went up on the roof to talk to Momma. Momma and Daddy have a disagreement.

[Lights fade in kitchen. Come up on roof.]

MR. BROOKS: Where is that Booker T.?

GAIL: She gave him this list of demands . . .

BOOKER T: Good morning, everybody. It sure is a pretty day, ain't it? How is everybody?

MRS. BROOKS: Unless you came to tell me that Mr. Brooks has agreed to my demands, the answer is no. Did you come to tell me that?

BOOKER T: Well, not exactly, Momma. I was just sort of hoping that you two could work out some kind of deal, you know, a compromise.

MRS. BROOKS: I don't have anything more to say unless you've brought that piece of paper signed.

[BOOKER T. *paces, exasperated.*]

BOOKER T: Hey, Gideon. Hey, man, look here. Why don't you try and talk to Momma, and get her to cut the old man a little slack.

GIDEON: Why don't you dig yourself, Sharrief? Daddy has been dead wrong for years, you know that, and yet you want me to talk to Momma. If you really knew what was happening you'd be for what's right, and not on anybody's side. Excuse me.

[MARVIN *crosses to* GAIL *and sits her at the kitchen table and begins preparing her a glass of hot milk.*]

MARVIN: Wow! I can see where your mother is coming from but I don't understand Gideon.

GAIL: And they are not coming back in this house until Daddy signs all the demands.

MARVIN: Picketing, taking over his father's shop, fighting in the streets. He knows you don't deal with the members of your family the same way you deal with your enemy. You can use those cold calculating tactics against outsiders, but with your family you should use another value system. You should practice a different kind of morality, one based on love and respect.

GAIL: I know. I agree with you, but try and tell that to somebody in this house. Daddy is so pigheaded.

MARVIN: Just relax, Gail, we'll figure something out.

BOOKER T: [*Looking at strategy map.*] Hey, Momma, there's no need for all this. I'm sure you and Dad can make a deal if you'll just call off those pickets and get Gideon's friends out of the barbershop.

GIDEON: She's already said no deals, man. [STORMY MONDAY *climbs down the ladder.*]

STORMY MONDAY: Come on, Gladys, let's get our planning session started. We're already late. All right. Gideon, will you please report what happened on phase one and two so we can get phase three started.

GIDEON: Right. Well, we took over the barbershop. That was phase one. In phase two we set up pickets around the house. Phase three is where you come in, Stormy Monday.

STORMY MONDAY: Right on. We're ready.

[*Does a karate kick.* STORMY MONDAY *and* MRS. BROOKS *climb the ladder to the upper section and* GIDEON *goes back to his planning.* SWEET-MEAT *enters the kitchen.*]

GAIL: Dad. Dad. [MR. BROOKS *enters.*] Dad, we're going outside for a walk.

MR. BROOKS: What! Deserting me at a time like this. You women always stick together.

GAIL: Aw, Daddy, you don't understand anything. You never listen. All we're trying to do is communicate with you. Listen, Dad, Momma is not a robot or a machine. She has feelings, she has needs and you've been taking her for granted all these years. All Momma wants to do is express herself.

MR. BROOKS: Express herself — Hmmmph!

BOOKER T: Momma, come on, I know the old man is rough at times, but I thought you loved him.

MRS. BROOKS: I do, I love your father. We all love him, but nobody wants to live with him, that's the trouble.

MARVIN: Mr. Brooks, this whole thing is so simple. Gideon is saying let me go so I can be a man, a real man. He doesn't want to follow in your footprints. He wants to make his own tracks.

MRS. BROOKS: Let's face it. We are not a big happy family.

MARVIN: Gideon wants to make his own decisions about life and define his own role as a black man in this screwed-up society.

MRS. BROOKS: We could be if someone could talk some sense into that selfish, self-centered man down there.

MARVIN: Mr. Brooks, Gideon is just searching, looking for new answers, that's all. And all he and your wife want you to do is love them as they really are and not in some image that you've created for them.

GIDEON: Hey, man, you'd better go back downstairs and talk to Dad.

STORMY MONDAY: Yeah, man, you can see the pickets and the takeover are just light action.

GIDEON: If Daddy don't give in, we gonna sock it to his case. [*Exits.*]

STORMY MONDAY: Right on.

BOOKER T: You know, Momma, I really thought you and Dad were a beautiful couple.

MRS. BROOKS: You've got a lot to learn about women, son. Just remember this— never make a woman do anything that will make her lose her self-respect.

BOOKER T: Momma, you're out of sight. I'm going to talk with Dad. I think I know a way to bring him around.

SWEETMEAT: Remember how you've always said that a good businessman doesn't limit his market?

MR. BROOKS: That's what I calls a truism, Sweetmeat. Of course I remember. So what?

SWEETMEAT: And since everybody is wearing naturals now, we are most definitely limiting our market by not cutting them.

MR. BROOKS: Hmmph!

SWEETMEAT: And you've said all along that we needed a manicurist in the shop. The way I figure it, letting Mrs. Brooks do it is a good idea. It'll give the place a little class. And the salary you pay her will remain in the family, if you know what I mean.

MR. BROOKS: Ohhhhhhhh. I seeeeeeee.

SWEETMEAT: Now I don't know about all them demands on that list . . .

GAIL: Come on, Marvin. Let's go upstairs . . .

[MARVIN, GAIL *and* BOOKER T. *are heard in the hallway.*]

BOOKER T: You know, we've got a dynamite woman for a mother. I just got turned on to her.

MR. BROOKS: What did your mother say, boy?

BOOKER T: [*Enters.*] Dad, you've been had.

MR. BROOKS: Had! Had! Boy, what are you talking about?

BOOKER T: Momma is stone out of sight. Got a mind like Gillette and a heart as big as a watermelon.

MR. BROOKS: Razor blades. Watermelons. What's come over you, Booker T.? Gail, you talk to him. He's crazy.

MARVIN: What's happening, man? What's going on?

BOOKER T: Why Dad's knee deep in a fight. Here, Dad. You'd better sign this while you're still ahead!

GAIL: What's come over you? What's going on?

BOOKER T: If the picketing and the take-over don't work they plan to picket the bank where you keep your account.

MR. BROOKS: Oh God! No! No! No!

GAIL: Wow.

BOOKER T: She's got her communication thing together, too. She's going to print up some leaflets, sort of like her position paper and have the kids pass them out in the community.

MR. BROOKS: Position papers!

BOOKER T: And dig this. She's setting up the machinery for a press conference. She's already contacted the *Amsterdam News*. And she's working on a contact at C.B.S.

MR. BROOKS: C.B.S.!! I'll crush her with my very hands!

BOOKER T: And in case there is any rough stuff, she's got a group of women karate experts waiting. Stormy Monday is the commanding officer.

SWEETMEAT: You'd better get you a lawyer, man.

BOOKER T: Momma's already spoken to three lawyers. And the one who was on your side told Momma that the least she could get in a settlement was everything in the apartment and all the money.

MR. BROOKS AND SWEETMEAT: All the money!

GAIL: You mean Momma's into all that?

BOOKER T: Why, she's even considering asking for a Congressional investigation.

MR. BROOKS: Children, what are we going to do?

BOOKER T: What you mean "we," baby?

MR. BROOKS: What did you say, Booker T. ?

GAIL: Come on, Marvin.

MR. BROOKS: Gail! Marvin! Come back. Ah, no matter, you're still beside me, Booker T. We'll figure something. There must be some way . . . Booker T.! What are you doing? Where are you going?

BOOKER T: I've got to go downstairs and talk to a lady.

MR. BROOKS: A lady?

BOOKER T: Yea, Dad. A lady. A sister.

MR. BROOKS: A sister? Whose sister? Sharrief, my son. Come back. Oh no! No. Oh no, no! The bad guys are winning.

SCENE 2

TIME: *The next day. The wedding, which has taken place at the church, is over.* MRS. BROOKS, RUBY *and* SLIM *[who drove them in his car, from the wedding] are the first to arrive. While* SLIM, *who is not on stage, is bringing up boxes of presents from his car which is parked downstairs,* MRS. BROOKS *starts putting glasses on the table.* RUBY *starts making punch. In the center of the table stands a large wedding cake with a black bride and groom on the top. There is another table in the kitchen where the "hard" liquor is kept.* MRS. BROOKS *and* RUBY, *dressed in their Sunday best, enter hurriedly and start working.*

MRS. BROOKS: Come on, Ruby, we've got to hurry. Everybody will be here in a little while.

RUBY: Gladys, you've got to give me time. When you've got as much as me to carry around, you've got to go slow and easy with it.

MRS. BROOKS: I'll start making the punch, and we'll start setting up the table.

RUBY: I still can't believe it, girl. How you got that man to sign that piece of paper is way beyond me. You ought to be mighty proud of yourself. Un, uh! Just think, you got Mr. Brooks to promise to straighten up after all these years.

MRS. BROOKS: I thought he was going to break down and cry when he was signing it, but afterwards he swore that he would try to live up to every single item.

RUBY: If somebody had told me last week that something like this could happen I would have called them a whole croker sackful of liars to their faces.

MRS. BROOKS: It was easy once I made up my mind to do it, girl.

RUBY: Well, I still got to hand it to you, Gladys, it took a lot of gumption to stand up to Mr. Brooks like you did.

MRS. BROOKS: Well, I had a lot of help. And I want to thank you too, Ruby.

RUBY: Ah, it was nothing, Gladys. I didn't do nothing but carry a picket sign. It was fun. Say, I wonder if something like that would work on my Wilbur?

[*The* DOORBELL *rings.*]

MRS. BROOKS: That must be Slim. Get that, will you, Ruby?

RUBY: Hold on, I'm coming. Just hold your horses. [SLIM *enters carrying wedding presents.* RUBY *follows him in.*] Where do you want him to put these, Gladys?

MRS. BROOKS: Right over there. And, Ruby, why don't you leave the door open? Everybody will start coming pretty soon. Slim, would you like to try some of my punch? Ruby, why don't you offer the gentleman some of my punch?

RUBY: Would you like to try some punch, Mr. Slim?

SLIM: Don't mind if I do. [RUBY *adds to* SLIM'*s glass of punch from a bottle.*] Thank you. Whoooo!! This sure is some mighty potent stuff.

MRS. BROOKS: Thank you. Do you know if John Henry is coming with Sweetmeat?

SLIM: I'm not sure. John Henry disappeared right after the wedding. The last time I saw him he was with Gideon. That was a surprise.

MRS. BROOKS: Yes, they made up last night, too. Both of them were so funny, just like two little boys. Both of them had tears in their eyes. Talk about two happy people. John Henry told Gideon he could be anything he wanted to be, as long as he too was the best at it.

RUBY: That sounds like Mr. Brooks, all right.

SWEETMEAT: [*Enters with camera.*] Hold that pose. [*Takes a picture of* RUBY *and* MRS. BROOKS.] Beautiful, beautiful! Howdy, Mrs. Brooks. Slim.

SLIM: You're early, but you're late.

MRS. BROOKS: Sweetmeat, have you seen John Henry? I thought he was coming with you.

SWEETMEAT: He didn't come with me, he told me to go on.

MRS. BROOKS: I wonder where he is. Oh, Sweetmeat, I want you to meet my friend, Ruby. Ruby, this is Sweetmeat.

SWEETMEAT: Pleased to meet you, ma'am.

RUBY: Your face looks awfully familiar. Haven't I seen you somewhere before?

MRS. BROOKS: You probably saw him at the	SWEETMEAT: You don't

| barbershop, Ruby. He | know me, |
| works with John Henry. | woman. |

SWEETMEAT: Say, what are you drinking, Slim?

SLIM: Punch. I told you you were early, but you're late. Pass the ice, man.

SWEETMEAT: Down home you all don't drink nothing but that white lightning. You ain't used to this good J & B. You stick with me, and I'll make you a big-time operator like me.

SLIM: You'd better be careful that you don't end up like my cousin, Elmo.

SWEETMEAT: What happened to your cousin, Elmo?

SLIM: He drove himself to death.

SWEETMEAT: Oh yeah? How did he do that?

SLIM: He drove around in his Volkswagen all last summer with the windows up so people would think that he had air-conditioning. And he suffocated.

SWEETMEAT: Ah, man! You sure are low. Setting up your man, and sounding on him like that. How are you gonna show?

GIDEON: Get ready, everybody, get ready! They're coming! [*Enters carrying rice.*] This is fun. We must have thrown a ton on them already. Here, take some rice, Momma. [*Gives rice to* MRS. BROOKS, RUBY, SLIM *and* SWEETMEAT.]

[SAMPSON *stands by the door pretending to be blowing a trumpet, as* NIA *and* STEPHANIE *file past him.*]

BOOKER T: Da de da de daaaaaaaaaa.

ALL: [*Chanting.*] Black is so bad!

MRS. BROOKS: Gail! I'm so happy for you. Congratulations, son. See, I told you everything was going to work out just fine.

MARVIN: [*Overlaps above.*] Thank you, Mrs. Brooks.

RUBY: Nice going, Gail, you sure are a pretty bride.

SWEETMEAT: That's it. [SWEETMEAT *takes a picture.*] Now let me kiss the bride.

BOOKER T: Welcome to the family, bro.

MARVIN: I'm the luckiest man in the world.

MRS. BROOKS: [*Overlaps above.*] Gideon, have you seen your father? He should have been here by now.

GIDEON: Not since we left the church. Excuse me, Momma. Everybody. I think it's time to propose a toast to our newlywed king and queen.

SAMPSON: Hey, man, Stormy Monday said she was going to make that toast.

GIDEON: Well, where is she?

ALL: Where is Stormy Monday?

STORMY MONDAY: [*Enters, posing at the entranceway.*] I'm here, I'm here, I'm right here. Now I want you all to know that I was up half the night getting this number together. Now if someone will get me that chair — Thank you. Now I need a drink. Thank you. All right. May your tribe increase. May your feet always point toward Mecca. May happiness hound you like a tax collector. And whether you love wisely or foolishly, may you always love. O.K., let's start dancing before I do something foolish like crying.

GIDEON: We'll get that, Stormy. [GIDEON *and* NIA *cross to the record player.*]

STORMY MONDAY: Gladys, we did it, we did it.

MRS. BROOKS: Thanks to you, Stormy. Stormy, have you seen John Henry?

STORMY MONDAY: No, Gladys, I haven't seen Mr. Brooks, that is not since the wedding.

MRS. BROOKS: Oh, Stormy, I want you to meet a friend of John Henry's. Slim, this is Stormy Monday. Stormy, this is Slim.

[*The music begins — rhythm and blues, for dancing fast. As the music begins the younger generation begins to dance. At that moment* FUN LOVING *enters.*]

FUN LOVING: Hey, look out, let a man come in.

[FUN LOVING *slaps five with most of the males in the room and then starts everyone dancing by twirling* GAIL *around and dancing with her. Everyone joins the dancing, including* MRS. BROOKS *under the guidance of* GIDEON *and then* RUBY *under the guidance of* FUN LOVING. *Sampson starts a line. As the line is moving the record sticks.* MRS. BROOKS *removes the needle and the younger generation begins a chant of* "WE DON'T NEED NO MUSIC" *to replace the sound of the record and the dancing continues.* MR. BROOKS *enters wearing a loud Dashikie and various emblems around his neck, including a necktie.*]

MR. BROOKS: Somebody give me five. Give me five — on the black hand side.

[*The following six speeches are spoken together.*]

SLIM: Man! Look at John Henry!

RUBY: They say that wonders will never cease.

STORMY MONDAY: Get a load of Mr. Brooks strutting around. Got enough stuff around his neck to start a five and ten cent store.

STEPHANIE: Mr. Brooks is really way out there.

BOOKER T: Hey, Dad, you are really out of sight.

GIDEON: Yea, Dad, you're really a gas.

MR. BROOKS: Don't let me stop you all from dancing. [*Turns to* GAIL.] I told you I was going to dance at your wedding. [*Picks her up and twirls her around.*]

SWEETMEAT: Hold that pose everybody.

MR. BROOKS: Hold it there, Sweetmeat. Gideon, come over here and join us. I want to hang this picture in the barbershop for good luck.

SWEETMEAT: All right, you're getting too serious. Let's get the family together for the big one. It's picture-taking time and I'm steady setting fire to every twig in sight.

[STORMY MONDAY *and* SWEETMEAT *set out directing the family and all concerned into a suitable pose for the big picture.* JOHN HENRY *is the last one in place.*]

SWEETMEAT: Good job, sister Cloudy. Fine job. Fine as the wine you drink as you dine. Hold it steady, everybody.

BOOKER T: [*Who has been talking to* STEPHANIE.] Hey, Gideon, how's that for a starter?

GIDEON: That's beautiful, man. Bea-uti-ful.

BOOKER T: Right on.

SWEETMEAT: Now everybody say cheese.

ALL: Cheese. [*The younger generation says* BLACK IS SO BAD.]

STORMY MONDAY: And don't forget your light meter.

[*Curtain.*]

Ted Shine

CONTRIBUTION

Contribution by Ted Shine
© 1973, Ted Shine

TED SHINE

Attended public schools in Dallas, and obtained his bachelor's degree from Howard University in Washington, D.C. where his writing was encouraged by Owen Dodson and Sterling Brown, and his master's degree from the State University of Iowa. Later, he received his doctorate from the University of California, Santa Barbara.

He is a frequent contributor to various magazine publications, has many professional and non-professional productions to his credit, and two PBS projects. His professional productions include *Ancestors, Baby Cakes, Hamburgers are Impersonal, Baker's Dream, The Night of Baker's End,* and *Contributions.* Other produced plays include *Come Back after the Fire, The Woman who was Tampered with in Youth, Idabel's Fortune,* and *Herbert the Third.* He wrote approximately 65 half-hour scripts for PBS-TV's *Our Street* Series, and wrote *Shoes,* produced by Barbara Shultz for PBS' *Visions.* He co-edited with James Hatch, *Black Theatre USA: Plays By African Americans From 1847 To Today.*

Currently, Shine is teaching at Prairie View A&M University in Prairie View, Texas. He has also taught at Howard University and Dillard University in New Orleans.

CHARACTERS

MRS. GRACE LOVE   A Negro woman in her seventies

EUGENE LOVE   Her grandson, a twenty-one year old college stu
dent

KATY JONES   Her neighbor, thirty–eight

SCENE: MRS. LOVE's *kitchen. Clean, neatly furnished. A door upstage center leads into the backyard. A door, right, leads into the hall. In the center of the room is an ironing board with a white shirt resting on it to be ironed.*

AT RISE: KATY *sits at the table drinking coffee. She is ill at ease.* MRS. LOVE *stands beside her mixing cornbread dough. Now and then she takes a drink of beer from the bottle resting on the table.*

MRS LOVE: [*Singing.*] Where he leads me
IIIIIII shall follow!
Where he leads me
IIIIIII shall follow!
Wwwwwwhere he leads me
IIIIIII shall follow!
IIIIIII'IIIII go with him—

EUGENE: [*Offstage.*] Grandma, please! You'll wake the dead!

MRS. LOVE: I called you half an hour ago. You dressed?

EUGENE: I can't find my pants.

MRS. LOVE: I pressed them. They're out here. [EUGENE *enters in shorts and undershirt, unaware that* KATY *is present.*]

EUGENE: I just got those trousers out of the cleaners and they didn't need pressing! I'll bet you scorched them! [*He sees* KATY *and conceals himself with his hands.*]

MRS. LOVE: You should wear a robe around the house, boy. You never know when I'm having company. [*She tosses him the pants.*]

EUGENE: I'm . . . sorry. 'Mornin', Miss Katy. [*He exits quickly.*]

KATY: Mornin', Eugene. [*To* MRS. LOVE.] He ran out of here like a skint cat. Like I ain't never seen a man in his drawers before.

MRS. LOVE: [*Pouring cornbread into pan.*] There. I'll put this bread in the oven and it'll be ready in no time. I appreciate your taking it down to the Sheriff for me. He'd bust a gut if he didn't have my cornbread for breakfast. [*Sings.*]

I sing because I'm happy —
I sing because I'm free —

KATY: I'm only doing it because I don't want to see a woman your age out on the streets today—

MRS. LOVE: [*Singing.*]

His eye is on the sparrow
And I know he watches me!

KATY: Just the same I'm glad you decided to take off. White folks have been coming into town since sun up by the truck loads. Mean white folks who're out for blood!

MRS. LOVE: They're just as scared as you, Katy Jones.

KATY: Ain't no sin to be scared. Ain't you scared for Eugene?

MRS. LOVE: Scared of what?

KATY: That lunch counter has been white for as long as I can remember— and the folks around here aim to keep it that way.

MRS. LOVE: Let 'em *aim* all they want to! The thing that tees me off is they won't let me march.

KATY: Mrs. Love, your heart couldn't take it!

MRS. LOVE: You'd be amazed at what my heart's done took all these years, baby.

EUGENE: [*Entering.*] Where's my sport shirt? The green one?

MRS. LOVE: In the drawer where it belongs. I'm ironing this white shirt for you to wear.

EUGENE: A white shirt? I'm not going to a formal dance.

MRS. LOVE: I want you neat when you sit down at that counter. Newspaper men from all over the country'll be there and if they put your picture in the papers, I want folks to say, "my, ain't that a nice looking, neat, young man."

EUGENE: You ask your boss how long he'll let me stay neat?

MRS. LOVE: I ain't asked Sheriff Morrison nothin'.

EUGENE: He let you off today so you could nurse my wounds when I get back, huh?

MRS. LOVE: You ain't gonna get no wounds, son, and you ain't gonna get this nice white shirt ruined either. What's wrong with you anyway? You tryin' to — what yawll say — "chicken out"?

EUGENE: No, I'm not going to chicken out, but I am nervous.

KATY: I'm nervous too—for myself and for all you young folks. Like the Mayor said on TV last night the whites and the colored always got on well here—

MRS. LOVE: So long as "we" stayed in our respective places.

KATY: He said if we want to eat in a drug store we ought to build our own.

EUGENE: Then why don't you build a drug store on Main Street with a lunch counter in it?

KATY: Where am I gonna get the money?

MRS. LOVE: Where is any colored person in this town gonna get the money? Even if we got it, you think they'd let us lease a building—let alone buy property on Main Street.

KATY: I know, Mrs. Love, but—

MRS. LOVE: But nothin'! If I was a woman your age I'd be joinin' them children!

KATY: I'm with yawl, Eugene, in mind—if not in body.

EUGENE: Um–huh.

KATY: But I have children to raise—and I have to think about my job.

MRS. LOVE: Why don't you think about your children's future? Them few pennies you make ain't shit! And if things stay the same it'll be the same way for those children too, but Lord knows, if they're like the rest of the young folks today—they're gonna put you down real soon!

KATY: I provide for my children by myself—and they love me for it! We have food on our table each and every day!

MRS. LOVE: Beans and greens! When's the last time you had steaks?

KATY: Well . . . at least we ain't starvin'!

EUGENE: Neither is your boss lady!

KATY: Mrs. Comfort says yawl *are*—*communists*!

MRS. LOVE: I'll be damned! How come every time a black person speaks up for himself he's got to be a communist?

KATY: That's what the white folks think!

MRS. LOVE: Well ain't that somethin'! Here I am—old black me—trying to get this democracy to working like it oughta be working, and the democratic white folks say wait. Now tell me, why the hell would I want to join another bunch of white folks that I don't know nothin' about and expect them to put me straight? [*To Eugene.*] Here's your shirt, son. Wear a tie and comb that natural! Put a part in your hair!

EUGENE: Good gracious! [*He exits.*]

KATY: "Militant"! That's what Mrs. Comfort calls us — "militants"!

MRS. LOVE: [*Removing bread from oven.*] What does that mean?

KATY: Bad! That's what it means — bad folks!

MRS. LOVE: I hope you love your children as much as you seem to love Miss Comfort.

KATY: I hate that woman!

MRS. LOVE: Why ?

KATY: I hate all white folks — don't you?

MRS. LOVE: Katy Jones, I don't hate nobody. I get disgusted with 'em, but I don't hate 'em.

KATY: Well, you're different from me.

MRS. LOVE: Ummmmmm, just look at my cornbread!

KATY: It smells good!

MRS. LOVE: [*Buttering bread and wraps it.*] Don't you dare pinch off it either!

KATY: I don't want that white man's food! I hope it chokes the hell outta that mean bastard!

MRS. LOVE: I see how come your boss lady is calling you militant, Katy.

KATY: Well, I don't like him! Patting me on the behind like I'm a dog. He's got that habit bad.

MRS. LOVE: You make haste with this bread. He likes it hot.

KATY: Yes'em. I ain't gonna be caught dead in the midst of all that ruckus.

MRS. LOVE: You hurry along now. [*Gives* KATY *the bread and* KATY *exits.* MRS. LOVE *watches her from the back door.*] And don't you dare pinch off it! You'll turn to stone! [*She laughs to herself, turns and moves to the hall door.*] You about ready, son?

EUGENE: I guess so.

MRS. LOVE: Come out here and let me look at you.

EUGENE: Since when do I have to stand inspection?

MRS. LOVE: Since *now*! [EUGENE *enters.*] You look right smart. And I want you to stay that way.

EUGENE: How? You know the Sheriff ain't gonna stop at nothing, to keep us out of that drug store.

MRS. LOVE: Stop worrying about Sheriff Morrison.

EUGENE: He's the one who's raisin' all the hell! The mayor was all set to intergrate until the Sheriff got wind of it.

MRS. LOVE: Yes, I know, but—don't worry about him. Try to relax.

EUGENE: How can I relax?

MRS. LOVE: I thought most of you young cats had nerve today.

EUGENE: And I wish you'd stop embarrassing me using all that slang!

MRS. LOVE: I'm just tryin' to talk your talk, baby.

EUGENE: There's something wrong with a woman eighty years old trying to act like a teenager!

MRS. LOVE: What was it you was telling me the other day? 'Bout that gap — how young folks and old folks can't talk together?

EUGENE: The generation gap!

MRS. LOVE: Well, I done bridged it, baby! You dig?

EUGENE: You are ludicrous!

MRS. LOVE: Well, that's one up on me, but I'll cop it sooner or later.

EUGENE: I know you'll try!

MRS. LOVE: Damned right!

EUGENE: That's another thing — all this swearing you've been doing lately —

MRS. LOVE: Picked it up from you and your friends sitting right there in my living room under the picture of Jesus!

EUGENE: I . . .

MRS. LOVE: Don't explain. Now you know how it sounds to me.

EUGENE: Why did you have to bring this up at a time like this?

MRS. LOVE: You brought it up, baby.

EUGENE: I wish you wouldn't call me baby — I'm a grown man.

MRS. LOVE: Ain't I heard you grown men callin' each other baby?

EUGENE: Well...that's different. And stop usin' 'ain't' so much. You know better.

MRS. LOVE: I wish I was educated like you, Eugene, but I *aren't*!

EUGENE: Good gracious!

MRS. LOVE: Let me fix that tie.

EUGENE: My tie is all right.

MRS. LOVE: It's crooked.

EUGENE: Just like that phoney sheriff that you'd get up at six in the mornin' to cook cornbread for.

MRS. LOVE: The sheriff means well, son, in his fashion.

EUGENE: That bastard is one dimensional — all black!

MRS. LOVE: Don't let him hear you call him black!

EUGENE: What would he do? Beat me with his billy club like he does the rest of us around here?

MRS. LOVE: You have to try to understand folks like Mr. Morrison.

EUGENE: Turn the other cheek, huh?

MRS. LOVE: That's what the Bible says.

EUGENE: [*Mockingly.*] That's what the bible says!

MRS. LOVE: I sure do wish I could go with yawl!

EUGENE: To eye–witness the slaughter?

MRS. LOVE: You young folks ain't the only militant ones, you know!

EUGENE: You work for the meanest paddy in town — and to hear you tell it, he adores the ground you walk on! Now you're a big militant!

MRS. LOVE: I try to get along with folks, son.

EUGENE: You don't have to work for trash like Sheriff Morrison! You don't have to work at all! You own this house. Daddy sends you checks which you tear up. You could get a pension if you weren't so stubborn — you don't have to work at your age! And you surely don't have to embarrass the family by working for trash!

MRS. LOVE: What am I suppose to do? Sit here and rot like an old apple? The minute a woman's hair turns gray folks want her to take to a rockin' chair and sit it out. Not this chick, baby. I'm keepin' active. I've got a long time to go and much more to do before I go to meet my maker.

EUGENE: Listen to you!

MRS. LOVE: I mean it! I want to be a part of this 'rights' thing — but no, yawl say I'm too old!

EUGENE: That's right, you are! Your generation and my generation are complete contrasts — we don't think alike at all! The grin and shuffle school is dead!

MRS. LOVE: [*Slaps him.*] That's for calling me a "Tom"!

EUGENE: I didn't call you a "TOM," But I have seen you grinning and bowing to white folks and it made me sick at the stomach!

MRS. LOVE: And it put your daddy through college so he could raise you with comfort like he raised you—Northern comfort which you wasn't satisfied with. No, you had to come down here and "free" us soul brothers from bondage as if we can't do for ourselves! Now don't try to tell me that your world was perfect up there — I've been there and I've seen! Sick to your stomach! I'm sick to my stomach whenever I pick up a paper or turn on the news and see where young folks is being washed down with hoses or being bitten by dogs — even killed! I get sick to my stomach when I realize how hungry some folks are — and how disrespectful the world's gotten! I get sick to my stomach, baby, because the world is more messed up now than it ever was! You lookin' at me like that 'cause I shock you? You shock me! You know why? Your little secure ass is down here to make history in your own way — And you are scared shitless! I had dreams when I was your age too!

EUGENE: Times were different then. I know that —

MRS. LOVE: Maybe so, but in our hearts we knowed what was right and what was wrong. We knowed what this country was suppose to be and we knowed that we was a part of it — for better or for worse — like a marriage. We prayed for a better tomorrow — and that's why that picture of Jesus got dust on it in my front room right now — 'cause the harder we prayed — the worser it got!

EUGENE: Things are better now, you always say.

MRS. LOVE: Let's hope they don't get no worse.

EUGENE: Thanks to *us*.

MRS. LOVE: If you don't take that chip off your shoulder I'm gonna blister your behind, boy! Sit down there and eat your breakfast!

EUGENE: I'm not hungry.

MRS. LOVE: Drink some juice then.

EUGENE: I don't want anything!

MRS. LOVE: Look at you — a nervous wreck at twenty–one — just because you've got to walk through a bunch of poor white trash and sit at a lunch counter in a musty old drug store!

EUGENE: I may be a little tense — it's only natural — you'd be too!

MRS. LOVE: I do my bit, baby, and it don't affect me in the least! I've seen the blazing cross and the hooded faces in my day. I've smelled black flesh burning with tar, and necks stretched like taffy.

EUGENE: Seeing those things was your contribution, I guess?

MRS. LOVE: You'd be surprised at *my* contribution!

EUGENE: *Nothing* that you did would surprise me at all! You're a hard headed old woman!

MRS. LOVE: And I'm *justified* — justified in whatever I do. [*Sits.*] Life ain't been pretty for me, son. Oh, I suppose I had some happiness like when I married your granddaddy or when I gave birth to your daddy, but as I watched him grow up I got meaner and meaner.

EUGENE: You may be evil, but not mean.

MRS. LOVE: I worked to feed and clothe him like Katy's doin' for her children, but I had a goal in mind. Katy's just doin' it to eat. I wanted something better for my son. They used to call me "nigger" one minute and swear that they loved me the next. I grinned and bore it like you said. Sometimes I even had to scratch my head and bow, but I got your daddy through college.

EUGENE: I know and I'm grateful — he's grateful. Why don't you go and live with him like he wants you to?

MRS. LOVE: 'Cause I'm stubborn and independent! And I want to see me some more colored mens around here with pride and dignity!

EUGENE: So that Sheriff Morrison can pound the hell out of it every Saturday night with his billy club?

MRS. LOVE: I've always worked for folks like that. I worked for a white doctor once, who refused to treat your grandaddy. Let him die because he hated black folks. I worked for him and his family and they grew to love me like one of the family.

EUGENE: You are the *true* Christian lady!

MRS. LOVE: I reckon I turned the other cheek some — grinned and bowed, you call it. Held them white folks' hand when they was sick. Nursed their babies—and I sat back and watched 'em all die out year by year. Old Dr. Fulton was the last to go. He had worked around death all his life and death frightened him. He asked me—black me—to sit with him during his last hours.

EUGENE: Of course you did.

MRS. LOVE: Indeed! And loved every minute of it! Remind me sometimes to tell you about it. It's getting late. I don't want you to be tardy.

EUGENE: I bet you hope they put me under the jail so that you can Tom up to your boss and say, "I tried to tell him, but you know how—"

MRS. LOVE: [Sharply.] I don't want to have to hit you again, boy!

EUGENE: I'm sorry.

MRS. LOVE: I've got my ace in the hole—and I ain't nervous about it either. You doin' all that huffin' and puffin'—the white folks' are apt to blow you down with a hard stare. Now you scoot. Us Loves is known for our promptness.

EUGENE: If I die—remember I'm dying for Negroes like Miss Katy.

MRS. LOVE: You musta got that inferior blood from your mama's side of the family. You ain't gonna die, boy. You're coming back here to me just as pretty as you left.

EUGENE: Have you and the Sheriff reached a compromise?

MRS. LOVE: Just you go on.

EUGENE: [Starts to the door. He stops.] I'll be back home, grandma.

MRS. LOVE: I know it, hon. [He turns to leave again.] Son!

EUGENE: Ma'am?

MRS. LOVE: The Bible says love and I does. I turns the other cheek and I loves 'til I can't love no more. [EUGENE nods.] Well...I reckon I ain't perfect—I ain't like Jesus was, I can only bear a cross so long. I guess I've "had it" as you young folks say. Done been spit on, insulted, but I grinned and bore my cross for a while—then there was peace—satisfaction—sweet satisfaction. [EUGENE turns to go again.] Son, you've been a comfort to me. When you get to be my age you want someone to talk to who loves you, and I loves you from the bottom of my heart.

EUGENE: [Embarrassed.] Ahhh, granny...I know...[He embraces her tightly for a moment. She kisses him.] I'm sorry I said those things. I understand how you feel and I understand why you—

MRS. LOVE: Don't try to understand me, son, 'cause you don't even understand yourself yet. Gon' out there and get yourself some dignity — be a man, then we can talk.

EUGENE: I'll be damned, old lady —

MRS. LOVE: Now git!

EUGENE: [*Exiting.*] I'll be damned! [MRS. LOVE *watches him exit. She stands in the doorway for a moment, turns and takes the dishes to the sink. She takes another beer from her refrigerator and sits at the table and composes a letter.*]

MRS. LOVE: [*Writing slowly.*] "Dear Eugene, your son has made me right proud today. You ought to have seen him leaving here to sit–in at the drug store with them other fine young colored children." Lord, letter writin' can tire a body out! I'll let the boy finish it when he gets back.

KATY: [*Offstage.*] Miss Love! Miss Love!

MRS. LOVE: [*Rising.*] Katy? [KATY *enters. She has been running and stops beside the door to catch her breath.*] What's wrong with you, child? They ain't riotin', are they? [KATY *shakes her head.*] Then what's the matter? You give the sheriff his bread? [*She nods, yes.*]

KATY: I poked my head in through the door and he says: "'What you want, gal?" I told him I brought him his breakfast. He says, "all right, bring it here." His eyes lit up when he looked at your cornbread!

MRS. LOVE: Didn't they!

KATY: He told me to go get him a quart of buttermilk from the icebox, then he started eatin' that bread and he yelled at me — "Hurry up, gal, 'fore I finish!"

MRS. LOVE: Then what happened?

KATY: I got his milk and when I got back he was half–standin' and half–sittin' at his desk holding that big stomach of his'n, and cussin' to high heaven. "Gimme that goddamned milk! Can't you see these ulcers is killin' the hell outta me?"

MRS. LOVE: He ain't got no ulcers.

KATY: He had something all right. His ol' blue eyes was just dartin' about in what looked to be little pools of blood. His face was red as a beet —

MRS. LOVE: Go on, child!

KATY: He was panting and breathin' hard! He drank all that milk in one long gulp, then he belched and told me to get my black ass outta his face. He said to tell all the Negroes that today is the be all and end all day!

MRS. LOVE: Indeed!

KATY: And he flung that plate at me! I ran across the street. The street was full of white folks with sticks and rocks and things — old white folks and young 'em — even children. *My* white folks was even there!

MRS. LOVE: What was they doin'?

KATY: Just standin' — that's all. They wasn't sayin' nothin' — just staring and watching. They'd look down the street towards the drug store, then turn and look towards the Sheriff office. Then old Sheriff Morrison come out. He was sort of bent over in the middle. He belched and his stomach growled! I could hear it clear across the street.

MRS. LOVE: Oh, I've seen it before, child! I've seen it! First Dr. Fulton a medical man who didn't know his liver from his kidney. He sat and watched his entire family die out — one by one — then let hisself die because he was dumb! Called me to his deathbed and asked me to hold his hand. "I ain't got nobody else to turn to now, Auntie." I asted him, "You related to me in some way?" He laughed and the pain hit him like an axe. "Sing me a spiritual," he told me. I told him I didn't know no spiritual. "Sing something holy for me, I'm dyin'!" he says. [*She sings.*]

I'll be glad when you're dead, you rascal, you!
I'll be glad when you're dead, you rascal you —

Then I told him how come he was dyin'.

KATY: He was a doctor, didn't he know?

MRS. LOVE: Shoot! Dr. Fulton, how come you didn't treat my husband? How come you let him die out there in the alley like an animal? When I got through openin' his nose with what was happenin', he raised up — red like the sheriff with his hands outstretched toward me and he fell right square off that bed onto the floor — dead. I spit on his body! Went down stairs, cooked me a steak, got my belongings and left.

KATY: You didn't call the undertaker?

MRS. LOVE: I left that bastard for the maggots. I wasn't his "auntie"! The neighbors found him a week later stinking to hell. Oh, they came by to question me, but I was grieved, chile, and they left me alone. "You know how nigras is scared of death," they said. And now the sheriff.

Oh, I have great peace of mind, chile, cause I'm like my grandson in my own fashion. I'm too old to be hit and wet up, they say, but I votes and does my bit.

KATY: I reckon I'll get on. You think you oughta stay here by yourself?

MRS. LOVE: I'll be all right. You run along now. Go tend to your children before they get away from you.

KATY: Ma'am?

MRS. LOVE: Them kids got eyes, Katy, and they know what's happenin' and they ain't gonna be likin' their mama's attitude that much longer. You're a young woman, Katy, there ain't no sense in your continuing to be a fool for the rest of your life.

KATY: I don't know what you're talkin' about, Mrs. Love!

MRS. LOVE: You'll find out one day—I just hope it ain't too late. I thank you for that favor.

KATY: Yes 'em. [She exits.]

EUGENE: [Entering. He is dressed the same, but seems eager and excited now.] Grandma! They served us and didn't a soul do a thing! We've intergrated!

MRS. LOVE: Tell me about it.

EUGENE: When I got there every white person in the county was on that street! They had clubs and iron pipes. There were dogs and firetrucks with hoses. When we reached the drugstore, Old man Thomas was standing in the doorway. "What yawl want?" he asked. "Service," someone said. That's when the crowd started yelling and making nasty remarks. None of us moved an inch. Then the Sheriff came down the street from his office. He walked slowly like he was sick—

MRS. LOVE: Didn't he cuss none?

EUGENE: He swore up and down! He walked up to me and said, "Boy, what you and them other niggers want here?" "Freedom, baby!" I told him. "Freedom my ass," he said. "Yawl get on back where you belong and stop actin' up before I sic the dogs on you." "We're not leaving until we've been served!" I told him. He looked at me in complete amazement—

MRS. LOVE: Then he belched and started to foam at the mouth.

EUGENE: He was mad, grandma! He said he'd die before a nigger sat where a white woman's ass had been. "God is my witness!" he shouted. "May I die before I see this place intergrated!" Then he took out his whistle—

MRS. LOVE: Put it to his lips and before he could get up the breath to blow, he fell on the ground—

EUGENE: He rolled himself into a tight ball, holding his stomach. Cussing, and moaning and thrashing around—

MRS. LOVE: And the foaming at the mouth got worse! He puked—a bloody puke, and his eyes looked like they'd popped right out of their sockets. He opened his mouth and gasped for breath.

EUGENE: In the excitement some of the kids went inside the drugstore and the girl at the counter says, "Yawl can have anything you want— just don't put a curse on me!" While black faces were filling that counter, someone outside yelled—

MRS. LOVE: "Sheriff Morrison is *dead*!"

EUGENE: How do you know so much? You weren't there.

MRS. LOVE: No, son, I wasn't there, but I've seen it before. I've seen—

EUGENE: What?

MRS. LOVE: Death in the raw. Dr. Crawford's entire family went that away.

EUGENE: Grandma . . .?

MRS. LOVE: Some of them had it easier and quicker than the rest—dependin'.

EUGENE: "Dependin" on what?

MRS. LOVE: How they had loved and treated their neighbor—namely *me*. [*Unconsciously she fumbles with the bag dangling from around her neck, which she removes from her bosom.*]

EUGENE: What's in that bag you're fumbling with?

MRS. LOVE: Spice.

EUGENE: You're lying to me. What is it?

MRS. LOVE: The spice of life, baby.

EUGENE: Did you . . . Did you do something to Sheriff Morrison?

MRS. LOVE: [*Singing.*]

In the sweet bye and bye
we shalllllll meet . . .

EUGENE: What did you do to Sheriff Morrison!??!

MRS. LOVE: I helped yawl intergrate — in my own fashion.

EUGENE: What did you do to that man?

MRS. LOVE: I gave him peace! Sent him to meet his maker! And I sent him in grand style too. Tore his very guts out with my special seasoning! Degrading me! Callin' me "nigger"! Beating my men folks!

EUGENE: [*Sinks into chair.*] Why?

MRS. LOVE: Because I'm a tired old black woman who's been tired, and who ain't got no place and never had no place in this country. You talk about a "new Negro" — Hell, I was a new Negro seventy–six years ago. Don't you think I wanted to sip me a coke–cola in a store when I went out shopping? Don't you think I wanted to have a decent job that would have given me some respect and enough money to feed my family and clothe them decently? I resented being called "Girl" and "Auntie" by folks who weren't even as good as me. I worked for nigger haters — made 'em love me, and I put my boy through school — and then I sent them to eternity with flying colors. I got no regrets, boy, just peace of mind and satisfaction. And I don't need no psychi-atrist — I done vented my pent–up emotions! Ain't that what you're always saying?

EUGENE: You can be sent to the electric chair!

MRS. LOVE: Who? Aunt Grace Love? Good old black auntie? Shoot! I know white folks, son, and I've been at this business for a long time now, and they know I know my place.

EUGENE: Oh, grandma . . .

MRS. LOVE: Cheer up! I done what I did for all yawl, but if you don't ap-preciate it, ask some of the colored boys who ain't been to college and who's felt ol' man Morrison's stick against their heads — they'd ap-preciate it. Liberation! Just like the underground railroad — Harriett Tubman — that's me, only difference is I ain't goin' down in history. Now you take off them clothes before you get them wrinkled.

EUGENE: Where're you going?

MRS. LOVE: To shed a tear for the deceased and get me a train ticket.

EUGENE: You're going home to daddy?

MRS. LOVE: Your daddy don't need me no more, son. He's got your mama. No, I ain't going to your daddy.

EUGENE: Then where're you going?

MRS. LOVE: Ain't you said them college students is sittin' in in Mississippi and they ain't makin' much headway 'cause of the governor? [EUGENE *nods.*] Well . . . I think I'll take me a little trip to Mississippi and see what's happenin'. You wouldn't by chance know the governor's name, would you?

EUGENE: What?

MRS. LOVE: I have a feeling he just might be needing a good cook.

EUGENE: Grandma!

MRS. LOVE: Get out of those clothes now. [*She starts for the door.*] And while I'm downtown I think I'll have me a cold ice cream soda at Mr. Thomas'! Ain't much left, Lord . . . I wonder who'll be next? I'll put me an ad in the paper. Who knows, it may be you . . . or you . . . or you . . . [*Sings as she exits.*]

Where he leads me
I shallllll follow . . . .
Where he leads me
I shallllll follow . . . .

[EUGENE *sits stunned as the old woman's voice fades.*]

[*Curtain.*]

Don Evans

ONE MONKEY DON'T STOP NO SHOW

DON EVANS (Donald T.)

Was born in Philadelphia just before the Second World War. He attended Philadelphia's public schools and graduated not long after the Korean War. Because he was busy with The United States Marine Corps, he missed the early days of the Civil Rights Movement, but did manage to march while attending Cheyney State University and Temple University's School of Drama. Somewhere between Martin Luther King, Jr. and Malcolm X he managed to meet playwrights Ron Milner and Alice Childress, both of whom helped convince him that it was better to write plays than to write about them. His first plays were produced during the Vietnam Crisis and he continued to write through Grenada, The Middle East Crisis and still has a pen in hand as the troops move to Bosnia.

Among the plays to come from the playwright are *It's Showdown Time, Blues for a Gospel Queen, The Trials and Tribulations of Staggerlee Brown, Miss Lydia, Sugarmouth Sam Don't Dance No More, Orrin*, and a few others that have faded from memory but are still good plays. The playwright has lectured and read his works extensively in universities in this country and abroad but continues to say "axe" when he means "ask." He is the Chair of African-American Studies at Trenton State College and boasts of two grandsons, a Martin and a Malcolm. His new play entitled *When Miss Mollie Hit the Triple Bars* received a staged reading during "GENESIS '96: A Celebration of New Voices in African American Theatre" at Crossroads Theatre Company.

FROM THE WORDS OF THE PLAYWRIGHT

Writing about the plays is more difficult than writing them. They come from a lot of different places. Like, *One Monkey* . . . has something to do with watching a production of Shaw's *Man and Superman* and wondering what it would be like if Tanner talked like my soulmate Kenny. The kid with the glasses is somehow a mixture of myself and my oldest son when he was all edges and wishes. And then, of course, there's the fact of coming home from work every day and meeting interesting folk in the process. They get mixed up in the pot, too. I mean, I live in a world of words . . . poetry by people who don't know they're poets and humorists who think they're sages (and sometimes are). Don't lay those memorable moves down near me because I'll steal them. I dust them off, shape them up and call it a play.

And when you ask me about funny writing, I have to admit that I don't know. I don't remember jokes so I never tell them. People do funny things and I remember them. Hell, I do funny things and, try as hard as I might, they stay around until I polish them up and put them on the stage. The strange part of it all is that they weren't meant to be funny when I did them . . . or you did them or whoever provided the germ for the laugh you experienced when the play finally got to the stage. The problem is to find the TRUTH of the moment and just lay it out there. The laughs will follow. I mean, hey, life is funny sometimes. Mostly it's funny when you recognize that today has no choice but to become tomorrow and all the heavy stuff that you can't deal with now you still won't be able to deal with then and, if you can make sense out of all this, you'll know exactly why folks say my stuff is funny . . . sometimes.

CHARACTERS

MYRA HARRISON	A well kept woman in her late forties.
FELIX HARRISON	Myra's "all American colored-boy" son of nineteen. He is "preppy" and hates it.
AVERY HARRISON	Myra's husband, a former athlete but currently a preacher.
CALEB JOHNSON	a streetwise man of thirty with a penchant for telling the truth.
BEVERLY HARRISON	An attractive young woman of twenty who lets baggy jeans cover her razor sharp com mon sense.
L'IL BITS	Felix's streetwise girlfriend.
MRS. CALDWELL	L'il Bits' hardworking mother.
MOZELLE	A fine looking beautician who could pass for anything.

ACT ONE

SCENE ONE

TIME: *The Present.*

PLACE: *The almost gaudy apartment of* THE REVEREND AND MRS. AVERY HARRISON *in the suburbs of Philadelphia. The furniture is white and gold, probably French provincial and definitely not quite paid for. There is a gold and white fireplace that sports an imitation fire even in the summer time. Against the upstage wall is a large painting of an Italian Villa, the kind that "go with the furniture". Ashtrays are held by little cherubic figures, discreetly garbed in swirls of cloth. A bookshelf with matching, but unread sets of bound volumes rests against the left wall. Upstage right is an imposing desk, properly choreographed to appear busy, but not cluttered. A sofa stands behind an ornate coffee table, on which a shiny tea set rests. Two chairs (one with a hassock) balance the room. In short, these "colored folks act like they're living."*

AT RISE: MYRA *and the* REVEREND DOCTOR HARRISON, *both in "funeral garb", are in the living room. The* REVEREND *is at his desk, laboriously pondering the monthly bills.* MYRA *is seated downstage pondering the latest issue of "The Lamba Nu Newsletter" while* FELIX, *their son, peers through the window. He is anxious. He, too, wears a dark suit, but without a jacket or tie. In the background quiet music can be heard. It is the kind of lush sound generally associated with dentists' offices — noncommittal, unobtrusive and totally uninteresting.* MYRA *looks up from her magazine.*

MYRA: Junior . . . come away from that window. Have my drapes all wrinkled.

FELIX: Just wanna see when Caleb gets here.

MYRA: [*Going back to her magazine.*] Humph! If he don't never come it'll be too soon for me.

AVERY: [*Looking up from his bills.*] Myra, what in the name o' sense is this here "Les Femmes du Jardin"? [*He pronounces it as he sees it and that ain't hardly French.*] Three hundred dollars?

MYRA: My garden club. That's the plant fee. Also covers our trips. Junior, I done told you to get away from that window.

FELIX: I think he's comin' right now.

AVERY: Weeds in the ground cost three hundred dollars?

MYRA: [*Haughtily.*] We ain't just stickin' plants in the ground, Avery . . . we're studyin' horriculture.

FELIX: "Horticulture", Mom. I think he's comin' . . . [*Offstage sound of a dog barking, a very small dog . . . like a toy poodle.*]

MYRA: [*Closing her book, rising.*] Junior, take Frou-Frou for a walk around the block.

FELIX: But Caleb's comin' up the walk. Do I have to?

AVERY: [*Putting the bills in the drawer.*] Beverly oughta be back here by now.

FELIX: People laugh at me when I walk her.

MYRA: I don't know why . . . much as I paid for that dog. [*More barking, followed by a chiming of the doorbell. From offstage we hear* CALEB'*s voice. "Get the hell outta here! Git." Junior rushes to the door.*]

CALEB: [*In the doorway.*] You'd better call this damn dog.

MYRA: Don't you hurt Frou-Frou, Caleb Johnson. Junior, do what I said.

FELIX: Hi, Cal. Beverly went to the store. [*Enter* CALEB, *an impeccably dressed man in his early thirties.*]

MYRA: Junior.

FELIX: I'm goin', Ma. Soon's I get the leash. [AVERY *crosses to* CALEB.]

AVERY: Good to see you, Mister Johnson... even under these trying circumstances.

CALEB: Yeah... well, where the hell is she?

MYRA: You mean my niece, Beverly, I presume.

CALEB: No, I mean that teenaged millstone.

AVERY: Well, now... if you feel that way... I mean, you don't have to take her unless...

MYRA: [*Interrupting.*] Avery.

CALEB: Oh, yes, I do. Big Ed took care of that. I don't raise his daughter, I lose my share of the club. Sucker ain't did nothin' legal in his whole damned life. Kick the bucket an' tie me with a pimple pusher.

[FELIX *re-enters carrying a dog leash.*]

FELIX: Beverly ain't no "pimple pusher". She's...

MYRA: Junior, just walk the dog.

CALEB: [*To* FELIX.] You let people see you with that thing?

MYRA: That "thing" cost me five hundred dollars. It's got a protogee.

FELIX: Pedigree, Mom.

MYRA: I done tol' you about correctin' me.

[FELIX *exits as the dog begins barking again.*]

CALEB: [*Laughing.*] Whyn't y'all get a real dog?

AVERY: Mr. Johnson, I hope you will respect the sadness in this family. My brother an' I, we lived different lives... an' I can't honestly say that I agree with his decision to leave my niece in your care .. but that was his wish...

MYRA: [*Muttering.*] The man was cemented, if you ask me.

AVERY: Demented, Myra.

MYRA: That's what I said... demented.

CALEB: Look, forget the speeches . . . just gimme the broad.

AVERY: Now, there's certain things that hafta be understood. I mean, your lifestyle ain't exactly what . . .

CALEB: I said... where's the broad? Hell, I don't like you no better than you like me so can the speeches an' let's get on with the business.

MYRA: Avery, that brother of yours musta been crazy . . . musta been stone outta his mind.

CALEB: He was a bookie ... that's what he was. All the time playin' the long shots. [*To* AVERY.] You oughta be ashamed. Up there tellin' all them lies ... "He loved his Jesus." Only reason that cat went to church was to find out the hymn number so he could drop a dollar on it an' get hisself some coins. You oughta be ashamed. I kept thinkin' Big Ed was gon' jump outta that box an' start kickin' ass.

AVERY: Have some respect for the dead, Mr. Johnson.

CALEB: Damn the dead! I'm the one in pain!

MYRA: [*Changing the subject.*] Wasn't he put away nicely? Looked just like he was sleeping, didn't he?

CALEB: I don't know. I never slept with him. Did you?

AVERY: Now, wait just a minute.

MYRA: Don't tell him nothin'. I'm tryin' to be polite. Don't get my blood pressure up, Mister. You're in my house.

CALEB: An' I'm probably the only "street niggah" you let in here, too.

MYRA: If you mean them lowlifes over on the avenue, you're right. Not only ain't they been here, they ain't gon' get here.

AVERY: Now, calm down, Myra. Don't let him get you upset.

MYRA: I'm calm. Been calm.

CALEB: Yeah, I'm wise ... but you'd be real cool if Big Ed had left the club to you now, wouldn't you?

MYRA: What would we look like runnin' a nightclub?

AVERY: [*Muttering.*] Like we could pay for this furniture, maybe.

MYRA: We have a position in society, Mister Caleb Johnson ... an' I don't mean just black society. [FELIX *enters. He is followed by* BEVERLY, *a young woman about twenty years old and wearing overalls, her hair in braids.*]

FELIX: [*To* MYRA.] I put the dog in the cellar. [*To* CALEB] This is Beverly ... my cousin.

BEVERLY: [*Brightly*.] Hi. [*A moment in which the two principals look each other over.* CALEB *is shocked. He had expected a younger girl. If not younger, at least, neater.*]

CALEB: [*Abruptly.*] How old are you?

MYRA: An' good afternoon to you, too. [*Muttering.*] Ain't got no manners.

BEVERLY: I'm Beverly.

CALEB: [*To* AVERY.] You're lyin'.

AVERY: I beg your pardon.

CALEB: That broad's old enough to look out for herself. [*Points to the sky.*] Dead or alive, sucker, you ain't hangin' nothin' like this on me.

BEVERLY: [*Innocently.*] Is somethin' wrong?

CALEB: Damn right there's somethin' wrong! I come up here to pick up a little girl. [*Points to* BEVERLY.] This ain't no girl... [*Turns to her.*] Honey, I don't mean no harm, but you're on your own... [*Looks around.*] Who took my coat?

AVERY: Now, wait a minute. You just can't . . .

CALEB: [*Commanding.*] Who took my coat? [FELIX *goes quickly to get the coat.* AVERY *moves to* CALEB *and attempts to reason with him, but quietly.*]

AVERY: Now, you know I'd let her stay here with me . . . [*Looks at her.*] Send her to charm school or somethin'... but you'd hafta work out somethin' as far as her expenses go . . . don't pay all this no mind. [*Gestures to the room.*] I'm a poor preacher livin' all the good will of.. . [CALEB *sends him a withering glance that warns him to try another tack.*]

BEVERLY: What's the matter? You don't even know me, Uncle Caleb an' yet . . .

CALEB: Look here, girl... get up off that "uncle" jive.

BEVERLY: But my daddy said you was a good man . . . an' Aunt Rose said so too. If I'da knowed you was gon' act like this . . . I'da stayed down home. I only come up here 'cause Daddy's dyin' wish was that I should not be dependin' on nobody . . . an' since you was his friend an' he did leave you part o' the club ... [*Starting to whine a bit.*] You at least oughta act like you're glad I come . . .

MYRA: Poor thing.

CALEB: Oh, stop that snivelin'. How the hell do you expect me to act? Cat tell me my share in the club is dependent on me settin' his child straight . . . He don't say his "child" is a woman . . . a dumb country broad that don't . . .

BEVERLY: [*Through the feigned tears.*] I ain't dumb.

MYRA: [*Moving to her with an arm of comfort.*] We'd keep you here, Love . . . but you wouldn't be happy . . . the social responsibilities would be a bore . . . [BEVERLY *lays her head on* MYRA'S *shoulder, but* MYRA *cautions her and places a handkerchief on her shoulder.*] Just a minute, baby . . . I just got this dress outta the cleaners . . .

CALEB: [*Reluctantly.*] I'm sorry . . . about callin' ya dumb, I mean. I'd like to do this thing... 'cause, well... you look like a ... nice girl ... but, I just ain't set up to be takin' care o' no full grown woman. Ask your uncle over there ... hell, I stay up all night, sleep all day ... drink liquor an' chase women ... right now I'm shacked up with a six-foot lady wrestler ...

FELIX: For real?

CALEB: [*Waving* FELIX *quiet.*] You oughta stay on up here with your aunt an' uncle ... where they can introduce you to the right kinda people ...

MYRA: Now just one minute. We've got Felix an'...

BEVERLY: I wanna see my club that daddy left me half of right now an' two thirds of in one year ...

CALEB: That's all you want? Shoot, you can come down the club anytime you want ...

AVERY: When can we get the business straight?

CALEB: Man, be cool. I tryin' to get my partner to agree.

BEVERLY: [*Pulling herself together.*] I ain't stayin' here.

CALEB: What?

BEVERLY: My daddy wrote me that he had a little apartment over top the club ... that he ain't even stay there hisself 'cause he was fixin' it up for me. That's where I wanna stay ... be walkin' on floors that belong to me. Last thing Aunt Rose said to me on this earth ... I say it like that cause she done come to me in dreams a couple times... last thing she said was "Beverly, don't never be beholdin' to nobody ... not if you can help it." Now, that's what she said.

CALEB: [*Sarcastically.*] Dead folks talk to you, right?

BEVERLY: Aunt Rose do ... an' she told me this was gon' be a troublesome venture ... that I was gon' meet a tall, dark stranger with no backbone who was gon' turn his back on a promise ...

FELIX: Dig it . . . dude can't keep a promise to the dead, he ain't nothin'...

AVERY: Junior, keep outta grown folks conversations.

BEVERLY: But she said it would be all right in the end 'cause the gentleman was kind an' good...

MYRA: Well, my record's clean. We've offered our house ...

BEVERLY: An' I appreciate it, too . . . but I don't wanna be nobody's burden . . .

CALEB: Nobody but mine.

BEVERLY: . . . so I'm gon stay out the weekend an' then go on back to Wall Hollow . . .

CALEB: As your legal guardian, I think that's the best thing for you to do . . .

BEVERLY: [*With a smile that just barely hides the guile.*] . . . an' then I wanna come back an' claim my two thirds of the Shake–Shake Club . . .

CALEB: Oh, no you're not.

BEVERLY: [*Innocently.*] I can go to the Wall Hollow Junior College o' business an' learn all about runnin' it . . . then I can be your partner for true . . . 'cept two thirds of it belong to me . . .

CALEB: [*Recognizing that this is not a simple country girl.*] Heyyyy, now, you just cool it over there. That club belongs to me!

BEVERLY: Fifty-fifty until I get to be twenty-one . . . then two-thirds, one third. [*Turns to* AVERY.] I guess I'd better take up business administration, don't you think?

CALEB: [*Warning her.*] Don't bully me, girl . . . an' throw that partners-jive outta your mouth 'cause I still run that place . . . an' right now what I say goes . . .

BEVERLY: [*Playing it, but not meaning it.*] Yessir.

CALEB: An' don't be sirrin' me either . . .

BEVERLY: Well, what must I say?

CALEB: Say "Yeah" and "un-hunh" . . . talk like ya got some trainin' . . . get your coat.

BEVERLY: My coat? But . . .

FELIX: He's gon take you with him.

MYRA: Junior, hush. [*He nods to* AVERY.] Say it, now.

AVERY: [*Ministerially.*] Well, I just want you to remember . . . that . . . uh . . . that child is my blood an' . . . well . . . she's also a young woman . . .

MYRA: An' we don't want her hangin' out with none of them low-lifes . . . them musicians an' preverts . . .

FELIX: "Perverts," Mom . . .

MYRA: Boy, if you don't stop correctin' me.

AVERY: If it wasn't that we had Junior here to educate . . .

MYRA: We can still introduce her to some nice young men. Reverend Thompson's boy ain't too dark an' he's got right nice hair . . . but you keep your eye on that girl, Caleb Johnson. You hear me . . . 'cause I know if she on Avery's side of the family, she's mighty hot natured . . .

AVERY: My side?

MYRA: It's that West Indian blood.

FELIX: Me, too, Ma?

AVERY: Quiet, Felix.

MYRA: Breed like rabbits.

CALEB: [*Resigned to his fate.*] Don't look to me like she gotta be worried.

BEVERLY: Humph . . . you wait 'til I get my good clothes on . . . my *orlon* dress with the white platforms . . .

CALEB: Get your coat on.

MYRA: You can't go anywhere just yet.

CALEB: [*To* BEVERLY.] You hear me? Get your things.

BEVERLY: But I fixed dinner . . . special 'cause you was comin'.

FELIX: Smells good, too.

CALEB: [*Pointing to* BEVERLY.] First law of good business . . . be on time. An' I gotta open the club. [BEVERLY *pouts.* MYRA *takes charge.*]

MYRA: It is considered polite . . . for folks to stay when they're offered dinner . . . especially when it's French.

CALEB: [*Looking at her directly.*] What's that mean?

BEVERLY: Aunt Myra loaned me her cookbook. Its called Beef-Barkin' On . . .

CALEB: [*Starting for the door.*] Sorry.

MYRA: [*Nastily.*] You'd stay if it was red beans an' rice. [CALEB *stops dead in his tracks.*]

CALEB: What's that supposed to mean?

MYRA: It means that you ain't got the culture to give her the culture that she needs to be cultured . . . a little French food ain't gon' do nothin' but tickle your palace . . .

AVERY: Palette, Myra.

CALEB: An' give me gas . . . Bloods all up an' down the avenue bustin' folks in the head to get hot-dog money an' y'all up here greasin' on things I can't even say.

AVERY: Don't be lookin down your nose at us, Mr. Johnson. Everything we have is provided by the Almighty . . .

CALEB: The Almighty dollar . . . at the expense of some poorass domestic worker . . . some broad tryin' to buy a piece o' heaven by feedin' you Beef Barkin' on.

MYRA: [*Haughtily.*] White folks ain't the only ones got a right to ĕat good. We'll eat our beef. You see can you buy some o' them starvin' brothers a hotdog. [*To* FELIX.] Set the table, Junior.

BEVERLY: I just wanted somethin' extra fancy so we could get off on the right foot. Aunt Rose always said . . .

CALEB: [*Tired of Aunt Rose.*] HEAT IT, I'LL EAT IT!!! An' after that, Miss Lady, you get your stuff together so we can get outta here. [FE-LIX *exits quickly.* BEVERLY *follows.*]

FELIX: [*As he exits.*] I'll set the table.

BEVERLY: Aunt Myra, you gotta help me. I ain't used to all this fancy cookin' . . . [*They all exit except* CALEB *and* AVERY.]

CALEB: Bourguignonne.

AVERY: What?

CALEB: Bourguignonne . . . it's Beuf a la Bourguignonne. [AVERY *looks at him in disbelief a moment and then exits, repeating the words over and over so as not to forget them.* CALEB *lights a cigarette and sits on the arm of a chair.*] Every now an' then ya gotta bust a balloon, y'understand what I mean? These preacher-teacher intellectuals get up so high they forget . . . start actin' like they're the only ones that know what's happenin . . . Many leftovers from white folks parties as I ate, I know about some fancy cookin' . . . like, I can tell you about how them folks live . . . The thing that gets you is folks like Miss Myra an' Avery . . . tryin' to put me down 'cause I work with the "funky folk" . . . like, I run a bar an' he's a preacher so he got all the answers an' I'm just a dummy. You oughta dig the cat's church . . . two flights up over a grocery store . . . Yeah, that's right . . . . two flights over top of a grocery store . . . cat hangs a clergy sign on the fire plug on Sunday so he'll have space to park his long black Cadillac with the whitewall tires . . . . Can't too much blame him though. I mean, the brethern and sisteran must dig it, they payin' for it. But I'm s'posed to be the hustler . . . me an' his dead brother . . . Wouldn't be half so bad if the broad wasn't so country . . . but, like I can see it . . . leave a chick like that with these bourgie niggahs an' they have her feelin' worse than dog do-do . . . tryin' to change her up for one o' them phony-time fraternity boys . . . sons of the preacher-teachers . . . Now, don't get me wrong . . . I ain't got nothin' against professional Negroes . . . folks oughta get as much as they can . . . . but don't be lookin' down on me 'cause I ain't got it . . . [*Puffs his cigarette.*] . . . Yeah, I gonna take the broad back with me . . . if I don't I might lose my club an' I ain't hardly playin' no games with that . . . So, I wanna straighten her out . . . dress her up an' teach her how to count . . . like, I've always wanted to make me a woman . . . start from scratch an' just make any kind o' woman I want . . . [*Sympathetically.*] an' this child is so ready . . . an' so much in need . . . .

[*End of Scene One.*]

SCENE TWO

BEVERLY *enters wearing an apron over her jeans — another point of incongruity —*

BEVERLY: [*Shyly.*] You ain't mad, is ya?

CALEB: About what?

BEVERLY: Well, I did kinda hogtie you into dinner . . .

CALEB: Forget it . . . anyway, I'm hungry.

BEVERLY: They serve food down the club? . . . 'Cause if they don't, I'd gladly cook up . . .

CALEB: [*Interrupting.*] Barbecue ribs an' chicken . . .

BEVERLY: I'm a real good cook.

CALEB: Don't make no difference. I eat out.

BEVERLY: [*Sitting.*] Why're you so evil?

CALEB: What?

BEVERLY: You talk like you mad all the time. That 'cause you ain't with your wife?

CALEB: What wife? I ain't got no wife. An' don't be pryin' into my affairs either.

BEVERLY: Wasn't her name Mildred? Daddy wrote me all about her.

CALEB: The divorce papers are framed on my wall. I don't mention her name and don't you mention her name. That broad almost ruint me.

BEVERLY: Ain't no reason to be bitter. Whole lotta folks mess up on marriage. My folks saw the trouble so they didn't even bother to take the step. I never even knew my momma . . . 'cept what Aunt Rose tell me about her . . . that she was a tap dancer.

CALEB: She was a stripper.

BEVERLY: I know. Aunt Rose fibbed every now an' then if she thought it would do you some good. You see her anymore? Mildred, I mean.

CALEB: Yeah, every time I miss one o' them checks she have me down there at 1801 Vine Street. I see her . . . but with a judge standin' between us . . . Change the subject, baby 'cause I ain't into no marriage . . . Don't need no hammerhead all the time complainin' . . . beggin' an complainin' . . . Every time I go see my kids, she act like she doin' me a favor . . . But I ain't bitter. Un-unh, I'd go to that chick's funeral any day in the week. [*Looks at* BEVERLY.] Where's my food? I ain't got all night. I got things to do. [*The phone rings.* BEVERLY *starts to answer it, but is cut off by* FELIX, *who bolts into the room and answers the phone.*]

FELIX: Hello?

BEVERLY: [*Shrugs.*] Reckon, I'll get things on the table.

FELIX: [*Into the receiver.*] This is him . . . I mean he . . . [*Excited.*] Oh, yeah. [*Looks around as if to ask that everyone leave.* BEVERLY *exits.* CALEB *sits in the chair and begins reading a copy of* Ebony *that is on display.*] I can't get it upstairs . . . mom's up there. What'd you call for anyway? I said I'd . . . you' lyin' . . . you ain't seen nothin'? No signs? [*Looks around to make sure no one is listening.*] Well, look, I can't talk about it right now . . . how late are you? Two weeks, damn . . . Now don't panic . . . I mean . . . these things happen . . . but . . . Well, look . . . I'll see if I can get the car an' . . . no, no, don't do that. I'll come over there . . . oh, come on . . . you know better better'n that. I told you . . . they're just . . . not too worldly . . . Okay . . . right . . . don't call me, I'll call you. [*He hangs up. Sits dejectedly.*] Hooooly Cow! What am I gonna do now?

CALEB: Sweat it out. That's about all you can do . . . [*Turns to him.*] Treat the broad real nice . . . *extra* nice . . . an' pray for the flood.

FELIX: I don't know what you're talkin about. I was talkin' to Butch.

CALEB: Then you really do have a problem . . .

FELIX: [*Deciding to play it straight. Disgusted.*] She didn't come on.

CALEB: I'm wise.

FELIX: An' it was only the first time, too. [FELIX *sits dejectedly.*]

CALEB: Pay it no mind. It happens to the best of us. Probably a false alarm.

FELIX: Damn you, Alex Comfort!

CALEB: Who?

FELIX: That's what started it all. [*He looks around to make sure they are alone and then goes to the closet and rummages around for a book.*] I bought her a copy of this . . . I mean, I don't really know too much about women . . . I thought it would heat her up.

CALEB: [*Taking the book.*] Damn, boy. They lock you up in Wichita for lookin' at stuff like this . . . give ya pimples.

FELIX: [*Reaching for the book, but* CALEB *maintains his grip.*] You never looked at dirty pictures, I guess.

CALEB: Still do . . . but these cats ain't for real . . . No sweat . . . eyes open an' all that. They'd have to catch the blood on record . . . draw 'em with they' mouth wide open, screamin' . . . These cats is jivin' . . .

FELIX: You don't think . . . it's "freakish"? Readin' books, I mean?

CALEB: Hell no! . . . I learned how to type readin' a book . . . Got better at it when I bought me a typewriter though. Dig where I'm comin' from?

FELIX: [*Elated that he isn't a freak.*] Gosh, Cal . . . I knew you were cool. I thought somethin' was wrong with me 'cause I really dig that book, y'know.

CALEB: I ain't say wasn't nothin' wrong with you. I said wasn't nothin' wrong with readin' the book.

FELIX: Hunh?

CALEB: You need a woman.

FELIX: [*Sadly.*] You sure got that right. I even voted yes on the co-ed question back at school. It's rough, Cal . . . I mean, it's murder . . . no women . . . nothin' but nuns . . .

CALEB: [*Sympathizing.*] An' you don't get none from a nun . . .

FELIX: [*Excited, like the cat's out there.*] Yeah . . . but sometimes, I get these wild thoughts . . .

CALEB: About the nuns?

FELIX: [*On his feet animatedly.*] Y'see, I'm not really the cat you see here.

CALEB: [*Amused.*] No?

FELIX: Heck no. I mean, the glasses an' the books. This corny cat here . . . it ain't me.

CALEB: Well, just who the hell are you. Like, I could swear . . .

FELIX: Aww, man . . . inside . . . I'm a tiger . . . A roarin' tiger just waitin' to break loose from all this bourgeois-good-little-boy jive . . .

CALEB: Yeah, break loose an' get you a woman, right?

FELIX: [*Strutting, jitterbug style.*] Damn right . . . I mean, no. . . hell, no . . . Not just one woman. I want a whole flock of 'em . . . Lay 'em all out on the floor . . . buck neckid . . . paint their bellies with Crisco an' just sliiiiiide from one end to the other . . . [*Mah man is flying now.*] Awwwww, Man, you just don't know!

CALEB: [*Handing him the book.*] I know you'd better get rid o' that book for they hafta lock you up somewhere.

FELIX: [*Beseeching.*] How do I get cool, Cal? Hell, I'm nineteen years old an' a virgin minus one. What kind o' black man is that?

CALEB: One that don't know how to lie. That's somebody's myth about black men jumpin' in an' outta bed from the time they ol' enough to pee straight. Whole lotta liars runnin' the streets today, man.

FELIX: But I wanna break out.

CALEB: You better make sure that broad come *on* before you break *out*. Forget them lyin' cats . . . when a dude can't brag about nothin else, he get to lyin' about his lovin' . . . [MYRA, *now wearing a low-cut, flowing lounging robe enters and poses long enough for* CALEB *to see it.*]

MYRA: I just came to get you for dinner. [FELIX *remembers the book and quickly puts it behind him.*] If you'd like to use the laboratory it's right out there. [FELIX *shifts the book and tries to make a quick exit to the powder room.*] Junior . . . ain't you got no manners? Let the guest go first.

FELIX: Ma'am?

MYRA: [*Her irritation showing.*] Let the man go first boy. Can't ya hear? [*To Caleb.*] Young people just ain't raised like we were.

CALEB: No ma'am . . . like I started to step on that roach over there by the door, but I was raised better'n to mess other people's bugs . . . [MYRA, *shocked and frightened, turns quickly toward the door.* CALEB *snatches the book from* FELIX *and jams it under the seat of the chair.*]

MYRA: [*Outraged.*] What roach? I know ain't no roach in the world bold enough set up camp in Miss Mattie Lou's house . . . [*She gives it a good look-see and then turns to* CALEB.] Which way did it go? . . . You musta brought it with you.

CALEB: [*Innocently.*] Maybe I was mistaken. You look so nice I was probably just dazzled an' started seein' things.

FELIX: A mirage, Momma. It was a mirage.

MYRA: [*Smiling at the compliment.*] You better get outta here with your ol' timey talk . . . a roach? Not in my house. Humph . . . any bugs walk around in this house . . . in this neighborhood . . . well, they won't be no colored folks bugs, you can bet a fat man on that . . . Now, come on let's eat . . . [FELIX *and* CALEB *start out.*] Had me scared to death.

CALEB: Is your name really Mattie Lou . . . ?

MYRA: [*Quickly.*] No! [*Her attention falls on the chair. She starts over to it.*] Junior, I done told you about comin' in my livin' room an' messin' up. Got the pillows all bottomside uppers . . . [*She is at the chair and tries to straighten the pillow.* FELIX *is already on his way over to divert her attention.*] Can't have nothin' around here . . .

FELIX: Mom . . . can't you leave that . . . ?

MYRA: [*She has it in her hand.*] OHHH. [*Reads.*] The Joys of . . . [*The word won't come. She stands frozen.*] Take it outta my hand .. . [FELIX, *too, is frozen.* CALEB *comes to the rescue.*] TAKE IT OUTTA MY HAND!!! [CALEB *quickly takes the book as* MYRA *falls into the chair.*]

CALEB: Ain't nothin' but a book. Give it here.

MYRA: Lord, I wish I was white so I could faint . . . [CALEB *throws the book on the end table.*] Don't leave it there. You brought that nasty thing in here.

CALEB: Me?

MYRA: Nobody but a lowlife Negro like you would bring something as un-decent as that in a Christian home. [*To* FELIX.] Call your daddy, Junior . . . we gon' run this black-slaver outta town. At least, outta this neighborhood.

CALEB: When do we eat, woman? I got places to go.

MYRA: Guardian? You better start lookin' for a job mister 'cause my niece ain't goin' nowhere with you an' you ain't gon' run my brother-in-laws nothin' . . .

FELIX: Mom . . .

MYRA: Junior, get your daddy like I said. You done heard too much already . . . [*Having heard the noise,* AVERY *enters, followed by* BEVERLY.]

AVERY: What, in the name o' sense, is goin' on here?

MYRA: [*Rising. Boldly.*] Your brother . . . may he rest in peace . . . left your niece . . . poor thing . . . in the custody of a PREVERT . . .

CALEB: WHO'S a pervert? I ain't bring that thing in here.

AVERY: What thing? [MYRA *rushes to the book and thrusts it at her husband.*]

MYRA: Just look at that. [AVERY *takes the book and leafs through it.* FELIX *shifts nervously.*]

AVERY: [*Appreciatively.*] Ummumh . . . good gracious alive

MYRA: [*Sharply.*] What?

AVERY: I mean . . . [*Indignantly.*] Ummmmmmmmmm-umh . . . good gracious. [*Interested.*] Whose book is it?

MYRA: Why're you askin? You know whose it is. Wouldn't nobody but a . . .

CALEB: [*Interrupting.*] You said that before. [*Look at his watch.*] I'm losin' my appetite.

AVERY: [*With full ministerial dignity.*] You . . . brought this . . . into my house?

CALEB: Naw, Baby, but y'all look like you can use it.

FELIX: [*Gathering his strength.*] Well . . . y'see, Pop . . . Actually . . .

BEVERLY: [*Interrupting.*] I bought it in. It's mine. [*Takes the book from* AVERY.] It's a text. We used it in our Abnormal Behavior class.

FELIX: [*Relieved.*] It's hers.

MYRA: You mean to tell me they let you read this . . . this . . . garbage in school?

BEVERLY: [*Lightly.*] Of course . . . it's a best seller. All the right people are reading it.

MYRA: Who?

CALEB: Right, Miss Myra. She said "right" people.

FELIX: We even read down at St. Bonaventures . . .

CALEB: Coupla nuns drew the pictures.

AVERY: No kiddin'?

MYRA: [*Impressed.*] Best seller. Hummmm. I ma hafta write to my Book of the Month about this. They s'posed to keep me up to date . . . [*To* AVERY.] Colored folks got to be up on what's happenin' . . . preacher or no preacher.

AVERY: I didn't say . . .

MYRA: Come on. Let's get this dinner on an' off the table.

CALEB: [*Checking the time once again.*] Sorry . . . y'all done blew it. I gotta get 'cross town. [*To* BEVERLY.] Got your things? [*He starts for the suitcases she left by the door.* MYRA *"insinuates" herself in front of him.*]

MYRA: We don't make no stew like this everyday. I helped an' that much work requires a guest.

FELIX: You'll like it . . . I guess.

CALEB: Lookahere, I'm a businessman. When you say dinner in ten minutes I expect it in nine. [CALEB *takes* BEVERLY's *bags and starts for the door. Not knowing what else to do,* BEVERLY *follows.*]

MYRA: [*Nastily.*] That's just why we ain't no further than we are. Ain't got no respect. [AVERY *moves to the table and sneakily fingers the book.*]

FELIX: [*Calling to* BEVERLY.] Be cool, Beverly . . . an' thanks for you know what . . . [BEVERLY *and* CALEB *are about to exit, but when they open the door they find someone already standing there.*]

CALEB: What the . . . who're you?

WOMAN'S VOICE: Do Felix Harrison live here? [*Hearing the voice,* FELIX *bolts into the kitchen, leaving a frightened yelp behind him.*]

AVERY: Boy, what's the matter with you?

MYRA: [*Not noticing* FELIX.] That somebody at the door?

CALEB: Some broad want Felix. [AVERY *crosses to the door.*]

AVERY: A girl? For Junior? [*At the door.*] Well, come right on in. [*He ushers in a young girl in her late teens. The girl is strikingly big busted and plump-rumped. We can see this in spite of the jacket she pulls tightly around her.*]

CALEB: [*Digging the girl's walk.*] An he wants to break out? Damn!

AVERY: [*Looking around for* FELIX.] Who shall I say is calling?

WOMAN: Just tell 'im Li'l Bits is here.

AVERY: Who?

CALEB: Li'l Bits. Tell 'im Li'l Bits is here. [AVERY *nods his understanding and crosses to the kitchen door.*]

MYRA: [*Eyeing her and not approving.*] What you wanna see my son for?

AVERY: [*Calling.*] Junior . . . Miss Bits is out here to see you.

CALEB: [*To* BEVERLY.] I got to watch this.

BEVERLY: What?

CALEB: This.

AVERY: Junior? I say Miss . . .

BEVERLY: [*Crossing to* LI'L BITS, *laughing.*] What's your name? I mean, your real name?

LI'L BITS: [*Laughing.*] Ain't that somethin? Folks been callin' me that for so long I almost forget I got a name. It's Josephine. Josephine Nefertiti Caldwell. You work here?

BEVERLY: Humh?

LI'L BITS: Felix ain't got no sister . . . an' if he had one he wouldn't have her walkin' 'round in no overalls like that . . . that's a high class nig-gah . . . nossir.

CALEB: Dig that. The broad done peeped your card.

AVERY: I can't seem to find him anywhere, but I know he's around. [*Extends his hand.*] I'm Reverend Harrison . . . an' this is my wife . . . Mrs. Harrison.

MYRA: [*Affectedly.*] Beverly . . . our niece.

AVERY: An' that is her guardian . . . I mean . . . I think that's what he is . . .

LI'L BITS: Guardian? You been in jail or somethin'?

CALEB: Naw, baby, I'm the one got the life sentence.

LI'L BITS: [*Recognizing* CALEB.] I know you . . . you run that place on the corner where they play all that ol' timey music.

CALEB: I changed my mind. I think I am gonna leave.

LI'L BITS: I ain't mean no harm, but I can't dance off that stuff . . . my momma like it though. [*To* AVERY.] You say Felix ain't here? An' I come all the way over here on the bus, too. Ol' bus driver come pat-tin' me on my behind . . . I betcha he don't pat no more.

CALEB: [*Enjoying the whole thing.*] Why don't you stay for dinner? [*Turns to* BEVERLY.] Ask her to dinner, baby. Where's your manners?

MYRA: This is *my* house, Mister Man!

CALEB: [*Ceremoniously.*] But the Man Upstairs pays the rent.

MYRA: [*Reluctance, covered by phony hospitality.*] If you don't mind French food you're welcome. [FELIX *can be heard trying to sneak out the door.*]

AVERY: Junior? Where you goin'? You've got company.

MYRA: [*Muttering.*] An' I may see you about it later on. [FELIX *pauses, looks sheepishly into the room.*]

FELIX: Company?

AVERY: Miss Bits is here.

BEVERLY: Caldwell, Uncle Avery.

AVERY: Oh.

FELIX: Hi.

LI'L BITS: I told you I was comin' over. [*She starts to take off her coat.* AVERY *rushes to help her.*] You oughta be like your ol' man Felix . . . helpin' people off with their coats. [*Once the coat is off, we see that she's wearing a pair of ass-hugging pants over which is a maternity blouse. Everyone is dumbfounded, except* CALEB *who bursts into laughter.*]

FELIX: BUT YOU SAID . . . oh, no . . .

CALEB: Get him, tiger.

MYRA: Jesus, keep the record.

AVERY: [*Handing her the coat again.*] Here. Put it back on.

BEVERLY: [*Crossing to* FELIX *who is about to pass out.*] You all right, Junior?

FELIX: It ain't mine.

LI'L BITS: What ain't?

MYRA: Let me tell you somethin' right now, Miss Fast, ain't no need in you comin' over here like that thinkin' you gon' rope my boy into nothin' . . . he's gon' be a dentist an' you can just change your mind an' hit the street!

CALEB: That's called the morality of the bourgeoisie, Miss Caldwell. Instead of givin' you some praise for bringin' a new warrior into the world, they worryin' about what folks gon' say . . .

AVERY: Now, you keep outta this, Mr. Johnson, this is a family matter . . . Praise the Lord.

LI'L BITS: I don't know what y'all talkin' about. [*Gestures to her shirt.*] You mean this here? . . . Humph, I just wore this 'cause my gray sweater with the scoop neck is in the cleaners. What you say about French food?

FELIX: I lost my appetite.

BEVERLY: Dinnah . . . is served.

AVERY: Amen. [*They begin to file into the other room.*]

LI'L BITS: [*To* AVERY *as they exit.*] I ain't never had no French food except french fries . . .

[*The lights dim out.*]

SCENE THREE

TIME: *An hour later.*
PLACE: *The same.*
AT RISE: BEVERLY *eases through the door and we hear the sound of loud talking coming from the dining room. The word "fool" can be heard every now and again. It is often followed by similar compliments. Beverly laughs, shakes her head and reaches into the pocket of her apron and takes out a napkin. Opening the napkin, we see that she has a leg of chicken, fried nice and crisp. She settles herself, starts eating and then looks up at the audience.*

BEVERLY: That French food is fine for the French . . . but I had to get me some chicken . . . somethin' I know about . . . Wonder if they had chickens in Africa? . . . [*Laughs.*] Lord, these northern men are somethin' else . . . Politics . . . religion . . . the revolution . . . Back home they do more eatin' then talkin' . . up here it's more talkin' then eatin' . . . [*Munches the chicken.*] Ain't he fine? . . . Daddy tol' me I was gon' like him . . . if I ever got him to shut up long enough . . . Anyway, I like older men . . . Ain't none o' the young ones got no job . . . Women under twenty-five got it hard . . . but I knew what I wanted 'long time ago . . . My daddy used to write to me about the club . . . an' about him, too . . . In fact, he wrote mostly about him. Seems like I knew him when I had never met him, so when I got outta high school an' Daddy asked me what I wanted, I said Caleb Johnson . . . [*Laughs.*] I did . . . I was a bold little hussy . . . [*Looks at the audience, maybe moves to them.*] Sure wish I had enough chicken to give y'all some, but I know y'all gon' get some later on anyway. I fry mine in Crisco. Don't use nothin' but Crisco . . . [*Bites the chicken.*] Daddy kept me down there in the south . . . thinkin' he was gon' keep me innocent. Well, I am . . . but I ain't dumb . . . an' I know what I want. [*Sits musing.*] I just wish I was a little more . . . sophisticated . . . a little more high class. That's what these northern men like . . . [*Leans close.*] But you can bet your granmammy's drawers I ma work at that. Yes, I am.

AVERY: [*Enters, muttering.*] Neanderthal dummy! Whole history of black folks in America starin' him in the face an' too dumb to read the words. I thank my saviour for not makin' me stupid. [CALEB *enters. They square off with their eyes.*]

AVERY: [*A pronouncement.*] If a Republican president had a Republican congress . . .

CALEB: [*Interrupting.*] He'd be king! Man, don't you understand the Republican party ain't never done nothin' but make poor people destitute? Ain't nothin' happenin' but welfare when them cats take charge . . .

AVERY: [*Taking the cigar back.*] Democrat.

CALEB: Hey, man . . . don't hang that on me. I ain't rich enough to be damn Democrat . . . an' I ain't dumb enough to be no Republican. [MYRA *enters with* L'IL BITS. FELIX *lurks behind them.*]

MYRA: [*Affectedly.*] Yes, I belong to a sorority . . . but I'm much more active in my bridge club. You do play bridge, don't you?

LI'L BITS: That's a card game, ain't it? . . . Now, I don't play that but I can get into some tonk an' bid whist . . . sometimes I shoot craps with the cats down the alley, but they fight too much. Cat lose his bread an' wanna go upside your head.

CALEB: [*Belches. Speaks to* BEVERLY.] An' I don't dig that French stew neither.

AVERY: Come to a man's house an' run down his politics . . . complain about the food. Jus ain't got no manners.

CALEB: Don't need no manners when I payin' for my own food.

BEVERLY: [*Putting the napkin in her pocket.*] I thought it was pretty good myself.

MYRA: [*Inspecting* LI'L BITS *once again.*] You know, you'd look real nice with a permanent . . .

LI'L BITS: Not me. Never will I let them chemicals be eatin up my scalp.

AVERY: [*With a forced calm.*] Jealousy is not new to me . . . forward looking black folks have always had to suffer the wrath of the do-nothings who frequent bars like the one you run . . . frequent bars an' drink their money away . . .

CALEB: Cats ain't poor 'cause they drink. They drink because they're poor, dig it? They're poor an' cats like you ain't helpin' 'em. Get your coat, Beverly, let's go.

MYRA: [*Casts her a disdainful look and continues.*] An' take good care of our niece, too, y'hear?

AVERY: I'll pray for you, child.

CALEB: [*Putting on his jacket.*] You do that, brother. You keep right on prayin'.

MYRA: [*To* CALEB.] You could've said "thank you." Most people say "thank you" when they've been treated with hostility.

CALEB: Yeah, well I thank you all right . . . thank you for helpin' me understand Big Ed. [*To* LI'L BITS.] You need a ride over the bucket, baby?

LI'L BITS: Felix will take me home.

BEVERLY: Uncle Cal, let's go.

MYRA: [*Wanting* LI'L BITS *out as quickly as possible.*] Uh . . . since they're goin' your way, Miss Uh . . . Caldwell . . . why don't you catch a ride? That way Junior won't have to drive the Cadillac down there . . .

FELIX: Awww, Mom . . . I can take the car.

MYRA: [*He ought to get the message.*] It *is* a pretty rough neighborhood, isn't it?

LI'L BITS: Oh, he don't hafta worry as long as he's with me.

CALEB: [*With mock graciousness.*] An' on that, I takes me leave. [CALEB *exits with* BEVERLY *trailing behind saying quick goodbyes. Once they are out of sight,* AVERY *and* MYRA *show their relief.*]

MYRA: Thank god . . . I need me a "sensitive" . . . that man got me all upset.

LI'L BITS: [*Looking at* MYRA.] A what?

FELIX: [*Quickly.*] Sedative. She said "sedative."

LI'L BITS: Oh, I think he's cute.

AVERY: [*Rises, stretches and then folds newspaper.*] Oh, he's a familiar type. Don't know how to deal with quality folks. One of the crosses we must bear. [*He starts out, pauses.*] Make a good sermon . . . crabs in the barrel, brother . . . I say, crabs in the barrel don't ever make it to the promised lands . . . [MYRA, *who is now preparing the leave, emptying ashtrays, etc.*] How's that sound?

MYRA: Some Negroes sure need it. I swear to God, they do. [MYRA *and* AVERY *exit.*]

AVERY: I'll work on that . . . "crabs in the barrel . . . " [FELIX *checks to see that they are well our of earshot. Satisfied that they cannot hear him, he rushes to* LI'L BITS.]

FELIX: [*Anxiously.*] Well, did ya? I mean . . .

LI'L BITS: [*Coldly.*] Ain't no need in you askin' me nothin'. I seen the way you looked when you saw that dress. I just wore it to see how you'd act.

FELIX: Did ya come on or didn't ya?

LI'L BITS: That's for me to know an' for you to find out.

FELIX: You come all the way out here to play games?

LI'L BITS: S'pose I didn't? What would you do?

FELIX: [*Knowing he's trapped.*] Uhhhhh . . . I would . . . uh . . . I'd do the right thing.

LI'L BITS: [*Suspiciously eyeing him.*] Ol' liar!

FELIX: Honest to God I would.

LI'L BITS: [*Rising, walking around the room. Inspecting.*] Yeah, well, you better start makin' plans.

FELIX: [*Frantic.*] You mean ain't nothin' happened?

LI'L BITS: [*Affectedly.*] My "visiter" has not yet arrived.

FELIX: Can't you make it come on? Take a hot bath or somethin'?

LI'L BITS: You think you're too good for me, don't ya? Just cause you go to college an' live up here with all these white people. You ain't say that when we was in the back seat o' that Volkswagon. You ain't say that then.

FELIX: An' I ain't sayin' it now, either. Just because I don't wanna get married . . .

LI'L BITS: [*Confronting him.*] See there' I knew you was lyin'. [*Mimicking him.*] "I'd do the right thing" . . . ol' liar.

FELIX: [*Coming out of hiding.*] Hey, girl . . . Don't nobody be havin' no babies on accident! They got the pill, the coil, the IUD, the damn foam an' a whole lotta kinds o' jellies.

LI'L BITS: [*Meeting him in full.*] Yeah, an' they also got them rubber things, too! [*The comment was unexpected.* FELIX *pauses, momentarily puzzled.*]

FELIX: Rubbers? Un-unn, baby. Them things are unnatural. I don't put nothin' unnatural on me.

LI'L BITS: [*Getting the full picture.*] I see . . . well, I'll tell you what you do . . . you sweat out these next few weeks. You sweat 'em out 'cause I ain't hardly into no baby-bumpin'. I leave that to you "high class coloreds." [*She takes her coat, throws it over her shoulder and exits, leaving* FELIX *momentarily stunned. Regaining his composure, he rushes to the door and calls.*]

FELIX: How're you gonna get home?

LI'L BITS: [*Offstage.*] Walk! [AVERY *enters with his bible, notebook, etc. He crosses to the desk and prepares to write his sermon.*]

AVERY: What was that all about?

FELIX: She's gonna walk.

AVERY: Good. Saved yourself some gas.

FELIX: [*Crossing to his father.*] You don't like her do you Pop? I know Mom doesn't.

AVERY: Now, I wouldn't exactly say that.

FELIX: She ain't high class enough for you.

AVERY: [*Remembering his calling.*] Son . . . in the eyes of The Maker we're all the same . . . high class an' low class. All his people. I will say this much, she ain't exactly what we had in mind.

FELIX: [*Moving from him, disgusted.*] I knew it! She's right.

AVERY: [*Irritated at being interrupted again, he patiently closes his book.*] Now, what did I say that she's right about?

FELIX: You an' Mom . . . an' me. [*The thought amazes him.*] Yeah . . . me, too! I'm one o' them hincty negroes upon the hill. Me. An' I always thought I was a liberal. [*The young man has just announced his entry into a period of crisis. He exits quickly, leaving* AVERY *to figure out the meaning of the past few moments.*]

AVERY: [*Calling after him.*] Junior!!!! [*Pauses. Mutters to himself.*] Boy talk more foolishness. [*He picks up his "sermon" and begins to move about, silently rehearsing and then making corrections. He winds up near the closet where* The Joys Of Sex *finally ended up. He pauses, tries the sermon again, but can't get himself to sustain the interest. He begins to whistle nonchalantly and looks out into the hallway. Satisfied that no one is about, he then pulls the blinds and stealthily takes out the book, turns on some quiet music and settles himself into a chair for a comfortable moment alone with his fan-*

tasies. He reads with considerable interest, nodding and wrinkling his brow, crossing his legs until, finally, he eases the book down from in front of his face and looks out at the audience. Caught with his hands in the cookie jar.] I'm human . . . an' anyway . . . there's some first class art work in this . . . [*Starts to show it to the audience. Changes his mind.*] Take my word for it. "A preacher must be *of* the world . . . but not *in* it." That's what they told us at the seminary. I'm just reading this so I can get a little more of it. [*He pauses as the words come back to him.*] What I mean to say is . . . no, that's exactly what I mean. It's hard when you're a preacher . . . [*Afterthought.*] In fact, it's that way most of the time . . . when you're a preacher. Colored people like their preachers to look like they can . . . but they run you outta town if ya do. Don't think you're holy 'less you're castrated. But I'm a man . . . an' a hot natured one, too. Like Myra said, it's that West Indian blood. But the hottest thing I get right now is a Saturday night bath. I mean, since I got "the call" I've got to call an' call an' call . . . an' still she don't answer . . . except every now an' then. Y'see, it wouldn't be so bad, but I grew up in a close knit family. Three rooms an' bath; Mom, Pop an' four kids. Beaverboard walls. I useta think the folks were really saved, don'tcha know. Sometimes I'd wake up in the middle of the night an' I'd hear Pop yellin, "Jesus, Jesus, Jesus . . . Lord have mercy." We all thought he was prayin'. Time I was half grown I knew he wasn't. Kinda took on the habit myself . . . 'til Myra tol' me it wasn't decent to be callin' on the Lord. Now, I just bite my lips an' grunt. Know what I mean? [*Picks up the book.*] But I'm fifty now. Lookin' at this book I realize I've been missin' a whole lot. They done improved it since I was in the swim. Well, I'm gon' break out . . . an' I'm takin' Myra right along with me. Shoot, I might not be as young as I used to be, but I can sure 'nough deliver anything I can promise. An' you just better-black believe it. [MYRA *enters wearing an apron over her dinner frock. She carries a "butler" and busies herself with emptying ashtrays and generally putting the room back into "showcase shape."*]

MYRA: Who're you talkin' to? [*She looks up and sees* AVERY *as he tries to put the book behind him.*] Oh. Best seller or no, it's still filthy. That's why young folks don't know nothin' but fornicatin' in the wilderness now . . . [*Raised eyebrows.*] An' I don't know why you keep lookin' at it.

AVERY: [*Bringing the book out again and deciding to tell it like it is.*] Well . . . seem to me . . . we oughta be givin this here thing some serious consideration.

MYRA: [*Haughtily.*] For what? Can't do nothin' but get black folks into trouble.

AVERY: [*Moving to her, flipping through the pages.*] Not everything in here leads to baby-makin'. Some of it's just plain pleasure. Kinda like havin' your cake an' . . . [*The words freeze as he comes upon a page that is particularly explicit.*]

MYRA: Say what?

AVERY: [*Closing the book.*] Different strokes for different folks.

MYRA: Lemme see that thing. [*Takes off her apron and crosses to the sofa where she settles herself with the book. AVERY crosses behind the sofa and looks over her shoulder.*] O . . . , my goodness. Look at that, Avery. [*Turns a page.*] Um, um, um. I swear white folks do near 'bout anything. [*AVERY has started to rub her shoulders and neck. MYRA is, at first, too wrapped up in the book to notice. When she catches on, she straightens in all her pristine glory. Icily.*] Reverend Doctor Avery Harrison . . . I don't know what you call yourself doin', but I know you better take yourself in hand right now. [*AVERY moves quickly around to sit next to her.*]

AVERY: Myra . . . I wanna put them two single beds together. Right now. Tonight.

MYRA: For what? The way you thrash around an' snore I oughta put you in Junior's room. They too close as it is now.

AVERY: Now, I know you ain't forgot how it used to be. How I used to rub my feet on yours when we had that old bed.

MYRA: Dry an' hard as them ol' dogs is now, you better keep 'em to yourself.

AVERY: Sex ain't nasty, Myra. Not no more, it ain't.

MYRA: [*Running out of patience as he tries to kiss her.*] No, an' tonight ain't Thursday. Ain't no need in you gettin' no "Thursday thoughts" on a Saturday evenin'! [*Pushing him away.*] I don't know how you expect to lead your flock to grace when you can't keep your own hands on the plow. You need prayers!

AVERY: [*Miffed.*] Prayers ain't what I want.

MYRA: [*Rising, getting her apron.*] A preacher actin' like one o' them lowlifes in your brother's bar. Messin' up my hair an' I've got a sorority meetin' tomorrow. Go there lookin' all beat out. [*AVERY decides to take the plunge. He moves behind her, turns her to him and plants a big kiss in the right place. MYRA is taken aback.*] Avery, are you crazy?

AVERY: Mattie Lou Henderson, you're still the finest lookin' woman I know. Twenty-two years an' I still wanna . . . [*He reaches for her again, but she manages to catch hold of his hands. She presses them together.*]

MYRA: Avery! Avery! Pray with me. Ask the Lord an' He'll help you. [AV-
ERY *struggles to free his hands as* MYRA *begins singing "Yield Not To
Temptation."* AVERY *continues in his attempt to kiss her and hold her.* FELIX
*appears at the doorway. He carries an overnight bag and a stack of books.
Seeing* FELIX, AVERY *tries to cool his "attack" and pins the song.* MYRA,
wrapped up in the fervor of the song.] Amen . . . praise the Lord! [*She exits in the fullness of the spirit, secure that the proper path has been shown.*
AVERY *kind of shrugs it off and turns his back on the perplexed* FELIX *as he
tucks his shirt in.*]

AVERY: [*Covering.*] That new sermon's gon' be dynamite! [*Turns back to see*
FELIX *with the bag.*] Goin' somewhere?

FELIX: [*As he thinks an adult should act.*] I'd appreciate it if you wouldn't be
gettin' on my case tonight. I'm doin' what I hafta do.

AVERY: [*Gesturing.*] An' you need your suitcase to do it?

FELIX: Pop, it's time I was leavin' home. I mean, I'm not a kid anymore.
I'm nineteen an' there are . . . things . . . I oughta be doin'. Things I
gotta be doin'.

AVERY: An' you can't do 'em at home?

FELIX: Heck no. I mean, I respect you an' Mom too much for that. An'
also I don't wanna be what she said I was when she was talkin' about
you an' Mom. Also, I don't wanna be that.

AVERY: [*Not understanding but playing it through.*] Wouldn't nobody in the
world wanna be that . . . especially if he knew what it was she said we
were.

FELIX: Bourgie niggahs.

AVERY: [*Disbelieving.*] She said that?

FELIX: But it's true, Pop.

AVERY: Don't you ever believe that, boy. We might be a little bit on the
"Bourgie" side, but I'll be damned if I'll own up to that other!

FELIX: I don't wanna be none of it.

AVERY: You ain't gon' be nothin', you don't stay in school.

FELIX: School contributes to it. I lose sight of the real world and the political realities of my existence in this oppressive culture . . . also ain't
no women down at Saint Bonaventures.

AVERY: Oh, now that throws a different light on the situation.

FELIX: [*Moving to him.*] Pop, I like Li'l Bits. She . . . she . . . well, she's got . . .

AVERY: Never mind. I already know.

FELIX: You ain't mad? You ain't gon' rat on me to Mom? [AVERY *crosses to the doorway and checks that* MYRA *is out of earshot. Turns to* FELIX.]

AVERY: Son, there are two times in a man's life when he gets to feelin' what you're feelin' . . . once when he's your age . . . an' once again when he's my age.

FELIX: [*Pondering the comment.*] You lookin' for a woman, Pop?

AVERY: [*Making certain that no one overheard that!*] Uh . . . Junior . . . y'see . . . uh . . . I've got mine right here . . . [*Confidentially.*] She just don't know that she's what I'm lookin' for, y'understand?

FELIX: [*Weighs it.*] Un-unh.

AVERY: It's like . . . when you're young, ya think about all the things you're gonna do when you get older. When ya get there, get older, I mean . . . that's when you think about the things you are doin' . . . an' how well you're doin' 'em. [*Realizing that he has said more than is proper.*] I mean, dependin' on what it is you're doin' . . . at any particular time, that is.

FELIX: [*Puzzled by the whole exchange.*] Are you impotent, Pop?

AVERY: [*Defensively.*] Boy, you'd better hush! I'm in the prime of my life!!!!

FELIX: [*Delighted at his father's sudden statement of virility.*] Holy cow! I didn't know ol' folks got horny!

AVERY: [*The boy's laughter reminds him that this conversation has gone far enough.*] I assume you're leavin', boy. Where are you plannin' on goin'?

FELIX: Cross town.

AVERY: Cross town? You're leavin' home an' goin' across town?

FELIX: Well, I figure I can get a job over at the club with Cal. Learn about life an' be back here before the semester starts. He probably needs a bouncer an' with my karate . . .

AVERY: [*Let down.*] Goin' across town an' goin' be back home in September. [*Shakes his head. Lights his pipe.*] Across town.

FELIX: [*Following his father.*] Y'see Dad, I need time to be independent. Make my own money an' have my own place. Make some new friends an' live around black people an' get to know my roots. Then when I get back to school I can concentrate on ghetto dentistry. Learn how to put in gold teeth an' all that.

AVERY: Well . . . given the fact that you're gon' be back here in September an' it's already August, I guess you'd better get movin' . . . [FELIX *is dumbfounded at his father's willingness. He extends a manly hand for a shake as* MYRA *enters.* AVERY *begins to hum and crosses to his chair to hide behind his paper: leaving the matter up to his son.*]

MYRA: [*Seeing his overnight bag.*] Junior, I done told you about leavin' things around this house. An' where you think you're goin' this time o' night anyway? [FELIX *quickly picks up his bag and "stands his ground", after a quick look at* AVERY.]

FELIX: Ma . . . sit down. I want to tell you somethin'.

MYRA: Avery, you see my Lamda Nu monthly newsletter?

FELIX: Ma.

MYRA: [*Looking in the bookcase.*] Felix, I'm listenin' to you. [*Muttering.*] I put that thing right up yesterday.

FELIX: Ma, I'm breakin' out.

MYRA: Well, I don't wonder . . . hangin around with that Li'l Bits. You liable to have anything. [AVERY, *exasperated that* MYRA *won't hear, puts his paper aside and rises.*]

AVERY: Just get on outta here, son. Call when you get settled.

FELIX: [*Quickly, exuberantly.*] Right on, Pop. See ya later, Mom. [*He exits before* MYRA *can get herself to protest.*]

MYRA: [*To* AVERY.] See ya later? Where's he goin' this time o' night?

AVERY: Mattie, the boy's growin' up.

MYRA: [*Moving to the door.*] Grown or not, he ain't got no business roamin' 'round out here at night. [*Calls.*] Junior! [*To* AVERY.] Where's he goin?

AVERY: He's movin' in with Caleb.

MYRA: What?

AVERY: I said . . .

MYRA: Over there with them pimps an' pre-verts . . . them prostitives?

AVERY: Myra, the boy got to sow his "wild oats."

MYRA: [*Definite.*] No, he don't'! He's gon' be a dentist!

AVERY: There comes a time when all young men hafta leave home. S'pose I hadn't left? We'd never met.

MYRA: Oh, you'da found some way.

AVERY: [*Looking out the window.*] He's gon' be all right. [*Pulls the blind.*] But ya know what? . . . That means ain't nobody home . . . [*Puts the lock on the door.*] but you an' me. [*Kinda "leers" at her.*] Sweetheart . . .

MYRA: Now, Avery . . . we've been through that already . . .

AVERY: [*Stalking her.*] Book say you oughta try different places an' different ways . . .

MYRA: [*As he blocks her exit.*] Man, you better get yourself together. [AVERY *pulls her to the sofa.*]

AVERY: [*As he tries to kiss her.*] An' keep the light on . . .

MYRA: Avery, you're gon' mess up the sofa. Now, get outta here! [*She pushes him away and stands up. She starts out in a huff, but feeling his eyes on her, she stops and sees him smiling sneakily.*] Avery . . . you all right? What're you lookin' at me like that for? [AVERY *motions to her to come to him. She backs off as he rises and goes after her, smiling and grinning all the way.*]

[*Dimout to black.*]
[*End of Act One.*]

ACT TWO

SCENE ONE

TIME: *Later that evening.*
PLACE: CALEB's *apartment above the Shake-Shake Club. It is a large space that doubles as sleeping space and office. The room is dominated by a large bed at center. Against the left wall is a component set set in what is called "as music center" and surrounded by records. It is playing as the lights come up; a Miles Davis record. A large recliner is downstage left; a desk, littered with papers and empty glasses, is downstage right. The walls are decorated with various art objects of African orientation. Magazines are stacked here and there. There is a large closet in the left wall.*
AT RISE: CALEB *enters followed by* BEVERLY *carrying her suitcase and looking approving around the room.*

BEVERLY: This where you stay?

CALEB: [*As if it hurt him to speak.*] Right.

BEVERLY: Where you cook?

CALEB: [*Putting his jacket in the closet.*] Don't. I go out.

BEVERLY: [*Inspecting a wall plaque.*] Cheaper if you cook. [*Taking off her coat.*] You play that music all the time? Even when you ain't here?

CALEB: [*Gesturing for her to put her coat in the closet.*] Right.

BEVERLY: Make you feel less lonely when you talk in an empty room.

CALEB: Wrong.

BEVERLY: I useta play mine like that, but Aunt Rose said it run up the electricity. [*Gesturing to the record player.*] That's Miles . . . my daddy wrote me all about him. Useta send me records all the time. Specially after I started goin' to that business school. Said he didn't want me to get around all them white folks an' forget about my culture. [*Looking at a picture on the shelf; a woman's picture.*] Sure wish I knew him better.

CALEB: [*Taking a bottle from his desk and pouring a drink.*] Who?

BEVERLY: My daddy. What was he like?

CALEB: Quiet. Didn't talk much.

BEVERLY: Like you?

CALEB: [*Ignoring her comment.*] Cat was a prince . . . if he like you, I mean. [CALEB *crosses to the record player and begins searching for another record.*]

BEVERLY: I know he like music. Tol' me to always trust a man who likes music.

CALEB: Miles, Bird, Billie . . . all he ever talked about. Diz an' Sarah. I useta hang out around *The Moonglow* . . . wasn't nothin' but a kid, but all the "real" musicians played *The Moonglow*. Some of 'em never made it big, but them cats knew how to play pretty for the people. I'd be standin' out there . . . tryin' to be cool without a penny in my pocket an' knowin' damn well I wasn't old enough to go in. Soakin' up the sounds an' plannin' what I was gon' do when I got my chance. Mostly though, I'd be waitin' for Big Ed to drive up there in that big black Buick an' tap me on the shoulder . . . "Hey, youngblood, you still hangin' 'round here? Ain't you got no home?" Then he'd nod his head an' tell me to follow him. I'd sit there with him an' his broad smile he tell everybody I was his boy an' how I was gon' blow Clifford an' Diz both right off the stand. [*Laughs.*] He be sayin' that an' the cat ain't never heard me play. [*Puts his drink down.*] Got so I'd go over to his place an' hang out . . . listenin' to his records. [*Gestures to the shelves.*] Most of these are his. We'd talk about gettin us a club . . . a musicians club. Place where cats could come an' jam . . . get some free grease . . . a clean place to crash an' no cash registers bangin' when they played. Yeah . . . we'd dream the world away.

BEVERLY: [*Quietly. Admiringly.*] Wasn't all dreams. You got your place.

CALEB: [*With an edge of bitterness.*] Yeah . . . when the cat was too sick an' beat up to dig on it. After all the giants had passed on an' the streets too ugly for folks to come out at night no matter how much they dig the music. Anyway them cats what can still hit hot chord done gon' disco mad . . . priced themselves right outta black folks pockets. We got our club all right.

BEVERLY: [*Sympathetically.*] You don't play no more? Daddy always said . . .

CALEB: I know what he said. The cat lied.

BEVERLY: Oh.

CALEB: Pay it no mind. Just 'cause you can't dance don't mean you can't dig the beat. [*Crosses to the closet, gets a robe and towel.*] I'm goin' down the hall an' get cleaned up. Set the clock for nine. You can use the john when I get finished. [*He exits.* BEVERLY *takes a snoop around the room, being sure to take a longer look at the woman in the picture. She shrugs it off and then turns to the audience.*]

BEVERLY: [*Elated.*] Now, tell me I wan't right. You can always trust a man your daddy likes . . . especially if he likes music, too. Most of the times, that is. Depends on whether or not you like your daddy. [*Laughs.*] You know something . . . [*Quieter.*] he's got the same kinda hurt my daddy had . . . the kinda hurt that only comes to good men. I ain't never met Mildred an' I don't make a habit o' talkin' about folks I don't even know, but there's some women who don't know how to deal with a good man. I mean, a man who wanna do for ya an' treat you the best he can. A man like that, most women call simpleminded . . . say he's weak. The sisters be runnin' all over top of 'em . . . an' you know I'm tellin the truth, too. Ain't good for a woman to spend too much time listenin' to other women talkin' about their men. That's why I'm glad I had my daddy to talk to . . . even if it was only by letter. He told me all about life . . . an' about that one just walked outta here, too. His bloodson he called him. But what I remember most is how he'd try to explain to me about him an' my momma . . . how they couldn't never get back together again. Seem like when you're close to somebody an' they walk off an' leave you . . . or things just don't work out right . . . it's like they take a part of you with 'em. I guess whatever it is they take you can't grow back . . . just leave an empty hole. That Mr. Johnson out there . . . he boxin' so hard 'cause he scared somebody might make somethin' grow . . . get through that protection an' make him feel somethin'. Humph! Don't make me no nothermind . . . 'cause me, myself . . . I know how to treat a good man. [*The door opens and* CALEB *reenters. He is now wearing his robe and pajamas. He goes right to the bed and begins getting it ready for the night.*]

CALEB: Your turn. An' be sure you turn the spigot off tight. [BEVERLY *gets her things and rummages through her bag, taking sneaky looks at* CALEB *as he hangs up his robe.*]

BEVERLY: I sure do appreciate everything you're doin' for me . . . fixin' up the bed an' all.

CALEB: Can't sleep unless the covers are straight.

BEVERLY: Giving up you bed an' everything.

CALEB: [*Pauses.*] Doin' what?

BEVERLY: [*Her things in hand, she glances out the window.*] I don't see how you can sleep with that light flashin' outside the window. [*Laughs.*] I remember when I first went to Aunt Myra's . . . that dog just barked all night. Couldn't sleep no kinda way . . . [*She starts out, but notices* CALEB *in the bed.*] Counta that dog . . . barkin' . . . all night long. You sleepin' there?

CALEB: [*Yawns.*] It's my bed, ain't it?

BEVERLY: [*Stifling the panic.*] Where am I supposed to sleep? [CALEB *pats the space next to him and pulls the covers up about his head. It is obvious that sleep is the only thing he is interested in.*]

CALEB: Turn the record player off when you come back.

BEVERLY: [*Amazed at his boldness.*] Un-unh. I ain't sleepin' in no bed with you. I don't even know you.

CALEB: [*Too tired to be bothered.*] Hey, look . . . I ain't had time to find you a proper place. Hell, I thought you were gonna be one o' them teenaged pimple pushers. You wouldn't raise no hell if you had to sleep with your daddy, would you? Well, I'm your guardian.

BEVERLY: [*Definitely.*] I ain't no pimple-pusher. You ain't my daddy an' I ain't gettin' in that bed with you.

CALEB: [*He doesn't care.*] Suit yourself. You've got the bathtub or the floor. Don't forget to turn the water off.

BEVERLY: [*Not certain what to do, she wanders to the chair.*] You've got a hell of a nerve . . . an' I don't even cuss. [BEVERLY *stands a minute, weighing her alternatives. In a sudden burst she charges to the bed and snatches the blanket.*]

CALEB: [*Leaping up angrily.*] What the hell's the matter with you, woman?

BEVERLY: Do you mind if I cover up in the bathtub? . . . Or ain't I allowed to have a blanket either?

CALEB: Take the damn thing! [*He goes to the closet, muttering unheard obscenities, and takes out another blanket. Returning to the bed, he covers his head, leaving his feet sticking ingloriously out.*]

BEVERLY: If you was a gentleman you give me your bed.

CALEB: [*His patience at end.*] This is a double bed. Plenty of room for two.

BEVERLY: [*Knowingly.*]You mighty bold with your stuff, ain't ya? Just come right out a say what you want.

CALEB: [*Pauses. The thought of her thought amazes him.*] What? . . . You think . . . no . . . you couldn't . . . [*He begins to laugh.*] Lookahere, Beverly . . . you ain't got to worry about nothin' like that. Anyway, what makes you think I'd try somethin?

BEVERLY: [*Sarcastically.*] Oh, we gon' lay there in that bed an' you ain't gon' do nothin'. I might look dumb, mister, but I got plenty o' sense.

CALEB: Fine, but I'm sleepin' in the bed I paid for. You can do what the hell you want. [*Begins arranging his covers, muttering.*] Got some nerve . . . [*Aloud.*] What makes you think I'd be interested in you anyway. You ain't been up here that long to be that lucky! [*With that he gets into the bed and covers himself up, fully and completely.* BEVERLY *is aghast at his "verbal ugliness."*]

BEVERLY: [*Angry, near tears.*] I can't stand you, Caleb Johnson! You ain't nothin' but a conceited . . . bowlegged, beady-eyed nigga. An' whether you think I got somethin' or not, I can sure find somebody who do! [*She boots him in the butt with her foot and makes a fast exit, carrying the blanket with her.* CALEB *jumps up and sneers after her. In his exasperation he turns to the audience.*]

CALEB: I don't understand not a damn one of 'em! First she mad 'cause she think I want her to sleep with me . . . then she mad 'cause she think I don't want her to sleep with me. Why the hell couldn't Big Ed have a son? All I'm tryin' to do is treat her like a buddy . . . but no, she don't want that. Can't treat no broad like that. Soon as you act half way decent to 'em they think you tryin' to get into their pants. An' don't try to talk to 'em . . . let 'em know where you really comin' from. Tell 'em the truth an' they turn around a whip you with it. I'm sick o' the whole damn thing. Sick of it. [*Moves to straighten the bed, but the anger wells up anyway.*] Dig it . . . if it wasn't for the fact that she is a broad . . . I could lay it all out there . . . "Look here, Baby . . . I am temporarily in a jam for space. I just didn't get around to fixin' up that place across the hall but you can camp out here for the night." Hell, I'd do that much for a stranger! Ya just can't treat no woman like a friend. [*Looks out at the audience.*] Tell me somethin' . . . an' I'm just talkin' to the men out there . . . how many of you all got a woman that you can call a friend? [*Pause.*] Yeah . . . well, I believe you lyin'. She just paid for the ticket an' you don't wanna make her feel bad . . . else you tryin' to work up on somethin' an' wanna be sneaky. But I'ma tell you 'bout myself . . . I ain't got no time for them games. First thing in the mornin' I'ma call somebody an' ge that broad outta my hair! [*He turns off the record player and gets in the bed as the door opens and* BEV-ERLY, *wrapped Indian-style in the blanket, re-enters.*]

BEVERLY: [*Pouting.*] The bathtub's cold an' the faucet leaks. [*Crosses to the chair and begins putting her clothes back in the suitcase. She is wearing a nightgown.*] I'ma sleep here in the chair . . . see can't I dream I was back home where folks at least try to talk nice to you. [CALEB *turns over in the bed so as not to face her, a movement that only makes* BEVERLY *mad. She accidentally knocks her suitcase to the floor.* CALEB, *under the covers, starts.* BEVERLY'S *concern turns to enjoyment as she begins to plot other ways of disturbing his sleep. She picks up the suitcase and bangs it around, practices opening and closing it; anything to make sleeping hard for* CALEB. *Each time she makes a noise she plays it off when he looks at her like a "clumsy child". Finally,* CALEB *can't stand it anymore. He leaps from the bed and shouts at her.*]

CALEB: HERE, TAKE THE DAMN THING!!!!

BEVERLY: I DON'T WANT IT!!

[CALEB, *realizing that the best thing to do is ignore her, goes back to bed.* BEVERLY *sits in the chair, her feet propped on the suitcase and tries to make herself comfortable. This results in much shifting and turning. Finally she is comfortable but only for a minute. She rises and kneels next to the chair. All of this has been disconcerting to* CALEB, *who now looks over at her.*]

CALEB: [*Slowly.*] What the hell are you doin' now?

BEVERLY: [*Snapping.*] I'm saying my prayers! Do you mind? [*Returns to her praying, but with a watchful eye to see that* CALEB *is listening. She mumbles just enough to be overheard.*] Dear Lord . . . thank you for bringing me up here on this fearful journey . . . bless . . . Aunt Myra . . . Uncle Avery . . . Felix . . . an' . . . Frou-Frou. [*Smiles, knowing that* CALEB *has noted the fact of his deletion.*] An', Dear Lord . . . please protect me from this . . . man among whom you have set me down . . .

CALEB: [*Impressed.*] You say your prayers every night?

BEVERLY: If I gotta stay here with you, I ma start sayin' 'em in the mornin', too. [*Tying up prayer.*] Amen. [*Rises, begins resettling herself in the chair.*] Somethin' wrong with sayin' your prayers?

CALEB: No. I just don't know too many women who . . . uh . . . sho do that anymore. [*Pauses.*] My momma . . . all the time I was growin' up . . . I remember her gettin' down on her knees. Almost every night, she'd say her prayers. I'd be wonderin' who she was thankin' an' for what. Poor an raggedly as we were, seemed to me she shoulda been askin' some heavy questions.

BEVERLY: Most likely she was prayin' for you. Askin' The Lord to knock some o' the devil outta your behind. Don't do to pray for yourself.

CALEB: Yeah . . . she probably was. [BEVERLY *settles herself in the chair. CALEB stares off into the darkness. Neither person is interested in sleep. CALEB reaches over and turns on the record player. A John Kleinmet selection plays softly, moodily, in the background. Self-consciously, like one unaccustomed to saying or doing anything gently.*] Hey, Beverly . . .

BEVERLY: Hunh?

CALEB: I'm sorry . . . about what I said; hollarin' at you an' all. I didn't mean it.

BEVERLY: You was just mad.

CALEB: Right.

BEVERLY: Aunt Rose say when you get mad you just have to ask The Lord to . . .

CALEB: [*Interrupting her, not hardly ready for a sermon.*] Now, look, I said I was sorry. I don't wanna talk about it no more. [*His snappiness amuses* BEVERLY, *she curls down into the chair and blanket. She is satisfied.* CALEB *scrunches under the covers, now ready for sleep.*]

BEVERLY: [*After a pause.*] Cal. . .

CALEB: [*Tired of the talk.*] Hunh?

BEVERLY: [*Cooingly.*] Can I take back my half of the bed?

CALEB: [*Sharply. Hiding his soft side.*] I wish you'd make up your mind, girl! In the bed or outta the bed! [BEVERLY *pulls the blanket tightly around her so that she resembles a cold Apache and ambles over to the bed. She has never slept with a man and, although she feels a bit more secure with* CALEB, *she is taking no chances. She stands next to the bed and does not speak.* CALEB *is turned from her. Sensing her standing there.*] Well, ya gettin' in or ain't ya? [BEVERLY *pauses, takes a deep breath and gets quickly in the bed, still wrapped in her blanket. Feeling the weight of her falling onto the bed,* CALEB *turns to see her wrapped up. Irritated.*] Damn woman! You can take the blanket off. Ain't nobody gon' bother you.

BEVERLY: [*Pouting as she tries to spread the blanket.*] You ain't got to hollar so much. [*The awkwardness of the situation amuses* CALEB. *He begins to smile and shake his head in amazement.*]

CALEB: You ain't never slept with a man before, have you?

BEVERLY: [*Indignant.*] That ain't none o' your business. [*Pauses, holding the blanket by a corner.*] . . . an' you better not tell nobody I was in here with you tonight!

CALEB: [*The idea of virginity is amusingly incongruous to him.*] You're kidding.

BEVERLY: Well, what do you think I am? [*Muttering as she finishes spreading the blanket.*] Shoot . . . I wish I thought it.

CALEB: That's just it, I don't know. Every time I think I've got a handle on you, you go changin' up.

BEVERLY: [*Not sure she likes the implication.*] What you mean?

CALEB: You really are just a sweet kid, aren't you?

BEVERLY: [*Getting into the bed as if it was "old hat."*] Not so sweet as you think. I got my shameful thoughts same as anybody else.

CALEB: [*Devilishly.*] I'll bet you have.

BEVERLY: Well, I do.

CALEB: [*Teasing.*] Yeah, tell me.

BEVERLY: [*Teasingly petulant.*] I said they was shameful.

CALEB: Awww, come on. Tell me.

BEVERLY: You won't say nothin' to nobody?

CALEB: Hey, baby . . . this here's your guardian. Hell, it's my job to marry you off.

BEVERLY: Well, you can just forget that.

CALEB: Oh, you ain't makin' that scene, right?

BEVERLY: [*She is sure of herself on this matter.*] I might . . . someday.

CALEB: In the meantime you just have nasty thoughts.

BEVERLY: [*Quickly, a sharp edge.*] I ain't say "nasty." I said shameful!

CALEB: [*Before she can change her mind.*] Like what?

BEVERLY: [*Looks at him, weighing it all. Finally . . .*] Like . . . well . . . meetin' somebody I like a whole lot . . . an' not holdin' nothin' back on 'em.

CALEB: [*Taken back by her frankness.*] Nothin'!

BEVERLY: Nothin'! I meet a lot o' folks I like. Like, maybe they've got nice personalities an' they be a lotta fun to be with. Guys I never would marry even if I had a mind to. I ain't sure I wanna marry nobody just yet, but I know I want me a house full o' kids. Course, that's only if I got me a real good man or a good job.

CALEB: Either one, right?

BEVERLY: [*As logical as hell.*] Sure! What I need somebody always fussin' an' cussin' at me if I can take care of 'em by myself? I just don't wanna go through life not knowin' that part o' me just cause I ain't never got married, that's all. My cousin, Inez, is like that. She never got married so she never "knew" herself . . . with no man, I mean. Not me. I know what it takes to make me happy . . . an' if I don't find it in no man, that's all right. Long as I can take care o' me an' mine.

CALEB: Sound to me like you just wanna be loose.

BEVERLY: Un-unh! I just wanna do what the men do without gettin' my name dragged all in the street an' havin' to suffer for it. It ain't like I wanna be . . . "personal" with every man I see. That ain't what I mean. Shoot, sometimes I see men I just wanna be gentle with . . . lay up in their arms an' talk quiet to 'em . . . tell 'em things I ain't never tol' nobody an' have them tell me things. I'd like to do that once. Get to know somebody like that. [CALEB *has been watching her closely during this last speech. He finds himself drawn to her.*]

CALEB: Yeah?

BEVERLY: [*Looks at* CALEB. *Sees the gentleness the last few moments have generated.*] That's . . . what I be thinkin' . . . I mean . . . [CALEB *is embarrassed by his own thoughts. He looks away and then back to her. Finally, he yawns, stretches a bit bigger than necessary, so that his arm seems to surround* BEVERLY. *He falls back on the pillow, careful to keep the arm ready for* BEVERLY *to lie on. One eye open, he looks sidewise at her.* BEVERLY *smiles and cuddles next to him, her head on his shoulder as the lights dimout and we are left with the record player's comment.*]

[*End of Scene One.*]

SCENE TWO

The backyard of LI'L BITS' *home. It is dominated by a high fence with lots of graffiti. Most likely there is a clothesline strung across the area and several trashcans against the fence. Downstage center there are several crates turned on their sides to form a sitting place.*
AT RISE: *We hear the sound of trashcans being overturned as someone runs through the dark and the voices of neighbors raising their windows and calling out things like, "What the hell is goin' on down there?" "Y'all better cut out that noise, I gotta go to work" . . . etc.* FELIX *rushes onstage, wrapped in a blanket. He looks behind him and then moves quickly to the nearest hiding place. He is soon followed by* MRS. EMMA CALDWELL, *a woman in her forties. She is wearing a bathrobe pulled tightly around her, a cap covering her curlers and brandishes a length of lead pipe. The lady is angry.*

MRS. CALDWELL: I see you. Ain't no need in you tryin' to hide. [*She feints toward* FELIX, *he moves.*] An' if I catch you . . .

FELIX: [*When he is clear of her.*] Please, Ma'am . . . can't I get my clothes?

MRS. CALDWELL: You got your clothes, mister . . . an' you better see that I get my blanket back!!!

FELIX: But it wasn't what it looked like. I swear to God, it wasn't.

MRS. CALDWELL: You better pat your feet an' hit the street fo' I lose my patience. [*She makes another move toward him, pipe waving threateningly.*]

LI'L BITS: [*Entering.*] Felix! [*Seeing her mother, she stops dead in her tracks.*]

MRS. CALDWELL: I hope you brought your clothes, Miss Fast 'cause you ain't puttin' nary foot in the house back there!!

FELIX: But Mrs. Caldwell . . . [*Turning quickly to* FELIX, *brandishing the pipe like an extension of her finger.*] I done tol' you, boy. You better get on back up there with them "muckety-mucks you live with."

LI'L BITS: But Ma . . .

MRS. CALDWELL: Don't you say a word to me, child. I ain't goin' out here everyday at that factory so you can be loose with them ol' high saditty niggas across town . . . [*She's just getting wound up.*] I ain't out here makin' myself old an' raggedy so you can have them muckety-mucks layin' up in the bed anytime you think I ain't around.

FELIX: I just wanna get my clothes.

LI'L BITS: We wasn't doin' nothin' but talkin'.

MRS. CALDWELL: Don't be lyin' to me, girl. Ain't nobody teach you to be "talkin" in your bedroom! What kinda conversation gotta be carried on in your drawers? Don't you talk to me like I'm no fool.

LI'L BITS: Awww, momma.

MRS. CALDWELL: [*Feinting with the pipe.*] Was he tryin' to force you, child? Please tell me he was tryin' to hurt my little girl!

FELIX: *We wasn't doin' nothin!*

MRS. CALDWELL: Oh, you just took off your clothes so you could be cool, hunh? An' your daddy's a preacher, too! [*To* LI'L BITS.] Well, I ain't gon' have no hussies in my house. You like him? Then you can live with him!

FELIX: I just want my clothes!

MRS. CALDWELL: That's what you want? Well, I'm gon give it to you. Give both of you just what you want. You wait right here. [*She starts off* LI'L BITS *rises.*]

LI'L BITS: Momma, you ain't bein' fair. I can get my own clothes . . . an' if you don't want me stayin' in your house I can go. I won't be the first one of your children you done put out in the street.

FELIX: That's right. We can take care of ourselves.

MRS. CALDWELL: Boy, you better not be givin' me none o' your muckety-muck lip! Have you walkin' 'cross town in your drawers! I know all about you college boys. Come down here slummin' an' then grab your hat.

FELIX: I ain't slummin. I like Li'l Bits.

MRS. CALDWELL: [*To* LI'L BITS.] Girl, I never thought I'd see the day . . . never thought you'd hurt me so. Bringin' your trashy ways right here in front of my eyes. Never in the world thought I'd see that day. But that's okay. You wait right here. You like him . . . live with him! [*She exits into the house.* LI'L BITS *sits disgusted on one of the crates.*]

FELIX: [*Seeing that they are alone.*] You never answered my question.

LI'L BITS: What?

FELIX: Did he come? . . . Your "visitor" . . . did he come?

LI'L BITS: I think so . . . I mean, I don't think nothins wrong, but I ain't takin' no more chances specially since we got to live together.

FELIX: [*The thought is unsettling.*] Live together!!!!!

LI'L BITS: Well, I gotta stay somewhere . . . an' it was your fault!

FELIX: You didn't have to let me in.

LI'L BITS: [*Melting him with her eyes.*] Yes, I did. Leastways, I wanted to.

FELIX: [*Softening.*] Well . . . don't you worry. I'll work something out.

LI'L BITS: I know. That's what I like about you.

FELIX: [*Sitting next to her.*] Yeah. I can get a job. Maybe talk Cal into let-tin' us stay down there at the club 'til I get things together. [*The idea doesn't exactly fit in with* LI'L BITS' *plans.*]

LI'L BITS: In a bar? You want me to stay in a bar?

FELIX: Just 'til I get things together.

LI'L BITS: You ain't goin' back to college?

FELIX: [*The idea of a job and independence more and more interesting to him.*] Maybe later. Right now, I've got to do my "man-thing" . . . I'll go back to school later. After we're married.

LI'L BITS: [*Not one to allow dreams.*] Humph. Don't be writin' no checks you can't cash.

FELIX: No, I mean it. I'm crazy about you.

LI'L BITS: If you so crazy about me, you better stop talkin' about gettin' a job an' livin' in a bar!

FELIX: What's the matter with livin' in a bar?

LI'L BITS: [*Looking away from him.*] Humph!

FELIX: An' everybody I know got a job.

LI'L BITS: You suit yourself, but I ain't marryin' no ordinary workin' man. I want me a dentist! A school teacher at the very least . . . an' I ain't too hip on them 'cause they ain't makin' no money.

FELIX: You wouldn't marry me like I am?

LI'L BITS: [*Rising.*] Felix, I'd be a fool to marry you just because you loved me. Any-ol-body can love you. I want me somebody who can *support* me! I don't intend to be workin' in that supermarket all my life.

FELIX: An' you call me a "bourgie niggah"!

LI'L BITS: [*Right with him.*] I said I didn't like being with 'em! I ain't say I didn't want to be one myself. I don't like bein' poor an' if you don't like me enough to be a dentist you don't like me at all. What I wanna be stayin' in a bar for when your daddy get that fine house up there? You don't make no sense. [*"Common sense" doesn't sit too easy with* FE-LIX, *especially this kind of non-logical common sense.*]

FELIX: [*Indignantly.*] Li'l Bits, I hope you don't mean what you just said.

LI'L BITS: [*With a withering look.*] Diana Ross is Chinese if I don't!

FELIX: [*Whining as he moves from her.*] But you said you liked me.

LI'L BITS: I do, but I'll like you longer an' stronger when you're a dentist an' can feed me three squares a day.

FELIX: [*Amazed at the degree of her "innocence."*] Don't you see what you're saying? I mean, that's the epitome of middle class, American capitalism! That's the language of our oppressor!

LI'L BITS: Call it what you want, but it damned sure beats welfare an' foods stamps.

FELIX: That's what comes from listening to white folks!!!!

LI'L BITS: Poor folks, baby! I've been listenin' to *poor folks*!!!!

FELIX: [*Taking his stand.*] Well, I'm not going back to school.

LI'L BITS: Suit yourself . . . sucker! [LI'L BITS *turns to leave, but meets Mrs. Caldwell with a laundry bag full of clothes. She puts the bag in* LI'L BITS' *hand and moves directly to* FELIX.]

MRS. CALDWELL: That's right! I'm puttin her out 'til she learn some respect, but blood don't forget blood an' if you mistreat her, I'm comin' after you, y'understand?

FELIX: You'd better find somebody else to go after 'cause she ain't comin' with me!

MRS. CALDWELL: Say what?

FELIX: I said she ain't comin' with me. Mrs. Caldwell, your daughter's a snob! She think she's too good for me, too good for the real people! [MRS. CALDWELL *quickly turns to her daughter.*]

MRS. CALDWELL: What? Girl, you better act like you got some sense!

LI'L BITS: That's just what I'ma do . . . act like I've got some sense. [*She takes her laundry and exits toward the house.*] Bye.

FELIX: [*Calling after her.*] Go on! I don't care. I may get me a *real funky woman.* Make you look like one o' them sorority girls. You ol' bourgie, capitalist, hammer head!!!

MRS. CALDWELL: [*Not having understood a word of it.*] Now, you just watch what you callin' my daughter.

FELIX: I thought you didn't have no daughter. [MRS. CALDWELL *is finished with it all. She turns and exits. Muttering,* FELIX *takes a joint from behind his ear. He begins looking along the curb for a match. Finding the match, he rummages in his pants pocket* — MRS. CALDWELL *has thrown them to the ground* — *and comes up with a joint. He lights up as we hear* MRS. CALD-WELL *knocking at her door.*] I don't need her. Get me any woman I want . . . a real funky sistuh. No . . . I'll get me a white girl. That'll show her . . . an' don't you think I can't either. Them girls from St. Cecelia's always checkin' me out. Be just like my daddy always say . . . one monkey don't stop no show. She don't do right somebody else will. [*Loudly to the house.*] Damn you, Li'l Bits!

MRS. CALDWELL: [*Offstage.*] Josephine . . . you better open this door.

FELIX: An' that goes for your momma, too!!! [*He picks up his "stuff" and exits. The lights dim on the following offstage line.*]

MRS. CALDWELL: [*Off.*] Now, sugar . . . this ain't no way to treat your momma! Open the door!

[*Blackout on Scene.*]

SCENE THREE

CALEB's *apartment. The next morning. Music still plays quietly as the sun sneaks around the edges of the window blinds.* BEVERLY *is curled up in the bed, holding the pillow tightly in her arms. After a moment* CALEB *enters from the corridor. He is wearing only his trousers, a towel thrown across his shoulder. He crosses to the dressing table and puts on his watch. Looking at the time, he then turns and lightly swats* BEVERLY *on the butt with the towel. She exits laughing.* CALEB *finds that he can't hold back his own smile. Now, dressed except for his jacket, he crosses to the phone, dials.*

CALEB: [*Muttering as he dials.*] Uncle Cal . . . broad's enough to drive you crazy . . . [*Into the receiver.*] Where the hell are you? Said you was gon' be here first thing in the morning! . . . Yeah, we've been ready. Waitin' on you . . . the works. Everything from the skin out . . . awwww, come on, you know better'n that. She ain't nothin' but a kid. I don't care what he said, she's a kid . . . an' what the hell he doin' spyin' on me that time o' night, anyway? . . . That's right . . . right here. I stayed on my side an' she stayed on hers . . . [*Laughs.*] I swear to God! . . . Hey, everybody ain't like you. Look baby . . . move your buns an' get on around here, I got work to do. Yeah . . . you, too. All the time . . . don't do nothin' but think about my lady. [*He hangs up the phone and crosses to the mirror and begins putting the finishing touches on his clothing. Admiringly.*] Don't know what you got, Mr. Cal Johnson, but the women sure dig it. [BEVERLY *bursts into the room wearing a pair of "bib overalls", a sweatshirt, and her hair still in braids. She goes directly to her suitcase and begins putting her things away.*]

BEVERLY: [*Brightly.*] Okay, what's on the agenda?

CALEB: [*Crossing to his desk and opening an address book.*] Well, I'm gon' see can't I book some music in this place an' you're gon' go get your hair done.

BEVERLY: What?

CALEB: [*Studying the address book.*] The hairdresser, baby. You know what that is?

BEVERLY: [*Touching her hair, pouting.*] I don't want my hair all fried up. I like it like it is.

CALEB: [*Puts down the address book, reaches for a magazine.*] Then you're gon' go downtown an' get yourself some clothes.

BEVERLY: [*Her irritation growing.*] But I brought clothes. [CALEB *tosses the book at her. It is a fashion magazine.*]

CALEB: In the nightclub business...beauty is a commodity. Can't hang around here with your hair all plaited up an' wearin' them farmer Browns.

BEVERLY: [*Looking at her jeans.*] Want me to put on somethin' else?

CALEB: Naw, let it pass 'cause I'm sure what you got ain't much better than what you're wearin'. Gon' get you some new clothes; teach you how to make up your face. [BEVERLY *is disgusted. She flops onto the bed, holding the magazine.*]

BEVERLY: That stuff breaks my face out.

CALEB: [*Exasperated.*] Now look . . . [*Decides to use the fatherly approach.*] Trust me. You ain't ready for the "fast crowd." Like, you're a sweet kid an' all that, but I gotta hip you to what's happenin' up here. Get you ready for the night-time people.

BEVERLY: [*Quietly.*] S'pose I don't wanna be like them?

CALEB: Say what?

BEVERLY: [*Pointing to a picture in the magazine.*] I'd catch my death o' pneumonia with my bosoms all hangin' out like that...

CALEB: Then maybe you oughta go back up there with your preacher uncle. [BEVERLY *is stung by the thought that he might be rejecting her.*] Now, look, don't go gettin' all long in the mouth. Like I say, you're a nice kid, but comin' outta the fatback an' greens bag you're a sittin' duck.

Every jivetime player on the avenue be hittin' on you. If you're gon' help me run this place, you gotta swat them cats away like flies. To do that you gotta change the image a little bit. Uncle Cal's payin' for it. [*She thinks about it for a moment.*]

BEVERLY: Just one question. You gon' like me better when I'm all dressed up like you say?

CALEB: [*Carelessly.*] Hell, yeah. Don't nobody like a bear!

BEVERLY: [*Ruined.*]A bear!!!! [*Sighs.*] Well . . . let's get goin'. [*Sitting on bed.*] If you gon' "make me over" we oughta get started. Sounds like it ain't gon' be no easy job.

CALEB: [*Writing notes from his book.*] Don't let it throw you all outta shape. I've seen worse. [BEVERLY *glances at herself in the mirror. There is a knock at the door.* CALEB *crosses quickly to open it.*] That must be her.

BEVERLY: Her who? [CALEB *opens the door to admit* MOZELLE, *a woman whose bearing seems to say "I've been around." She is attractive in a worldly way and made up to the teeth. She looks fine, but very definitely at bargain rates.*]

MOZELLE: [*Smiling provocatively at* CALEB.] Hey, Big Daddy. Momma missed you. [*They move easily into each other's arms and the kiss removes all doubt as to the nature of their relationship.*]

CALEB: Thought about you all night.

MOZELLE: Stop lyin'. From what I hear you had your hands full.

CALEB: Well, you heard wrong.

BEVERLY: [*The sister's jaws are tight.*] Well, don't mind me. [MOZELLE *moves from* CALEB *to give* BEVERLY *the once over.*]

MOZELLE: [*With grown folks condescension.*] Ohhh, this must be Big Ed's little girl. How're you doin', honey? My name's Mozelle.

BEVERLY: [*Putting her on, but very obviously on the nasty side.*] Must I call you "Aunt"?

MOZELLE: [*Taken back by the cutting quality of the greeting.*] Waaaaait a minute. We'd better run this thing again from the top. My name is Mozelle. [*Satisfied that she has struck a blow,* BEVERLY *rises and moves in front of* MOZELLE, *conducting her own inspection.*]

BEVERLY: [*Overly polite.*] It wasn't my intention to offend you, ma'am, but my Aunt Rose always say you don't never grow up to your family. You're always a baby to them . . .

CALEB: What's the matter with you, girl?

BEVERLY: [*Sharply.*] Well, she ain't my father, mother, sister or brother and, to my knowledge, we ain't cousins. But since she insist on callin' me "little girl", she must be my aunt. [*Turns quickly to face* MOZELLE.] How d'ya do, Aunt Mo?

MOZELLE: [*Not at all amused.*] What you say your name was?

BEVERLY: Beverly! Miss Beverly Harrison!

MOZELLE: [*Turns to* CALEB.] You sure you want me to take this child out?

BEVERLY: I appreciate your offer, but me an' my guardian was just on our way to buy some decent clothes, wanna go?

MOZELLE: [*To* CALEB.] You better straighten this mess out. I got a houseful o' customers. I could be making me some money today.

BEVERLY: [*Aside.*] I'll bet you could. I didn't know y'all worked in the daytime, too.

CALEB: Hey, girl, you better check yourself.

MOZELLE: Don't tell her nothin'. [*Putting* BEVERLY *in her place.*] I'm a hairdresser, baby. An' I thought I was takin' a day off to help a friend . . . at least, I think he's a friend.

CALEB: That's right.

MOZELLE: All this ugliness ain't my bag, so I'm just gon' go out here in the hallway an' smoke me a cigarette while my friend fills you in on what's happenin'. But when I come back . . . I'm gon' speak pleasant . . . an' everybody in this room gon' talk pleasant . . . or else I'ma haft tell this fresh behind little hussy where to get off.

[MOZELLE *makes a confident exit into the hallway.* CALEB *closes the door behind her and turns to* BEVERLY.]

CALEB: [*Whispering.*] What the hell's the matter with you, woman?

BEVERLY: [*Putting her things in her bag.*] That's your ol' lady, ain't it? Come in here sloppin' all over you like a hound-dog in heat! An' in front o' people, too!

CALEB: That's what got your jaws all tight, hunh?

BEVERLY: [*Hot.*] My jaws ain't tight! They loose! I just don't like no painted streetlady callin' me a child, that's all.

CALEB: [*Commanding.*] Get your coat. Ain't nobody got all day to mess with you.

BEVERLY: No, you just mess with "Mo-zelle"! [*Mimics.*] "Mama missed you. Did you miss Momma"?

CALEB: Cut that out.

BEVERLY: Don't holler at me!

CALEB: I'll do more than that you don't shut your mouth an' get that coat on. That woman's takin a day off from her work just to take you downtown an' help you to pick out some clothes.

BEVERLY: I can pick out my own clothes!

CALEB: I'm wise. That's why you look like you do.

BEVERLY: An' I'm tired o' you tellin' me I'm ugly. You want me to look like her?

CALEB: Damn right I do. That's a woman . . . an' you oughta be thankful she . . . [MOZELLE *opens the door and leans in.*]

MOZELLE: Can I come in now?

CALEB: No! [MOZELLE *closes the door.*]

BEVERLY: Why should you care what I look like? That your woman. [CALEB *is afraid that* MOZELLE *will overhear that last statement. He makes sure the door is closed.*]

CALEB: [*An angry whisper.*] That ain't my woman an' if she was it ain't none o' your business. [*Realizing that she has scored a hit,* BEVERLY *raises her voice to the occasion.*]

BEVERLY: [*Loudly so* MOZELLE *can hear.*] YOU AIN'T say that last night WHEN I WAS LAYIN' UP IN THE BED WITH YOU!!!

CALEB: [*Amazed.*] Layin' in the bed? Hey, girl . . . [*Loud enough for* MOZELLE *to hear his side of it.*] I lay up in the bed with any woman I want. . . . but DON'T NO BROAD GET NO STRINGS ON CAL JOHNSON . . . y'understand? [*Takes* BEVERLY *by the arm.*] If it wasn't for that woman out there, you'd be campin' on that bed again tonight, but no, I call that chick on the phone an' tell her how I'm temporarily in a jam for space . . . how Big Ed's little girl ain't hardly no little girl at all . . . an' that woman . . . the one you can't find nothin' good to say about . . . she turn around an' offer you her pad until I can get things straightened out . . .

BEVERLY: I ain't stayin' over there with her!

CALEB: You ain't got to. She's comin' over here. Now, get your coat. [MOZELLE *opens the door again.*]

MOZELLE: Now?

BEVERLY: No! [*As* MOZELLE *closes the door.*] Man, you must be crazy! I'm s'posed to stay over her place while you an' her "shack up" over here? [*Moves quickly to her suitcase and begins gathering her things.*]

CALEB: What you got to do with what two grown folks do?

BEVERLY: [*Angry and hurt at the same time.*] Nothin! . . . Not a doggoned thing . . . but I got a whole lot to do with what I do, Mr. Caleb Johnson! I ain't gon' be in your way an' I don't want yo' ol' night club neither! [BEVERLY *starts for the door, but is stopped by* CALEB.]

CALEB: Where do you think you're goin'?

BEVERLY: [*Her anger wide open now.*] Maybe I'll buy me some new clothes or maybe get my "hair" done. Maybe I'm gon' learn how to talk real "hip" an' wear purple paint on my eyebrows . . . Or maybe I'm just gettin' away from you!!! [*She strides for the door as* MOZELLE *steps aside to clear her path. To* MOZELLE.] Move outta my way!!! [*She is gone.* MOZELLE *moves fully into the room and sits on the bed observing* CALEB *pacing angrily about.*]

CALEB: [*Muttering.*] Ol' simpleminded, country-assed broad. [*To* MOZELLE.] What the hell's the matter with her? Just tol' her I was gon' buy her some clothes an' fix her up . . . teach her how to run the business. Gon' turn her into somebody . . . 'cause the broad ain't bad-lookin' an' with a little help, I don't think she's dumb. She's just raw . . . unhip. I don't straighten her out some o' them jivetime dudes out there on the corner have her spittin' wooden nickles an' barkin' at the moon. Yeah, but let her tell it, I ain't worth a damn! Everything I say is wrong. [*Sits on the bed, ponders and then turns quickly to* MOZELLE.] An' I ain't even touch her last night. Just let her lay there like a baby . . . lay there . . .

MOZELLE: [*Feeding him.*] . . . in your arms.

CALEB: [*Not having paid attention.*] Like a baby . . . talkin' about music . . . an' saying prayers. [*Looks at* MOZELLE.] You say your prayers at night?

MOZELLE: [*The wisdom of the cold world.*] Well, let's just say I've been known to call His name once in awhile . . . but I don't think you'd call it "praying."

CALEB: [*Becoming angry again.*] Now, what the hell I'ma do? That simple ass broad runnin' loose in West Philly. [*Pause.*] The hell with her. She left on her own, she'll come back on her own. If I'm gon' be her guardian, she gon' hafta mind!

MOZELLE: That's what you' gon be, Cal? Her guardian? [*Moves to him, fixes his collar.*] What I mean is . . . if you're gon' be her watchdog . . . an' that's all you're gon' be . . . then everything's cool. Otherwise, Miss Mo gotta beat the bushes an' see can't she find a new pastime. [*She leans to kiss* CALEB, *but his mind is elsewhere, he turns from her.*]

CALEB: Ain't but one place she can be . . . back there with that preacher uncle of hers.

MOZELLE: [*Musing aloud.*] I see . . . time to call on the claws . . . [*Sweetly.*] Cal . . . you still want me to do that shopping?

CALEB: Hunh?

MOZELLE: Your charge card, baby.

CALEB: [*Still busy with* BEVERLY.] Oh, yeah. [*Takes card from his wallet and hands it to her.*] That's why I can't stand no young broads . . . can't depend on 'em to think! [MOZELLE *takes the card and very deliberately puts it in her purse.* CALEB *starts for the door.*] Wait here. I'll be back. I might catch her before she gets the bus . . . ol' simpleminded . . . [*He exits muttering.* MOZELLE *watches him out, turns to the audience.*]

MOZELLE: Miss Mozelle gon' get herself a goin' away present . . . an' ain't gon' feel no ways guilty. While he's lookin' for her I'm gon' do some lookin' on my own . . . startin' with some new shoes, coat, underwear . . . maybe a dress or two . . . might even get me one o' them battery operated radios for the shop. I mean, it's no more than I'm due. Like, what I've been givin' up ain't hardly second class. Now, don't get me wrong. Y'see, Cal ain't my man . . . never was. That don't mean I don't like him. It just means I don't want him—not for no longer than an occasional night, I don't. Wakin' up lookin' at the same face every mornin' would bore me to death. With Cal . . . it's all animal. I dig the man's body . . . the way he be wearin' them low-slung pants an' his shirt unbuttoned to the belly button . . . shoot . . . I had a good time . . . an' I ain't loose either. Like me a man who can go the distance . . . most women do, they just don't say it out loud. You see a dude walkin' down the street with everything altogether, you be lookin' . . . lookin' an thinkin', "umph, I sure would like to get next to that!" Women do it all the time, they just don't say nothin' about it. [*Moving to balcony.*] An' don't come askin' me why neither 'cause you know good an' well that if a woman talk to a man the way a man talk to a woman, she'd be by herself an' lonesome. That's right. Man walk up to you an' say, "Momma, you sure got a fine hine," you s'-posed to be flattered. You say the same thing to him an' he run for the hills . . . call you fifty 'leven different kinds o' hussy, too. [*Pauses.*] But I put all that aside. Figured you ain't gon' get nothin' outta life 'cept maybe a coupla good meals an' some good lovin', if ya lucky . . . an' I ain't missin' out on neither one just because I'm too polite to ask for it. Me an' Cal was a good thing. He don't B.S. an neither do I . . . but it's quittin' time. That young sister got his nose wide open an' he don't even know it. An', lemme tell you somethin' . . . when a man's with you . . . but he thinkin' about somebody else . . . that's when he turn bad. Get evil an start hollerin' at you cause he feels guilty, I'd drop in on that sister an' give her some of my old tactics . . . if I wasn't such a "bee-eye-itch." Well, why not? Long as a horse got one race left in him ain't right to put him out to pasture just 'cause he found a new rider. [*Blackout as she takes the card from her purse, flashes it and exits.*]

[*End of Act Two.*]

ACT THREE

SCENE ONE

THE HARRISON's. *Several days later. It is early morning. As the lights come up we see* BEVERLY *and* MOZELLE *entering from the kitchen.* MOZELLE *is dressed in a white uniform and carries a small satchel.* BEVERLY *is dressed in a bathrobe and is carefully wigged and made-up. There has been quite a transition from the "raw" country girl of Act Two.*

BEVERLY: [*Looking at herself in a hand mirror.*] But I don't know why you're doin' all this, Mozelle. Specially after the way I talked to you last time.

MOZELLE: [*Sitting.*] Just pay it no mind, girl. It's like, well . . . when I was comin' up my momma didn't like for us to leave no food on the plate an' now that I'm grown, I can't stand to see no worthwhile man go to waste. [*Gesturing to the make up.*] How does it look up close?

BEVERLY: I can't really tell . . . but I sure feel pretty.

MOZELLE: You're a fox.

BEVERLY: I guess bein ugly is a state o' mind, ain't it?

MOZELLE: Not since Max Factor an' Flori Roberts it ain't.

BEVERLY: [*Sits.*] You know somethin'? After I left that place I went around with my mouth all poked out . . . eyes all swoll up from cryin' . . . I was a mess. Looked just like what he said I looked like. Standin' there brushin' my teeth one mornin' with all that ugliness starin' out at me. I knew I had to get myself together.

MOZELLE: What you gonna do now?

BEVERLY: Buy me some clothes. [*Picks up* Vogue *and shows it to* MOZELLE.]

MOZELLE: [*Suspiciously.*] This is the book you got from Cal, ain't it?

BEVERLY: Un hunh.

MOZELLE: Throw it away.

BEVERLY: But.

MOZELLE: But nothin! . . . Throw it away. That's what he would wear if *he* was a woman. I know that man, an' lemme tell ya, if he was a woman he'd be a stone skunk. You buy for Beverly. One person try to·make another one, they always wind up with a monster. Be yourself.

BEVERLY: [*Takes the book, drops it in the trash, smiles.*] Mozelle, I'm so glad you come up here.

MOZELLE: It even surprised me. [*They laugh as* MOZELLE *rises and prepares to leave.*]

BEVERLY: Mozelle . . . you think he's gon' call?

MOZELLE: I hope you ain't sittin' here waitin' on him to call!

BEVERLY: Well, what must I do?

MOZELLE: Get yourself a man . . . have a ball!

BEVERLY: You mean go out with somebody else?

MOZELLE: Except for a slight variation in shape, size and color, they're all the same honey.

BEVERLY: I don't think I could do that. Anyway, Cal would . . .

MOZELLE: [*Interrupting.*] No, he wouldn't. Men are funny, baby. They all talk about "pioneerin'," but when the get down time comes they really want the ground to be lightly traveled, if you know what I mean. All Cal got to do is think somebody shakin' your tree, he'll do right.

BEVERLY: An' if he don't, I might not even care, right?

MOZELLE: Ain't it the truth! [*They share a laugh.*]

BEVERLY: If my Aunt Rose could hear me talkin' like this! [*Pauses. Seriously.*] But ya know somethin, Mozelle . . . I'm scared.

MOZELLE: [*Moving to her, sisterly.*] Oh, I was too . . . once . . . a *long* time ago.

BEVERLY: I really do like Cal an' . . .

MOZELLE: Do like I say, girl. Them boys your aunt keep throwin' up in your face? You go out with 'em. Y'see, women like me spoil Cal. He get burned one time an' we be hangin' around to pick up the pieces. Truth be told, we're just as scared of a real involvement as he is.

BEVERLY: You was married once?

MOZELLE: Once . . . when I was sixteen. Once when I was twenty-two . . . an once more when I'm forty. [*Looks at her watch.*] Which means I got to get outta here. Got a three o'clock appointment with a foot doctor . . . who is not too recently divorced an' very much interested in takin' care o' that corn on my little toe.

BEVERLY: Mozelle . . . thank you. [MOZELLE *gives her a friendly touch and gathers her things.*]

MOZELLE: Like I said . . . that's too much man to be runnin' around here loose. [*As she starts for the door,* AVERY *enters wearing a sweat suit. He is perspiring.*]

AVERY: [*As he enters.*] Beverly, baby . . . why don't you run upstairs an' get me . . . a towel . . . [*Aware that she is being admired* MOZELLE *smiles provocatively.*]

MOZELLE: The Reverend Mr. Harrison, I presume.

BEVERLY: This is my friend, Mozelle.

AVERY: Mighty pleased to meet you, Miss Mozelle.

BEVERLY: I'll get the towel. [BEVERLY *exits.* MOZELLE *sits demurely, but certain as to the whereabouts of all her attributes.*]

MOZELLE: You run every mornin'? [AVERY *begins to double time in place.*]

AVERY: Oh, yes, ma'am. Got to keep the ol' body in shape.

MOZELLE: [*Giving him a once over on the sly.*] Seems like you could miss a day.

AVERY: Well, really I couldn't but . . . what I mean is . . . uh . . . do you run?

MOZELLE: Me?

AVERY: I was just noticin' . . . your . . . legs. I mean you have "strong" legs.

MOZELLE: [*Teasing.*] Reverend . . . [*Stops double timing. Sits, panting.*]

AVERY: [*Quickly.*] I didn't mean any harm. It's just that . . . well, I didn't expect to see you here an' . . . do you really think I've got a good body? For my age I mean?

MOZELLE: [*Leans to him.*] Does it work? Then it's good. They tell me that a body's like a car . . . gotta turn the engine over every now an' then just to keep it runnin'. [MOZELLE's *conversation upsets* AVERY. *He likes it, but knows he shouldn't.*]

AVERY: [*Nervously.*] I guess that was a kind o' out of place question to ask you. I mean, I don't even know you an' uh . . . my niece . . . she . . .

MOZELLE: Tol' me all about you . . .

AVERY: She did? What'd she say?

MOZELLE: That you were a fine upstandin' . . . pillar of society. [*Looks around to make sure they can't be overheard.*] An' ain't nothin' no more borin' than bein' a "pillar of society."

AVERY: [*Sits.*] Ain't it the truth?

MOZELLE: [*Quietly.*] All that pressure an' responsibility . . . wears you down. Oh, I could tell. Soon as you walked in that door, I . . .

AVERY: Ran. I "ran" in.

MOZELLE: I said to myself . . . that man needs a good time . . . needs to learn how to relax . . . burn off that energy . . .

AVERY: [*Checking to see that they are alone.*] How? You just tell me how.

MOZELLE: Y'see . . . I can do things with your body that you never thought possible . . .

AVERY: [*Mesmerized, anxious.*] Yeah? Un-hunh.

MOZELLE: [*Reaches into her bosom and passes a small card to* AVERY.] Come an' see me sometime.

AVERY: [*Not looking at the card.*] Do what?

MOZELLE: Call first . . . just to avoid confusion.

[MYRA *enters carrying a towel. She pauses as she sees the two of them head to head.*]

MYRA: [*No play here.*] Good mornin'. [*To* MOZELLE.] An' who might I ask are you?

AVERY: [*Leaping to his feet.*] A friend o' Beverly's . . .

MOZELLE: [*Cool as can be.*] We met down at the club . . . Beverly an' I. I told her I'd give her a beauty treatment an' see if I couldn't . . .

MYRA: All that paint on her face, I figured somethin' had happened to her. [*Cattily.*] I hope you weren't workin' on my husband just now. With your beauty treatment, I mean.

MOZELLE: [*Laughs.*] Oh, I don't think he needs that. I was just on my way out an' thought I ought to take the time to drum up a little business. You're welcome to come down, too, if you'd like to.

AVERY: The three of us?

MOZELLE: Why not? Don't knock it til you try it!

MYRA: Avery . . . I'm gon' turn my back an' concentrate on the plants in my window. When I see your face again, that front door better be closed with that . . . woman . . . on the other side.

MOZELLE: Now, wait a minute. You better look at my card. [*She takes the card from* AVERY *and gives it to* MYRA.] I am a hairdresser . . . an' I also have a license as a physical therapist which means I give massages an' rubdowns. An' when I'm talkin' to a man an' he can't get his eye above my legs, I know he needs a rubdown. If you won't give it, I will . . . only mine cost fifteen dollars. Tell Beverly I'll give her a call. [MOZELLE *picks up her things and exits.*]

MYRA: Avery, you oughta be ashamed!

AVERY: Of what?

MYRA: I saw the way that woman was perusin' your body!

AVERY: Not "perusin", Myra.

MYRA: All these years . . .

AVERY: An' anyway, you've got it backwards. It was she who was perusin' my body!

MYRA: I don't doubt it! This house ain't been the same since that brother o' yours died. All kinds o' people knockin' at the door . . .

AVERY: [*Thinking about his previous statement.*] That's right . . . it was my body. [*Takes the card back from* MYRA.] Gimme that.

MYRA: You wouldn't dare!

AVERY: You don't know, do you? I might like havin' a fine lookin' lady put her hands all over my body . . . I just might like that.

MYRA: [*Starts to leave. Chin held high.*] I don't even want to discuss it.

AVERY: You'd better.

MYRA: [*Stops.*] What?

AVERY: I say, "You'd better." That woman done give me a new lease on life. Mattie, did it ever occur to you that some woman might find me attractive? Might like my body?

MYRA: Your body?

AVERY: I just might like havin' my body rubbed. Might check it out to see what else . . . else is up for grabs.

MYRA: You wouldn't dare.

AVERY: [*Desperately.*] I want a rubdown, Myra. I want somebody to kiss me right smack in the middle of my back. Use some o' that Vaseline Intensive Care lotion you got up there in the room. An' then when I finish getting mine, I'll turn around and give you one.

MYRA: I didn't hear that. Ain't no way in the world my ears could've preserved such a thing. I'm going upstairs and see how my niece made out with her date, which I arranged for her an' then I'm putting on my clothes an' going out in the fresh air . . . out of this den of iniquity. [*The "grand dame" exits.* AVERY *stands a minute. He looks at the card again.*]

AVERY: [*Musing.*] In six months and some odd days . . . I will be fifty years old. Every day I cross the street, I think how easy it is to get hit by a car. Last month I buried a man half my age who died of a heart attack . . . ! High blood, ulcers, blindness and bad breath waitin' around the corner for me. Flat feet, hemorrhoids, the flu . . . both German an' Hong Kong, punchin' holes in my system every day I draw breath . . . an' I can't get a little rubdown. The hell you talk! [AVERY *starts for the door.* MYRA *pops into the room.*]

MYRA: Avery! Don't you go down there to that woman! . . . I might . . . try it one time. But don't let it get good to you . . . Miss Myra ain't nobody's pre-vert! [*He stops, looks at her. A smile eases its way across her face and they are soon laughing as they start out and upstairs.*]

[*Lights out.*]

SCENE TWO

Several days later. More of the "Muzak" sound introduces us to the HARRISON's living room. BEVERLY, *well dressed and very attractive, is at the door talking to someone.*

BEVERLY: [*Airishly.*] Thank you so much, Roger. I ain't never enjoyed a luncheon so much in my life! [*Pause.*] Dinner? But we just got back from . . . [*Laughs.*] All right. Pick me up about six. I just can't understand why you want to spend so much time with me!

[*She slowly closes the door. Once it is closed she moves quickly to the win-*

dow and looks out, careful that she is well hidden. She laughs quietly and exits to her room; her stride a bit jauntier than we have previously seen it. Once she is out of the room, MYRA *enters. She has a robe pulled about her and her hair is a slight disarray. She looks around the room.*]

MYRA: Beverly? [*Pause.*] I coulda swore l heard somebody come in that door. [*She crosses to the door and checks that it is locked. She then moves to the window. As she starts out, she stops to pick up a pillow that has fallen from the sofa. As she bends* AVERY *also in a robe, sneaks into the room and pats her on the behind.* MYRA *starts.*] Whoooo! [*Turns to* AVERY.] Man, if you don't stop actin' the fool around here!

AVERY: [*In his best bedroom manner.*] When I see one I just gotta touch it!

MYRA: [*Smiling in spite of herself.*] Must be crazy . . . ol' as you are. [MYRA *pats the pillow, picks up an* Ebony *and sits on the sofa.* AVERY *sits very deliberately next to her, grinning nastily.* MYRA *moving to give him room.*] Do you mind? [AVERY, *thinking himself to be very sexy, kisses her on the neck or thereabouts.* MYRA *trying to play it hard.*] Feelin' better?

AVERY: You come on back upstairs with me an' I'll show you how I feel.

MYRA: [*Girlishly.*] I ain't. An' you better put on some clothes 'fore that child come back here.

AVERY: Mattie-my-love, these past few days I ain't felt like puttin' on no clothes-never-no-time.

MYRA: [*Doing her duty, but liking it all the same.*] Now, you just stop all that talk!

AVERY: Gimme some sugar an' I won't say a word. [*He leans for another kiss, placing his hand on her leg as he does so.*]

MYRA: [*Moving his hand.*] You done had your sugar, mister. Now, sit over there somewhere.

AVERY: [*Devilishly.*] An' it was good, too, wasn't it?

MYRA: [*Sharply.*] Just because I . . . "let myself go" ain't no cause for you to be talkin' like that!

AVERY: What's wrong with it? It's the truth, ain't it?

MYRA: It don't sound decent.

AVERY: Did I lie?

MYRA: [*Try as hard as she will, she can't keep from enjoying* AVERY's *boldness.*] I ain't said you was lyin'. I said it wasn't decent . . . an' it ain't. [*Knowing that he's got her moving again, he leans to her, moving his arms about her shoulders. Her resistance is "polite."*]

AVERY: I oughta be ashamed of myself . . . for likin' my ol' lady's eyes . . . and her neck . . . [*Kisses her lightly.*] . . . an', Lord-have-mercy . . . them old, but smooth shoulders . . . momma, don't you know you've got the . . . [MYRA, *not liking the heat that is starting to generate is up and stepping back from* AVERY.]

MYRA: [*Pulling her "dignity" together.*] We can stop it right there. Don't need to go no further than the shoulders! Man, I don't know what done got into you! Must be on your change!

AVERY: [*Moving to her, satisfied.*] You know somethin', baby . . . I'll never forget the first time I made you blush. Never! Finest lookin' thing I ever saw . . . still are! [*Still teasing.*] An' if I wasn't married! [*Repeats the pat on the butt that started the scene and strides off, smiling as* MYRA *watches, confused and amused. Once he is out of sight, she addresses the audience.*]

MYRA: OO . . . , ain't he somethin'? An' I wanna thank you. I ain't know the ol' rascal had so much life in him! [*Moves to the audience with a funky-freedom to her gait.*] Yessir! Surprised me, An' don't you think I don't like it either. I don't care how long you been together, you don't never let him know everything! Nevah! He think them rubdowns is somethin' new . . . shoot, Miss Myra ain't even in second gear yet. Y'see, I come up the old fashioned way . . . the old fashioned "colored" way. Soon as you hit that first danger sign, momma call you aside an' lay it all out there for ya . . . "Keep your drawers up an' your dress down." That's what she say. [*Looks to make sure she is alone with her audience.*] Now, I ain't sayin' momma was right . . . an' I ain't tellin' you whether I followed her advice . . . but I sure learned how to act like I was followin' it whether I was or not. [*Points.*] Some o' you know exactly what I mean . . . 'cause you see, accordin' to the old folks women didn't have no sex drive no way. They "did their duty" . . . *after* the fact, the "fact" bein' marriage. Tell ya what I believe though . . . that gettin' happy took care of a whole lotta late night dreamin'. You ever notice who be doin' all the shoutin' and hollerin'? That's right . . . got the old and decrepit men . . . or they ain't got nobody. You check that out next Sunday . . . but this one here. Avery . . . I never would've believed it. I mean, I was willin' to do what I was s'-posed to do. In fact, I was anxious, But . . . [*Checks around again. Speaks confidentially.*] . . . truth be told . . . wasn't nothin' but routine. Got so I'd even pick the day in the week. Two days before my sorority meetin' an' five days after my last visit to the hair dresser. Then the old fool hit them middle years. Got curious an' got to readin' all them books, worryin' 'cause old age starin' him in the face. Gon try to get it all before it goes away. But lemme tell you . . . the best thing that ever happened to a middle aged woman is male menopause! Everything up to that point ain't nothin' but rehearsal. [*Looks out cockily, sure of her footing.*] Am I lyin'? I ask you, am I lyin? Shoot . . . don't worry about your hair. Do like Miss Myra . . . get yourself a wig! [*There is a knock at the door.* MYRA *starts to open, but* BEVERLY *appears in the doorway, dressed in a fine looking white suit.*]

BEVERLY: Don't open it.

MYRA: Hunh?

BEVERLY: Ain't nobody but that ol' Caleb. Been followin' me all day. [*She crosses to the window and looks out.* MYRA *follows. Whispering.*] Seen his car drive up from the window. See. [*Points out the window.*]

MYRA: Ol' fool . . . [*Remembering that she is not "dressed" in her usual fashion.*] Oh . . . uh . . . how long have you been home?

BEVERLY: [*Moving from the window.*] Followed me all up an' down Market Street. Even came into the restaurant when we ate lunch!

MYRA: [*Trying to make her hair presentable.*] Just decided I'd sleep in today. [*More knocks,* BEVERLY *just stands.*] He knock one more time, I'ma call the cops. This ain't no ghetto for him to bangin' on people's doors! [*Slight pause.*] You say you went out to lunch? Then you ain't been long come in, right?

BEVERLY: [*Back at the window.*] He's gettin' back in the car. [*Pause.*] He's just sittin' there! Waitin' on Roger I'll betcha.

MYRA: Don't you let him hurt that boy. He's just jealous, that's all.

BEVERLY: Stoppin' people on the street an' pointin' at us.

MYRA: That's how they do. Soon's you get yourself a man worth somethin', they go to actin' up . . . but don't you let it worry you. That Roger is just what the doctor ordered. Your daddy would be proud of you.

BEVERLY: No, he wouldn't either. He'd be just like Cal. That's what makes me so mad.

MYRA: [*Sits, still primping.*] Yes, I guess he would be. He was one of them "low-classed coloreds," too.

BEVERLY: [*Flopping onto the sofa.*] Well, what am I supposed to do? Sit around here an' wait 'til Caleb Johnson decides that havin' big feet an' talkin' flat ain't the worst thing in the world? Roger likes my feet . . . an' my talk, too.

MYRA: Honey, the better class of people like you just the way you are . . . especially when you learn to fix up what you got. [*Sound of a car horn. MYRA leaps to her feet. Angrily.*] He better stop that noise! He ain't back there in Coontown! [*Horn again.*]

BEVERLY: I'll go talk to him!

MYRA: No, you don't. I'm call the cops. They'll take care o' his behind. They know don't no colored people belong in this neighborhood. [*Crosses to the phone.*] They even picked up Avery one time. [AVERY *enters, still in his robe and carrying the* Joy Of Sex *under his arm.*]

AVERY: What's all the racket out there?

MYRA: [*Covering the now obvious tracks.*] Oh, finished your nap, dear?

BEVERLY: It's Cal. Been followin' me all day. [MYRA *motions to the book which* AVERY *hides under the pillow again.*]

MYRA: I was gon' call the cops.

AVERY: That's all right. I'll straighten him out. [BEVERLY *crosses to the door and opens it.*]

BEVERLY: You an' Aunt Myra oughta go an' put your clothes on. I can talk to Cal. [AVERY *and* MYRA *look at each other and start out.* BEVERLY *folds her arms and waits for* CALEB *to enter, which he does. He walks past her and into the room as if he owned it.* BEVERLY, *directly.*] What you bangin' on that horn for?

CALEB: I saw you.

BEVERLY: So, maybe we'll have three more weeks o' bad weather.

CALEB: Don't get smart with me, girl. An' you need to take that wig off your head, too.

BEVERLY: It's my head an' I'll put anything I want on it.

CALEB: Walkin' around the street with all that make-up and that thing slapped up on your head. Look like a black fool!

BEVERLY: Well, that's better than what you said I looked like before. Anyway, some people like it.

CALEB: An' I saw that, too. You oughta be ashamed.

BEVERLY: I am . . . but in a way you'll never understand. What you come up here for?

CALEB: In case you forgot, you are my legal responsibility.

BEVERLY: I ain't your legal nothin' an' I'm getting' me a job so I won't hafta be dependin' on you for nothin' . . . ever!

CALEB: Oh, you been up here with your preacher-uncle an' you don't need the club no more!

BEVERLY: I don't *want* it! It ain't makin' no money no way.

CALEB: It could if you'd help.

BEVERLY: [*Turns from him. Looks out the window.*] I'm too ugly . . . ain't "hip" enough.

CALEB: [*Moving to her.*] You look better now . . . just take off that wig.

BEVERLY: [*Matter of factly.*] Go to hell, Caleb Johnson. An' who do you think you are followin' me around an' pointin' at me like I'm some kinda freak?

CALEB: Hey, girl, what you're into is definitely freaky. Don't no broad what think nothin' of herself be seen, public or private with no cat like that.

BEVERLY: He treats me nice.

CALEB: Oh, I'll just bet he does. [BEVERLY *sits, determined not to let* CALEB's *sarcasm get to her. He paces the room, winding up on the sofa. A moment of silence as he tries to figure out what to say to her. After pause. Gruffly.*] I'm sorry. That what you want to hear?

BEVERLY: No.

CALEB: Well, I am. I mean . . . what I said back there. You're not so . . . [*He has difficulty looking at her.*] Well, you're attractive . . . when you're not wearin' that halloween wig an' all that slop on your face.

BEVERLY: [*Coldly.*] Mozelle wears it.

CALEB: [*Sharply.*] You wanna be like her, I guess!!!

BEVERLY: [*Quietly.*] Cal, why don't you go on back to the club an' leave me alone? You don't want me. Ain't nothin' about me that you like. You just all razzed up 'cause you seen me with Roger.

CALEB: Damn right I am "razzed up." You can't find nobody else to go out with? Let you off the farm an' right away you go runnin' after the whities.

BEVERLY: [*Rising.*] Right. 'Cause up to now, I've just been runnin' with the "brothers." Herman, that was my first boyfriend. He all the time tellin' me how I was his woman but I was too aggressive, that I didn't know nothin' about bein' "feminine" . . .

CALEB: That's the way some o' y'all come on.

BEVERLY: [*Continuing.*] So, I quit him an' started goin' out with Tyrone but he went in the service. Time he get back all he want is somebody to smoke that dope an' help him find them powders. An' Leon... mad at me 'cause I had a little piece o' job an' he couldn't get none. Like it was my fault.

CALEB: Beverly, it's hard out there.

BEVERLY: I ain't finished! There's one more. The only one that ever counted. A hurt man . . . gun shy. Lumped every black woman under one heading . . . 'Fore I even get to know him good, he runnin' me down. [*With intensity.*] Don't you see, Cal. . . it all means the same thing. *Y'all don't want us!*

CALEB: An' Roger does? [BEVERLY *doesn't answer.*] Hey, Beverly... them cats been hawkin' y'all since the first boat touched land. A broad like you ain't nothin' new to Roger-dodger. He just comin' to the front door now. He comin' after you 'cause his own woman don't want him . . . she too busy beatin' the bushes for the blood. The cat tried to keep her locked up in the big house, but she broke loose, y'dig?

BEVERLY: [*Levelly. A challenge.*] So, what're you gon' do about it?

CALEB: It ain't on me! Hell, I did the best I could with the one I married. Take a fool to jump out there twice. I'm just tryin' to hip you. Let you know ain't nothin' so special just 'cause you got some honky's nose open.

BEVERLY: [*Sharply.*] But I am. I'm very special . . . an' if you don't see that an' Roger does, well, I'd be loose in the head to waste my time with you now, wouldn't I?

CALEB: [*Coldly.*] Like I said, you ain't ready for the fast crowd. I just hope Tyrone or one of the boys back home got over first. I'd hate to see that white boy turn you out. [BEVERLY *slaps him soundly across the face. Surprised by the blow,* CALEB *grabs her and pulls her to him. Before he can give vent to his anger, he finds himself kissing her hard. The kiss over, they stand looking at each other until* CALEB *impulsively attempts to repeat the act.* BEVERLY *pushes him from her gently.*]

BEVERLY: Un-unh. [*He persists.*] I said "no." [*She moves from him, avoiding his eyes. She struggles to maintain her own composure.*]

CALEB: [*After a pause. Embarrassed.*] I know what you're thinkin' . . . but I didn't plan it like that.

BEVERLY: I ain't thinkin' nothin' . . . 'cept how I wish you'd stayed down there where you was.

CALEB: [*Irritated with himself as much as with her.*] Damn, woman! You think I wanted to come up here?

BEVERLY: [*Challenging.*] Then why did you?

CALEB: [*Direct, afraid to let his true feelings show. He almost sounds angry.*] 'Cause I fixed up those two rooms across the hall an' you can have them if you want 'em.

BEVERLY: That ain't no reason.

CALEB: [*Ignoring her comment.*] Figured it's time I started you out down at the place . . . on a part time basis kinda. Let you see how the place runs 'cause I'm thinkin' bout branchin' out. Goin' after the cabaret trade. Hit on a few of them saditty clubs like your aunt an' them belong to. You'd be good at that. Go out to their meetin's an' sell 'em on the idea of havin' their functions at The Shake-Shake. [*He looks at her, but sees that she is still unimpressed.*] We could even change the name y'know. Get fancy. Somethin' like The C and B Lounge. Somethin' with class. You be the "official hostess." Wear one o' them spangled gowns.

BEVERLY: [*Icily.*] Which you pick out.

CALEB: [*Ignoring the ice.*] You could stand there at the door . . . greetin' people . . . pinnin' flowers on their lapel . . . smilin'! [*Seeing that she still does not react.*] Hey . . . I thought I was talkin' to you.

BEVERLY: I heard you.

CALEB: Well, you coulda fooled me. I mean, most chicks woulda been a little bit excited.

BEVERLY: [*Coolly at first.*] I was. For just a li'l ol' minute there, I was excited. No, that ain't the truth. I waltzed through this town all day long . . . floated down the street and danced around the corner. Every time I turned an' saw you dartin' in an' out of this or that doorway, heard you honkin' on that horn to let me know you was still somewhere around. I was excited then. An' when you . . . let yourself go back there . . .

CALEB: [*Defensively.*] That's what you wanted wasn't it?

BEVERLY: I almost thought you was kissin' me . . . but I know you was just punchin' Roger!

CALEB: [*Sharply.*] That's a lie! I kissed you because [*He can't say it.*] . . . because . . .

BEVERLY: [*Tightly.*] See what I mean? You can't even say it! [*She starts for the door, but* CALEB *takes her arm and stops her exit.*]

CALEB: [*Quietly. Intensely.*] You're muddyin' the waters, baby. What you're lookin' for I can't be an' don't wanna be. That ol' gotcha to the grave jive done played out . . . at least it has for me. Beverly, you're the most . . . comfortable . . . broad I know. An' I want you around. We can have a good time together.

BEVERLY: [*Pulling from him.*] I'm wise.

CALEB: I ain't no saint. Ain't nothin' platonic in what I'm talkin' about. I want you to use me an' I'm gonna use you . . . but I won't hurt you an' you won't hurt me. If it gets raggedy, you split an' won't be no questions asked. Same goes for me. Hey, Beverly, you're young, but I've been through it all an' I know. This is the best thing for right now. We grow as the relationship grows. Hey, just pick my brains; share my soul . . . 'cause you're the only one I want to have it. [BEVERLY *looks at him. She sees him differently and is warmed by what she sees, warmed but not satisfied.*]

BEVERLY: [*Noncommittal in spite of the words.*] I'll get my things. [*She exits up the stairs.* CALEB *looks after her, sighs and turns to the audience.*]

CALEB: Well, I had to do somethin! An' it ain't like I was lyin' 'cause I do care about the broad. When I saw her breakin' bread with that . . . other dude, well, I knew I had to get my program together. Like, ain't nothin' I wouldn't do to keep my woman mine . . . 'cept for one o' those long term contracts an' all that jive. An' I'm a treat her good, too. Just like I told her old man I would 'cause, y'see, the first time I saw her, I had a reaction. Can you dig it?

[*Knocks at the door.* LI'L BITS *enters wearing a chic white suit and carrying a small bouquet of flowers.*]

LI'L BITS: [*Looking around, calling.*] Mother Harrison! "Whoooooohoooo"! Mother Harrison!

CALEB: Mother who?

[*She responds by extending her hand and showing a wedding band.*]

LI'L BITS: Ain't got no stone yet, but I can wait. [CALEB *bursts into laughter and collapses into a chair.* LI'L BITS *crossing to the stairs.*] Laugh all you want, Mister . . . but I got what I want! [*Calls.*] Mother Harrison!

[MYRA *comes quickly into the room.*]

MYRA: Who that callin' me "Mother . . . "? [*Seeing* LI'L BITS, *impressed by her appearance.*] Ohhhhhhhh, turn around an' let me see it from the back. [*As* LI'L BITS *models*.] Now, that's taste. I mean, you really wearin' that suit! You just graduate from school or somethin?

CALEB: [*Laughing.*] Naw, Miss Mattie. She just did somethin' real fine for the family!

MYRA: [*It hasn't connected.*] You just keep that "Miss Mattie" outta your mouth! [*Back to* LI'L BITS.] Now, what did you say?

LI'L BITS: Me an' Felix . . . we decided it was time . . . [*Before she can finish, the door opens and* MRS. CALDWELL *enters carrying a suitcase. She is also dressed.*]

MRS. CALDWELL: [*She speaks rapidly.*] How're y'all doin'? Where you want these things, Josephine?

LI'L BITS: Just put 'em in the middle room?

MYRA: What "middle room"? I know you ain't talkin' about that room upstairs!

MRS. CALDWELL: [*To* LI'L BITS.] Girl, you done set yourself down in a pot o' honey. I ain't even know colored folks live like this. [*To* MYRA.] Y'all got a fine place here . . . an' I wanna thank you!

MYRA: WHO IS THIS WOMAN?

LI'L BITS: That's my momma. Y'all just about sisters now.

[MRS. CALDWELL *takes the box and continues off.*]

MRS. CALDWELL: Yeah, child . . . a pot o' honey! [*She exits.*]

MYRA: [*Starts after* MRS. CALDWELL, *turns back to* LI'L BITS.] Somebody better tell me somethin' . . . folks walkin' all over my house!

CALEB: Go on, Li'l Bits . . . lay it on her.

LI'L BITS: That ain't my name no more . . . not since ten fifteen this mornin', it ain't.

[AVERY *enters, buckling his belt.*]

AVERY: What in the name o' sense is goin' on here? I'm sittin in the bathroom an' this strange woman come openin' the door all . . .

MYRA: Avery, I'm scared to say what my mind is thinkin'. [*They both look at* LI'L BITS. *She extends her hand, showing them the ring.*] Where is Felix? Where is that little sapsucker?

LI'L BITS: Got married this mornin' over in Delaware . . . but I tol' Felix there wasn't gon' be no honeymoon 'til he come back here and worked out how he was gon keep on going to school even though he had a wife to support.

MYRA: [*Weak, staggering.*] I've got to sit down.

LI'L BITS: Well, I know y'all don't want no child o' yours living down there in the ghetto. [*Sound of a truck outside.*]

CALEB:.[*Enjoying the whole scene.*] That must be the groom pulling into the driveway now . . . in a pick-up!

MYRA: A pick-up? He parkin' a pick-up in our driveway!

MRS. CALDWELL: [*Offstage, yelling.*] Josephine! If that's Arthur, tell him I'll be right down to help him unpack. [MYRA *rushes to the window to look at the truck.*]

LI'L BITS: Momma figured we need a few things to start us off so she give up her ol' kitchen set. Arthur, that's her boyfriend, he figured it would be easier to bring it all over at one time rather than piece by piece so he loaned us his pick-up.

MYRA: It's got cement all over it! [*Yelling out.*] JUNIOR, YOU GET THAT RATTLE-TRAP OUTTA THERE AN "BRING YOUR- SELF ON IN HERE"!!!

AVERY: Myra, will you stop hollarin'. The neighbors will think it's ours!

[MRS. CALDWELL *re-enters.*]

MRS. CALDWELL: Yeah, y'all got a fine place here an' you can bet a fat man I'm gon' be a frequent caller. Give me someplace to get away from them niggahs in the ghetto.

[FELIX *enters. He is wearing a blue suit with a flower in his lapel and car- ries a chair. When he appears, the room becomes suddenly quiet until* CALEB *rushes up to him and shakes his hand.*]

CALEB: More power to you, blood. Hope you lotsa happy. [*Puts an arm around him and faces the group. It is obvious that* MYRA *has disowned him. She looks the other way.*]

FELIX: I was gonna tell you, but . . .

MRS. CALDWELL: [*Interrupting.*] Girl, these young folks today don't tell you nothin'. [*Moving toward the doorway.*] I'm gon' go out here an' help Arthur. [*Pauses, looks around again.*] Yeah, child . . . a pot o' honey! A place like this an' your momma could retire in style! [*She exits.*]

MYRA: [*A reprimanding whisper to* FELIX.] I wanna talk to you, Mr. Man. Married or not, you gon' stay in this house 'til we get this mess straightened out!

CALEB: An' no more bike ridin' either, Junior!

FELIX: [*Calling on his adulthood.*] But you don't understand, Ma. [*Takes* LI'L BITS' *hand.*] This is my wife. Mrs. Felix Harrison . . . an' we kinda think there might be somebody else, too.

LI'L BITS: Hannibal if it's a boy an' Cleopatra if it's a girl.

MYRA: [*Unable to speak from shock and disappointment.*] But you . . . uh . . . I . . . Avery, say somethin'.

[*He helps her to her seat, props a pillow behind her back.*]

CALEB: An' I tried to warn the cat, too.

AVERY: [*With ministerial compassion.*] Well, son . . . uh . . .

MYRA: [*Pained to the bone, muttering.*] All my plans . . .

AVERY: Marriage is an important step . . .

MYRA: Could've given us some warnin' . . . an' a baby, too.

AVERY: [*Definite, but not abusive.*] Mattie, will you hush!

MYRA: I beg your pardon. The name is Myra.

AVERY: [*Ignoring her.*] Welcome to the family, Miss Bits. I hope it's a boy. [*He hugs* LI'L BITS, *shakes his son's hand.*] . . . but about that middle room . . . I think maybe you all better . . . [BEVERLY *enters with a suitcase.*]

BEVERLY: Uncle Avery, some people are out there tryin' to get a table through the kitchen door. What's goin' on here?

CALEB: Felix took the plunge . . . much to the surprise of his mommy an' daddy.

BEVERLY: You mean . . . [LI'L BITS *flashes her ring.* BEVERLY *embraces her.*] I'm so happy for you. For both of you.

MYRA: [*Suddenly.*] When's the baby due?

LI'L BITS: Don't worry momma. I took a ball point pen an' back dated the license. Everything's cool.

CALEB: An' they live happily ever after. [*To* BEVERLY.] Get your things. [BEVERLY *motions to her bag.* CALEB *goes to pick it up.*]

AVERY: You're leavin'?

CALEB: That's right. She's movin' in with me. [*He takes her hand and starts for the door.*]

FELIX: You're lyin'.

AVERY: For what?

MYRA: Humph.

CALEB: [*To* MYRA.] Wrong! We just happen to like each other. Want to take care of each other an' we feel good together.

AVERY: Now, Beverly, remember I'm a preacher. [MRS. CALDWELL *enters from the kitchen.*]

LI'L BITS: [*Bringing her mother up to date.*] They movin' in together.

MRS. CALDWELL: Girl don't you do that. He ain't gon' treat you worth a damn, anyway can't even take him to court.

MYRA: [*Surprised that she is agreeing.*] He wanna sleep in the same bed with you, make him do it right! Ol' lowlife slickster.

CALEB: [*To* MYRA.] You the one with your mind in the gutter!

MYRA: That's cause I know you!

MRS. CALDWELL: An' if she don't, I do. That livin' in ain't worth a damn . . . an' any man what ask you to do that don't respect you in the first place!

CALEB: [*Angrily.*] Don't be washin' my face with your outdated colored morals! They's more to a relationship than just sleepin' in the same bed. There's havin' somebody around you who understands you . . . who appreciates you. I need that in my life. I can always find somebody to sleep with. [AVERY *clears his throat.*] That's right. I happen to think I've got somethin' I want to share with Beverly an' she must feel the same way or else she wouldn't be comin' down there with me . . . like, I'm glad Junior had the heart to tighten it up with this child here. Everybody oughta try it once, but I had mine once. [*Looks at* BEVERLY.] An' anyway, I dig this broad too much to be throwin' some marriage at her.

AVERY: Now, that's about the craziest thing I ever heard of. Beverly, take that suitcase on back upstairs!

BEVERLY: That's my club! My daddy left it to me an' that's where I'ma stay.

CALEB: He don't understand nothin' like that. Only reason he so heavy into that matrimonial bag is 'cause folks slip him some green every time he put on that robe.

AVERY: [*Hot.*] That's a blasphemous lie! Sometimes I don't even take that money.

[*There is a knock at the door.* MRS. CALDWELL *crosses to open it causing*

MYRA *to snort her disapproval of her taking the liberty of answering the door unasked.*]

MRS. CALDWELL: Don't nobody named Beverly live here.

BEVERLY: That's me.

MRS. CALDWELL: [*Coming back into the room.*] For real? Some white man was out there looking for you. I was about to tell him he had the wrong house.

BEVERLY: Oh, no.

MRS. CALDWELL: How did I know? [MRS. CALDWELL *looks suspiciously at* BEVERLY. BEVERLY *crosses to the front door.*] You go out with white men?

CALEB: [*Magnanimously.*] Break it to him easy, baby . . . he give you any static, you come get me. [BEVERLY *looks at him as if he were crazy and exits. We hear her call once, "Roger."*]

MYRA: I don't understand it. Child got her self a white man . . . a real estate broker an' she'd rather live with [*Points to* CALEB.] with . . . that!

CALEB: Miss Myra, don't you know you're a relic! Them ol' "white is right" days is gone!

MRS. CALDWELL: Tell her about it. 'Course, it ain't my business. [BEVERLY *re-enters, looking anxiously about the room.*]

BEVERLY: Anybody see my white purse?

LI'L BITS: [*Taking it from the end table.*] Here it is.

CALEB: Where're you goin'?

BEVERLY: [*Taking the purse.*] Oh . . . the bag's over there. Don't wait up for me. Just leave the light on. [*She starts out again.*]

CALEB: BEVERLY, YOU COME BACK HERE!

BEVERLY: [*At the doorway.*] I ain't got time now. Roger's waitin'.

CALEB: I fixed that place up for you an' you said you was gon' live in it an' that's just what the hell you're gon' do right now.

BEVERLY: [*Amazed at his certainty.*] No, I ain't. "Right now" I'm goin' out to dinner with a gentleman.

CALEB: [*Accusingly to* AVERY.] See that! I offer that broad the world an' she turn it down . . . for a white boy!

BEVERLY: I did not.

MYRA: Don't waste your time. The car's runnin'.

BEVERLY: I'm comin' down there just like you said. [*With an edge.*] An' we're goin' have just the kind of relationship you said. "Marriage is outdated, outmoded an' somethin' black folks don't need to be bothered with." Fine, but I ain't gon' play like I got the real thing when I ain't got nothin' but a *cheap imitation!* [*Supportive comments from the others.*] An' you don't need to worry none . . . 'cause Roger ain't my type . . . black or white. But I'll tell you one thing, you better watch out . . . 'cause right now his offer is a damn sight lot more better than yours. I can shack up with any ol' body.

CALEB: [*Besides himself.*] You gon' make me say it, ain't ya?

BEVERLY: You ain't got the heart. Scared you' gon' commit yourself!

AVERY: [*To* MYRA.] Say what . . . [*She hunches him to be quiet.*]

CALEB: The hell I ain't.

BEVERLY: [*Taking an "I dare you" pose.*] I'm waiting. [*Knowing he is on the spot,* CALEB *moves from her, trying to get his nerve together. The family folk stare at him as one does at a man who has just bitten off more than he can chew.*]

CALEB: All right . . . All right. I . . . I, uh . . . [*Seeing the others looking at him.*] What the hell're y'all lookin' at? [BEVERLY *sighs as if "bored."* CALEB, *running it together.*] Beverly, I don't want you to go out there with that dude 'cause I'm crazy about you, that good enough? [*The others are both surprised and seemingly relieved.*]

BEVERLY: [*Smiling as she moves to him.*] For me to move into my apartment across the hall from you? Oh, that's more than enough. But for me to give you exclusive rights, you gotta come a little stronger than that! An' for me to get you what I feel . . . what I feel for you . . . [*Abruptly.*] Don't wait up for me, just leave a light on! [BEVERLY *exits with determined strides.* CALEB *moves about the room, trying to play it off and hold onto the remainder of his "cool."*]

CALEB: See that! Ya can't never satisfy a sister! Never! [MYRA *rises, smiles benignly at* CALEB *and turns.*]

MYRA: Well, since it seems like our family proliferatin', I guess we'd better be about makin' a quick announcement to the public an' havin' a reception . . . I'll make up the guest list. You all can help with the menu.

MRS. CALDWELL: That's fine with me. Just don't be invitin' none o' them ol' juiceheads off the avenue, 'cept maybe for my boyfriend, Arthur an' Sneaky-Pepe Patterson! [MYRA *shakes her head as the trio exits chattering.*]

AVERY: [*Winking at* FELIX.] Well, looks like things gon' be all right after all. [FELIX *rises and he and* LI'L BITS *prepare to leave.*]

CALEB: [*Still sulking.*] I could half way deal with it if the cat was a blood.

LI'L BITS: Humph! Most o' them thinkin' just like you: tryin' to get over, get down an' stay loose! [*Looks sweetly at* FELIX.] 'Cept for some. [*They also exit, hand in hand.* LI'L BITS, *calling after them.*] An' all you middleclassed blacks actin' like it all right . . . like, that's the way things s'posed to be!

AVERY: [*Stretching, rising.*] Now, I'll tell ya . . . me, myself . . . I ain't prejudiced . . . but I read in *Ebony* where . . .

CALEB: [*Sharply.*] Damn an' *Ebony*! I'm talkin' about my woman.

AVERY: Said the same thing in *Jet*! Y'all must ain't doin' somethin' right. G'night. [*He exits, leaving* CALEB *slouched in the chair, hat covering his eyes. The lights begin to dimout.*]

CALEB: [*Snatching his hat from his eyes and leaping to his feet.*] Hold them damn lights! I ain't finished. Don't no broad get the last word on Cal Johnson. . . [*Moving toward the audience.*] An' you bet' no laugh either 'cause I knew this was gon' happen. They do it every damn time. Soon's you get your program together, here come some ol' tackhead to make a punk an' a liar outta you. I knew it when I kissed the broad. Once a chick know she got your nose open, she gon' make you crawl . . . lead you around like a seein' eye dog do a blind man! . . . [*Muttering.*] Tryin' to make somebody say they love her. [*Bold.*] Well, I do! . . . an' I'm scared to death behin' all them weddin' bells . . . an' them toasters . . . his an' hers towels an' don't say nothin' about them Sunbeam mixmasters! [*Wide open.*] The hell with her! Let her go on with Roger!!!! He needs her. He ain't got no women . . . just "persons" . . . Fire persons! An' police persons! Let him have her . . . [*Pause.*] For tonight, that is. Tomorrow, she's mine! . . . yeah, I know, it's a bourgie plot! But ya got to give it to the old boy, I was cool. Right down to the very end, the kid was cool. [*Smiles, satisfied with himself.*] Hey, light man . . . you can turn 'em out now. I'm through.

[*Curtain.*]

George C. Wolfe

THE COLORED MUSEUM

GEORGE C. WOLFE

Producer of the New York Shakespeare Festival/Joseph Papp Public Theater and the author of *The Colored Museum*. (Crossroads Theatre, NYSF, The Royal Court Theatre). For the Public Theatre: adapted and directed *Spunk*, three tales by Zora Neale Hurston; curated two seasons of a Festival of New Voices (as an NYSF Artistic Associate); directed Brecht's *Caucasian Chalk Circle* (adapted by Thulani Davis), Anna Deavere Smith's *Twilight: Los Angeles, 1992*, which moved to Broadway and *Blade to the Heat*. For "American Playhouse" he directed *Fires In The Mirror* and co-directed for *Great Performances, The Colored Museum*. For Broadway: writer and director of *Jelly's Last Jam*, director of Tony Kushner's *Angels in America: Millennium Approaches* (Tony Award) and *Perestroika*. He was recently honored as a "Living Landmark" by the New York Landmarks Conservancy. Other awards include Drama Desk, Outer Critics Circle, Obie, AUDELCO, Oppenheimer, Hull-Wariner and, most recently, "The Spirit of the City" Award and a LAMBDA Liberty Award. Mr. Wolfe is the co-creator of *Bring in 'da Noise, Bring in 'da Funk* [*a Tap/Rap Discourse on the Staying Power of the Beat*] (Five Tony Awards).

THE CAST

An ensemble of five, two men and three women, all black, who perform all the characters that inhabit the exhibits. A little girl, seven to twelve years old, is needed for a walk-on part in Lala's Opening.

THE STAGE

White walls and recessed lighting. A starkness befitting a museum where the myths and madness of black/Negro/colored Americans are stored.

Built into the walls are a series of small panels, doors, revolving walls, and compartments from which actors can retrieve key props and make quick entrances.

A revolve is used, which allows for quick transitions from one exhibit to the next.

MUSIC

All of the music for the show should be pre-recorded. Only the drummer, who is used in Git on Board, *and then later in* Permutations *and* The Party, *is live.*

THERE IS NO INTERMISSION

THE EXHIBITS

Git on Board
Cookin' with Aunt Ethel
The Photo Session
Soldier with a Secret
The Gospel According to Miss Roj
The Hairpiece
The Last Mama-on-the-Couch Play
Symbiosis
Lala's Opening
Permutations
The Party

CHARACTERS

Git on Board
    MISS PAT

Cookin' with Aunt Ethel
    AUNT ETHEL

The Photo Session
    GIRL
    GUY

Soldier with a Secret
    JUNIE ROBINSON

The Gospel According to Miss Roj
    MISS ROJ
    WAITER

The Hairpiece
    THE WOMAN
    JANINE
    LAWANDA

The Last Mama-on-the-Couch Play
    NARRATOR
    MAMA
    WALTER-LEE-BEAU-WILLIE-JONES
    LADY IN PLAID
    MEDEA JONES

Symbiosis
    THE MAN
    THE KID

Lala's Opening
    LALA LAMAZING GRACE
    ADMONIA
    FLO'RANCE
    THE LITTLE GIRL

Permutations
    NORMAL JEAN REYNOLDS

The Party
    TOPSY WASHINGTON
    MISS PAT
    MISS ROJ
    LALA LAMAZING GRACE
    THE MAN (from *Symbiosis*)

GIT ON BOARD

Blackness. Cut by drums pounding. Then slides, rapidly flashing before us. Images we've all seen before, of African slaves being captured, loaded onto ships, tortured. The images flash, flash, flash. The drums crescendo. Blackout. And then lights reveal MISS PAT, *frozen. She is black, pert, and cute. She has a flip to her hair and wears a hot pink mini-skirt stewardess uniform.*

She stands in front of a curtain which separates her from an offstage cockpit.

An electronic bell goes "ding" and MISS PAT *comes to life, presenting herself in a friendly but rehearsed manner, smiling and speaking as she has done so many times before.*

MISS PAT: Welcome aboard Celebrity Slaveship, departing the Gold Coast and making short stops at Bahia, Port Au Prince, and Havana, before our final destination of Savannah.

Hi. I'm Miss Pat and I'll be serving you here in Cabin A. We will be crossing the Atlantic at an altitude that's pretty high, so you must wear your shackles at all times.

[*She removes a shackle from the overhead compartment and demonstrates.*]

To put on your shackle, take the right hand and close the metal ring around your left hand like so. Repeat the action using your left hand to secure the right. If you have any trouble bonding yourself, I'd be more than glad to assist.

Once we reach the desired altitude, the Captain will turn off the "Fasten Your Shackle" sign . . . [*She efficiently points out the* "FASTEN YOUR SHACKLES" *signs on either side of her, which light up.*] . . . allowing you a chance to stretch and dance in the aisles a bit. But otherwise, shackles must be worn at all times.

[*The* "FASTEN YOUR SHACKLES" *signs go off.*]

MISS PAT: Also, we ask that you please refrain from call-and-response singing between cabins as that sort of thing can lead to rebellion. And, of course, no drums are allowed on board. Can you repeat after me, "No drums." [*She get the audience to repeat.*] With a little more enthusiasm, please. "No drums." [*After the audience repeats it.*] That was great! Once we're airborn, I'll be by with magazines, and earphones can be purchased for the price of your first-born male.

If there's anything I can do to make this middle passage more pleasant, press the little button over-head and I'll be with you faster than you can say, "Go down, Moses." [*She laughs at her "little joke".*]

Thanks for flying Celebrity and here's hoping you have a pleasant take off.

[*The engines surge, the "Fasten Your Shackles" signs go on, and over-articulate Muzak voices are heard singing as* MISS PAT *pulls down a bucket seat and "shackles-up" for takeoff.*]

VOICES: Get on board Celebrity Slaveship
Get on board Celebrity Slaveship
Get on board Celebrity Slaveship
There's room for many a more!

[*The engines reach an even, steady hum. Just as* MISS PAT *rises and replaces the shackles in the overhead compartment, the faint sound of African drumming is heard.*]

MISS PAT: Hi. Miss Pat again. I'm sorry to disturb you, but someone is playing drums. And what did we just say . . . "No drums." It must be someone in Coach. But we here in Cabin A are not going to respond to those drums. As a matter of fact, we don't even hear them. Repeat after me. "I don't hear any drums." [*The audience repeats.*] And "I will not rebel."

[*The audience repeats. The drumming grows.*]

MISS PAT: [*Placating.*] OK, now I realize some of us are a bit edgy after hearing about the tragedy on board The Laughing Mary, but let me assure you Celebrity has no intention of throwing you overboard and collecting the insurance. We value you!

[*She proceeds to single out individual passengers/audience members.*]

Why the songs *you* are going to sing in the cotton fields, under the burning heat and stinging lash, will metamorphose and give birth to the likes of James Brown and the Fabulous Flames. And you, yes *you*, are going to come up with some of the best dances. The best dances! The Watusi! The Funky Chicken! And just think of what *you* are going to mean to William Faulkner.

All right, so you're gonna have to suffer for a few hundred years, but from your pain will come a culture so complex. *And*, with this little item here . . . [*She removes a basketball from the overhead compartment.*] . . . you'll become millionaires!

[*There is a roar of thunder. The lights quiver and the "*FASTEN YOUR SHACKLES*" signs begin to flash.* MISS PAT *quickly replaces the basketball in the overhead compartment and speaks very reassuringly.*]

MISS PAT: No, don't panic. I'm here to take care of you. We're just flying through a little thunder storm. Now the only way you're going to make it through this one is if you abandon your God and worship a new one. So, on the count of three, let's all sing. One, two, three ...

Nobody knows de trouble I seen

Oh, I forgot to mention, when singing, omit the T-H sound. "The" becomes "de". "They" becomes "dey". Got it? Good!
Nobody knows ...
Nobody knows ...

Oh, so you don't like that one? Well then let's try another——

Summer time
And de livin' is easy ...

Gershwin. He comes from another oppressed people so he understands.

Fish are jumpin' ... come on.
And de cotton is high.

Sing, damnit!

[*Lights begin to flash, the engines surge, and there is wild drumming.* MISS PAT *sticks her head through the curtain and speaks with an offstage* CAPTAIN.]

MISS PAT: What?

VOICE OF CAPTAIN [*Offstage.*]: Time warp!

MISS PAT: Time warp! [*She turns to the audience and puts on a pleasant face.*] The Captain has assured me everything is fine. We're just caught in a little time warp. [*Trying to fight her growing hysteria.*] On your right you will see the American Revolution, which will give the U.S. of A exclusive rights to your life. And on your left, the Civil War, which means you will vote Republican until F.D.R. comes along. And now we're passing over the Great Depression, which means everybody gets to live the way you've been living. [*There is a blinding flash of light, and an explosion. She screams.*] Ahhhhhhhhhh! That was World War I, which is not to be confused with World War II ... [*There is a larger flash of light, and another explosion.*] ... Ahhhhh! Which is not to be confused with the Korean War or the Vietnam War, all of which you will play a major role in.
    Oh, look, now we're passing over the sixties. Martha and Vandellas ... Malcolm X. [*There is a gun shot.*] ... "Julia" with Miss Diahann Carroll ... and five little girls in Sunday school ... [*There is an explosion.*] Martin Luther King ... [*A gun shot.*] Oh no! The Supremes just broke up! [*The drumming intensifies.*] Stop playing those drums. I said, stop playing those damn drums. You can't stop

history! You can't stop time! Those drums will be confiscated once we reach Savannah. Repeat after me. I don't hear any drums and I will not rebel. I will not rebel! I will not re—

[*The lights go out, she screams, and the sound of a plane landing and screeching to a halt is heard. After a beat, lights reveal a wasted, disheveled* MISS PAT, *but perky nonetheless.*]

MISS PAT: Hi. Miss Pat here. Things got a bit jumpy back there, but the Captain has just informed me we have safely landed in Savannah. Please check the overhead before exiting as any baggage you don't claim, we trash.

It's been fun, and we hope the next time you consider travel, it's with Celebrity.

[*Luggage begins to revolve onstage from offstage left, going past* MISS PAT *and revolving offstage right. Mixed in with the luggage are two male slaves and a woman slave, complete with luggage and I.D. tags around their necks.*]

MISS PAT: [*With routine, rehearsed pleasantness.*]

Have a nice day. Bye bye.
Button up that coat, it's kind of chilly. Have a nice day. Bye bye.
You take care now.
See you.
Have a nice day.
Have a nice day.
Have a nice day.

COOKIN' WITH AUNT ETHEL

As the slaves begin to revolve off, a low-down gutbucket blues is heard.
AUNT ETHEL, *a down-home black woman with a bandanna on her head,*
revolves to center stage. She stands behind a big black pot and wears a re-
assuring grin.

AUNT ETHEL: Welcome to "Aunt Ethel's Down-Home Cookin' Show,"
where we explores the magic and mysteries of colored cuisine. Today,
we gonna be servin' ourselves up some . . . [*She laughs.*] I'm not gonna
tell you. That's right! I'm not gonna tell you what it is till after you
done cooked it. Child, on "The Aunt Ethel Show" we loves to have
ourselves some fun. Well, are you ready? Here goes.

[*She belts out a hard-drivin' blues and throws invisible ingredients into the*
big, black pot.]

First ya add a pinch of style
And then a dash of flair
Now ya stir in some preoccupation
With the texture of your hair

Next ya add all kinds of rhythms
Lots of feeling and pizzaz
Then hunny throw in some rage
Till it congeals and turns to jazz

Now you cookin'
Cookin' with Aunt Ethel
You really cookin'
Cookin with Aunt Ethel, oh yeah

Now ya add a-heap of survival
And humility, just a touch
Add some attitude
Oops! I put too much

And now a whole lot of humor
Salty language mixed with sadness
Then throw in a box of blues
And simmer to madness

Now you cookin'
Cookin' with Aunt Ethel, oh yeah

Now you beat it — Really work it
Discard and disown
And in a few hundred years

Once it's aged and fully grown
Ya put it in the oven
Till it's black
And has a sheen
Or till it's nice and yella
Or any shade in between

Next ya take 'em out and cool 'em
'Cause they no fun when they hot
And won't you be surprised
At the concoction you got

You have baked
Baked yourself a batch of Negroes
Yes you have baked yourself
Baked yourself a batch of Negroes

[*She pulls from the pot a handful of Negroes, black dolls.*]

But don't ask me what to do with 'em now that you got 'em, 'cause child, that's your problem [*She throws the dolls back into the pot.*] But in any case, yaw be sure to join Aunt Ethel next week, when we gonna be servin' ourselves up some chitlin quiche...some grits-under-glass,

And a sweet potato pie
And you'll be cookin'
Cookin' with Aunt Ethel
Oh, yeah!

[*On* AUNT ETHEL's *final rift, lights reveal...*]

THE PHOTO SESSION

...a very glamorous, gorgeous, black couple, wearing the best of everything and perfect smiles. The stage is bathed in color and bright white light. Disco music with the chant: "We're fabulous" plays in the background. As they pose, larger-than-life images of their perfection are projected on the museum walls. The music quiets and the images fade away as they begin to speak and pose.

GIRL: The world was becoming too much for us.

GUY: We couldn't resolve the contradictions of our existence.

GIRL: And we couldn't resolve yesterday's pain.

GUY: So we gave away our life and we now live inside *Ebony Magazine.*

GIRL: Yes, we live inside a world where everyone is beautiful, and wears fabulous clothes.

GUY: And no one says anything profound.

GIRL: Or meaningful.

GUY: Or contradictory.

GIRL: Because no one talks. Everyone just smiles and shows off their cheekbones. [*They adopt a profile pose.*] Last month I was black and fabulous while holding up a bottle of vodka.

GIRL: This month we get to be black and fabulous together.

[*They dance/pose. The "We're fabulous" chant builds and then fades as they start to speak again.*]

GIRL: There are of course setbacks.

GUY: We have to smile like this for a whole month.

GIRL: And we have no social life.

GUY: And no sex.

GIRL: And at times it feels like we're suffocating, like we're not human anymore.

GUY: And everything is rehearsed, including this other kind of pain we're starting to feel.

GIRL: The kind of pain that comes from feeling no pain at all.

[*They then speak and pose with a sudden burst of energy.*]

GUY: But one can't have everything.

GIRL: Can one?

GUY: So if the world is becoming too much for you, do like we did.

GIRL: Give away your life and come be beautiful with us.

GUY: We guarantee, no contradictions.

GIRL/GUY: Smile/click, smile/click, smile/click.

[*They adopt a final pose and revolve off as the "We're fabulous" chant plays and fades into the background.*]

A SOLDIER WITH A SECRET

Projected onto the museum walls are the faces of black soldiers—from the Spanish-American thru to the Vietnam War. Lights slowly reveal JUNIE ROBINSON, *a black combat soldier, posed on an onyx plinth. He comes to life and smiles at the audience. Somewhat dim-witted, he has an easy-going charm about him.*

JUNIE: Pst. Pst. I know the secret. The secret to your pain. 'Course, I didn't always know. First I had to die, then come back to life, 'fore I had the gift. Ya see the Cappin sent me off up ahead to scout for screamin' yella bastards. 'Course, for the life of me I couldn't understand why they'd be screamin', seein' as how we was tryin' to kill them and they us. But anyway, I'm off lookin', when all of a sudden I find myself caught smack dead in the middle of this explosion. This blindin' burnin', scaldin', explosion. Musta been a booby trap or something, 'cause all around me is fire. Hell, I'm on fire. Like a piece of chicken dropped in a skillet of cracklin' grease. Why, my flesh was justa peelin' off of my bones. But then I says to myself, "Junie, if yo' flesh is on fire, how come you don't feel no pain!" And I didn't. I swear as I'm standin' here, I felt nuthin'. That's when I sort of put two and two together and realized I didn't feel no whole lot of hurtin' cause I done died. Well I just picked myself up and walked right on out of that explosion. Hell, once you know you dead, why keep on dyin', ya know? So, like I say, I walk right outta that explosion, fully expectin' to see white clouds, Jesus, and my Mama, only all I saw was more war. Shootin' goin' on way off in this direction and that direction. And there, standin' around, was all the guys. Hubert, J.F., the Cappin. I guess the sound of the explosion must of attracted 'em, and they all starin' at me like I'm some kind of ghost. So I yells to 'em "Hey there Hubert! Hey there Cappin!" But they just stare. So I tells 'em how I'd died and how I guess it wasn't my time cause here I am, "Fully in the flesh and not a scratch to my bones." And they still just stare. So I took to starin' back.

[*The expression on* JUNIE'S *face slowly turns to horror and disbelief.*]

Only what I saw . . . well I can't exactly to this day describe it. But I swear, as sure as they was wearin' green and holdin' guns, they was each wearin' a piece of the future on their faces.

Yeah. All the hurt that was gonna get done to them and they was gonna do to folks was right there clear as day. I saw how J.F., once he got back to Chicago, was gonna get shot dead by this police, and I saw how Hubert was gonna start beatin' up on his old lady which I didn't understand, 'cause all he could do was talk on and on about how much he loved her. Each and every one of 'em had pain in his future and blood on his path. And God or the Devil one spoke to me and said, "Junie, these colored boys ain't gonna be the same after this war. They ain't gonna have no kind of happiness."

Well right then and there it come to me. The secret to their pain.

Late that night, after the medics done checked me over and found me fit for fightin', after everybody done settle down for the night, I sneaked over to where Hubert was sleepin', and with a needle I stole from the medics . . . pst, pst . . . I shot a little air into his veins. The second he died, all the hurtin-to-come just left his face.

Two weeks later I got J.F. and after that Woodrow . . . Jimmy Joe . . . I even spent all night waitin' by the latrine 'cause I knew the Cappin always made a late night visit and pst . . . pst . . . I got him.

[*Smiling, quite proud of himself.*]

That's how come I died and come back to life. 'Cause just like Jesus went around healin' the sick, I'm supposed to go around healin' the hurtin' all these colored boys wearin' from the war.

Pst, pst. I know the secret. The secret to your pain. The secret to yours, and yours. Pst. Pst. Pst. Pst.

[*The lights slowly fade.*]

THE GOSPEL ACCORDING TO MISS ROJ

The darkness is cut by electronic music. Cold, pounding, unrelenting. A neon sign which spells out THE BOTTOMLESS PIT *clicks on. There is a lone bar stool. Lights flash on and off, pulsating to the beat. There is a blast of smoke and, from the haze,* MISS ROJ *appears. He is dressed in striped patio pants, white go-go boots, a halter, and cat-shaped sunglasses. What would seem ridiculous on anyone else,* MISS ROJ *wears as if it were high fashion. He carries himself with total elegance and absolute arrogance.*

MISS ROJ: God created black people and black people created style. The name's Miss Roj...that's R.O.J. thank you and you can find me every Wednesday, Friday and Saturday nights at "The Bottomless Pit," the watering hole for the wild and weary which asks the question, "Is there life after Jherri-curl?"

[A waiter enters, hands, MISS ROJ *a drink, and then exits.]*

Thanks, doll. *Yes*, if they be black and swish, the B.P. has seen them, which is not to suggest the Pit is lacking in cultural diversity. Oh no. There are your dinge queens, white men who like their chicken legs dark. *[He winks/flirts with a man in the audience.]* And let's not forget, "Los Muchachos de la Neighborhood." But the speciality of the house is The Snap Queens. *[He snaps his fingers.]* We are a rare breed.

For, you see, when something strikes our fancy, when the truth comes piercing through the dark, well you just can't let it pass unnoticed. No darling. You must pronounce it with a snap. *[He snaps.]*

Snapping comes from another galaxy, as do all snap queens. That's right. I ain't just your regular oppressed American Negro. No-no-no! I am an extra-terrestrial. And I ain't talkin' none of that shit you seen in the movies! I have real power. *[The waiter enters.* MISS ROJ *stops him.]* Speaking of no power, will you please tell Miss Stingy-with-the-rum, that if Miss Roj had wanted to remain sober, she could have stayed home and drank Kool-aid. *[He snaps.]* Thank you.

[The waiter exits. MISS ROJ *crosses and sits on bar stool.]*

Yes, I was placed here on Earth to study the life habits of a deteriorating society, and child when we talkin' New York City, we are discussing the Queen of Deterioration. Miss New York is doing a slow dance with death, and I am here to warn you all, but before I do, I must know...don't you just love my patio pants ? Annette Funicello immortalized them in *Beach Blanket Bingo*, and I have continued the legacy. And my go-gos? I realize white after Labor Day is very gauche, but as the saying goes, if you've got it flaunt it, if you don't, front it and snap to death any bastard who dares to defy you. [*Laughing.*] Oh ho! My demons are showing. Yes, my demons live at the bottom of my Bacardi and Coke. Let's just hope for all concerned I dance my demons out before I drink them out 'cause child, dancing demons take you on a ride, but those drinkin' demons just take you, and you find yourself doing the strangest things. Like the time I locked my father in the broom closet. Seems the liquor made his tongue real liberal and he decided he was gonna baptize me with the word "faggot" over and over. Well, he's just going on and on with "faggot this" and "faggot that," all the while walking toward the broom closet to piss. Poor drunk bastard was just all turned around. So the demons just took hold of my wedges and forced me to kick the drunk son-of-a-bitch into the closet and lock the door. [*Laughter.*] Three days later I remembered he was there. [*He snaps.*]

[*The waiter enters.* MISS ROJ *takes a drink and downs it.*]

Another!

[*The waiter exits.*]

[*Dancing about.*] Oh yes-yes-yes! Miss Roj is quintessential style. I corn row the hairs on my legs so that they spell out M.I.S.S. R.O.J. And I dare any bastard to fuck with me because I will snap your ass into oblivion. I have the power, you know. Everytime I snap, I steal one beat of your heart. So if you find yourself gasping for air in the middle of the night, chances are you fucked with Miss Roj and she didn't like it. Like the time this asshole at Jones Beach decided to take issue with my coulotte-sailor ensemble. This child, this muscle-bound Brooklyn thug in a skintight bikini, very skin-tight so the whole world can see that instead of a brain, God gave him an extra thick piece of sausage. You know the kind who beat up on their wives for breakfast. Well, he decided to blurt out when I walked by, "Hey look at da monkey coon in da faggit suit." Well, I walked up to the poor dear, very calmly lifted my hand, and .... [*He snaps in rapid succession.*] A heart attack, right there on the beach. [*He singles out someone in the audience.*] You don't believe it? Cross me! Come on! Come on!

[*The waiter enters, hands* MISS ROJ *a drink.* MISS ROJ *downs it. The waiter exits.*]

[*Looking around.*] If this place is the answer, we're asking all the wrong questions. The only reason I come here is to communicate with my origins. The flashing lights are signals from my planet way out there. Yes, girl, even further than Flatbush. We're talking another galaxy. The flashing lights tell me how much time is left before the end. [*Very drunk and loud by now.*] I hate the people here. I hate the drinks. But most of all I hate this goddamn music. That ain't music. Give me Aretha Franklin any day. [*Singing*] "Just a little respect. R.E.S.P.E.C.T." Yeah! Yeah!

Come on and dance your last dance with Miss Roj. Last call is but a drink away and each snap puts you one step closer to the end.

A high-rise goes up. You can't get no job. Come on everybody and dance. A whole race of people gets trashed and debased. Snap those fingers and dance. Some sick bitch throws her baby out the window 'cause she thinks it's the Devil. Everybody snap! *The New York Post.* Snap!

Snap for every time you walk past someone lying in the street, smelling like frozen piss and shit and you don't see it. Snap for every crazed bastard who kills himself so as to get the jump on being killed. And snap for every sick muthafucker who, bored with carrying around his fear, takes to shooting up other people.

Yeah, snap your fingers and dance with Miss Roj. But don't be fooled by the banners and balloons 'cause, child, this ain't no party going on. Hell no! It's a wake. And the casket's made out of stone, steel, and glass and the people are racing all over the pavement like maggots on a dead piece of meat.

Yeah dance! But don't be surprised if there ain't no beat holding you together 'cause we traded in our drums for respectability. So now it's just words. Words rappin'. Words screechin'. Words flowin' instead of blood 'cause you know that don't work. Words cracklin' instead of fire 'cause by the time a match is struck on 125th Street and you run to midtown, the flame has been blown away.

So come on and dance with Miss Roj and her demons. We don't ask for acceptance. We don't ask for approval. We know who we are and we move on it!

I guarantee you will never hear two fingers put together in a snap and not think of Miss Roj. That's power, baby. Patio pants and all.

[*The lights begin to flash in rapid succession.*]

So let's dance! And snap! And dance! And snap!

[MISS ROJ *begins to dance as if driven by his demons. There is a blast of smoke and when the haze settles,* MISS ROJ *has revolved off and in place of him is a recording of Aretha Franklin singing, "Respect."*]

THE HAIRPIECE

As "Respect" fades into the background, a vanity revolves to center stage. On this vanity are two wigs, an Afro wig, circa 1968, and a long, flowing wig, both resting on wig stands. A black WOMAN *enters, her head and body wrapped in towels. She picks up a framed picture and after a few moments of hesitation, throws it into a small trash can. She then removes one of her towels to reveal a totally bald head. Looking into a mirror on the "fourth wall, she begins applying makeup.*

The wig stand holding the Afro wig opens her eyes. Her name is JANINE. *She stares in disbelief at the bald woman.*

JANINE: [*Calling to the other wig stand.*] LaWanda. LaWanda girl, wake up.

[*The other wig stand, the one with the long, flowing wig, opens her eyes. Her name is* LAWANDA.]

LAWANDA: What? What is it?

JANINE: Check out girlfriend.

LAWANDA: Oh, girl, I don't believe it.

JANINE: [*Laughing.*] Just look at the poor thing, trying to paint some life onto that face of hers. You'd think by now she'd realize it's the hair. It's all about the hair.

LAWANDA: What hair! She ain't got no hair! She done fried, dyed, de-chemicalized her shit to death.

JANINE: And all that's left is that buck-naked scalp of hers, sittin' up there apologizin' for being odd–shaped and ugly.

LAWANDA: [*Laughing with* JANINE.] Girl, stop!

JANINE: I ain't sayin' nuthin' but the truth.

LAWANDA/JANINE: The bitch is bald! [*They laugh.*]

JANINE: And all over some man.

LAWANDA: I tell ya, girl, I just don't understand it. I mean, look at her. She's got a right nice face, a good head on her shoulders. A good job even. And she's got to go fall in love with that fool.

JANINE: That political quick-change artist. Everytime the nigga went and changed his ideology, she went and changed her hair to fit the occasion.

LAWANDA: Well at least she's breaking up with him.

JANINE: Hunny, no!

LAWANDA: Yes child.

JANINE: Oh, girl, dish me the dirt!

LAWANDA: Well, you see, I heard her on the phone, talking to one of her girlfriends, and she's meeting him for lunch today to give him the ax.

JANINE: Well it's about time.

LAWANDA: I hear ya. But don't you worry 'bout a thing, girlfriend. I'm gonna tell you all about it.

JANINE: Hunny, you won't have to tell me a damn thing 'cause I'm gonna be there, front row, center.

LAWANDA: You?

JANINE: Yes, child, she's wearing me to lunch.

LAWANDA: [*Outrage.*] I don't think so!

JANINE: [*With an attitude.*] What do you mean, you don't think so?

LAWANDA: Exactly what I said, "I don't think so." Damn, Janine, get real. How the hell she gonna wear both of us?

JANINE: She ain't wearing both of us. She's wearing me.

LAWANDA: Says who?

JANINE: Says me! Says her! Ain't that right, girlfriend?

[*The* WOMAN *stops putting on makeup, looks around, sees no one, and goes back to her makeup.*]

JANINE: I said, ain't that right!

[*The* WOMAN *picks up the phone.*]

WOMAN: Hello ... hello ...

JANINE: Did you hear the damn phone ring?

WOMAN: No.

JANINE: Then put the damn phone down and talk to me.

WOMAN: I ah ... don't understand.

JANINE: It ain't deep so don't panic. Now, you're having lunch with your boyfriend, right?

WOMAN: [*Breaking into tears.*] I think I'm having a nervous breakdown.

JANINE: [*Impatient.*] I said you're having lunch with your boyfriend, right!

WOMAN: [*Scared, pulling herself together.*] Yes, right ... right.

JANINE: To break up with him.

WOMAN: How did you know that?

LAWANDA: I told her.

WOMAN: [*Stands and screams.*] Help! Help!

JANINE: Sit down. I said sit your ass down!

[*The* WOMAN *does.*]

JANINE: Now set her straight and tell her you're wearing me.

LAWANDA: She's the one that needs to be set straight, so go on and tell her you're wearing me.

JANINE: No, tell her you're wearing me.

[*There is a pause.*]

LAWANDA: Well?

JANINE: Well?

WOMAN: I ah . . . actually hadn't made up my mind.

JANINE: [*Going off.*] What do you mean you ain't made up you mind! After all that fool has put you through, you gonna need all the attitude you can get and there is nothing like attitude and a healthy head of kinks to make his shit shrivel like it should!

That's right! When you wearin' me, you lettin' him know he ain't gonna get no sweet-talkin' comb through your love without some serious resistance. No-no! The kink of my head is like the kink of your heart and neither is about to be hot-pressed into surrender.

LAWANDA: That shit is so tired. The last time attitude worked on anybody was 1968. Janine girl, you need to get over it and get on with it. [*To the* WOMAN.] And you need to give the nigga a goodbye he will never forget.

I say give him hysteria! Give him emotion! Give him rage! And there is nothing like a toss of the tresses to make your emotional outburst shine with emotional flair.

You can toss me back, shake me from side to side, all the while screaming, "I want you out of my life forever!!!" And not only will I come bouncing back for more, but you just might win an Academy Award for best performance by a head of hair in a dramatic role.

JANINE: Miss hunny, please! She don't need no Barbie doll dipped in chocolate telling her what to do. She needs a head of hair that's coming from a fo' real place.

LAWANDA: Don't you dare talk about nobody coming from a "fo' real place," Miss Made-in-Taiwan!

JANINE: Hey! I ain't ashamed of where I come from. Besides, it don't matter where you come from as long as you end up in the right place.

LAWANDA: And it don't matter the grade as long as the point gets made. So go on and tell her you're wearing me.

JANINE: No, tell her you're wearing me.

[*The* WOMAN, *unable to take it, begins to bite off her fake nails, as* LAWANDA *and* JANINE *go at each other.*]

LAWANDA:	JANINE:
Set the bitch straight. Let her know there is no way she could even begin to compete with me. I am quality. She is kink. I am exotic. She is common. I am class and she is trash. That's right. T.R.A.S.H. We're talking three strikes and you're out. So go on and tell her you're wearing me. Go on, tell her! Tell her! Tell her!	Who you callin' a bitch? Why, if I had hands I'd knock you clear into next week. You think you cute. She thinks she's cute just 'cause that synthetic mop of hers blows in the wind. She looks like a fool and you look like an even bigger fool when you wear her, so go on and tell her you're wearing me. Go on, tell her! Tell her! Tell her!

[*The* WOMAN *screams and pulls the two wigs off the wig stands as the lights go to black on three bald heads.*]

THE LAST MAMA-ON-THE-COUCH PLAY

A NARRATOR, *dressed in a black tuxedo, enters through the audience and stands center stage. He is totally solemn.*

NARRATOR: We are pleased to bring you yet another Mama-on-the-Couch play. A searing domestic drama that tears at the very fabric of racist America. [*He crosses upstage center and sits on a stool and reads from a playscript.*] Act One. Scene One.

[MAMA *revolves on stage left, sitting on a couch reading a large, oversized Bible. A window is placed stage right.* MAMA's *dress, the couch, and drapes are made from the same material. A doormat lays down center.*]

NARRATOR: Lights up on a dreary, depressing, but with middle-class aspirations tenement slum. There is a couch, with a Mama on it. Both are well worn. There is a picture of Jesus on the wall . . . [*A picture of Jesus is instantly revealed.*] . . . and a window which looks onto an abandoned tenement. It is late spring.
      Enter Walter-Lee-Beau-Willie-Jones [SON *enters through the audience.*] He is Mama's thirty-year-old son. His brow is heavy from three hundred years of oppression.

MAMA: [*Looking up from her Bible, speaking in a slow manner.*] Son, did you wipe your feet?

SON: [*An ever-erupting volcano.*] No, Mama, I didn't wipe my feet! Out there, every day, Mama is the Man. The Man Mama. Mr. Charlie! Mr. Bossman! And he's wipin' his feet on me. On me, Mama, every damn day of my life. Ain't that enough for me to deal with? Ain't that enough?

MAMA: Son, wipe your feet.

SON: I wanna dream. I wanna be somebody. I wanna take charge of my life.

MAMA: You can do all of that, but first you got to wipe your feet.

SON: [*As he crosses to the mat, mumbling and wiping his feet.*] Wipe my feet . . . wipe my feet . . . wipe my feet . . .

MAMA: That's a good boy.

SON: [*Exploding.*] Boy! Boy! I don't wanna be nobody's good boy, Mama. I wanna be my own man!

MAMA: I know son, I know. God will show the way.

SON: God, Mama! Since when did your God ever do a damn thing for the black man. Huh, Mama, huh? You tell me. When did your God ever help me.

MAMA: [*Removing her wire-rim glasses.*] Son, come here.

[SON *crosses to* MAMA, *who slowly stands and in an exaggerated stage slap, backhands* SON *clear across the stage. The* NARRATOR *claps his hands to create the sound for the slap.* MAMA *then lifts her clinched fists to the heavens.*]

MAMA: Not in my house, my house, will you ever talk that way again!

[*The* NARRATOR, *so moved by her performance, erupts in applause and encourages the audience to do so.*]

NARRATOR: Beautiful. Just stunning.

[*He reaches into one of the secret compartments of the set and gets an award which he ceremoniously gives to* MAMA *for her performance. She bows and then returns to the couch.*]

NARRATOR: Enter Walter-Lee-Beau-Willie's wife, The Lady in Plaid.

[*Music from nowhere is heard, a jazzy pseudo abstract intro as the* LADY IN PLAID *dances in through the audience, wipes her feet, and then twirls about.*]

LADY: She was a creature of regal beauty
who in ancient time graced the temples of the Nile
with her womanliness.
But here she was stuck being colored
and a woman in a world that valued neither.

SON: You cooked my dinner?

LADY: [*Oblivious to* SON.] Feet flat, back broke,
she looked at the man who, though he be thirty,
still ain't got his own apartment.
Yeah, he's still livin' with his Mama!
And she asked herself, was this the life
for a Princess Colored, who by the
translucence of her skin, knew the
universe was her sister.

[*The* LADY IN PLAID *twirls and dances.*]

SON: [*Becoming irate.*] I've had a hard day of dealin' with the Man. Where's my damn dinner? Woman, stand still when I'm talkin' to you!

LADY: And she cried for her sisters in Detroit
Who knew, as she, that their souls belonged

in ancient temples on the Nile.
And she cried for her sisters in Chicago
who, like her, their life has become one colored hell.

SON: There's only one thing gonna get through to you.

LADY: And she cried for her sisters in New Orleans
and her sisters in Trenton and Birmingham,
and
Poughkeepsie and Orlando and Miami Beach
and
Las Vegas, Palm Springs.

[*As she continues to call out cities, he crosses offstage and returns with two black dolls and then crosses to the window.*]

SON: Now are you gonna cook me dinner?

LADY: Walter-Lee-Beau-Willie-Jones, No! Not my babies!

[SON *throws them out the window. The* LADY IN PLAID *then lets out a primal scream.*]

LADY: He dropped them!!!!

[*The* NARRATOR *breaks into applause.*]

NARRATOR: Just splendid. Shattering.

[*He then crosses and after an intense struggle with* MAMA, *he takes the award from her and gives it to the* LADY IN PLAID, *who is still suffering primal pain.*]

LADY: Not my babies . . . not my . . . [*Upon receiving the award, she instantly recovers.*] Help me up, sugar. [*She then bows and crosses and stands behind the couch.*]

NARRATOR: Enter Medea Jones, Walter-Lee-Beau-Willie's sister.

[MEDEA *moves very ceremoniously, wiping her feet and then speaking and gesturing as if she just escaped from a Greek tragedy.*]

MEDEA: Ah, see how the sun kneels to speak
her evening vespers, exalting all
in her vision, even lowly tenement
long abandoned.

Mother, wife of brother, I trust
the approaching darkness finds you
safe in Hestia's busom.

Brother, why wear the face of a man

in anguish. Can the garment of thine
feelings cause the shape of your
  countenance to disfigure so?

SON: [*At the end of his rope.*] Leave me alone, Medea.

MEDEA: [*To* MAMA] Is good brother still going on and on and on about He
  and The Man.

MAMA/LADY: What else?

MEDEA: Ah brother, if with our thoughts and
  words we could cast thine oppressors
  into the lowest bowels of wretched
  hell, would that make us more like the
  gods or more like our oppressors.

No, brother, no, do not let thy rage
  choke the blood which anoints thy
  heart with love. Forgo thine darkened
  humor and let love shine on your
  soul, like a jewel on a young maiden's hand.

[*Dropping to her knees.*]

I beseech thee, forgo thine
  anger and leave wrath to the gods!

SON: Girl, what has gotten into you.

MEDEA: Juilliard, good brother. For I am no
  longer bound by rhythms of race or
  region. Oh, no. My speech, like my
  pain and suffering, have become
  classical and therefore universal.

LADY: I didn't understand a damn thing she said, but girl you usin' them
  words.

[LADY IN PLAID *crosses and gives* MEDEA *the award and everyone ap-
  plauds.*]

SON: [*Trying to stop the applause.*] Wait one damn minute! This my play. It's
  about me and the Man. It ain't got nuthin' to do with no ancient temples on the Nile and it ain't got nuthin' to do with Hestia's busom.
  And it ain't got nuthin' to do with you slappin' me across no room.
  [*His gut-wrenching best.*] It's about me. Me and my pain! My pain!

THE VOICE OF THE MAN: Walter-Lee-Beau-Willie, this is the Man. You
  have been convicted of overacting. Come out with your hands up.

[SON *starts to cross to the window.*]

SON: Well now that does it.

MAMA: Son, no, don't go near that window. Son, no!

[*Gun shots ring out and* SON *falls dead.*]

MAMA: [*Crossing to the body, too emotional for words.*] My son, he was a good boy. Confused. Angry. Just like his father. And his father's father. And his father's father's father. And now he's dead. [*Seeing she's about to drop to her knees, the* NARRATOR *rushes and places a pillow underneath her just in time.*] If only he had been born into a world better than this. A world where there are no well-worn couches and no well-worn Mamas and nobody over emotes.

If only he had been born into an all-black musical.

[*A song intro begins.*]

Nobody ever dies in an all-black musical.

[MEDEA *and* LADY IN PLAID *pull out church fans and begin to fan themselves.*]

MAMA: [*Singing a soul-stirring gospel.*]
Oh why couldn't he
Be born
Into a show with lots of singing
and dancing

I say why
Couldn't he
Be born

LADY: Go ahead hunny. Take your time.

MAMA: Into a show where everybody
Is happy

NARRATOR/MEDEA: Preach! Preach

MAMA: Oh why couldn't he be born with the chance
To smile a lot and sing and dance
Oh why
Oh why

Oh why
Couldn't he
Be born
Into an all-Black show
Woah — woah

[*The* CAST *joins in, singing do-wop gospel background to* MAMA's *lament.*]

Oh why
Couldn't he
be born
[He be born]
Into a show where everybody
Is happy
Why couldn't he be born with the chance
To smile a lot and sing and dance
Wanna know why
Wanna know why

Oh why
Couldn't he
Be born
Into an all-Black show
A-men

[*A singing/dancing, spirit-raising revival begins.*]

Oh, son, get up
Get up and dance
We say get up
This is your second chance

Don't shake a fist
Just shake a leg
And do the twist
Don't scream and beg
Son son son
Get up and dance

Get
Get up
Get up and
Get up and dance — All right!
Get up and dance — All right!
Get up and dance!

[WALTER-LEE-BEAU-WILLIE *springs to life and joins in the dancing. A foot-stomping, hand-clapping production number takes off, which encompasses a myriad of black-Broadwayesque dancing styles—shifting speeds and styles with exuberant abandonment.*]

MAMA: [*Bluesy.*] Why couldn't he be born into an all–Black show

CAST: With singing and dancing

MAMA: Black show

[MAMA *scats and the dancing becomes manic and just a little too desperate to please.*]

CAST: We gotta dance
We gotta dance
Get up get up get up and dance
We gotta dance
We gotta dance
Gotta dance!

[*Just at the point the dancing is about to become violent, the cast freezes and pointedly, simply sings:*]

If we want to live
We have got to
We have got to
Dance...dance...dance...

[*As they continue to dance with zombie-like frozen smiles and faces, around them images of coon performers flash as the lights slowly fade.*]

SYMBIOSIS

The Temptations singing "My Girl" are heard as lights reveal a BLACK MAN *in corporate dress standing before a large trash can throwing objects from a Saks Fifth Avenue bag into it. Circling around him with his every emotion on his face is* THE KID, *who is dressed in a late-sixties street style. His moves are slightly heightened. As the scene begins the music fades.*

MAN: [*With contained emotions.*] My first pair of Converse All-stars. Gone. My first Afro-comb. Gone. My first dashiki. Gone. My autographed pictures of Stokley Carmichael, Jomo Kenyatta and Donna Summer. Gone.

KID: [*Near tears, totally upset.*] This shit's not fair man. Damn! Hell! Shit! Shit! It's not fair!

MAN: My first jar of Murray's Pomade.
My first can of Afro-sheen.
My first box of curl relaxer. Gone! Gone! Gone!
Eldridge Cleaver's *Soul on Ice.*

KID: Not *Soul on Ice!*

MAN: It's been replaced on my bookshelf by *The Color Purple.*

KID: [*Horrified.*] No!

MAN: Gone!

KID: But—

MAN: Jimi Hendrix's "Purple Haze." Gone.
Sly Stone's "There's A Riot Goin' On." Gone.
The Jackson Five's "I Want You Back."

KID: Man, you can't throw that away. It's living proof Michael had a black nose.

MAN: It's all going. Anything and everything that connects me to you, to who I was, to what we were, is out of my life.

KID: You've got to give me another chance.

MAN: *Fingertips Part 2.*

KID: Man, how can you do that? That's vintage Stevie Wonder.

MAN: You want to know how, Kid? You want to know how? Because my survival depends on it. Whether you know it or not, the Ice Age is upon us.

KID: [*Jokingly.*] Man, what the hell you talkin' about. It's 95 damn degrees.

MAN: The climate is changing, Kid, and either you adjust or you end up extinct. A sociological dinosaur. Do you understand what I'm trying to tell you? King Kong would have made it to the top if only he had taken the elevator. Instead he brought attention to his struggle and ended up dead.

KID: [*Pleading.*] I'll change. I swear I'll change. I'll maintain a low profile. You won't even know I'm around.

MAN: If I'm to become what I'm to become then you've got to go ... I have no history. I have no past.

KID: Just like that?

MAN: [*Throwing away a series of buttons.*] Free Angela! Free Bobby! Free Huey, Duey, and Louie! U.S. out of Viet Nam. U.S. out of Cambodia. U.S. out of Harlem, Detroit, and Newark. Gone! ... *The Temptations Greatest Hits!*

KID: [*Grabbing the album.*] No!!!

MAN: Give it back, Kid.

KID: No.

MAN: I said give it back!

KID: No. I can't let you trash this. Johnny man, it contains fourteen classic cuts by the tempting Temptations. We're talking, "Ain't Too Proud to Beg," "Papa was a Rolling Stone," "My Girl."

MAN: [*Warning.*] I don't have all day.

KID: For God's sake, Johnny man, "My Girl" is the jam to end all jams. It's what we are. Who we are. It's a way of life. Come on, man, for old times sake. [*Singing.*]

I got sunshine on a cloudy day
Dum–da–dum–da–dum–da–dum
And when it's cold outside

Come on, Johnny man, sing

I got the month of May

Here comes your favorite part. Come on, Johnny man, sing.

I guess you say
What can make me feel this way
My girl, my girl, my girl
Talkin' 'bout

MAN: [*Exploding.*] I said give it back!

KID: [*Angry.*] I ain't givin' you a muthafuckin' thing!

MAN: Now you listen to me!

KID: No, you listen to me. This is the kid you're dealin' with, so don't fuck with me!

[*He hits his fist into his hand, and* THE MAN *grabs for his heart.* THE KID *repeats with two more hits, which causes the man to drop to the ground, grabbing his heart.*]

KID: Jail! Jail! Jail!

MAN: Kid, please.

KID: Yeah. Yeah. Now who's begging who ... Well, well, well, look at Mr. Cream-of-the-Crop, Mr. Colored Man-on-Top. Now that he's making it, he no longer wants anything to do with the Kid. Well, you may put all kinds of silk ties 'round your neck and white lines up your nose, but the Kid is here to stay. You may change your women as often as you change your underwear, but the Kid is here to stay. And regardless of how much of your past that you trash, I ain't goin' no damn where. Is that clear? Is that clear?

MAN: [*Regaining his strength, beginning to stand.*] Yeah.

KID: Good. [*After a beat.*] You all right man? You all right? I don't want to hurt you, but when you start all that talk about getting rid of me, well, it gets me kind of crazy. We need each other. We are one ...

[*Before* THE KID *can complete his sentence,* THE MAN *grabs him around his neck and starts to choke him violently.*]

MAN: [*As he strangles him.*] The ... Ice ... Age ... is ... upon us ... and either we adjust ... or we end up ... extinct.

[THE KID *hangs limp in* THE MAN'S *arms.*]

MAN: [*Laughing.*] Man kills his own rage. Film at eleven. ˉ[*He then dumps* THE KID *into the trash can, and closes the lid. He speaks in a contained voice.*] I have no history. I have no past. I can't. It's too much. It's much too much. I must be able to smile on cue. And watch the news with an impersonal eye. I have no stake in the madness.

Being black is too emotionally taxing; therefore I will be black only on weekends and holidays.

[*He then turns to go, but sees the Temptations album lying on the ground. He picks it up and sings quietly to himself.*]

I guess you say
What can make me feel this way

[*He pauses, but then crosses to the trash can, lifts the lid, and just as he is about to toss the album in, a hand reaches from inside the can and grabs hold of* THE MAN's *arm.* THE KID *then emerges from the can with a death grip on* THE MAN's *arm.*]

KID: [*Smiling.*] What's happenin'?

[*Blackout.*]

LALA'S OPENING

Roving follow spots. A timpani drum roll. As we hear the voice of the AN-
NOUNCER, *outrageously glamorous images of* LALA *are projected onto the
museum walls.*

VOICE OF ANNOUNCER: From Rome to Rangoon! Paris to Prague! We
are pleased to present the American debut of the one! The only! The
breathtaking! The astounding! The stupendous! The incredible! The
magnificent! Lala Lamazing Grace!

[*Thunderous applause as* LALA *struts on, the definitive black diva. She has
long, flowing hair, an outrageous lamé dress, and an affected French accent which she loses when she's upset.*]

LALA: Everybody loves Lala
Everybody loves me
Paris! Berlin! Rome!
No mattèr where I go
I always feel at home

Ohhhh
Everybody loves Lala
Everybody loves me
I'm tres magnifique
And oh so unique
And when it comes to glamour
I'm chic–er than chic

[*She giggles.*]

That's why everybody
Everybody
Everybody–everybody–everybody
Loves me

[*She begins to vocally reach for higher and higher notes, until she has to
point to her final note. She ends the number with a grand flourish and
bows to thunderous applause.*]

LALA: I-love-it-I-love-it-I-love-it!

Yes, it's me! Lala Lamazing Grace and I have come home. Home
to the home I never knew as home. Home to you, my people, my
blood, my guts.

My story is a simple one, full of fire, passion, magique. You may
ask how did I, a humble girl from the backwoods of Mississippi, come
to be the ninth wonder of the modern world. Well, I can't take all of
the credit. Part of it goes to him. [*She points toward the heavens.*]

No, not the light man, darling, but God. For, you see, Lala is a star. A very big star. Let us not mince words, I'm a fucking meteorite. [*She laughs.*] But He is the universe and just like my sister, Aretha la Franklin, Lala's roots are in the black church. [*She sings in a showy gospel style.*]

That's why everybody loves
Swing low sweet chariot
That's why everybody loves
Go down Moses way down in Egypt land
That's why everybody everybody loves me!!!

[*Once again she points to her final note and then basks in applause.*]

Thank you. Thank you.

Now, before I dazzle you with more of my limitless talent, tell me something, America. [*Musical underscoring.*] Why has it taken you so long to recognize my artistry? Mother France opened her loving arms and Lala came running. All over the world Lala was embraced. But here, ha! You spat at Lala. Was I too exotic? Too much woman, or what?

Diana Ross you embrace. A too-bit nobody from Detroit, of all places. Now, I'm not knocking la Ross. She does the best she can with the little she has. [*She laughs.*] But the Paul la Robesons, the James la Baldwins, the Josephine la Baker's, who was my god-mother you know. The Lala Lamazing Grace's you kick out. You drive...

[*Singing.*}

Away
I am going away
Hoping to find a better day
What do you say
Hey hey
I am going away
Away

[LALA, *caught up in the drama of the song, doesn't see* ADMONIA, *her maid, stick her head out from offstage. Once she is sure* LALA *isn't looking, she wheels onto stage right* FLO'RANCE, LALA's *lover, who wears a white mask/blonde hair. He is gagged and tied to a chair.* ADMONIA *places him on stage and then quickly exits.*]

LALA: Au revoir — Je vais partier maintenant
Je veux dire maintenant
Au revoir
Au revoir

Au revoir
Au revoir
A–ma–vie

[*On her last note, she sees* FLO'RANCE *and, in total shock, crosses to him.*]

LALA: Flo'rance, what the hell are you doing out here looking like that. I haven't seen you for three days and you decide to show up now?

[*He mumbles.*]

I don't want to hear it!

[*He mumbles.*]

I said shut up!

[ADMONIA *enters from stage right and has a letter opener on a silver tray.*]

ADMONIA: Pst!

[LALA, *embarrassed by the presence of* ADMONIA *on stage, smiles apologetically at the audience.*]

LALA: Un momento.

[*She then pulls* ADMONIA *to the side.*]

LALA: Darling, have you lost your mind coming onstage while I'm performing. And what have you done to Flo'rance? When I asked you to keep him tied up, I didn't mean to tie him up.

[ADMONIA *gives her the letter opener.*]

LALA: Why are you giving me this? I have no letters to open. I'm in the middle of my American debut. Admonia, take Flo'rance off this stage with you! Admonia!

[ADMONIA *is gone.* LALA *turns to the audience and tries to make the best of it.*]

LALA: That was Admonia, my slightly overweight black maid, and this is Flo'rance, my amour. I remember how we met, don't you Flo'rance. I was sitting in a cafe on the Left Bank, when I looked up and saw the most beautiful man staring down at me. "Who are you," he asked. I told him my name...whatever my name was back then. Yes, I told him my name and he said, "No, that cannot be your name. Your name should dance the way your eyes dance and your lips dance. Your name should fly, like Lala." And the rest is la history. Flo'rance molded me into the woman I am today. He is my Svengali, my reality, my all. And I thought I was all to him, until we came here to America, and he fucked that bitch. Yeah, you fucked 'em all. Anything black and breathing. And all this time, I thought you loved me for being me.

[*She holds the letter opener to his neck.*]

Well, you may think you made me, but I'll have you know I was who I was, whoever that was, long before you made me what I am. So there!

[*She stabs him and breaks into song.*]

Oh, love can drive a woman to madness
To pain and sadness
I know
Believe me I know
I know
I know

[LALA *sees what she's done and is about to scream but catches herself and tries to play it off.*]

LALA: Moving right along.

[ADMONIA *enters with a telegram on a tray.*]

ADMONIA: Pst.

LALA: [*Anxious/hostile.*] What is it now?

[ADMONIA *hands* LALA *a telegram.*]

LALA: [*Excited.*] Oh, la telegram from one of my fans and the concert isn't even over yet. Get me the letter opener. It's in Flo'rance.

[ADMONIA *hands* LALA *the letter opener.*]

LALA: Next I am going to do for you my immortal hit song, "The Girl Inside." But first we open the telegram. [*She quickly reads it and is outraged.*] What! Which pig in la audience wrote this trash? [*Reading.*] "Dear Sadie, I'm so proud. The show's wonderful, but talk less and sing more. Love, Mama." First off, no one calls me Sadie. Sadie died the day Lala was born. And secondly, my Mama's dead. Anyone who knows anything about Lala Lamazing Grace knows that my mother and Josephine Baker were French patriots together. They infiltrated a carnival rumored to be the center of Nazi intelligence, disguised as Hottentot Siamese twins. You may laugh but it's true. Mama died a heroine. It's all in my autobiography, "Voilá Lala!" So whoever sent this telegram is a liar!

[ADMONIA *promptly presents her with another telegram.*]

LALA: No doubt an apology. [*Reading.*] "Dear Sadie, I'm not dead. P.S.

Your child misses you." What? [*She squares off at the audience.*] Well, now, that does it! If you are my mother, which you are not. And this alleged child is my child, then that would mean I am a mother and I have never given birth. I don't know nothin' 'bout birthin' no babies! [*She laughs.*] Lala made a funny.

So whoever sent this, show me the child! Show me!

[ADMONIA *offers another telegram.*]

LALA: [*To* ADMONIA.] You know you're gonna get fired! [*She reluctantly opens it.*] "The child is in the closet." What closet?

ADMONIA: Pst.

[ADMONIA *pushes a button and the center wall unit revolves around to reveal a large black door.* ADMONIA *exits, taking* FLO'RANCE *with her, leaving* LALA *alone.*]

LALA: [*Laughing.*] I get it. It's a plot, isn't it. A nasty little CIA, FBI kind of plot. Well let me tell you muthafuckers one thing, there is nothing in that closet, real or manufactured, that will be a dimmer to the glimmer of Lamé the star. You may have gotten Billie and Bessie and a little piece of everyone else who's come along since, but you won't get Lala. My clothes are too fabulous! My hair is too long! My accent too French. That's why I came home to America. To prove you ain't got nothing on me!

[*The music for her next song starts, but* LALA *is caught up in her tirade, and talks/screams over the music.*]

My mother and Josephine Baker were French patriots together! I've had brunch with the Pope! I've dined with the Queen! Everywhere I go I cause riots! Hunny, I am a star! I have transcended pain! So there! [*Yelling.*] Stop the music! Stop that goddamn music.

[*The music stops.* LALA *slowly walks downstage and singles out someone in the audience.*]

Darling, you're not looking at me. You're staring at that damn door. Did you pay to stare at some fucking door or be mesmerized by my talent?

[*To the whole audience.*]

Very well! I guess I am going to have to go to the closet door, fling it open, in order to dispell all the nasty little thoughts these nasty little telegrams have planted in your nasty little minds. [*Speaking directly to someone in the audience.*] Do you want me to open the closet door? Speak up, darling, this is live. [*Once she gets the person to say "yes."*] I will open the door, but before I do, let me tell you bastards one last thing. To hell with coming home and to hell with lies and insinuations!

[LALA *goes into the closet and after a short pause comes running out, ready to scream, and slams the door. Traumatized to the point of no return, she tells the following story as if it were a jazz solo of rushing, shifting emotions.*]

LALA: I must tell you this dream I had last night. Simply magnifique. In this dream, I'm running naked in Sammy Davis Junior's hair. [*Crazed laughter.*]

Yes! I'm caught in this larger than life, deep, dark forest of savage, nappy-nappy hair. The kinky-kinks are choking me, wrapped around my naked arms, thighs, breast, face. I can't breath. And there was nothing in that closet! And I'm thinking if only I has a machete, I could cut away the kinks. Remove once and for all the roughness. But then I look up and it's coming toward me. Flowing like lava. It's pomade! Ohhh, Sammy! Yes, cakes and cakes of pomade. Making everything nice and white and smooth and shiny, like my black/white/black/white/black behiney. Mama no! And then spikes start cutting through the pomade. Combing the coated kink. Cutting through the kink, into me. There are bloodlines on my back. On my thighs. It's all over. All over ... all over me. All over for me.

[LALA *accidentally pulls off her wig to reveal her real hair. Stripped of her "disguise" she recoils like a scared little girl and sings.*]

Mommy and Daddy
Meet and mate
The child that's born
Is torn with love and with hate
She runs away to find her own
And tries to deny
What she's always known
The girl inside

[*The closet door opens.* LALA *runs away, and a* LITTLE BLACK GIRL *emerges from the closet. Standing behind her is* ADMONIA.]

[*The* LITTLE GIRL *and* LALA *are in two isolated pools of light, and mirror each other's moves until* LALA *reaches past her reflection and the* LITTLE GIRL *comes to* LALA *and they hug.* ADMONIA *then joins them as* LALA *sings. Music underscored.*]

LALA: What's left is the girl inside
The girl who died
So a new girl could be born

[*Slow fade to black.*]

PERMUTATIONS

Lights up on NORMAL JEAN REYNOLDS. *She is very Southern/country and very young. She wears a simple faded print dress and her hair, slightly mussed, is in plaits. She sits, her dress covering a large oval object.*

NORMAL: My mama used to say, God made the exceptional, then God made the special and when God got bored, he made me. 'Course she don't say too much of nuthin' no more, not since I lay me this egg. [*She lifts her dress to uncover a large, white egg laying between her legs.*] Ya see it all got started when I had me sexual relations with the garbage man. Ooowee, did he smell. No, not bad. No! He smelled of all the good things folks never shoulda thrown away. His sweat was like cantaloupe juice. His neck was like a ripe-red strawberry. And the water that fell from his eyes was like a deep, dark, juicy-juicy grape. I tell ya, it was like fuckin' a fruit salad, only I didn't spit out the seeds. I kept them here, deep inside. And three days later, my belly commence to swell, real big like.

Well my mama locked me off in some dark room, refusin' to let me see light of day 'cause, "What would the neighbors think." At first I cried a lot, but then I grew used to livin' my days in the dark, and my nights in the dark . . . [*She hums.*] And then it wasn't but a week or so later, my mama off at church, that I got this hurtin' feelin' down here. Worse than anything I'd ever known. And then I started bleedin', real bad. I mean there was blood everywhere. And the pain had me howlin' like a near-dead dog. I tell ya, I was yellin' so loud, I couldn't even hear myself. Noooooooo! Noooooo! Carrying on something like that.

And I guess it was just too much for the body to take, 'cause the next thing I remember . . . is me coming to and there's this big white egg layin' 'tween my legs. First I thought somebody musta put it there as some kind of joke. But then I noticed that all 'round this egg were thin lines of blood that I could trace to back between my legs.

[*Laughing.*] Well, when my mama come home from church she just about died. "Normal Jean, what's that thing 'tween your legs? Normal Jean, you answer me, girl!" It's not a thing, Mama. It's an egg. And I laid it.

She tried separatin' me from it, but I wasn't havin' it. I stayed in that dark room, huggin', holdin' onto it.

And then I heard it. It wasn't anything that coulda been heard 'round the world, or even in the next room. It was kinda like layin' back in the bath tub, ya know, the water just coverin' your ears . . . and if you lay real still and listen real close, you can hear the sound of your heart movin' the water. You ever done that? Well that's what it sounded like. A heart movin' water. And it was happenin' inside here. Why, I'm the only person I know who ever lay themselves an egg before so that makes me special. You hear that, Mama? I'm special and so's my egg! And special things supposed to be treated like they matter. That's why every night I count to it, so it knows nuthin' never really ends. And I sing it every song I know so that when it comes out, it's full of all kinds of feelings. And I tell it secrets and laugh with it and...

[*She suddenly stops and puts her ear to the egg and listens intently.*]

Oh! I don't believe it! I thought I heard...yes! [*Excited.*] Can you hear it? Instead of one heart, there's two. Two little hearts just pattering away. Boom-boom-boom. Boom-boom-boom. Talkin' to each other like old friends. Racin' toward the beginnin' of their lives. [*Listening.*] Oh, no, now there's three...four...five, six. More hearts than I can count. And they're all alive, beatin' out life inside my egg. [*We begin to hear the heartbeats, drums, alive inside* NORMAL'S *egg.*] Any day now, this egg is gonna crack open and what's gonna come out a be the likes of which nobody has ever seen. My babies! And their skin is gonna turn all kinds of shades in the sun and their hair a be growin' every which-a-way. And it won't matter and they won't care 'cause they know they are so rare and so special 'cause it's not everyday a bunch of babies break outta a white egg and start to live. And nobody better not try and hurt my babies 'cause if they do, they gonna have to deal with me. Yes, any day now, this shell's gonna crack and my babies are gonna fly. Fly! Fly!

[*She laughs at the thought, but then stops and says the word as if it's the most natural thing in the world.*]

Fly.

[*Blackout.*]

THE PARTY

Before we know what's hit us, a hurricane of energy comes bounding into the space. It is TOPSY WASHINGTON. *Her hair and dress are a series of stylistic contradictions which are hip, black, and unencumbered.*
Music spiritual and funky, underscores.

TOPSY: [*Dancing about.*] Yoho! Party! Party! Turn up the music! Turn up the music! Have yaw ever been to a party where there was one fool in the middle of the room, dancing harder and yelling louder than everybody in the entire place. Well, hunny, that fool was me! Yes, child! The name is Topsy Washington and I love to party. As a matter of fact, when God created the world, on the seventh day, he didn't rest. No child, he partied. Yo-ho! Party! Yeah! Yeah! But now let me tell you 'bout this function I went to the other night, way uptown. And baby when I say way uptown, I mean way-way-way-way-way-way-way-way uptown. Somewhere's between 125th Street and infinity.

Inside was the largest gathering of black Negro/colored Americans you'd ever want to see. Over in one corner you got Nat Turner sippin' champagne out of Eartha Kitt's slipper. And over in another corner, Bert Williams and Malcolm X was discussing existentialism as it relates to the shuffle-ball-change. Girl, Aunt Jemima and Angela Davis was in the kitchen sharing a plate of greens and just goin' off about South Africa. And then Fats sat down and started to work them eighty-eights. And then Stevie joined in. And then Charlie and Sly and Lightin' and Count and Louie! And then everybody joined in. I tell you all the children was just all up in there, dancing to the rhythm of one beat. Dancing to the rhythm of their own definition. Celebrating in their cultural madness. And then the floor started to shake. And the walls started to move. And before anybody knew what was happening, the entire room lifted up off the ground. The whole place just took off and went flying through space— defying logic and limitations. Just a spinning and a spinning and a spinning until it disappeared inside of my head. [TOPSY *stops dancing and regains her balance and begins to listen to the music in her head. Slowly we begin to hear it, too.*] That's right, girl, there's a party goin' on inside of here. That's why when I walk down the street my hips just sashay all over the place. 'Cause I'm dancing to the music of the madness in me. And whereas I used to jump into a rage anytime anybody tried to deny who I was, now all I got to do is give attitude, quicker than light, and then go on about the business of being me. 'Cause I'm dancing to the music of the madness in me.

[*As* TOPSY *continues to speak,* MISS ROJ, LALA, MISS PAT, *and* THE MAN *from* Symbiosis *revolve on, frozen like soft sculptures.*]

TOPSY: And here, all this time I been thinking we gave up our drums. But, naw, we still got 'em. I know I got mine. They're here, in my speech, my walk, my hair, my God, my style, my smile, and my eyes. And everything I need to get over in this world, is inside here, connecting me to everybody and everything that's ever been.

So, hunny, don't waste your time trying to label or define me.

[*The sculptures slowly begin to come to "life" and they mirror/echo* TOPSY's *words.*]

TOPSY/EVERYBODY: . . . 'cause I'm not what I was ten years ago or ten minutes ago. I'm all of that and then some. And whereas I can't live inside yesterday's pain, I can't live without it.

[*All of a sudden, madness erupts on the stage. The sculptures begin to speak all at once. Images of black/Negro/colored Americans begin to flash — images of them dancing past the madness, caught up in the madness, being lynched, rioting, partying, surviving. Mixed in with these images are all the characters from the exhibits. Through all of this* TOPSY *sings. It is a vocal and visual cacophony which builds and builds.*]

LALA:
I must tell you about this dream I had last night. Simply magnifique. In this dream I'm running naked in Sammy Davis Junior's hair. Yes. I'm caught in this larger-than-life, deep, dark tangled forest of savage, nappy-nappy hair. Yes, the kinky kinks are choking me, are wrapped around my naked arms, my naked thighs, breast, and face, and I can't breathe and there was nothing in that closet.

MISS ROJ:
Snap for every time you walk past someone lying in the street smelling like frozen piss and shit and you don't see it. Snap for every crazed bastard who kills himself so as to get the jump on being killed. And snap for every sick mutha fucker who, bored with carrying about his fear, takes to shooting up other people.

THE MAN:
I have no history. I have no past. I can't. It's too much. It's much too much. I must be able to smile on cue and watch the news with an impersonal eye. I

MISS PAT:
Stop playing those drums. I said stop playing those damn drums. You can't stop history. You can't stop time. Those drums will be confiscated once

have no stake in the madness. Being black is too emotionally taxing, therefore I will be black only on weekends and holidays. we reach Savannah, so give them up now. Repeat after me: I don't hear any drums and I will not rebel. I will not rebel.

TOPSY: [*Singing.*] There's madness in me
And that madness sets me free
There's madness in me
And that madness sets me free
There's madness in me
And that madness sets me free
There's madness in me
And that madness sets me free
There's madness in me
And that madness sets me free

TOPSY: My power is in my ...

EVERYBODY: *Madness!*

TOPSY: And my colored contradictions.

[*The sculptures freeze with a smile on their faces as we hear the voice of* MISS PAT.]

VOICE OF MISS PAT: Before exiting, check the overhead as any baggage you don't claim, we trash.

[*Blackout.*]

Thomas W. Jones, II

THE WIZARD OF HIP

THOMAS W. JONES, II

A director, writer, actor and composer. Born and raised in Queens, New York, Jones began writing at an early age. His gift for writing was further encouraged and honed during his years at Amherst College under the guidance of his mentor, internationally renowned writer, Sonia Sanchez. He graduated with honors from Amherst College majoring in Theatre Arts. His senior thesis, a play *Every Father's Child*, was written as a tribute celebrating his father's life. The play focuses on the family's dealing with a catastrophic illness and death of a father.

From this effort, the production company Jomandi was conceived as a vehicle to produce *Every Father's Child* in order to endow a memorial scholarship fund at Morehouse School of Medicine for his father, Dr. Thomas W. Jones, former Fulton County Deputy Commissioner of Health. Later that year (1978) Jomandi was incorporated.

The name "Jomandi" is an amalgamation of the names of members of Dr. Jones' immediate family: Jo for Thomas W. Jones, II; Ma for wife Angeline (Angie) Jones; An and Di for daughters Andrea and Diane. It was discovered sometime later that in a Senegalese dialect the word Jomandi means "People Gathered Together in Celebration." From its familial roots, the company adopted the credo, "And The Family Is Now."

Jones' role as Co–Artistic Director of Jomandi over the past seventeen years has opened the door to guest residencies and workshops around the country and abroad. Highlights of his work as an actor include the critically acclaimed performance of his one man tour de force, *The Wizard of Hip*, Off–Broadway, and appearance in the play, *Checkmates* at Washington's prestigious Arena Stage. He has written, directed and composed scores for numerous plays; notably his work *Bessie's Blues*, has garnered awards from the press on the West and East coasts. His fine directorial work has been seen on stages across the country including the Indiana Repertory, Oakland Ensemble, New Federal and Bushfire theatres. Tom's play, *Hip II, Birth of a Boom* was named "Best Theatrical Production, 1994" by the *Atlanta Journal & Constitution* and was presented for the "Cultural Olympiad" during the 1996 Olympic Games at the14th Street Playhouse. *Sophisticated Ladies* directed by Jones, was named "Best Local Theatre Production, 1995" by *Atlanta Magazine*. The outstanding reputation of Jomandi is attributable in a major way to his vision and talent.

FROM THE WORDS OF THE PLAYWRIGHT

So, I'm riding down the street the other day and I pull up next to a brother driving a broke down, torn down, raggedy ragamuffin auto... with a car phone. A Car Phone! Auto can't bust 35 mph but Ma Bell is riding right along with him. "Who he trying to fool? Oxymorons are out running a muck!

So this is the planet: Filled with anachronisms and contradictions. It's a journey filled with a majestic and non–majestic moments. Turn a corner, there's a hair weave. Walk thru a door, there's a brother in an Italian suit and a plastic cellophane cap talking to his people, poised as a question mark in the syntax of living.

I no longer question them. I inhale oxymorons and break to the bottom line: My people are funny. As Zora Neale Hurston remarked, they are "unapologetically colored."

And to be sure, I love 'em. The street corner C.E.O.'s standing on angles, hands majestically tugging their histories. The sistahs sitting in nail salons, bare feet being scrubbed cause it's been a long, long, week.

Yeah, I inhale them all and walk them into literature. Their stories keep me sane. Their lives are inextricably tied into my sanity. They are funny without restriction. And in giving order to their experience I give symmetry to my own journey. After all isn't that theatre.

So kick your heels off honey... put down the remote; open a window and watch the fun begin. The theatre of your life is one house down eating a neckbone sandwich with a side of slaw. And if you let it wash over you without censoring it; it just might heal ya. Say Amen Somebody!

ACT ONE

Afro–guy walks onto stage doing assorted warm–ups . . . moon walks and other traditional ethnic kinds of stuff . . .

[*Opening.*]

Yo, yo, yo, "What up?" We gon do this like Brutus, yo, what up, and for brothers in Poland, "Yo, what up upsky" . . . Before we can crank it up and kick it live I know you have that one anxious question looping around ya' mind . . . there's always that question that hangs in mid psyche at the top of any performance featuring an Afro–Guy. You're asking yourself right now, "Hey, Afro–guy is there going to be real, as in, very real Black Theatre . . . is it, huh? Is it? Inquiring minds want to know." I can feel the anxiety, you want some answer . . . hey should I move my seat closer to the exit just in case it get a wee bit too ethnic. I mean you never know when a choreopoem [*Ntozake moves.*] may break out . . . I mean just how much funk does my enter-tainment dollar buy? And you deserve an answer, a straight up, no frills response to a good, and I mean damn good question. Le me start by saying that for those of you who haven't noticed, I am Black, and there will be times when I'll be splittin' them infinitives. So the an-swer to the question is this, "Yes this is Black Theatre." How real this thing gets is still hanging in the wings. To begin, we shall begin at the beginning, which is an off–way of saying we have a title. The title is THE WIZARD OF HIP!! WHEN IN DOUBT SLAM DUNK . . . cute. I think . . . kind of a rockabilly funky word play. Why rockabilly? Cause I like the way that word sounds. Now I'll jive you a minute to say it to yourselves . . . . . .

That's enough, you said it too much. It's my title . . . "Wizard of Hip . . . huh . . ." None of the names that will be mentioned tonight have been changed 'cause the innocent never really get protected and those really guilty write a book and then does a movie of the week. So changin' up anything ain't in the order of things. Please note that be-cause dis heah (that of course is dialect) is Black Theatre there is al-ways the distinct possibility of a few folk getting happy . . . getting happy if you will, testifying in the middle of the aisles. For those of you who saw *Gospel at Colonus* you know just how frightening that can be. So for your protection, comfort, and safety, we do have theatre police standing in the back. If someone does get out of hand the the-atre police will remove you and forcibly make you sit, without bene-fit of intermission, thru every movie Madonna ever made. [*Shivers.*] That should keep your ass in your seats . . . 'Nuff said. We begin at the beginning, the premise, a precipise, a raison d'tre. That sounded good didn't it? Yeah I know, once again... raison d'tre. Watch yourself. "Give me a beat" Da nuh, Da nuh, Hit me!!! Hit me!!! If we had some money we'd have pumped in a real nasty bass line [*He demonstrates.*]. In here, since we don't let our own funk guide you... white folks fake it. The beat is...

Everybody wants to be different. But nobody wants to stand out. You see to stand out alone, all by yourself is risky business. So the aim is to be different in packs. We call this *Sub–culture*. It used to be called *Cult* but the idea of being in a cult got a real bad rap when its two major press agents Charles Manson and the good Guyana Rev. Jim Jones laid down the law. So the chic new term is Sub–culture... .frankly, that word seems a bit odd to me since culture simply means the sum total ways in which we exist in the world. So to be sub–cultured would be to exist beneath all those worldly ways. Sounds a bit hellish to me, but no matter, that's something for critics and archaeologists to uncover... and being neither former nor latter, I just want to be where the truly hip be, hand there where the hip hang, speak with a sculptured hip tongue, surround myself in an ultra–phonic quadrapletic euphoric, surreal and unique hipness. And if that be so, if that be... really be huh, "Somebody give me a Beat..."

Yeah you guessed it, there was supposed to be another grand effect with sirens blaring, a trio of back–up singers do–woping, neatly two–stepping as they descended from the sky. But as you already know this is a slum budget–affair. I mean they could only afford one actor and not even a real famous one... just me... so 86 the effect, go with your own flow. Close those eyes... and imagine I'm Sidney Portier... let your mind kick it live. We're on our own beat. Hep me ... and we be off... off to see the Wizard — Auntie Em — The Wonderful Wizard of Hip... as in what is hip? As in trying to ponder the directness of it all... as in the ultimate out of mind/body experience... as in the wonderment of where do I belong in the grand circuitry of the moment...

We're off to see the wizard... give me those slippers... the wonderful wizard... wha'd I tell you about them poppies Toto Give me a beat!!!

> Too damn hip
> Ya too damn hip
> Too damn hip

Got to take you down to where I'm goin'... tryin' to find it all Nirvana — like, the grand inquisition of sense or lack, thereof.

Nothin' but a buzz word for a specific locale to trust anything other than your own bass line is honest subvert rhythm. I mean if we're really honest nothing shocks us anymore. There are only events that serve to remind us of the first time we were shocked...cogent little reminders of a time when our every being was racked by the unexpected. So I repeat, as in being repetitive

What is hip?
Hip as in what is lost in hip
And is there hip after death...hip after life
Or is there life after hip...
Hip as elementary as
>Dip in the hip
>Glide in the stride...hip

Not to be confused with your white boy walking hip which is more your bounce boogetty bounce heel toe hip...for to walk that way in my neighborhood meant you might not make it home for dinner...but no matter, we're looking for the closest thing resembling proximity...that is tryin' to find a place somewhere...where we are ...so what to do and where to go...is it on the map...hey when in doubt go to the book. The book being Webster's World Book — must be de' place 'cause any book penultimately catalogued dis world gotta know, and so Webster says:

Hip 1:   Noun or verb...hipped and hipping...
is the projecting part on a person where
the leg joins the body, nauch the ball
and socket joint formed by the upper thigh
bone and the pelvis...which is to say the
hip is in joint, as we being hip is *the* joint...

But that only takes us to the anatomy of the hip which doesn't account for that which is soulful... so...read   on...

Hip 2:   the pod containing the ripe seed of a rose bush...I don't think so.

Hip 3:   An exclamation used in cheering, as in "Hip!! Hip!! Hurrah!"...Naw...I don't think so.

Hip 4:   Informed, up to date...could be

Hip 5:   Low spirits, the blues...Nein, that's only according to Jonathan Swift and I know Jonathan...he ain't that swift...

So...gotta go...into the hitherlands of aloof, into the belly of a beginning, to the birthright of definition, all in the name of trying to belong.

> Give me a beat
> Ya too damn hip
> Too damn hip

"Meet George Jetson, daughter Judy, Jane, his wife, his boy Elroy." Ya volt back to childhood. Rocket me back it all the way up to being a boy when the search for hip was the only occupation one had if you didn't have a dog — and I didn't. Then the only thing to do was put ya' sneakers in the wind and find the places where the mystery in the world jetissoned the mystery in your head . . . put U.S. Keds in the wind and give young Tom some beat . . .

[*Chanted.*] "Domino Nabisco I got a Vanilla Wafer . . . I've got a domino, you've got a domino, you've got a domino–oh–oh–oh . . . "

[*On knees.*] Bless me Father for I have sinned. It has been, oh let's say, two years since my last confession. Would have been back sooner 'cept I really didn't have a whole lot to report. Well it wasn't really me that sinned, it was my sisters. Father let me put it to you this way. Being a kid 'sucks.' Like it's tryin' my last nerve. See Father there are three of us and I'm the only boy, and the youngest. So you can see where this can get kind of sticky. Today the worst Father, ya see, my sisters were supposed to be watching after me, but they wanted to go to the movies with their friends. And you know girls, they hate it when little brothers are around. So instead of watching me, they ran off and left me. I tried to catch them but they're fast for girls. I mean real fast. And somewhere between them laughing and Linden Blvd. I got lost. Father being lost is hell. I mean like no matter how hard you try you just don't know where you is. My sisters found me two double features later eating a jelly doughnut and drinking a glass of milk at the 103rd St. Police station. They kept thanking the good policeman for doing such a fine job in finding their little brother. I was after all half retarded having suffered a bump on the head when my real mother, a she–wolf named Shazba, dropped me on the doorsteps in front of the house. The family took me in and treated me as one of their own, and even though I never fully recovered, they've tried to do their best to look after me. After that, my sisters took me from the safe arms of the police and threatened to dismember me if I said one word to Mom and Dad. And even though I don't know what dismember means Father, I'm not gonna say nothin' 'cause it sounds a whole lot more worse than what they did yesterday when they dragged me upstairs to the attic, tied me up, and tickled me til I peed on myself. So you see Father, I can't wait to grow up. 'Cause, this being a kid is shitty. What's that Father, it's a sin to cuss? So Father, I'll say three Hail Marys and pray my sisters to reform school. [*Chanted.*] "I've got a domino, you've got a domino, we've just run out of Vanilla Wafers."

Yeah, I used to be Catholic. I had to give it up though, 'cause I was deathly afraid of becoming a "Catho–holic." I found myself hanging out on street corners looking for priests, saying "Yo, yo Padre, You got that holy water. Two bucks a bottle, get our head straight."

I went to a Catholic school for a minute, not a joyride Catholic School. I mean, they have these...these...nuns [*Takes black scarf from pocket ties on head; adjusts white sweat band to give the affect of nun's habit.*] (talk about your women with bad habits, these some "bru–tall" women) Looking back now, I can semi–understand. I mean I'd be a bit testy too if I knew I was never gonna be able to get "none" either. I mean, all that sexual energy's got to go somewhere...where does it go? I figured it out — What happens is...and you can check this with Dr. Ruth...is that all that energy gets backed up and hides underneath the gowns, right beneath the rosary beads....it then travels from just below the rosary beads up the back and out of the mouth which makes these nuns sound like,

"Afro Jo, are you chewing gum? [*Pause.*] Well did you bring enough for everyone?"

And then it travels back down the spine, down the right arm and into a metal ruler...

"Afro Jo, you come here right now and let the whole class watch me beat your knuckles bloody!"

Yep not getting "any" regularly, I find, is the quickest way to elevate evil to an art form. Not getting "any" at all makes evil a way of life. So I gave up Catholicism and started hanging out in a Pentecostal Church. You know, one of these holy roller palaces where folk catch the holy ghost and jump and shout and get goofy with Jesus. Yep, I'd go in every Sunday morning at 9:00 a.m. and get out promptly on Tuesday. Yeah, it was loooooong! After a while this too played out. And then one Sunday I found my religion...I discovered the First Congregational Church of the N.B.A...the honorable Wilt Chamberlain presiding...the Right Rev. Willis Reed and Elgin Baylor taking it to the mount...the good deacon Earl the Pearl Monroe escorting Bro. Clyde Frazier in a soulful 2–step down the aisle of the free throw line...Dr. Julius Erving summoning a choir of "oooohs" and "ahhhs" above fiberglass alters...bodies weaving thru endless bodies in cascading fade aways...whirling arabesques, arching the air in a fall back baby...fall back...Dick Barnett style. We the anointed huddled on the massive shoulders of Wes Unseld and Gus Johnson...breaking backboards and rebounds thru and rave of Daves...Debussere and Stallworth...thru a rampage of Russells... Carrie and Bill...pump fakin' our every wish...we the followers from New York to Atlanta ridin' the Hudson, Lou Hudson, Baltimore to L.A...Jerry West Jump Shootin' caravans. We the fevered fervent faithful followers revering blocked shots and trickery dribbles cast thru hosannas of electric lighttheir shouts...hail the host of hallelujahs...hear the multitudes carry tumultuous cry:

Dee–fense...Dee–fense — Hallelujah Dee–fense...yeah fall back baby...fall back

Ah...swish...

It was at this point I came to realize that slam dunking was less aerial gymnastics and more a legitimate world view...

Overweight uncle spits turkey in your face at Christmas — slam dunk him.

Alarm clock buzzes to wake you every morning at 6:00 a.m. — slam dunk it.

Women find you repulsive and would rather you crawl slowly back into the sewer you surfaced from — slam dunk them.

You don't have to be in doubt, anymore...Hell if ya get good they'll pay you millions. There are all kinds of fringes and bonus baby incentives to be had if you can just slam, dammit.

Don't worry about being short...lower the rim...

Don't worry about being white...you can wear suits and coach

Hands too small?? Buy a Nerf Ball!!

Place the globe in the gut of your hands...and slam Sam. Make those uncontrollable blues, kiss the soles of your tennis shoes...don't delay send straight away...$29.95 guarantees you...a patent leather, weather–proof, money back guaranteed, 360 degree, over the rainbow juke jack, get back in ya face, slam dunk hit...In New Jersey dial Murray the "K"...In Hawaii. the number's listed...In Atlanta the number is Hi–Five. Be the first in your neighborhood to tower the insidious rage...as you whisper Air Jordan baby...Air Jordan...Ah Swish...Ah Swish...Ah too damn hip...hip as a remembrance of what is and what used to be...sometimes to hang out in what used to be ain't half bad...

I remember 13...some of you may remember looks hard. I

mean, some of yalls hairlines is starting back here. I want you to remember the pride in being a [*In echo.*] Teen–Ager . . . 13 is the nomi-
nating year of membership into an elite club of changing voices,
budding facial hair and revolutionary acne. Yeah it's coming back
now, isn't it? Acne's a bitch. I had that acne that staged daily
co–ups . . . took military control of my face . . . held it for years
without rest . . . without retrenchment. Oh yeah junta acne . . . wasn't
all that bad . . . when I got bored I'd connect the dots and make con-
stellations. I know big dipper, little dipper, Alpha Centurion. Every
day for lunch I'd have peanut butter and Clearasil sandwiches . . . did-
n't matter born to Oxy 5. But 13 is the year when you discover dances
in the dark . . . parties where all the boys would line up on one side of
the room and watch the girls clear on the other side. You'd hang with
the fellas and scheme over who'd get to slow dance with girls who actually had to wear a real bra. Man shoot . . . you'd wait like a vulture,
like perched on the wall with your Kool–Aid and Boone's Farm apple
wine — the drink of coo–el 13 year old men. Cool–el 13. Yeah coo–el
at 13 is the lst rung on the way to being hip . . . "cool" precedes "hip"
for those of you taking notes. Yeah, that was Back in the day when you
didn't have to talk to a girl . . . Hell no Jim . . . words was not a necessary commodity . . . those blessed with a righteous lean and sufficient
supply of suave or coo–el need only stalk the room and grab . . . in
much the same way one tugs an obedient coat. Of course these priv-
ileges weren't guaranteed at birth . . . I mean you had to know
the"how to" . . . how to hang . . . the most important in the "how to" .
. . was being appropriately clad . . . which meant wearing grey plaid
sharkskin pants which tailored symmetrically into black or grey
Playboy shoes . . . up top one wore your two–tone eye–talian Knit blah
. . . a black Huey P. Newton leather jacket topped ever so slantedly
with a crush blue beaver brim. Once attired you was ready for the
pelvic dance of doom . . . I, of course, had to buy my choices secretly
on Capitol Delancy St . . . stow it in a brown paper bag and change at
a buddy's house on dance–night 'cuz my parents were staunch advo-
cates of Macy's. They had taken solemn oath to polyester. Something
to do with the effect that their son would never leave their house
lookin' like a Puerto Rican. So as you can see, cleverness is a necessary pre–requisite to cooo–el. On dance day me and the fellas would
play about 8–9 hours of basketball, then we'd get dressed and do the
basement party scene. See, all the brothers know that there was nothing more compelling to the teen–age femme than the smell of sweat
and Hi Karate. "Brut" me who knew that Eau de la Funk and Old
Spice are the things of which dreams are made. There we were

B–boys hunched on the wall hanging like three days of bad news, waitin' in the must and musk of the aromatic perspiration waiting for just the right jam to blow from a mono record player...blow from the over–anxious speakers the chosen sound issuing a fate of wet dreams. And it did come, the jam, Eddi, "King of the virgins dreams" Holman...Blow Eddie!!!!

"Hey there lonely girl...lonely girl
let me mend your broken heart like new..."

[*Brother walks and grabs a girl and begins to grind.*]

"Hey there lonely girl...lonely girl
Don't you know this lonely boy loves you"

Ah, to be male and privileged enuf, to be runnin' with the right crowd...Ah to be 13...and [*In echo.*] a TEEN — AGER.

[*Begins to sing and does a do–wop 2–step.*]

"Oh what a night
                      To be wanting you
Oh what a night
                      To be needing you
Oh what a night
                      To be holding you
That's why.........I love you so."

Ohh...it's rough to be a kid...no squay bidness. Wouldn't lie about a think like that. What makes it so difficult bein' a kid is that there's no frame of reference for it, you know. I mean who really understands the immediacy of peer pressure. You see as I figure it, the culture changes much too rapidly from generation to generation for anyone older than you to be of any real assistance. One's addictions are re–invented with each passing age. The result is that growing up is hell...John Wayne hell...just no frame of reference for it...only parents who say:

"What do you mean it's hard?...Boy you don't know what hard times is. When I was your age..."

Now you know you've entered the cliche school of doom when you hear "When I was your age."

"Son, when I was your age I walked 100, no 365 miles barefoot. ..in the snow...one–way everyday...just to get an education. So you thank your lucky stars you got shoes at all."

"No, I'm just thankful I'm not stupid enuf to do something like that."

But do admit this...admit one into the unpleasantry of not knowing where to turn...

Yes sir buddy, growing up is such a hard hustle...trying to invent a place of comfort while having to negotiate that fine line between peer pressure and curfews. I don't want to say it, but I can't help it...or as James Brown would say...hep it...god God, wait a minute...hep me...hep me...somebody hep me...Good, Good huh...Maceo... take me to the bridge and hep me...wait a minute...wait one damn minute, please.

You see that's what it all comes down to...we're all in need of a little hep...because who other than the shadow really knows...This is why God invented mothers. The Almighty having a slightly wacked sense of humor created a gender who had a longer period of time to really understand what foolishness is. The Almighty is no fool. He doesn't thrust mothers into the world ill–prepared, oh no he's created places where women with kids, women expecting kids, women who are thinking about expecting kids, can go and learn the intricacy of absurdity. These places are of course, Mommy Universities. Now at Ma U...mothers learn things like how not to murder their children before age nine, followed by seminars in how to inflict bodily harm thru the Kung–fu head turn and stare...At Mommy U. there are all kinds of classes in how to grab a child's behind while holding purse, groceries, and subway straps at rush hour. Symposiums in the fine art of walking and or looking away indifferently while your child lies kicking and screaming on the floor of a department store, and of course the ever popular Intro to silly little ditties 101; this class is of course a prerequisite for all mothers, and must be passed before graduating. This is the course where mothers, after spanking their children in public, learn to say lines like, "You keep crying mister and I'll give you something to really cry about."..."I brought you in this world and I can surely take you out"...And the ever popular classic. .."As long as you live in my house..." and you can say this with me if you know it..."You do as I say do." My mother graduated Mommy U. with honors...summa cum by here and whip yo' butt boy...oh yeah...My mother had an incredible intellect. She could hit and talk to you at one in the same time.

"You have the Au – da – ci – ty to In – sin – u – ate and In – terr – o – gate me on the Ver – a – city— – put your hand down— – of my— – I said put your hand down— –Ac – cu – sa – tions."

"No Mom, I said don't hit me so hard, please..."

My mother was an incredible woman...a truly remarkable individual. She was one of a chosen few blessed with psychic hands...I know this cause she told me more than once,

"Boy, if you keep messin' with me I'm gonna slap you into the middle of next week."

It's pretty amazing to me that when pressed to anger mother's intellects are mysteriously inflated because they ask you questions they already know the answers to. You can't blame them for this...it's the law...they're bound to it...it's a Federal statute, they have to do it, have no choice...police are on call waiting to lock them up if they don't ask you stuff...you can't understand.

"What did you say, little camper, do you want me to come there and rip you tongue right out of your mouth? Well do you? Do you want me to knock the living daylights outta you? Huh?"

What a revelation this is. I had no idea daylight was even alive much less living in me...

"I'll slap you senseless...

"Not that Mom, I only have three cents left, slap me some dollar bills, will ya."

"Who do you think you are talking to?"

"It's only me and you in the room, Mom."

"Mister, do you hear me?"

"Right now Ghandi can hear you and is re–thinking."

Yeah. You know what they say. (And just who is this they.) Someone find them for me, quick! "Spare the rod and spoil the child." Kid response: "Spoil me, please spoil me."

See, now–a–days kids have a .gimmick...an out. My nephew, Deuce, is 5 and I mean if my sister even looks like she's going to move her hand in his direction he says:

"Ah Mom is that child abuse number toll free? That's right—how do you spell prison, Mom? I spell it H.B.O. all night...don't you?

But my mother was a "down" female though. She sold more wolf tickets than she did hit us...and I really can remember my sisters getting hit once or twice. I was hit probably...6......7 hundred times. I stopped counting after the fourth grade.

Now daddies...Daddies are a whole other twist of fate...there are no Universities for Daddydom. Probably because they don't really have to submit to any real pain in the life giving process. They more or less give up 10 quick minutes of their time lay around for nine months waiting for the festivities to begin, "Hey honey is it soup yet?" Daddies do go to school, but they don't need Daddy Universities. They rely on the inherited daddy logic passed on from daddies who proceeded them . . . reason being it's in their best interest to offer their kids the same choices their fathers offered them. It's important to note that there are 2 distinct daddydom categories here . . . Fathers and daughters being 1 . . . the other of course being fathers and sons. The way daddies behave towards their daughters is one I like to catalogue as your basic three D's. This being dilly, dally, and defer. When pressed into a solo confrontation with their little girls, daddies will inevitably enter a plea of no lo contendre:

"Daddy, can I stay out late tonight?"

What did you mother say?"

"She said to ask you."

"Well then, in that case go ask her what she thinks I should do?"

No Lo contendre, jack . . . I don't wanna get emotionally involved in any real decisions. The reason for this is that daughters learn at a painfully young age how to wrap these guys around their pointed little wishes. Girls hit mighty blows to the heart. Oh yeah, they counter punch daddies in their emotional breadbasket. They take these daddies . . . men of steel mind you . . . and in one phrase reduce them to whimpering vats of wheatina.

"Daddy, can I borrow the car tonight?"

"Of course not."

"Oh but Daddy, you're so kind and cute . . . that's why I love you so much."

"Oh you don't love me."

"No, it's not me, it's your mother you love . . . I'm just here."

"Oh but Daddy, you're so brave . . . and strong . . . and giving . . . so can I please borrow the car?"

"Aw hell, girl, you can have the car. Me and your mother will take the bus from now on."

Yeah, that's right, be a son and try it. Trust me, he will not buy it.

"Dad, Lookin' good ol' man, can I use the car?"

"Hell no, now go mow the lawn."

"Just checking."

See because the father and son deal is based on a completely different ethic. An inherited logic. One their daddies handed them and in return they pass it on to their sons . . . a legacy of machismo. Get a football . . . get a girl . . . get laid . . . get a job . . . get laid . . . get laid off. A simple philosophy. Think . . . one of value . . . they of course never tell you how to accomplish said objectives . . . they simply let you know this is indeed our function as a man and if for any reason you have slight misgivings about this as your sole role on the planet enter your plea of: "But Pop . . . ?" . . . there is but one response to quell your anxiety . . . " If you don't have a job, you don't have a voice . . .

'This is my house, I pay the mortgage here. You lucky you got a pot to piss in fella. When you start bringing in the bacon, then you can have something to say."

My father was a righteous healer . . . a leader of men and subsequently quite adept at handling me in the whole father/son scenario. See he believed in allowing me to understand my options thus putting the onus back on me to contemplate said options and arrive at a reasonable conclusion . . . If I was, say, feeling my come–uppance, he didn't get dictorial . . . noooo . . . he'd lay out several options and leave it up to me . . .

"Boy you sass me one more time and one of is is going to jail . . . the other one's going to hell, now what's it going to be?"

[*Pause.*] God, it ain't like what ya see on T.V . . . where is poppa Walton when you need him? When he does have to actually discipline you, he launches into lunacy from lack of experience . . .

"Alright, alright no food for a year . . . "

"But Pop . . . "

"And no more using the telephones."

"But Dad I don't use the telephone."

"And you'll never use it, now go mow the lawn . . . "

Then there are those times when my father would put me on punishment, confine me to quarters then forget . . .

"Son, you haven't left the house for 2 years, how come?"

And heaven forbid, him have to chastise one of his little girls . . . call the forest rangers, the Canadian mounties, Dr. Ruth, Pee Wee Herman, James Brown give this man some hep please . . . hep him Lawd . . . hep him . . . I remember my sister said something to him that was real fresh after he had asked her to do some mind boggling feat like unhook the Christmas tree lights. She just looked over her shoulder in that young Black female tonal sass . . . "Ah excuse me, and when did you lose all feelings in your legs?" Well sir, the look of sheer panic in this man's face scared me, I thought: okay, coronary . . . it's here . . . it has arrived . . . I mean, he was supposed to say . . . do . . . something. After all he was the daddy . . . but what? It was panic time . . . my sister knew he wasn't ready . . . she had him. She never turned around, kept filing her nails and watching Batman re–runs, "Holy swollen lip lore Batman" . . . it was terrible. Right there all the blood rushed from his face, his head bobbing like a new born baby that can't quite get that head and shoulder thing in sync . . . here it was a 15 year old sass kitten transforming my father into an albino with a Stevie Wonder twitch. He figured out that him gotta do something . . . so he did what all self–respecting fathers would do in this situation, he went upstairs to get my mother . . . who learned the tricks of the trade . . . probably said something to the effect of

"She didn't say that to me, but if I were you I'd cuff her little nappy ass around the block a few times." He came back downstairs . . . with color in his cheeks, and that look in his eyes that says, "Ah ha . . . I have been to the promised land, and I'm back . . . I am James Brown . . . back"

him promptly said,

"What did you say to me child?"

having to hear it again to make sure going upstairs wasn't a wasted trip. My sister, Holy Mark Twain, youth is really wasted on the young, not having see the transformation, re–sassed,

"I say–yed . . . when did you lose all feelings in your . . . "

We never heard the last word . . . Pops had cinemascoped the side of her cheek and lightly Sugar Rayed her face. Personally I didn't think the shot was all that severe . . . more a gentle warning that smart assed remarks couldn't live with the family anymore . . . but my sister . . . geezy weezy . . . call in the state troopers . . . for her it was over. She upped and did a Ginger Rogers 2–step around the basement [*Demonstrates.*] ran upstairs in a bevy of Scarlet O'Hara tears . . . ran to her room . . . lept air bound . . . jack–knifed into the bed and cried her a river . . . cried her a river. When my mother Kojacked her for the ABC of it all, she lifted up, threw back her head in a betta Gretta Barbo and whimped, "The beast struck me . . . " She really said that.

Now while all this was in motion, I was doin' my impersonation of an amoeba . . . just trying to reduce and appear inactive.

"And what you lookin' at boy?"

"Hey pop, nothin' . . . trust me on this one . . . I'm not lookin at a thing . . . I'm not even here . . . in fact, I don't think I've been born yet."

You could tell he was feeling it . . . he just turned and walked, no strutted, peacock–like up the stairs . . . he had a haunchback Humphrey Bogart kinda thing to him . . . he kept mumbling under his breath . . .

"Yeah, talk to me that way . . . I don't know who she thinks she is . . . I'm the daddy dammit . . . girl don't bring home no bacon . . . I'm the rooster in this barn yard . . . and don't forget it . . . "

He moved thru the house with a newfound verve. When he arrived at my mother, he looked at her and said,

"Baby, go down and get me a bologna sandwich."

With that, he turned, saddled his pride, and rebopped off into the bedroom...ride daddy...ride...yeah daddy. Yep, daddies are deep dudes...mommies, deep dudettes...they're just cow polk looking for a horse to ride... "scuse me while I gallop to the side.

> Ah too damn hip
> Too damn hip

Daddies work but you don't see it...so you figure they doin' what you do when you leave the house...playin' with their buddies, 'cept when they come back inside they don't be in bed by nine...Just a cowboy looking for a horse to ride. Mommies work, you know they work, you see them work; washing, ironing, pruning, groaning, moaning, for you to stop putting your underwear on saucers of half eaten cake and leaving it under the bed...

> 'scuse me while I step
> outside.

Daddies sit in undershirts and belch Miller Lite blues to home team homeys. Mommies strip wax off the kitchen floor...looking for a horse to ride.

Daddies watching Walter Cronkite's World in turmoil, him surgically implanted to the livingroom chair. Mommies rearranging furniture, her patron saint of domesticity... 'scuse me while I step, 'scuse me while I step outside...your mamma... 'scuse me while I step outside. We're just cowboys looking for a horse, looking for a horse, looking for a horse to ride.

> 'scuse me while I go outside.

What to do...do what...do the do...do a turn into a season of reasons turning you to other Do–wop–dudes and dudettes working just like you to walk thru adolescence with a steady calm...

Do the do do do ricochet cool...
Find somebody like you who knows the real deal
Find doin' the do do do righteous cool brothers
Doin' it without benefit of Directory assistance...Doin' the do do down is like...
quasi...

Yeah Bro. Quasi...brother whose name used to be Fred before he got annointedly hip and became Quasi...a brother who I could swear was a vegetarian 'cause he was always saying "salid, salid."
...was the first Quasi brother I ever saw grab his crotch. I thought that had to be the coolest statement in motion...brother

would just tug at it...tweak it slightly with thumb and forefingers, thusly...ritual fashion. As he did it, he'd give off a slight "Huh," not a James Brown "Huh" more a Barry White "Huh." Yeah, as if a "Rat On" was to follow. Of course it never did, just a slight "Huh." Man, brother was cool. I figure any brother who could tilt without benefit of wind or telephone pole, and grab his stuff should be president. To have that much style in the middle of the week was worthy of leadership. I had to ask why he did it...how he learned at such an early age that kind of street elegance. Brother told me...

"Yeah Slim, I check my shit from time to time to make sure..."

"Sure of what?"

"What, are you dense? 'Cause...make sure it's still intact. See I lost it once...Yeah, looked up and had my hood stone cold snatched. When I finally caught up to it, it was in a pawn shop on 15th Street. Pissed me off too, 'cause I had to wait in line while 8 other brother looked to see which ones was theirs. My Daddy used to grab his shit too...then he got married and gave it to my mamma for safe keeping. She kept it in a box and put it on a shelf in the bathroom next the Buffrin cause she knew if he kept it with him all the time he'd lose it. So I grab mine from time to time 'cause I ain't got nobody but me to keep it safe and I sure as hell don't want nobody else trying to snatch my shit and split."

First time I grabbed my crotch, my mother slapped my hands and my old man fell off the breakfast room chair in a humor spasm. See, my mother said it was disgusting and my pop, in between laughter, said I was too small to have anything to protect. It was right about this time they stopped sending me to my room. I've always wondered if there was a correlation.

"Oh what a night...to be needing you..."

Oh needing a reference to the right or left of blase...'cause if Quasi was the one unabridged side of too down...too chilly...too winter ain't got nothing on me cool...then what was the alternative? As in who occupied the other side. She was cruisin' on the lip of hip? Anti-hip. Alas, it all comes back. It was Alvin Bing. Yep, I remember Alvin Bing. Nice guy, really nie guy. A sweetheart of a really nice guy, but a dork. He had an older sister named Margaret...who was a Dorkette...only girl I knew that had bell bottom ankles...which is to say she is fat. Margaret tipped the scales right at quarter past humorous, when she walked, her breasts would jump up and slap her back. You could hear the girl well into the next block. Slap slap...

back, back...slap slap. We all thought she was an African 'cause she had that Funga Conga walk...Slap, slap...Back, back...Slap, slap.

Now Alvin. Alvin Bing was the homey who brought a whole new symmetry to bein' square. Brother was a rhombus. (Guess y'all ain't too hip to geometry, huh?) Alvin would wear blue and gold plaid polyester pants complete with pleats and cuffs, red argyle socks and 2 inch brown platform shoes. The boy was an adolescent test pattern in motion. During the summers he would get dressed up and work part time. Yeah, the Navy would hang his ass out at sea so ships could find their way home in the fog. The thing is Alvin was always doing little irky things to bug the shit of us like...like cutting the grass so neatly that there'd never be any green stains on the sidewalk...

"Why can't you be more like Alvin Binggg?...like...like writing book reports during summer vacation. Why can't you be more like Alvin Binggg?"

"How are you today, Alvin?"

"Oh, fine Mrs. McCaulley...I just re–sanded the roof and put a pile of aluminum siding up for my Dad..."

"How nice, Alvin."

I know, I know why can't I be more like Alvin Bing? The other thing that made Alvin an irksome quirksome ponky kind of guy, aside from the fact that he used to fight like a girl and let his tongue hang from the side of his mouth...

"Stop it!"

was whenever you tried to school this dumb ass in an argument. He'd always refute you and validate his ignance by deferring to a higher authority...that authority being, of course...his cousin "Butchie." To all of us, Butchie was postmarked the King of Swing.. . he of course was not a citizen of the boro of Queens...he was from the post–modern suburb, Teee...Neck...New Jersey...and after all "Butchie" had to know everything there was to know about everything. That was cause he lived just 2 houses down from the Isley Brothers. King of Swing "Butchie" says:

"If you pee inside a girl, she'll get pregnant."

"Naw, Butchie, that bogus, it don't go like that."

"Of course it does..."

"How do you know, you ever try it?"

"No, never...that's vile and disgusting..."

"Then how you know?"

"Because I read it...in a book."

"Yeah, well book the fuck on, Butchie..."

Butchie Bing, cousin of the man for no reason, Alvin being...

USDA son–of–a Mr. and Mrs. Bing . . . I remember nights if you were quiet and you listened very carefully you could hear the whispers of Mr. Bing to his Mrs. Bing . . .

"Baby, our children have no friends because they're lame. Next time I'll wear condoms." Why did the man wear a tuxedo to his vasectomy? If I'm gone be impo'tent, I might as well be impotent.

> Yeah, caught up in the
> mix of antihip
> holding a pause for a
> · cause that we can't find . . .

We just don't have no reference for it . . . no reference for a youth . . . no alms for the poor . . . gotta try and be John Wayne tuff in a Shirley Temple world . . . no reference for hip the way it was at the very start . . . but gotta find it . . . can't be lame . . . Oh no . . . can't be a chump . . . oh no . . . can't be obtuse . . . no use . . . oh no . . . got to be . . . reference for me . . . the Wizard of Hip . . . Chancellor or suave . . . the Constable of cool . . . make me the mystic mercantile master of making it . . . yeah baby, 'cause we're all just searching for the Great McDonald trying to reach Nirvana in a burger/fries existence . . . and if I gotta be young too . . . without a reference . . . I would rather, at the very least, press–on with the crowd on my side.

> Give me a beat
> Too damn hip
> Too damn hip
> Ya too damn hip
> Too damn hip
> 'scuse me while I step
> outside . . .

> "Oh yeah . . . yeah . . . well you ain't nothin' but a bloody,
> humped back, Bazooka–lipped Barbarella, broke
> down cootie carryin' — too cheap to have elec
> tricity in yo' house, welfare walkin', sissy
> sashshain' son of a sea biscuit . . . uh oh . . . "
> "Yeah well, yo' Momma married a man named Bubba . . . "
> "Man don't be talkin' 'bout my Momma uh–huh . . . not

today . . . put up your hands, your buns is done negro."

Yeah satellite time, orbit ego into a Muhammad Ali renaissance hip, a sauntering deft bobbing weaving motion, impressive enough to win favor from the fellas, eloquent stylish enough to catch the gaze of a passing teen femme. You can talk about my daddy, he can take care of himself, but my mama need a little image protection. Flash ya back in the fleetness of feet ... in the quickness of jabbing left tongue ...

"Uh–huh watch me now, no Frankie, don't hold me, don't hold me. Negro talked about my lineage. Him gonna have to learn some–thin', now ...

[Bobs and weaves.]

Don't hold me now ... uh–huh

[Bobs and weaves.]

Him gonna have to learn somethin' ... uh–huh

[Bobs and weaves.]

Betta' deal with this

[Bobs and weaves.]

Hold on a minute, I'm tired

[Stops.]

Uh– huh, alright, alright I'm ready

[Bobs and weaves then stops.]

Alright ... well cross this line, then ...

[Bobs and stops.]

[Bobs and weaves away.]

Yah, well hit me ... Now, I ain't start nothin' but I'm sho' gonna finish up, homey ... just hit me ... go 'head. I just know you ain't gonna hit me again ... I know that much ... Man, Frankie don't stop it ... nigger ain't gonna hit me twice, I know that much ...

[Stops.]

Man ... you are so luckeey ... you are sooo lucky my mother called me in to set the dinner table, cuz I was about to hurt you and you know that ... Awww right mom, I'm comin' ... Look man it don't matter if you can't hear her ... You ain't supposed to hear her, she's my mother ... I heard her ... I heard her, that's all that counts.

And I want this to be a lesson to you ... oh yeah, that's right ... if you still here when I'm finished eating and watching T.V. and doing my homework, I'm gonna hurt you ... later fellas."

"Oh what a night ... "

Bob and weave ... poke and jab ... punch and judy ... punchinello fellow ... in and out ... always important to enter and exit in style.

Makes no never mind how deeply you are asunder...to backstroke in
bullshit is nothing more than learning to come and go with finesse. A
learned affect...an impressive effect if used at the proper p.m. And
remember...Never enter a room full front...enter and exit on an
angle.

> In a minute ya'll
> Too damn hip
> Ya too damn hip.

[*End of Act One.*]

ACT TWO

Afro–guy comes out
bobbing and weaving...
jabbing and feinting...
> *slows down to a soft trot...*

Quick impression: Sidney Portier dancing in *To Sir With Love*

> [*Does so.*]

"Look"

> [*Keeps on feinting and bobbing.*]

I know...talk about your eclectic as hell...no general eclectic.
Here...dis here specific and local wattage...ya' got to find your heroes where you can...cuz outside of Mommies and Daddies house
passing few and far between...Give me a beat...

> "Reaching for the dream
> that spells tomorrow.
> I see another generation
> coming on..."

I was gonna Willie Mays my way into adulthood...round the hip
four base trip into travel and women and immortality...one small set
back...my old man said I couldn't hit the curve ball since I was too
lazy to actually man a protest/which move profoundly meant get a job
...we meaning he decided that I should go to a universe city...a col-
lage of arty liberal training...

> "Reaching for the dream"

Yes sir buddy, an academic and analytic hip!...trip ivy towers
embracing bastions intellectualism...a 4 year place to discover a

place where your personal race could be run. More importantly an independent sojourn where I could explore and soar and learn and turn in tradition and if truly blessed, lose my virginity...Oh yes...yes sir buddy...if there's any mandatory pre–requisite in establishing a premise...a hip realism...actually going all the way with an Afro–babe is the one...ya see up until that time Afro–guys simply hang out on midnight streets and lie about getting ovah...oh yeah.

"Yeah bro man, I've had more than you got socks...fact is I'd be
        in the rack with one of my femmes now it I hadn't pulled
a muscle playing B. ball today. Yeah, got to be at my best when I'm
    with the honeys."

It's a hard line one has to run when with the fellas...It's just too hard bein' the only one on your block whose only encounter with feminine anatomy was when you accidentally walked in the bathroom while your sister was steppin' out the shower...no sir, that doesn't count...and it's not until much later in life when the pressures off them you can realize you aren't the only one lying about it...So off to college and the increasing possibility of promiscuity in the dormitories with those who would not be promiscuous in your old man's Volkswagon...
Yes sir —
"Play on it...Play on it"
Try to just jump on it...
yeah

I remember vividly the excitement I felt the first time I had sex...it's too bad there was no one there to share it with me at the time...brrump bump

I used to go to college parties and fix two drinks, one for me and one for my left hand. When asked why, I'd tell folk I was tryin' to get my date drunk...

brrump bump

But into each male life a little "trim" must fall...and so it was...on an eventful rainy campus night. An autumn wind softly doing Tony Bennett riffs on my campus window. There arrived the moment I had wet–dreamed since early adolescence. She was a hell of a woman...an older woman...I was eighteen, she, nineteen. Candles had been lit; music slowly cascading from a corner turntable...filling the room with a la Carly Simon "Anticipation." We caressed, fondled... whispered widdle coos coos. She laughed...ha! ha!...I laughed... ho! ho! ho!...then she laughed...then I laughed again...The she grew impatient and I laughed again and again. Then she, also having

had a few childhood heroes, gave me a Sidney Poitier, "Look..." I
stopped laughing... see, I drew a blank. I was a victim of PG movies,
victim of "cut–aways" at the moment of truth. If it wasn't fondling, I
hadn't the foggiest idea of what came next. What to do? Admit it? Be
the say–hey kid and 'fess up... In your best male voice say

"I dunno... do you?

Hell no son... your hippness is at stake. You can't let the race
down... plow ineptly on... and hope; she won't notice.

Here the moment of truth and being sexually illiterate, I just went
full–speed–ahead for the first orifice I could find. I arrived at the
navel, issued un–holy hell on her belly button... I know... un–wise.
But in moments of extreme panic one reacts... one does not think.
There I was eighteen years of trembling emotional jello. My legs having served notice ten minutes before, that they were clocking out.
They were saying... "This is between you and the brains between
your legs, we're not in it." So my legs, they mutinied, and my knees,
they were beating in a cross counter rhythm, echoes of Ray Baddetto
and Mongo Santamariaa... and in that moment, that moment of
truth, I did what any self–respecting, red–blooded American
Afro–guy would do... I cooed in her ear "Is it good to you baby?" Oh
year, better to be thought kinky than unskilled. Ah, this thing... this
maleness thing... best understood in the precipice "leggo my ego...
"

She, on the other hand, being worldly in ways I had only slept
thru very patiently re–cooed "Freeze Jr. let's give it a rest before you
hurt somebody..."

No one wants to be defeated

Just how funky is the young male fight? Alas... alas again... just
can't be defeated... not the American way. But what if for a moment
... one shaky moment... there was a purge... a pimple of emotional
honesty... where Afro–Jo could confront Afro–femme and in ripened
honesty, maybe then the lot of us would stop getting busted for
male–fraud... maybe? Naw...

Too damn hip
Too damn hip
"Reaching for the dream that
spells tomorrow..."

Venture out Brodder guy... these 4 walls can't hold you.
Graduate from a city Universe... step from the liberal 4 year college
into the real universe... of paisley ties and coordinated fabric. Get
out there and make a way for yo'sef. Get a piece of the rock... own a

part of the planet. Cuz if you do, people will flock to you. They'll speak in a hushed, revered tone... "That Afro Jo, up–and–coming Afro guy." Graduate to hipper ideals, and maybe then it won't be nearly so difficult to get some "trim"... Come on admit it guy... that's what you're in it for... how do you spell relief... S–E–X... And if you get a lot... flaunt it... let your buddies know... brag about it... make everyone in your office revel in your dexterity... be the Monday morning matinee idol on your job... be aggressive and flaunt it... then hipness will surely follow 'cause we're all in search of the elusive cookie... so if you can own some planed; make a name for yourself, maybe you can barter... force an even exchange... makes her give you cookie for a little bit of your real estate... which then make you "Cookie Monster..."

"One cookie not enuf... me want to taste everybody's cookie..."

How to do? Aha, get more universe... build a monument, write a song... own more earth... get a jar big enough to hold more cookies... Step out young buck... be Master of the world... Master of the universe... Master of all you survey... Master–Bater.

[*Chants.*] "Gotta get... gotta get it... get ovah... gotta go get it... gotta... sho' nuff get it... gotta get a lotta shakalaka gotta... get ovah"

Get ovah the hellacious hustle of tryin' to get ovah... to hip... ness... yeah, gotta go... for it... you've heard it all before... the rain of the same refrain... hippness is as hippness does... get ovah hip... yeah... yeah... cuz maybe if I can stare squarely in the eyes of Afro–femme, one so adept at arousing this self–doubt and fear and survive the fear, then I'll be a man... Attention! Get ovah man... Get a job... get laid... get married... get laid... get bored... get laid on the side... get laid off... get divorced... get re–laid... ah, yes... Ah no... Ah so... it seems...

The 80's ain't easy... it's a hard road to toe... speak on it... you know the toe it is speakin' of... it's hard to hit the 80's Afro–femme with the big impress when she's pullin' down roughly 10 grand more than you.

Find yo'sef havin' to invent a new myth... Afro–femme makin' too much money to have to be patient with the old order. Your best respondevu is currently old news...

Your: "Yo ba–bee, I'd like to lasso you in an under–water lip–lock and make your vital organs scream for air..." is a Barry White riff in a Run DMC world...

Your: "Ba–bee, I'm a bidness man . . . here my bidness card . . .
call me and we do bidness . . . " is an elephant strut on a quick sand
road . . . you sinkin' . . . quickerly.

These are words of an ancient order . . . relics . . . semantic fossils
in the new age . . . I am now livin' in the age of automated lipstick . . .
astral–phonetic–cosmetics. Looks and sounds are constantly changing — zap — star wars–changin' — zap — now you know me — zap —
now you don't . . . If you don't like it the way it is . . . all you gotta do
is — zap — now you don't . . . If you don't even hafta use me not footsteps . . . just remote — bay–yah — to cable . . .

The new order agenda gentleman got to be SENSE–SI–TIVE . . .
Michael Jackson Sense–si–tive . . . if not you will beat it and beat it . . .
for real . . . shucks no one wants to be defeated . . . indeed . . .

Hard hustle to get ovah to the new age hip . . . an age where you
may see pink, but she sees mauve. And where the hell was I when the
color shifted? When did I become so a–symmetrical . . . I mean I'm
trying . . . tryin' to be sense–si–tive.

I take Afro–babes to restaurants deccoed in mauve, with quaint
Carmen Miranda bushes in the corner . . . places where waiters usher
in pyro–technic choreography and where menues are against the law.
One has to have mastered the Evelyn Wood speed listening technique
just to order a meal . . .

[*Properly British.*] "Hello, I'm Andre. I'll be serving you this
evening."

"Aw c'mon, Andre I don't wanna know your name, I don't wanna
get that emotionally involved . . . I just want something I can read."

"As you can see, we have no menues, so, I'll be rambling roughly
143 entrees and their prices and see if you can manage to remember
why you came out in the first place . . . first, we have a . . . "

"Save it Andre, just go to the last item on the list . . . "

"Yes sir, that will be the Veal Scalla Rambo in the Bette Davis
sauce."

Ah yeah, that's the one . . . and the only one making any head way
this nite is Andre cuz he oozes pyro–genetic sensitivity . . .

> Ah yes, to be in love is heavenly
> to not be horny devine . . .

And if you thought the quest for sex used to be rough, the new
age has made it damn near impossible. New Age sex can kill you. I
mean you can come and go in one stroke. Got to figure out how to
be Sense–Si–Tive . . . Cause if U.S.A. Today is right . . . and how could
it be wrong, it's too pictorially colorful . . . then the average man

thinks of sex every other minute while the average woman contemplates sex every ten minutes... That's why men are always looking at their watches... you can see right there, glaringly... there's a problem... compound those numbers over a 24 hour day and you can readily realize some new tactics are in order... my feeling is this... Gentlemen... give your main male organ... a name... make that little fella personable... Why? Cause women don't want to touch it... They don't... Why else is it that when you want to get intimate they say

"Oh no honey... please just hold me..."

They don't want to touch it!!!

This is... a problem... So give your companion a name... it will save you mornings of the little bugger waking you up... banging your chest...

"Yo... hey... cowboy... what's the deal? You been promising me company for a month now... What's up with you?"

Better name him. I gave mine a name... hell yeah. It took a while ... but I did it. I went through the obvious like Big Mac and Dr. Feelgood. Phill–up but I realized I had to settle on something comfy. Something appealing to Afro–femme. I named him Bert. Yeah... simple... boy next door homey... elegance. Now I simply say:

"Hello would you like to meet Bert, he'd sure like to meet you."

Bettah name that go–getter. Show you can be sensitive... cause the real deal is she doesn't want to touch it. You look on in disbelief... need further proof, dontcha? Alright... Find yourself fellas in a heated and passionate romantic interlude and let the phone ring. If you answer it all, it'll be a...

"Yo... Yeah... look... ah... I'm busy... Call ya back... Click"

Let that same phone ring, in that same interlude and let her answer and it'll be...

"Hey girl... how ya doin'... no... I'm not doin' nothin'... um hum... yeah... Afro Jo's here... so girl tell me 'bout what happened last night..."

I'm telling you. She doesn't want to touch it. Name that bad boy or devise some new design...

Ya' gots ta be sensitive... MJ sensitive... in the New Age... cause when women discovered orgasm way back in 1973, the old jig was up and yet how to arrive at a sensitive place in an insensitive world... ain't an easy thing... no sir... surely wasn't my legacy... surely wasn't easy try–as–they–might for an age of elder Afro guys who grew up in a world where their dreams got re–shuffled by...

"You can't sleep here, ride here, stay here, be here..."

Signs...surely ain't easy for young Afro–guy who grew up neu-
tralized by Prime Time TV assassinations...hard to be nice when
the grandest image of nice keeps gettin' cancelled...tends to
pre–empt a soft–touch:

> "What funeral we
> gonna watch this
> year, Daddy?"

To be sure, to be sensitive in this age is not an easy thing, daddy
man. Ain't hip to be sensitive and dead. Naw...no sir...make me
wanna holla, throw up both my hands; make me wanna find a fresh
21st century thang...make me wanna out last the outlaws...make
me wanna grab Bert and ride on...

> Give me a Beat...
> Too damn hip
> Ya too damn hip

To just get ovah...too damn hip...gotta be more...to damn
hip...gotta get through it to get to it...more...more than a
shakalaka...more to it...than knitted tweed places...gotta be...
maybe bout...planting a seed and raising a family...You know? Out
back waiting for the next harvest..

> Ah yeah, too damn hip

It's a quantum leap from a date to a procreate but the bottom line
is every Afro–Jo wants an Afro–infant...maybe just to insure there is
a hip after life. Cause if there is to be life after hip, somebody got to
be around to do the PR...

"C'mon youngun...lemma show you how I used to slam dunk.
Go on and get under the basket, son and throw me the ball back after I sink 'em."

"Howdy neighbor...yea this mine made 'em up with you own
two hands...yeah...Afro–momma carried 'em but hot damn if I
didn't cook up the recipe...yep looks just like me...go fetch the ball
youngun."

Need some young one to learn what you know been passed on by
those who knew it for you...

"Son get a job...get laid...get a life...mow the lawn..."

"And you I don't want to catch that little nappy headed fellow
over here when the sun goes down, you hear me girl?"

"And go on, you don't love me...it's your momma you love..."

Too damn *deja vu*...its gotta be more...this struggle to be...

struggle to be... to be immortal... gotta be immortality... hip gotta be immortality... gotta be more than just keeping warm bodies on the planet... yea, yeah ya gotta keep your name alive... hell, George Washington got his own currency... tain't too many of us got our name on a street... on a park or even their own holiday... most of us are a narrow cast memory... finally just forgotten... the anti–hip nightmare... not to be remembered for our having occupied a place on earth. Gotta plant a seed... raise a harvest... gotta tell an Afro–youngun

"Hell... dyin' ain't shit Jon... it's the world not knowing that I was here... that scares me... that's what you younguns are... you're life insurance. I invest in you cause if you make a loud enough noise on this earth... people will say had to be a helluva Afro–guy and girl to make up one with such a mighty sound... "

Kinda like grand Afro–elder use to say...

[*Woman dippin' snuff.*]

"If the Father was to let me know this was my last breath, you can believe I'd take that breath in, just as slow as I could, and hold it. You see, I don't want to leave 'fore my work is done... but just in case I do, you make sure you finish it up for me and let everyone know you was part of something and somebody's greater than you. Now go on and get me a ginger ale out of the box... "

Yeah, gotta keep the name alive... gotta connect the dots of what was to what is to what will be. You see, all my Granddaddy — men before me have met their Maker... Grandmommy memory women before me have gone and met their Maker. Daddy–man has hi–fived his Maker and now I am here in a subtler quiet... there's me and this lineage slowly drawn upon itself... there are but sisters and only the solo sound from the polo ground of a mother' voice binding this life to a legacy...

Mommie in your sleeping, I sing of silence

[*Whispers.*] Hey Momma, listen now... I have born you no children, grandly yet... still there are young voices hiding inside me... Momma you cannot leave me here alone... I am not yet sure of what pattern my feet make when they walk the path of you blood... Momma you are only sleeping now? Momma?... Momma...!?!

See it was a November, not long into an autumn ill wind when I stood upright in a hospital room with only the sounds of sonar, only the sights of geometric lines methodically pushing itself against a graph to signal life... and I watched you lying in silent convulsions wondering if it had all come to this... this memory of lineage and legacy concealed in the emptiness of a trembling hand...I remember whispering to you...

"Not yet...It cannot be time yet Mama...I am not ready to walk against a night of strangers. I am not ready to echo your voice to children who are not yet born to sound. I am not ready for your voice to lay passively inside my ears...

I am not ready to speak you...

I am not ready to just remember you...

Damnit wake up...Damn you...Wake up...

I am not ready for your memory

Wake up...

I am not ready...

Mama eyes now open...as if to say careless, selfish male child

I am still the wind that holds you upright

I am still...

I am falling now over the edge of the world, unable to scream...

But I am still

I am a mute...reconciled voice of an autumn morning

But I will yet hold your unborn children...I will yet move your fingers separately and help you feel the neutral edges of your heart

I will yet hold you...for

I am still...am still...still...with you...

[*Sing refrain "And When I Die and When I'm Gone."*]

And so a name...my name still celebrate...a sound resembling my face still resolute...a voice of my hip continuum still arcing on...still realized...still with me...

[*Refrain... "There'll be one child born in this world to carry on... "*]

"Hell boy...get a job...get a life...get an after life"

> "One child born in this
> world to carry on..."

Yeah, gotta find me a youngun...tell him that he gotta carry on a lineage...a memory...a legacy...

> "One child born in this
> world to carry on..."

And where the hell was I when the ground shifted...

"Say boy get your butt on in here, can't you see the street lights are on..."

And when exactly was it when I became my father's voice...

"Carry on"

Give me a beat...
Too damn hip
Too damn hip

So what it is Aunty Em, as in yo yo yo... what is it... now... as
in knowin' my voice now. Havin' it heard now... and whispered now
and remembered... when... as in hippness what hippness was... as
in maybe there's really no need to kneel at the altar of other media heroes... as in time now to press on to my own infinite place... a place
of word hipply wound around a whole... a whole life... as in bein'
born inside whole words that knit my like in a whole story... as in yo,
yo, yo light bulb time... maybe if you are taught a collective story,
not a solo story then don't no one body gotta live in a tenement
though... a high rise attitude... Dig what I'm saying as in yo, yo, yo
... wattage time. If you have to learn about everybody's story then no
one body get bent out of shape about something s simple as riding a
Bus tain't gotta bus nobody, nowhere if we all learnin' de same thing
... don't you know... Won't be so arr–o–gant in ig–no–rance yo...
yo... yo... like if you make it a living story about everybody then no
one somebody feels cheated cuz the story got iced... when somebody
gets left out you got trouble... Right here in River City and that
starts with "T" and that rhymes with "B" and that stands for body...
Aw, get nappy with it... Cuz the one somebody who ain't heard his
name in Da Book... get funky wid it...

The one in de book got a stick see... it's a stick of self–value... a
stick of self worth... while the one left outta de book gets oozed upside the head with da stick of self–denial and self–degradation...

"I don't know nothin' 'bout birthin' no babies"

Hell son got to make it a whole story... not his story or her story
... a whole of everybody don't leave nobody out...

Dig if you will, knowin' 'bout da world, the sounds of da world.
.. as in if you know and dig the rhythm of the world you be to busy
jukin' to ever think about nukin'... Why you wanna be a Russian,
man. Him just raisin' babies too...

"I tell you I don't know nuthin' 'bout birthin'... "

Wild when you don't know 'bout the collected logic of a planet.
.. make you wanna do things like call one music better than another.
. .

Call it in the air...
"Classical
Jazz
Classical

Jazz
Classical"

Yea, make you forget that ideology's nothing but a body of ideas. Kinda like a supermarket of ideas...kinda like socialism is cream corn lyin' on de shelf...And capitalism is green beans lyin' on da shelf and dependin' on what you taste be like depends on what you pick...kinda like K–Mart in though...kinda like why you wanna get mad at someone and tryin' to take dey marbles from 'em cuz dey like cream corn...not growin' up in the collected rhythm of sound make you do that "make" one arro–gant in ig–no–rance. Make you call someone out dey name...

Call 'em negro which begat negra which begat nigger which be-gat midnight...darkie...spook...coon...boot...spade...spick...guinea...

wop...do wop...shimmy shimmy co–co bop...

'N somebody please tell me who was the rocket scientist who came up with jigga boo...what the hell is a jigga boo? Don't sound like nothin' you can tie it no any kind of begat...jigga boo...it got no origin...probably be de same mind that calls the most vital part of a woman's anatomy...poon–tang...probably be de same mind that be callin' man who find compassion in man...faggot...same mind...same mind going going gone...who forgot about the hue in being...hue/man and hue/woman...

Yeah...gotta know everybody's story...Not knowin' the whole story make you wanna own the planet...not live on it...make you drop bombs on itty bitty island countries like Japan...like Vietnam...like South Philadelphia. I like my children without Napalm, please...not knowin' sounds of de world make you wanna make red people say: "Wom Pom." I knew an Indian once...he never said "wom pom"...Him say he mad paid reservation in homeland cancelled by guests he welcomed...him say he plenty tee–peed off bout the way the Manhattan deal went all the way down to L.A. Him say many things...but him never say wom pom.

Knowin' everybody's sound make you not sound off at young-blood who be pullin' him stereo on a dolley thru a corner part...him just tryin' to make the trees dance to him earthquake sound and sound to me if you don't wanna hear him why you let Panasonic put a volume knob on the box...anyway

Yeah, give me a beat...

A sound live in living color

Me got no use for Memorex
Give me words of living memory
Collected words of everybody

Swords... brazen daring darting defiant words... I wanna know
the wholeness of sound everybody's... don't leave nobody out... let
everybody sing a sho–nuff dooby dooby do...

Cuz I think maybe that if I can see you... "chances are" I might
get to know all about you... " and quite possibly I could not want to
hurt you or own you or capture you in my own myth and madness...
but just let you be... they say the difference between bein' artistic and
autistic is that you be... so I wanna just let you be... wanna merge
into a common traffic... lame of assertion

Jah–man
No ig–no–rance

Discover a place of collected truth. Preserve the integrity of dif-
ference — sanctify a chosen place — anoint the aloofness of hip...
so then maybe
Janet Jackson could sing
with the symphony. It's all sound.
And Shabadoo could lock–n–pop with the ballet. It's all motion
And Dizzy–n–Dexter–n–Grover–n–Bird–n–Monk could bump
on Top 40... It's all righteous
Rhythm–n–Boston Pops could hang out with Madonna... Okay
maybe not Madonna... but Prince could hit a lick one time stick and
James Brown could throw down...
Bob Marley–n–Beethoven could be heard at the same time in the
same ear in a common nod of yeah

[*Sing: "It's all right by me... "*]

It's on time 'bout to assert sound; not deny it... merge it to a finite abstraction, a non–muted tonality signifyin' sound of realism...
passive realism... peaceful realism... you be who you be–n–dooby
who dooby when we be doin' it to a righteous healin' place...
Yeah, and to hear it and feel it and believe it... is to finally be...

Give me a beat...
Too damn hip
Bein' who we be is
Too damn hip
But you know that...

Yo. Yo. Yo... one minor post script to an ending... Other day I'm
babysitting my niece Dara... she was taking a pause for the cause...

cuz when she's paired with her bro, the one Willie Deuce, and buzzing cousin Alyssia Jeanen, they become kids Quaddaffi, staging coups on any imposing room in their path...but this was a solo babysitting day with Dara...She looked at me and said...

"Unk Jo"
"Yes Dara"
"Unk Jo...I want to go to heaben..."
"That's nice Dara, you should want to go there..."
"Unk Jo...I want you to take me..."
"Sure baby, when the time comes I'll meet you there..."
"Unk Jo...I wanna go now..."
"Why Dara? Why now..."
"Cuz...Cuz...Cuz my teacher...Miss Little say heaben is nice place   where you can play all the time and you never have to go to bed   and you can have fun all the time...so I wanna go now."
"Well, you can't go now, Dara."
"Why Unk Jo? Why can't I go now?"
"Because you have to die before you can go to heaven, sweet heart..."
"You have to die?"
"Yes dear..."
"Oh.then could we go to Wendy's...?"
Yeah Dara...slam dunk it _____."

> Ya too damn hip
> Give me a beat...cuz we're
> outta here...we're
> history...post–dated...
> we're a memory...
> Ya too damn hip kid
> Just too damn hip
> But you know that...

[*End of Act Two.*]

Phyllis Yvonne Stickney

BIG MOMMA 'N 'EM

PHYLLIS YVONNE STICKNEY

A chameleon actress, a consummate artist, a griot, who celebrates the spirit of life, love and the universe through creations in theater, television, film and her unique, one-woman stand-up performances. After coming to NYC from the deep south, Stickney received training from the University of the Streets Theater, the Frank Silvera Workshop, and New Heritage Workshop, under the direction of the late Roger Furman, acclaimed playwright and director, who groomed her into a polished performer. She also produced several theatrical presentations after Furman's passing. Ms. Stickney introduced the award winning South African play *Woza Albert* to New York's black theater audience. In addition, she produced Beah Richard's *A Black Woman Speaks*, and the late Abram Hill's *Strivers Row*.

Ms. Stickney created a choreopoem for children called *The Crystal Pyramid*. She later went on to perform Wole Soyinka's Nobel Prize winning play *Death and the King's Horseman* at Lincoln Center. In 1993, Ms. Stickney did a stage reading from Gloria Naylor's *Bailey's Cafe* at Lincoln Center, which was presented in the 1994 spring season at the Hartford Stage Company. Comedy became the medium which would take Phyllis Yvonne Stickney most directly to stardom. Beginning at Small's Paradise in New York, Ms. Stickney performed before packed houses, weekly. She later seized first place in the Wednesday amateur night contest at the Apollo Theater on an evening where her motivation was to win enough money to give her brother train fare home. Ms. Stickney's first real break as a comedian came when she was personally requested to perform as the opening act for Roberta Flack during part of her 1986 tour. The early support she found in Roberta Flack as well as the acclaim she gained through her weekly Concrete Comedy performances in Washington Square in the Village led her to the likes of Andy Warhol and Bill Cosby. Ms. Stickney was featured in Warhol's *Interview* magazine in March of 1986 and his MTV special, *15 Minutes*. Stickney subsequently made screen appearances on *The Cosby Show*, *A Different World*, and became warm-up announcer for Cosby's television show during the 1986 and 1987 seasons. She was an opening act for the Patti LaBelle tour in 1991, and made her national television debut as Cora Lee in the ABC mini-series, *The Women of Brewster Place*. The mini-series also starred Oprah Winfrey and Cicely Tyson among other great talents. In the 1990 ABC sitcom *New Attitude*, she made TV history as the Afrocentric character Yvonne, with co-stars Sheryl Lee Ralph and Morris Day. Ms. Stickney returned to television in the February 1991 PBS' "Great Performances" production of George Wolfe's *The Colored Museum*, spotlighted in HBO's

The History Of Blacks In Comedy and appeared with Gregory Peck in *The Portrait*, a TNT original movie.

Her motion picture credits include: *New Jack City, Jungle Fever, Talkin' Dirty After Dark, Malcolm X, What's Love Got To Do With It?, The Inkwell* directed by Matty Rich, and most recently, *Die Hard With A Vengeance* starring Bruce Willis. Ms. Stickney produces "The Upper Room", a weekly poet writer's workshop, in Los Angeles and New York, as well as "The Comedy Connection", a weekly comedy venue production begun at New York's Cotton Club in 1991. She is currently working on the publication of an anthology of her original poetry as well as a debut album. As described in the 25th anniversary issue of *Essence Magazine* that was dedicated to "Extraordinary Women who Changed the World", Phyllis Yvonne Stickney "...with rootsy African beauty, snapping wit and affecting dramatic talent, she's working the crowd."

Awards: Roger Furman's adaption of Moliere's *Tartuffe*. (AU-DELCO); *Big Momma 'n 'Em* (AUDELCO); Custodian of the Cultural Consciousness Award.

FROM THE WORDS OF THE PLAYWRIGHT

I am writing these notes to be attached to the "script" of the work in progress known as *Big Momma n' 'Em* — my humble offering to the voices of the Black theatre experience. I received an invitation from Pamela Faith Jackson to include the work in this anthology. We were at a meeting of the Upperroom Poets and Playwrights Workshop that I produce in Harlem, New York every Monday night . . . We talked briefly and the next thing I knew I was at the keyboard trying to get this work in order. I certainly did not feel that the work on *Big Momma 'n 'Em* was finished. I could not however ignore the call. Documentation of the process of the work all began with a phone call. The idea that the making of the script of *Big Momma 'n 'Em* was supposed to happen just the way that it did, supports my firm belief that there are no coincidences.

The events in our lives are a special blend of fate, destiny, and prayer. So I guess I was supposed to get the call from George Wolfe. I was in Hartford, Connecticut. I was dog–tired from the grueling schedule of performances at the Hartford Stage production of Gloria Naylor's *Bailey's Cafe*. I'd slept on the couch with all my clothes on because I'd been too exhausted to climb up the five steps to the bedroom the night before. The phone rang and woke me up before I was actually ready to rise and shine, getting on my nerves. I answered the telephone in my best "I'm already up and have done three laps around the track" voice. The caller was none other than George Wolfe! Oh my God! THE George Wolfe was waking me up! Now I can't ask him to call me back not if I want to audition for The Public Theatre again (if you know what I mean). I wake up and focus through the fog of my fatigue and early morning maze and talk to Mr. Wolfe.

I met Mr. Wolfe some time ago before the *Colored Museum*. I counted him as friend even though our lives had taken us on different paths. He was a voice in the theatre that was proud and recognizably black. Black was definitely what I needed after the "snow" of Hartford. I was all ears and morning mouth. He asked me if I had something I wanted to do at the Public. He needed to fill a spot in his already publicized series. How could I say no? Why say no? I needed a next show so when I no longer had Jesse Bell and her eight page monologue or her weekly check I'd be able to pay Ma Bell or buy a few groceries — things I'd come to enjoy like you know, soap, bathroom tissue, water. I did not hesitate to say yes. But what would I do I asked? Looking back at it now, I'm sure George knew what he wanted, he had to get me to agree with him. Danitra Vance was very ill. He needed me to do *Big Momma n' 'Em*. Although he had seen the workshop productions in North Carolina and Georgia, he wanted a scripted show because he knew that I was MS. Improvisation. He was now challenging me to set the show. I could add the textures I'd always envisioned for the show, set, lights, sound design, and costumes. He was offering me a full production without the bill! It was definitely on! One thing I didn't factor into the equation — we had four weeks to pull this off! Four weeks to tell AND decide which stories would be written, four weeks to script and edit the show, light the show, design, build, set and sound. In four weeks! Since I believe in the magic of God and the theatre; I asked for someone to transcribe each days storytelling for me. I felt that transcription was essential to my being comfortable with accepting the challenge successfully.

An intense rehearsal schedule began almost immediately after the meeting in Hartford. I had to tell "stories" day after day and eventually weeks had passed and no transcribed pages from the myriad images touched upon in those Hartford sessions. With a dramaturg that was not typing...my mouth had been running for weeks. Some days the stories felt so rich I could hardly wait to read them.

After many long nights on the telephone with Trevor, my stage manager, the artistic team and crew, we made it to tech week. The sound was giving us hell. It was down to the wire — the weeks of rehearsing 10:00am to 6:00pm and then performing with a 7:00pm call. When everything looked as though it would break down, I could not. I PRAYED AND PRAYED AND PRAYED! That is how *Big Momma 'n 'Em* came to be. The night of first preview at the Public Theatre was cancelled. A decision made more difficult for Lonnie Berry, my director and George to make because we were sold out. — sold out for the entire run. So no matter what I felt about the readiness of the work; something in the work fed the people and they came every night. As *Big Momma* took the stage she prayed and prayed and prayed for all of us. Keep these thoughts in mind as you read these words and know that I will continue to be grateful to GOD to my Big Momma and the ancestors. To all who came to see the show in all of her forms; those who care and those who believe in the magic of theatre and prayer. I humbly offer these sisters to you.

CHARACTERS

BIG MOMMA

CAROL REED

VOICE OF HAROLD

HEATHER

VOICE OF HEATHER'S MOM

COOKIE

BENEFA

BIG MOMMA, *an older woman of extreme grace and regalness enters, in house coat and slippers kneels down by ottoman and proceeds to pray.*

BIG MOMMA: [*Voice-over.*] Blessed art thou oh lord God king of the universe who sanctify us with his commandments and who commands us to wash our hands.

Blessed art thou oh lord God king of the universe who sanctify us with his commandments and who commands us to wash our hands.

Blessed art thou oh lord God king of the universe who sanctify us with his commandments and who commands us to wash our hands.

Oh, I want to thank you Lord for wakin' me up this mornin' clothed in my right mind. I wanna thank you for the strength to get up out of bed this mornin' and the wisdom to give you the praise. I wanna thank you for the many blessings you bestowed upon me these sixty-seven years. I wanna thank you Father for the many blessings you have bestowed upon me this day, for Father this is a most special day.

And Father I want to extend my prayers for my people livin' and not—Lottie, Nathan, Leo, Aunt Lou Gracie, Bell, Elihugh, Pig, Welton, Malvonia, Fred and Felix, Cocoa—and all my grand babies.

Lord help me to keep your commandments and please to remember to bring every one of my spirit children something from Africa. That Bayzon fabric for Carol. Carol...

Cookin' currin' and cryin'. Every time I smell curry coming from a pot, I remember that girl come in here late that night. Came in here, Carol Reed, straight from the air boat, moved in next door and proceeded to be a good neighbor. Quiet. Except for that night she came in about nightfall.

The way that girl was wailin' was something terrible. I had to go see 'bout her. The more she cried the more she cooked. And come to find out, would you know it, all them tears was about a man. Seem like the similarity between us sometime remove all the difference, don't it? Cause in that moment, me and Carol were the same. Her pain was mine, her tears were mine. Oh, thank you Jehovah shammah my friend.

[BIG MOMMA *gets up, leaves.*]

[*Enter* CAROL REED, *a vibrant young woman dressed in colorful clothing, she reaches into her shoulder bag and withdraws an aerosol can and sprays the air.*]

CAROL: Everytime me ride upon da subway in da summer me miss Jamaica bad. White people smell like puppy dog. Me can't believe me been here tree years me live in Harlem. Already me want to go home but my papers no fix. I remember growin' up in Black River. Braidin hair from when me was a little youth until now always braidin' workin' in my braid shop business. Me can braid fast fast now. And all de people dat come out of Black River know about Carol's fingers. Me no braid no white girl hair in Jamaica, na seen? Jamaican beach picney can braid dem hair I and I never braid dem hair. One ting all dem always say about Carol. Me never take time for no romance.

And so me tink until de day he was walkin across Ms. Icy's. Ms. Icy makes da best rum punch and me love me rum punch. Me go dere me just sit and chat with Ms. Icy, and me look on da beach and me see dis man standin' dere. Me always did like a man with a nice bow legs, na seen? A swimmin' trunks, full. Me never let me elder know me gonna chat wit a man. Too much peppar dem a say.

So me just try to sit dere and acting like me pay attention. Ms. Icy talk about dis one stayin in de bungalow and what dis one do and dis next one. She just wanna chat about dem affairs. So me listen with half ear. De other half is listenin' out for dis man. So me just stare out into de ocean. Hoping maybe he will come back up the beach.

De next day me stop by Ms. Icy, have a cold fruit punch and don't see da man at all. So me just make me visit shorter. Da next day, me stop by Sun Splash and see Trevor, my bartender friend. Me see da same man dere! And me heart is just poundin. How me gonna get introduced to dis man — witout 'em tinkin' dat me a party girl.

So me just go and sit at de bar tell Trevor me have one rum punch, please. Me just sit dere and chat wit Trevor and me feel real nice. So now me just start to feel good enough to start hintin' bout da man dere.

Me say, "Trevor, you know Carol long time." "Uh Hm." "Ya ever seen me chase after a man?" "Uh Hm."

"So, if Carol inquire about a man you know it must be serious business." "Uh Hm."

Where da man born? Were 'em stayin'? Who travelin' with 'em? Any wife? Any pickney? Any white girl?" Him say "Daughter, me see da man 'pon da beach 'bout seven, eight years straight." "Me tink him a yankie man" "Him a yardy dat. Look at how him flex. Pure Jamaican dat."

Da man just come straight from da water to da bar. Me say, "Calm yourself, Carol." What me gonna do? Da man is standin' right dere. "Oh god." Ya don't know dis man. How you feel strong so? Da man got da serious bow legs dem. And beautiful face, big brown eyes, a nice little nose, nice little lips, a nice gap in between dose teeth. Me just wanna go and grab him up and just kiss 'em up right dere. "Calm yourself, Carol."

Me give Trevor the eye like you must introduce me. So Trevor just real cool and everyting and say, "What you want for drink man?"

Him sound like pure angel. I am hopin my mouth is not sittin open. Me give Trevor de eye again, Trevor get de message. And he say to me, "Carol, I want you to meet one of our guests." Me say, "What? Oh, yes Trevor ?" "Dis is Carol Reed, and dis here is Harold. Me not know your family name."

"Oh, God!" Don't tell me 'em last name. Me don't like dat. Em a yankie man. But still dem bow legs change my mind. Me never tink dis man would just occupy my heart and soul so fast.

Watchin' da sunset and gettin' tipsy. Walking home along the water edge talkin with Harold and laughing. Just laughin him love hearin' my laughter. Nobody can vex me from den.

Da next day at work me braidin' and braidin' when we hear. "Carol, come to da front." Me excuse meself and go up front. Oh God, it's Harold!! Me can't believe it. Harold white linen pants, white T-shirt, white flowers. "Calm yourself, Carol." Da man just make me feel pure, pure pure fire, hot, hot, hot.

HAROLD: [*Voice-over.*] I want to take you to dinner and then ride to the waterfall. I need to hear more laughter. May I? What time do you get off of work?

CAROL: 4:30 pass by for me. Now me hands can't braid fast enough. Me just braidin and braidin' and braidin'. Finish. Somewhere between da last braid and da first drop of shower water, me make a decision. I gonna leave Jamaica wit dis man, yes. Just as clear me know me want to make life and love wit dis one man.

So as me get meself ready put on little Frankenscense & Myrrh, smellin real nice feelin real nice, him did come, wearin' white, pure white. Oh God, me gonna strip 'em right dere and do 'em right dere.

Harold, you look like dinner may I take a bite. Everything goin' fine. We drive to Ochos Rios and so me just sit dere and listen to da waterfall. And Harold Miller, his last name, story about his life his friends and Washington Square Park. Dis man look dis sweet and smell dis sweet and sound so good but me know too many times foreign men come to find a girl in Jamaica. Do 'em business and den go. But Harold never try to touch me, disrespect me, or nutin. Dis man is too good.

When 'em did drop me off, me floated inside. Me never see mommy standin dere. "Just a friend, Mommy. Mommy don't trouble yourself, here?"

I and I gonna tell da man straight. Me want to know all about him and me want to go to America. All da dreams me did have from when me little girl. Me hear all kind of tings about America streets paved with gold, black people with plenty money and me know. Dis one Harold pure angel so me know dat America must be heaven. I and I gonna make dinner for Harold.

Every day for three weeks he just drop flower on my little work station. Write beautiful thoughts comparing me to queen dis and goddess dat. Me never tell mommy 'bout 'em. The night she spent at Lucy's I prepared Harold's dinner. He did come wearin' white again and smellin' so sweet. When 'em come inside 'em just look at and take in everyting. Every little flower, every little mat, every little glass, every little plate, everyting me did do for da man. Him just take notice. If he take dis kind of notice standin' straight up, what must be like in horizontal position?

"Calm yourself, Carol." Get da ginger beer dat ya made. Me want da man to know me can cook. Me decide me gonna do da man tonight. Me gonna get in his head for sure. So me did just fix da drinks and fixed little plate and we have nice conversation.

After we finish, we clean up, put everyting away. And me say, "Harold, ya ready for da rum punch?"

[CAROL *pulls out a very large glass.*]

I serve him in the biggest glass I can find cause me want to loose him up — quick. Dere's not much time.

[*Sitting on a stool she gestures between her legs.*]

"Harold, come here sit between me knees me want to do ya hair. Come now and let me do ya hair." You have nice hair. If we make baby, dey have beautiful hair. Him pure black, me pure black. Harold, tell me more about your family.

Me hear someting in his voice but I ignore it. "Harold will you take me to America?" And dere, it is out in de open.

Well everyting did stop. He takes me in his arms. He don't say nutin, just silent. My heart start beatin real fast in my chest like it's gonna beat out if I don't say someting.

HAROLD: [*Voice-over.*] We'll keep in touch. When I get things straightened, I'll send for you.

CAROL: One week turned to one month. One month turned to six months. At least me not give up no poohnanny. Him not take dat. He does have my heart and telephone number. He has everyting to keep in touch. Well after a whole year, me not so much vexed and 'embarrassed as determined. I must go to America.

24 hours a day I'm braidin'. I've gotta make da money to go to New York. Put all me money away. Now me have to get me passport. Have to call a friend of mine, if you know what I mean.

Two weeks and 700 dollars later, my passport and papers ready for travel. Well I tell mommy I'm goin to visit my friend in England. She don't mind. I have plenty family dere.

My cousin drives me to Montego Bay. I'm gettin' real excited about flyin' and seein' Harold. Me never did ride a plane but me act like me do so all da while. Da people just feed you and bring ya drink and pretzel and all kind of tings.

LaGuardia airport, New York City. Da lady on da passport don't look exactly like me, but I guess da bald head just see black face and white eyes, white teeth and say, "go." Carol in America legally, sort of.

A yardie spot me and just come and asked me where me wanna go. Harold talk about his friend Neville. Me remember Neville's number and where he stay. So me tell da cab driver "Espanlande Gardens". My sister say the fare ain't no more than 20 dollar. 20 dollar. Him know dat me a pure Jamaican woman and me not pay one penny more.

We arrive and me ask da driver to wait. Da doorman asks, "Can I help you?" I say "Why you twist up your face so? Is Neville here? Is Neville here?" "Last name please." First American frustration. In Jamaica the right city, street, house and first name that's enough information to find any man. Dis must be culture shock.

Me' get a little scared right now cause, in all the excitement me forget to remember me have no place to sleep. Me hurry back to da driver. "My sister sa ya can find me a room for cheap." Him laugh tell me his friend run a buildin' down da block and can find me a room for cheap.

It's a big apartment nice big rooms. Da whole of my family could stay here both sides. Oh God me have to call mommy so she no call England for me. Enough sightseeing for tonight. Me have but one ting on my mind. Find Washington Square Park.

Well after a while, one month, two months, I'm pretty good wit da train business. So me just one day put on a real nice white because Harold always like white.

So me get dere. His Washington Square Park. Me see da big arches and all da people dem just sittin around the vendors, musicians, playing and partyin.

Well, me can't believe it. Dere is Harold! Well, a part of me just wanna run and hug 'em up and kiss 'em up; tell 'em how much I and I miss him and such. But de other part is stopped dead cold. Because dere Harold sit wit a white girl. Me never did believe 'em see a white girl.

Me tink all da tings did say about nice Jamaican and nice black dis and a princess dat and a queen dis and 'em go on and so about how I love dis an I love dat and a black dis and black. And look see pure white girl.

I get my strength, walk over to dem. Chu. Him was so wrap up in talkin' to dis white girl 'em no see me, sit 'em don't even see me sit down. So me just listen to da sweet talk an da sweet conversation. Me hear Harold tell da woman da same ting he tell me. "Harold!" Pure fear take over da man face. "Why you never send for me? Is dis your wife dat?"

HAROLD: [*Voice-over.*] Uh Carol, uh Carol, me I tried to write.

CAROL: Just tell 'em "Lie. Is lie ya tell." True I was hurtin' inside but on de outside, me was strong because me see da white girl standin' dere.

HAROLD: [*Voice-over.*] She's a braider I met in Jamaica my last visit.

CAROL: Well dat was it? Just a braider? All da dream I had, all da love I had, all da feelin I and I have, just go so. Harold make me do something I never wanted to do. Just a braider. I looked in Harold Miller's eyes. I saw dat 'em never tink about hurt my feelings. 'Em never tink nutin' about da lie 'em tell, nutin.

So den, de white girl say to me maybe dat I can weave I can do her hair. "Calm yourself, Carol... Perhaps, sometime." "How much it cost?"

I look around at all my dread bretheren dere just make demself a clown and show for da white girl, struttin' and flexin'. Me decide right dere dat de only people hair me gonna braid here in America, de only people dat gonna pay for me services here in America, be's da white girl. She will pay for Carol to come. She will pay for Carol to be here. She will pay for Carol pain and she will pay well.

How much it cost? Five hundred dollar. For dese hands dat never touch white girl hair to braid your hair, five hundred dollar. So me give she da number. And, she did call dat night and make appointment and tell me she have other friends if my work is good. If my work is good. Chu.

[CAROL *takes out her spray can again, sprays the air, and exits.*]

BIG MOMMA: [*Voice–over.*] I have to give you thanks every day for my mother and father you will know a tree by the fruit it bears. Thank you lord for making dreams come true. You gave me a good life. Good children. With good sense, for most of the time. Lord don't let me forget to make up them herbs for Heather.

[*We hear Madonna's* Like a Virgin, *and a young attractive woman with long blond hair in exercise clothing jogs in and starts stretching.*]

HEATHER: And a one and a two and a three and four . . . Work those abs. Fourth of July is quickly approaching. And a six and a seven and a eight. Four more. And a one and a two, three, four. Good. Great workout.

[HEATHER *takes a towel and dries her forehead as she changes from her exercise clothing to street clothes.*]

BIG MOMMA: [*Voice-over.*] Wonder why people tryin' to be everything but what they is? Do things they ain't meant to do. Renting wombs and carryin' on, it's children already born need plenty lovin' — They don't have a whole bunch of proper guidance; role models. Some folk ya need need to grab hold of every now and then to set 'em straight. And some just in the wrong environment to be raised up. Like if a cat's tryin to raise puppies. What kind of confuseration is that? Lord, I don't know what have happened but somethings has got to be did.

HEATHER: Hi my name is Heather Leigh Hurst. I found out I was Black. Can you believe it. After all this time, my mother's keeping secrets? I mean, who do you trust? I never thought . . . Well, today, I mean, I was in the gym. I forget to get my hair out of my locker before I took my break. So, I'm going back in and Elaine and Phylicia are there. I don't want Elaine and Phylicia to know that I'm getting my hair out of my locker because everyone knows this is my real hair. So, I go in, the back but not before I hear Elaine's big mouth. She's talking to Phylicia about Todd. I overhear them saying that someone should tell

Heather that Todd doesn't like black girls. Duh! Then, I hear Elaine say, "But Heather doesn't even know that she's black. Can you imagine?"

They left and I went in to get my hair and made a bee line for the telephone. I've got some questions for my mother, OK. "Mom, I'm here at the gym, and I overheard something I really need you to address in like a major way. Is there something you have perhaps forgotten to tell me?" And I'm hysterical by this point. I'm like "Mom, they're saying that I'm black!"

MOM: [*Voice-over.*] Heather, you need to come over here, right now.

HEATHER: So, I power walk, there immediately. There are no clients, the receptionist is gone. Everything is like quiet and she takes me by the hand.

MOM: [*Voice-over.*] Heather, there's something I always wanted to tell you, but the time was never right.

HEATHER: She told me that she and dad had always wanted children. They couldn't have any — too many abortions and too many drugs. They decided to adopt but the waiting list was too long for babies that were white. And so they went to an agency and they made arrangements to adopt me all in one day. My mom tells me that I'm adopted — and that I'm black. Well, after I regained my consciousness, I came here to Blacks Anonymous.

[HEATHER *crosses to stool and sits.*]

CAROL: [*Voice-over.*] So about 9:30 in da evening my 6:00 is finished. Me just sittin down gettin nice glass of sorrell and everyting. Coolin, rollin a little splif, just chillin — and da buzzer ring. Da voice come back say Heather. She say she must get her hair done today. Heather the only black girl hair me weave. She tink she white. Me say, "Okay, you pay $500?"

HEATHER: After we'd gotten all the old hair taken out, Carol's looking at me in this really strange way, like really. Then, she suggested that I change my hair color. Something darker. She saw I wasn't buying it. I mean it wouldn't look right with my blue eyes.

CAROL: [*Voice-over.*] Well, if that's what you want. But it doesn't change who you are.

HEATHER: That's when I began to suspect that she knew. So, I told her all that I discovered.

CAROL: [*Voice-over.*] I want you to talk to somebody. You must let Big Momma give you a bath.

HEATHER: And I'm going like, "Duh, I am quite capable of bathing myself."

CAROL: [*Voice-over.*] No, no. What you have learned about yourself will require a lot of strength and a lot of protection to deal with.

HEATHER: So, I'm like, "OK. This Big Momma's gonna give me strength and protection? Is this what you're sayin' to me?"

CAROL: [*Voice-over.*] No, but people like us . . .

HEATHER: "Like US? I am an us?" I am a you people. Okay, like all of this is going really fast. Thank heavens for the Oreo Hotline.

Well, I figure this bath can't be worse than anything else on this given day. "All right, all right, all right!" And she dials the number and hands me the phone. And I get like a machine.

BIG MOMMA: [*Voice-over.*] You can call me Alma, or you can call me Momma or you can call me Big Momma. But you don't have to call me back. If you leave your name and number . . . Baby.

HEATHER: "This is Heather. I'm a friend of Carol's. Well, I'm a client of Carol's and she thought that I should call you. My home number is 516 555-2590. Please call." Well, Carol's grinning all over. I'm like whatever . . . I'm black! How am I gonna explain this to Elaine and Phylicia? I mean like everybody's gonna like know. All right, I won't think about it. But what will I do with my hair? This is my real hair. Well, Carol says she has an idea. Well, thank you Margaret Truman. She says that she'll do braids. She can still make them long — as long as I want. Okay. I don't have to do Cindy Crawford. I could do braids like Bo Derek. It would mean like seven hours of braiding. I'll think about it.

HEATHER: I get home and my message light is blinking like mad, really. The first five messages are from my mother. But I don't want to hear from her right now, Thank you. And then, there's this voice that comes on like . . .

BIG MOMMA: [*Voice-over.*] This is Big Momma. I got your message. I spoke to Carol. Be here Wednesday at 11:45 PM. Go get Florida water, blue balls, half a dozen lemons, half a dozen limes, sea salt, a quart of milk, whole milk, lady pompeii lotion, some white flowers and some green onions., Wrap you head in a white towel and don't be late."

HEATHER: Duh, Florida water?

BIG MOMMA: [*Voice-over.*] Check out your local botanical, baby.

HEATHER: Well, the next three days couldn't get there fast enough. I've got a date with Big Momma.

[HEATHER *exits, and renters in* BIG MOMMA'*s house with a towel wrapped around her head.*]

HEATHER: So I get uptown and I ring the buzzer.

BIG MOMMA: [*Voice-over.*] Come on in, the door is open.

HEATHER: It was like magical from the time I stepped through the door. She sets me in this little room there and she tells me to wait. She'll be back in a minute. And I'm getting goose bumps all over and I'm like oh my god, this is really weird.

And I'm thinking about all kinds of things *Friday the 13th* and Freddy Kreuger, Chucky and all kinds of things. No! Everything's fine. It's like this voice was talking to me the whole time and things I hadn't remembered since I was a little girl came back to me.

BIG MOMMA: [*Voice-over.*] Okay baby, I'm ready now.

HEATHER: And she comes and gets me and takes me to the bathroom. And everything is like so clean, I mean it's spotless clean. Not like what you hear about those people.

And there's, this old tub with feet and everything and she's got like all this water in it and it's got like smoke coming up and it's like really steamy in there and there's like lemons floating in the water.

BIG MOMMA: [*Voice-over.*] Take off your clothes now.

HEATHER: Everything was like a dream and I'm taking off my clothes and she's talking to me.

BIG MOMMA: [*Voice-over.*] You get in the water.

HEATHER: And it's hot, hot at first, so I have to stand there. With her hand she takes the water and she lets it fall down on my body. She just takes her hands like a cup and she just keeps putting water on my shoulders and my neck and my back.

And then she starts humming this song. I never heard it before. And then it seems like I am drifting and I hear a voice drifting out to me.

[*Sounds of African music layered with* BIG MOMMA *speaking in tongues fills the room.*]

BIG MOMMA: [*Voice-over.*] I want you to give everything to the water. Release all of your tensions, all of your fears to the water. Release all of your tensions, all of your fears to the water.

HEATHER: And she takes a lemon and she starts rubbing my face with it. She scrubs me and sings these songs and says these verses I never heard. And she explains what each thing is for, the lemons, the salt, the Florida water, the Pompeii lotion. And she says my ancestors want to help me through. Ancestors? She tells me a lot of stuff. Deep.

Inside I remember the words. At one point, I remember just crying uncontrollably.

When I was finished, she just tapped me all up and down my front side, then my back side, with these green onions.

BIG MOMMA: [*Voice-over.*] A little seasoning. To add some spice to your life.

HEATHER: I can kind of see all this stuff floating around me. It looked like a stew with lemons floating. And the milk she poured in and scallions ... The aromas mixing together ... It was intoxicating.

She wrapped me in a big white bath sheet and left me to sit and pray. I felt like a little girl. When she came back, she escorted me to the parlor, sat me in front of a big mirror.

BIG MOMMA: [*Voice-over.*] Behold yourself.

HEATHER: Me, Heather. Me, sitting there wrapped in white. I looked at my skin, for the first time. I never knew how rich it was.

Well the dream was over soon. Well, at least that part of it. It was time to go back to my world and try to fit in. And maybe not fit in. I tried to pay her but she wouldn't let me.

BIG MOMMA: [*Voice-over.*] Welcome home, my child. Who are you?

[HEATHER *removes the towel from her head to reveal a beautiful head of short black twists.*]

HEATHER: "I'm Heather — and this is my real hair."

[HEATHER *exits.*]

[*We hear some funk music layered with sounds of a more fiesty* HEATHER *then.*]

BIG MOMMA: [*Voice-over.*] Help us Lord to be more mindful, grateful and humble recognizing all that you do for us continually. Help us bear our load and help us to remember we are our sister's keeper.

[COOKIE *enters to a cacophony of sounds, of voices, echoes and lost souls. She pushes a baby cart full of unfulfilled dreams and memories.*]

COOKIE: I am not my circumstance. She taught me that. People be buggin', actin' like I got a disease. Hm. I don't want nothin' from 'em. Living in my peripheral existence. Wonderin' when it will end. Cause

I played the game by all the rules. So, here I am between residences. Homeless sounds like I don't care, don't know nothin, ain't been no where, lost a job. Nope, I enlisted. I signed up. I volunteered for this madness. Always volunteering. Got a new program, Cookie'll try it. Got some opportunities, Cookie'll take'm. Ebony made me reach higher, inspired me to keep on goin', keep on tryin'. From Upward Bound, Peace Corp...

CHORUS: [*Voice-over.*] Be all that you can be in the army reserves.

COOKIE: I'll take every night class every night course. I will do everything I can to keep my family together. I figure it is the perfect way to pay for an education. Get a degree, get a job, some experience. Me and Ebony were gonna see the world. Always good in school, always.

Weekends, once a month. Till January 15th. Got my orders. Who's gonna take care of Ebony. How long does it take the folks at Family Care Plan to find files misplaced and otherwise.

He declared war on Martin Luther King's Birthday. Didn't he know that Red Foxx was gone, Miles Davis... Give us time to mourn our heroes. Distracted by orders, 'Greetings and Salutations.'

GENERAL: [*Voice-over.*] Find someone to take care of your baby in 72 hours.

COOKIE: I can't say goodbye that fast. Sergeant Charlotte Brown reportin' for duty sir.

DRILL SERGEANT: [*Voice-over.*] Ya left Ya left left right left right had to go home with your left your right want to go back but ya can't your right. Sound off 1 2 Sound Off 3 4 Bring it on down 1 2 3 4. 1 2 3 4 ...

COOKIE: Everything else happened on time as decided by the powers that be. I never thought about goin' anywhere without Ebony. Where's the baby? All the right papers got to me got filed. How can you lose a baby? How can you? No, I am not crazy, just extremely pissed off! I went and fought for them, took their inoculations, took their abuse. U.S. Government issued inoculation for some unknown, unsaid, un-found disease. Genocide? You decide.

Why you lookin at me, brother? While you was on this corner selling dreams and illusions, I was dodgin' death in Kuwait. Couldn't wait to get back home. I got to find Ebony. We got places to go. Where is my baby? Did I do the wrong thing? It depends on who's lookin, who's doin' the talkin. Big Momma speakin' in tongues.

The first time I noticed her was on 145th Street and Seventh Avenue going into Pioneer on Wednesday afternoon. Shopping. I've seen her on the Avenue many times. But today there was something different, something special. She walked across the street. I was tickled to watch her dodging traffic, sometimes daring the cars, defying.

BIG MOMMA: [*Voice-over.*] Hold up now y'all, let me cross this street.

COOKIE: In front of the store, she stopped just long enough to hold my gaze and said.

BIG MOMMA: [*Voice-over.*] You are not your circumstance.

COOKIE: And she was gone into the store. I went to my spot on the median. On days that were warm and sunny like this one, I sat and contemplated my navel.

Seven months I had been in Harlem. I had my parameters. I knew my terrain. Shortly after my tour of duty was completed, I came home, New Haven, Connecticut.

Here I come Ebony. I can't wait to kiss them little fat cheeks and just hold her and smell the sweetness, of her the bananas and apple juice.

I miss my baby. I made a bee-line for Aunt Mayline's. The quietness and the 'emptiness of the front yard, there were no children playin', no cousins, no babies hollerin'. It was quiet but I thought well, maybe one of the relatives, one of the cousins, one of the girls in the neighborhood came by. Precious used to come by and baby-sit sometimes.

I didn't think anything was wrong until I saw this notice on the door, notice of eviction. And inside the mailbox was a letter addressed to me. I opened the letter and read it. Seems like Aunt Mayline had taken a bad turn with this Alzheimer's disease. They had to put her away.

Tina and Tony had taken Ebony. A college student and a 23 year-old Casanova? My baby cousins? They left partial information, "We at cousin Willie's." Cousin Willie's? I made a bee line to New York City. Harlem, USA. I thought it would be a simple task finding Ebony.

OPERATOR: [*Voice-over.*] The number that you have reached is not in service.

COOKIE: Peter Pan Bus Station. The number that you have reached is not in service. The 'A' train gets me uptown fast. Somewhere between 132nd and 158th Street is my life, my baby. I know the building when I see it. There it is. I go to the directory. No Willie Rice listed. So I ring the super.

SUPER: [*Voice-over.*] No aqui. Lo siento. Sorry.

WOMAN: [*Voice-over.*] He moved...Somewhere around here cause I see him from time to time.

COOKIE: How can nobody know?

WOMAN: [*Voice-over.*] He ain't my family, you don't know, ain't my family.

COOKIE: I find myself sitting in Mount Morris Park, hanging out at one of the paddle ball courts and one of the school yards — Hoping that cousin Willie, Tony and Tina, somebody, anybody would show up. Before I knew it, it was daybreak. Soon this was my routine.
    Well I'm daydreaming, thinking about all of this, wanderin off across the street just in time to see her coming out Pioneer loaded down with bags like she was going to give a party and the whole neighborhood was invited. Seemed like a lot for a little old lady. Hunger made me notice. She came out looking for something or someone. She waved her hand at me and moved in my direction.

BIG MOMMA: [*Voice-over.*] Come on here girl, come on, just come on. Get your bag and come on here now.

COOKIE: I was well raised. Elder speaks, you move. Plus curiosity, and missed meal blues got the best of me. The warmth and truth in her eyes, I hadn't seen in a while.
    We walked at her pace. Her gait was like somebody twenty years her junior. And she talked the whole way.

BIG MOMMA: [*Voice-over.*] Life is something like a card game. You got to learn to play the hand you's dealt.

COOKIE: Everybody knew Big Momma, the florist, the Korean grocery man, the shoe repair man, everybody. She was the matron saint of the community. I'm following her, because this is real human exchange. She didn't look at me like I was dirty or crazy.

CHILDREN: [*Voice-over.*] Big Momma!

COOKIE: The children all screamed and squealed as she came up and handed out little goodies to everybody and I thought, if this ain't my Aunt Mayline; if this ain't hope. [COOKIE *enters into* BIG MOMMA's *sitting room.*] Inside, the apartment is so clean, glossy hardwood floors, shiny pictures, baby pictures. It was the baby picture. I couldn't move. I was riveted, held there by this baby picture. How long had it been?

BIG MOMMA: [*Voice-over.*] I don't mean no disrespect but 'Cleanliness is next to Godliness' and the shower's waitin'. Third door on the left. I left a couple of thangs pick one and put it on.
    You like meatloaf? I use ground turkey.

[COOKIE *disrobes showers and changes.*]

COOKIE: Oddly enough, it was one of my favorites. I was showered and feelin' squeaky clean, zestfully clean. Well, it wasn't long before she got right down to business. She knew my pain. And in everything she said, there was a lesson. This woman could have lived in Bible times

BIG MOMMA: [*Voice-over.*] You are not your circumstance. You hear me.

COOKIE: I filled up the pitcher, set the table. I looked at the picture of the baby.

BIG MOMMA: [*Voice-over.*] That's Cocoa, my favorite. I don't tell everybody that.

COOKIE: I was Aunt Mayline's favorite. I looked closer at the picture of this little baby girl. "My baby's name is Ebony, that's what bought me here."

I spilled all of my insides and the tears flowed. It wasn't sadness, it was relief. Release. It was someone who dared to care in this moment, in this hour of my particular need.

The church hadn't done it. The people that were paid in positions of power hadn't been able to do what this women was able to do in an afternoon.

BIG MOMMA: [*Voice-over.*] Now you know we've go to do something about this. Figure this out. You's got to connect the dots.

COOKIE: She told me stories from the bible and stories from her child hood and stories about mothers, the seemingly insurmountable obstacles they had faced. Generations after generations after generations of mothers and children separated. Slave stories, every one strengthening me. Every one lifting the burden, the guilt, the feeling of failure that I had carried down in my gut. In an afternoon, her humming and her meatloaf makin' and my shower takin', I'd wash away the first layer of my fears. That was the first time I saw Big Momma.

The next day, I remember going to the Veteran's Administration. I was gonna get back some of what I had given. There were agencies available. There were more things than I could ever imagine available. And I had to make them work for me. I had to get Ebony back.

Couple weeks later, Big Momma sent word for me to stop by. She opened the door with the announcement

BIG MOMMA: [*Voice-over.*] Cocoa is taking me to Africa.

COOKIE: She was goin' home. She and Cocoa would be gone for a couple of months. And she had something she needed me to do for her. She needed somebody to drop by and make sure the plants were watered, the bowl got flushed, cause it wasn't good to let the water sit too long. Gets stagnant. She wanted to make sure there was somebody who was bringin' some life and some light into her home. And she was calling upon me to do that. I think I can handle this. She believed in me and helped me begin to believe in me.

BIG MOMMA: [*Voice-over.*] When I come back, I expect you and Ebony to greet me.

COOKIE: She gonna be gone just long enough for me to get it together and to remember no matter what. I am not my circumstance.

[COOKIE *exits, head up high pushing her baby carriage.*]

BIG MOMMA: [*Voice-over.*] God keep me steadfast and unfailing in my faith knowing that your light will shine bright as the noon day sun. Bring clarity to our purpose, dignity to our existence. Oh father let me get up off my knees before I can't and before Princess call.

[BENEFA, *a teenage girl with enough attitude to take on the world enters. She pulls up her very large baggy pants as she sits on* BIG MOMMA's *stoop and proceeds to roll her eyes.*]

BENEFA: Big Momma always on me about the way I talk and stuff like I can't get a job or something. I told her I could be a receptionist I could answer phones. For real though. I know how to answer them phones you know what I'm saying.

But she's always tryin to get on my case like I gotta learn how to talk right and stuff like that. I be like buggin' I be like dag why she always. I be like I can't even say dag I can't say nothin' right.

Because she say everytime I say something it's like I have an attitude. That's probably why the people at the group home, she call it all the time the facility that's why they want me to come over here because they want somebody to try to straighten me out.

She try to talk like she got it goin' on, you know like she all dat and a bag of chips. For real though. She need to go ahead somewhere.

And then one day I wasn't even really talking to her. It was something on the TV and I was like, 'Look at that bitch.' And she popped me in my mouth. My mother don't even pop me in my mouth you know. I was like OK this lady is really buggin'.

She didn't hit me hard enough to hurt me, that was true. But she had no business putting her hands on me. Everybody say it, record, TV. Dag. She say 'You ain't everybody. When you know better, you do better."

She was gonna try to tell me something about she know how I

was talking on the phone to dem boys and then she start bringing all this stuff she was feeling about me. And I was like dag. I knew it was time for me just to get my little stuff and just get up outta her house.

"Ya know you should not be running after no boys." And I was telling her I ain't running after no boys. I was only talking to them, right. And she said, "Well if you ain't doin' nuthin' why you gotta be sneakin it make it look like you're doin' something."

And I was like cause my mother won't let me talk to them and she be bugging every time I try to talk to somebody round my way.

There was this boy uptown that I always wanted to talk to. And den she looked at me and started telling me all this stuff 'bout bein special and bein' sacred and how when she was growing up how you waited for the boy to call you.

And there was a certain whatchacallit? Courtin' thing and stuff like that you know. And they would call your mother or your father or somebody. Somebody you know like older and stuff and ask for permission to come up there and talk to you and stuff like that.

She axed me how many times do you get on the phone when you up here? I said well you know . . . She said, if you go in that room and close that door I know you on the phone. Dag she got eyes in the back of her head.

She said I was young too. I'm just tryin' to help you because you wanna grow up and meet somebody nice and have a family and stuff like that. And she start telling me about when she met her husband Fred and how he used to come by her house and stuff like that.

And how he came by for a long time and they would just speak and stuff and finally he came and said something to her and the next thing you know he was talking to her mother and stuff. And the next thing you know, they were married and they were together all them years.

But if she had been loose like other girls, he would have just did what he can do and go on his way.

My mother never talked to me like that. And I was sitting there and thinkin' like everything she say and like I was talkin to my friend. And so she was telling me all this stuff about my body is a jewel and it's a treasure and it's something you have to protect and cherish and usin' all these words and stuff. And she made me feel like I was really special.

BIG MOMMA: [*Voice-over.*] Why you so angry Benefa?

[BENEFA *seems to pull within herself, reflective.*]

BENEFA: I was five years old and mom and 'em had give a party and they always invited Al Morgan. They wanted me to call him Uncle Al all the time but I knew he wasn't my uncle.

And everybody would like to always see me dance and give me a quarter or fifty cents to dance. So I remember I was just dancin'. I could always do the latest dances. I could do them first and I always like to dance.

Mom an 'em was in the kitchen fryin' chicken. They had brought hot dogs for the children and chili dogs. My mother's best friend Phoebe was there. And everybody was havin' a good time. They made such a big thing about me dancin'. Everybody was around in a circle. 'Go Nefa! Go Nefa!' They was clappin', eggin' me on to dance.

I was waitin' for my cousins, but they hadn't got there yet. So, Mister Al said he was gonna take me outside. Always like school. He know I like school and I could hardly wait till I was big enough to go cause I went to kindergarten but I wasn't in first grade yet because I wasn't six years old before September 1st or 30th or something. He said "Wanna play school?" I was so happy. That was my favorite game.

We was outside and he started asking me questions and I was answering them too. Every one he asked, I answered and I was right. He said that was wrong. I said "Nun uhn." I knew I was right. He said "I'm gonna give you a spankin'. You don't talk back to the teacher." I know I was right. He grabbed me and took me along side the building and pulled down my pants. He took his hands and put them there and pressed until his hand was inside of me. He was on his knees lookin' me in the eye, in my face.

And I knew what he was doin' was wrong, but I couldn't say nothing. I couldn't do nothing. I don't know when he stopped. I pulled my pants up. I ran inside and sat down. My cousin and 'em came in they had on their little dresses too. "Come on Nefa. Do that dance." I couldn't dance. I didn't want to be there no more. He had no business touchin' me like that, but I couldn't tell nobody. He was daddy's friend. I knew everybody was gonna get mad at me. They gonna say she was telling stories. But I was right. I knew I was right, just like I knew he was wrong.

Somebody should have came outside. Somebody should have came and seen about me.

[*Back in the present.*]

She held out her arms and she just rocked me. "Benefa I am so sorry. I wish that never did happen to you" and she was cryin' too. This time, it was like I knew that if she could have gone back in time and took my place, I believe she would have. And she was talkin' about what happened to babies today and how she feel bad that the babies don't get protected. And how she feel like so much had been changed and she wish she could make it right again.

And she let me ask her all kinds of questions about what it feel like to kiss somebody and what it feel like to have somebody you know being sweet to you and stuff like that. And then she told me that if I did real good in my classes and I didn't get in no trouble for two whole weeks, then she was going to let me see one of my friends. And I was like "I'll be good. I'll be good."

But she never, never, never tell my mother nothin'. If she say, she won't tell my mother. She won't tell my mother. She got way into my brain. I been thinkin' bout way way way in the beginning when I first met her and she was making me mad. I used to roll my eyes at her all the time. Now, when I be over there, she let me talk to my friends. So, and den, she said she think I might be ready real soon.

Everytime I come over there, she take me through what I should know to take care of myself, how to do everything like you know . . . like to do my fingernails and how to do my toe nails. She taught me so much stuff. I didn't even know that stuff about bein' no girl. She started calling me Princess too. That's her special name for me.

When I do real good and stuff she calls me Princess. She be makin' me smile all the time. My mother said she can see the difference too. I know I feel it inside. I know sometimes I try to be all hard, but I know.

It's been almost two weeks now. And I'm gonna get ready to go to the movies. We gonna go see *Crooklyn* or *The Inkwell* or some black movie cause my friend is very into his blackness. And that why I think she let me go out with him because he's into his blackness too and she like that. But I'm not ready for nuthin' but some talkin' though. I told her I promise her, I would never break my promise. Cause she kept my secret.

In a day, my two weeks is up. Big Momma said that she was going to get a present for me for when it was my graduation time. But it wasn't my graduation from regular school, it was my graduation from my Big Momma School. I was going on my first dinner date.

And so Big Momma had everything all fixed up that day. She had everything laid out on that bed, and it was all pretty stuff too. It was like stuff you see in magazines. I couldn't believe that it was for me. I was so happy. I was like, I was like dag ooooo weeeee! This for me. Big Momma dressed me up and he called and everything.

And he came by there, like he was on time and she made him sit in that room. "Where you takin' her and when she comin' back?" And all of that stuff like that. And "Because this is my Princess," and everything like that and I was feeling just like that, I was feeling just like I was from *Coming to America*.

And so we went and I remember everything she told me. I didn't let him put his hand on my knees or nothin'. I saw them other girls doin' that, but I said, um not me because my Big Momma will get mad at me and she got eyes everywhere. It's the best night I ever had.

I have to do something special for her. I got two mothers. Well, I got my mother and I got my Big Momma and so for Mother's Day I'll do something for Big Momma too. That's what I'm gonna do. She made me have the most fun I ever had. And so for Mother's Day, I wrote her a rap.

[BENEFA *stands and the music rises.*]

Back in the day
Back in the day
Sitting at home with my
Brothers and sisters
Looking at a photo album
Thumbing through some pictures
And to my dismay
I started thinking about today
Dag things have changed
'Cause I remember the way
We used to run around and play
Without being afraid
Of the aerial raid
Or having playgrounds sprayed
With the bullets ricocheted
Back in the day
Back in the day

[*The music rises as* BENEFA *dances off, and the lights fade to black.*]

[*Lights up on a very large fanny making its way on to the stage with a very large suitcase. The behind belongs to* BIG MOMMA, *who is dressed in a beautiful brocaded African wrap she struggles to right the suitcase and crosses to her throne like chair and sits.*]

BIG MOMMA: You reckon I forgot anything. Hardly anything in it for me. Taking some things to give away, Trade barter, like Cocoa say. Some dresses and things I don't wear toiletries soap tissues stuff like that.

Things we take for granted. I'm shedding this weight when I get there. Filling up with everything new.

Hand me downs was a tradition. Something was so nice you was waitin' hopin' you cousin or sister out grown it. Be watchin' her play wat and say don't mess up my dress. Sorta like what happened in my life. Having children for most of my young life. I was always the one teaching and knowing everthing about everthing. But it took me to have grandbabies to see the world thru different eyes. Transforming as Cocoa say. I have done a whole evolution form Nigga to a Goddess.

I used to eat Nigga food for example. Now don't go gettin' carried away, we didn't know no better. But when you know better you do better. But after Cocoa told me some things about the food we eat today said Jesus, we goin around carry around mess we don't need. Just full of mess. But you got to change your thinking. Got to transform.

Was a time I was a Negro didn't question nothing the government say, my husband, or the pastor, specially the government and my pastor. My husband, now that's a different story. Then my reading material changed. Whatever the children would be reading in school I'd read too. They'd leave'm layin' around here, I'd pick 'em up, and did you know for example Cleopatra was black as me. She didn't look like no Lizabeth Taylor.

I discovered through my reading things was a lot different than what we was taught in school. Evolution and Transformation from Nigga to a Goddess. I would have never thought about going to Africa before. Didn't know where it was even. They taught Africa was here and Egypt was waaaaaaay over there.

But I'm going to see for myself come 7:00. I'm goin to be on that train. Goin' to see the the original earth home of the Goddess. Get some knowledge about how to heal ya'll.

Cause I know what have happened and need to be did.

[*Light fade on* BIG MOMMA *rising and exiting.*]

[*Curtain.*]

Julius Harris and Members of the Negro Ensemble Company
God is a (guess what?) 1968

Arthur French, David Downing (standing), Julius Harris (sitting) and Esther Rolle
God is a (guess what?) 1968

Julius Harris and Frances Foster
God is a (guess what?) 1968

Julius Harris, Judyann Elder, Rosalind Cash, Hattie Winston
God is a (guess what?) 1968

Bernard Johnson's costume design for *God is a (guess what?)* 1968

Left to right: Willam Jay, Douglas Turner Ward, Esther Rolle, and Frances Foster
Happy Ending at St. Marks Playhouse (Negro Ensemble Company)

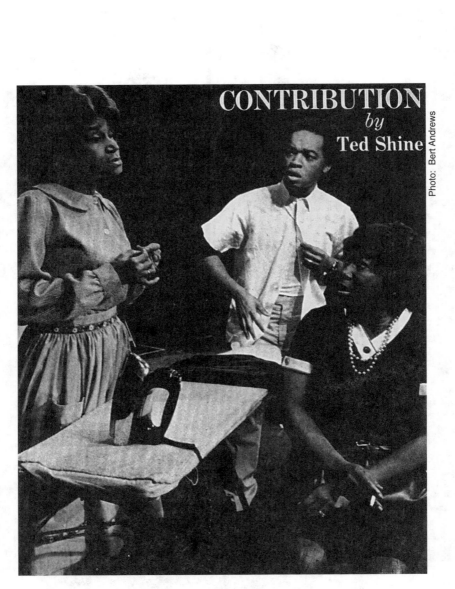

CONTRIBUTION
by
Ted Shine

Photo: Bert Andrews

Clarice Taylor (L) and Esther Rolle (R)
Negro Ensemble Company (1969)

Juanita Mahone and Charles Wilson in *Colored People's Time* (1981)

Chuck Patterson (l) in *Colored People's Time* (1981)
Negro Ensmble Company

Clarice Taylor (standing), Frances Foster (L) and Esther Rolle (C) in *Day of Absence*
Negro Ensemble Company (1969-1970)

Robert Hooks and Barbara Ann Teer in *Day of Absence* (1969-1970)
Negro Ensemble Company

David Downing and Rosalind Cash in *Day of Absence* (1970)
Negro Ensemble Company

Frances Foster (L), Frankie Faison, Judi Ann Mason (playwright) and Dean Erby
(Far Right group) with the cast of *Livin' Fat* (1975-1976)
Negro Ensemble Company

Photo: Bert Andrews

Frances Foster, Wayne Elbert, and Dean Erby in *Livin' Fat* (1975))

Photo: Bert Andrews

Dean Irby and Frankie Faison in *Livin' Fat* (1975)

Thomas W. Jones III in *The Wizard of Hip* (1990)

The Colored Museum (1986)
Back Row (L to R): Robert Jason, Arnold Bankston
Front Row: Myra Taylor, Vickilyn Reynolds, Olivia Virgil Harper

At the Public

BIG MOMMA 'N 'EM

An Outrageous Celebration of
Women Who Dare, Women Who Defy, Women Who Do and Women Who Don't

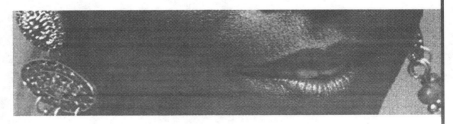

Conceived, Written and Performed by
PHYLLIS YVONNE STICKNEY
Directed by
LONI BERRY
Limited Engagement
MAY 20 - JUNE 5

Public Theatre (1994)

THE GIFT OF LAUGHTER

BY JESSIE FAUSET

The black man bringing gifts, and particularly the gift of laughter, to the American stage is easily the most anomalous, the most inscrutable figure of the century. All about him and within himself stalks the conviction that like the Irish, the Russian and the Magyar he has some peculiar offering which shall contain the very essence of the drama. Yet the medium through which this unique and intensely dramatic gift might be offered has been so befogged and misted by popular preconception that the great gift, though divined, is as yet not clearly seen.

Popular preconception in this instance refers to the pressure of white opinion by which the American Negro is surrounded and by which his true character is almost submerged. For years the Caucasian in America has persisted in dragging to the limelight merely one aspect of Negro characteristics, by which the whole race has been glimpsed, through which it has been judged. The colored man who finally succeeds in impressing any considerable number of whites with the truth that he does not conform to these measurements is regarded as the striking exception proving an unshakable rule. The medium then through which the black actor has been presented to the world has been that of the "funny man" of America. Ever since those far–off times directly after the Civil War when white men and colored men too, blacking their faces, presented the antics of plantation hands under the caption of "Georgia Minstrels" and the like, the edict has gone forth that the black man on the stage must be an end–man.

In passing one pauses to wonder if this picture of the black American as a living comic supplement has not been painted in order to camouflage the real feeling and knowledge of his white compatriot. Certainly the plight of the slaves under even the mildest of masters could never have been one to awaken laughter. And no genuinely thinking person, no really astute observer, looking at the Negro in modern American life, could find his condition even now a first aid to laughter. That condition may be variously deemed hopeless, remarkable, admirable, inspiring, depressing; it can never be dubbed merely amusing.

It was the colored actor who gave the first impetus away from this buffoonery. The task was not an easy one. For years the Negro was no great frequenter of the theater. And no matter how keenly he felt the insincerity in the presentation of his kind, no matter how ridiculous and palpable a caricature such a presentation might be, the Negro auditor with the helplessness of the minority was powerless to demand something better and truer. Artist and audience alike were in the grip of the minstrel formula. It was at this point in the eighteen–nineties that Ernest Hogan, pioneer comedian of the better type, changed the tradition of the merely funny, rather silly "end–man" into a character with a definite plot in a rather loosely constructed but none the less well–outlined story. The method was still humorous, but less broadly, less exclusively. A little of the hard luck of the Negro began to creep in. If he was a buffoon, he was a buffoon wearing his rue. A slight, very slight quality of the Harlequin began to attach to him. He was the clown making light of his trouble, but he was a wounded, a sore–beset clown.

This figure became the prototype of the plays later presented by those two great characters, Williams and Walker. The ingredients of the comedies in which these two starred usually consisted of one dishonest, overbearing, flashily dressed character (Walker) and one kindly, rather simple, hard–luck personage (Williams). The interest of the piece hinged on the juxtaposition of these two men. Of course these plays, too, were served with a sauce of humor because the public, true to its carefully taught and rigidly held tradition, could not dream of a situation in which colored people were anything but merely funny. But the hardships and woes suffered by Williams, ridiculous as they were, introduced with the element of folk comedy some element of reality.

Side by side with Williams and Walker, who might be called the apostles of the "legitimate" on the stage for Negroes, came the merriment and laughter and high spirits of that incomparable pair, Cole and Johnson. But they were essentially the geniuses of musical comedy. At that time their singers and dancers outsang and outdanced the neophytes of contemporary white musical comedies even as their followers to this day outsing and outdance in their occasional appearances on Broadway their modern neighbors. Just what might have been the ultimate trend of the ambition of this partnership, the untimely death of Mr. Cole rendered uncertain; but speaking offhand I should say that the relation of their musical comedy idea to the fixed plot and defined dramatic concept of the Williams and Walker plays molded the form of the Negro musical show which still persists and thrives on the contemporary stage. It was they who capitalized the infectious charm of so much rich dark beauty, the verve and abandon of Negro dancers, the glorious fullness of Negro voices. And they produced those effects in the *Red Shawl* in a manner of setting, by any latter–day companies.

But Williams and Walker, no matter how dimly, were seeking a method whereby the colored man might enter the "legitimate." They were to do nothing but pave the way. Even this task was difficult but they performed it well.

Those who knew Bert Williams say that his earliest leanings were toward the stage, but that he recognized at an equally early age that his color would probably keep him from ever making the "legitimate." Consequently, deliberately, as one who desiring to become a great painter but lacking the means for travel and study might take up commercial art, he turned his attention to minstrelsy. Natively he possessed the art of mimicry; intuitively he realized that his first path to the stage must lie along the old recognized lines of "funny man." He was, as a few of us recall, a Jamaican by birth; the ways of the American Negro were utterly alien to him and did not come spontaneously; he set himself therefore to obtaining a knowledge of them. For choice he selected, perhaps by way of contrast, the melancholy out–of–luck Negro, shiftless, doleful, "easy"; the kind that tempts the world to lay its hand none too lightly upon him. The pursuit took him years, but at length he was able to portray for us not only that "typical Negro" which the white world thinks is universal but also the special types of given districts and localities with their own peculiar foibles of walk and speech and jargon. He went to London and studied under Pietro, greatest pantomimist of his day, until finally he, too, became a recognized master in the field of comic art.

But does anyone who realized that the foibles of the American Negro were painstakingly acquired by this artist, doubt that Williams might just as well have portrayed the Irishman, the Jew, the Englishman abroad, the Scotchman or any other of the vividly etched types which for one reason or another lend themselves so readily to caricature? Can anyone presume to say that a man who traveled *north, east, south* and *west* and even abroad in order to acquire accent and jargon, aspect and characteristic of a people to which he was bound by ties of blood but from whom he was natively separated by training and tradition, would not have been able to portray with equal effectiveness what, for lack of a better term, we must call universal roles?

There is an unwritten law in America that though white may imitate black, black, even when superlatively capable, must never imitate white. In other words, grease paint may be used to darken but never to lighten.

Williams' color imposed its limitations upon him even in his chosen field. His expansion was always upward but never outward. He might portray black people along the gamut from roustabout to unctuous bishop. But he must never stray beyond those limits. How keenly he felt this few of us knew until after his death. But it was well known to his intimates and professional associates. W. C Fields, himself an expert in the art of amusing, called him "the funniest man I ever saw and the saddest man I ever knew."

He was sad with the sadness of hopeless frustration. The gift of laughter in his case had its source in a wounded heart and in bleeding sensibilities.

That laughter for which we are so justly famed has had in late years its over-tones of pain. Now for some time past it has been used by colored men who have gained a precarious footing on the stage to conceal the very real dolor raging in their breasts. To be by force of circumstances the most dramatic figure in a country; to be possessed of the wells of feeling, of the most spontaneous instinct for effective action and to be shunted no less always into the role of the ridiculous and funny—that is enough to create the quality of bitterness for which we are ever so often rebuked. Yet that same laughter influenced by these same untoward obstacles has within the last four years known a deflection into another channel, still productive of mirth, but even more than that of a sort of cosmic gladness, the joy which arises spontaneously in the spectator as a result of the sight of its no less spontaneous bubbling in others. What hurt most in the spectacle of the Bert Williams' funny man and his forerunners was the fact that the laughter which he created must be objective. But the new "funny man" among black comedians is essentially funny himself. He is joy and mischief and rich, homely native humor personified. He radiates good feeling and happiness; it is with him now a state of being purely subjective. The spectator is infected with his high spirits and his excessive good will; stream of well-being is projected across the footlights into the consciousness of the beholder.

This phenomenon has been especially visible in the rendition of the colored musical "shows," *Shuffle Along, Runnin' Wild, Liza,* which livened up Broadway recently for a too brief season. Those of us who were lucky enough to compare with the usual banality of musical comedy, the verve and pep, the liveliness and gayety of those productions will not soon forget them. The medley of shades, the rich colorings, the abundance of fun and spirits on the part of the players all combined to produce an atmosphere which was actually palpable, so full was it of the ecstasy and joy of living. The singing was inimitable; the work of the chorus apparently spontaneous and unstudied. Emotionally they garnished their threadbare plots and comedy tricks with the genius of a new comic art.

The performers in all three of these productions gave out an impression of sheer happiness in living such as I have never before seen on any stage except in a riotous farce which I once saw in Vienna and where the same effect of superabundant vitality was induced. It is this quality of vivid and untheatrical portrayal of sheer emotion which seems likely to be the Negro's chief contribution to the stage. A comedy made up of such ingredients as the music of Sissle and Blake, the quaint, irresistible humor of Miller and Lyles, the quintessence of jazzdom in the Charleston, the superlativeness of Miss Mills' happy abandon could know no equal. It would be the line by which all other comedy would have to be measured. Behind the banalities and clap–trap and crudities of these shows, this supervitality and joyousness glow from time to time in a given step or gesture or in the teasing assurance of such a line as: "If you've never been vamped by a brown skin, you've never been vamped at all."

And as Carl Van Vechten recently in his brilliant article, *Prescription for the Negro Theater,* so pointedly advises and prophesies, once this spirit breaks through the silly "childish adjuncts of the minstrel tradition" and drops the unworthy formula or unoriginal imitation of the stock revues, there will be released on the American stage a spirit of comedy such as has been rarely known.

The remarkable thing about this gift of ours is that it had its rise, I am convinced, in the very woes which beset us. Just as a person driven by great sorrow may finally go into an orgy of laughter, just so an oppressed and too hard driven people breaks over into compensating laughter and merriment. It is our emotional salvation. There would be no point in mentioning this rather obvious fact were it not that it argues also the possession on our part of a histrionic endowment for the portrayal of tragedy. Not without reason has tradition made comedy and tragedy sisters and twins; the capacity for one argues the capacity for the other. It is not surprising then that the period that sees the Negro actor on the verge of great comedy has seen him breaking through to the portrayal of serious and legitimate drama. No one who has seen Gilpin and Robeson in the portrayal of *The Emperor Jones* and of *All God's Chillun* can fail to realize that tragedy, too, is a vastly fitting role for the Negro actor. And so with the culminating of his dramatic genius, the Negro actor must come finally through the very versatility of his art to the universal role and the main tradition of drama, as an artist first and only secondarily as a Negro.

Nor when within the next few years, this question comes up — as I suspect it must come up with increasing insistence, will the more obvious barriers seem as obvious as they now appear. For in this American group of the descendants of Mother Africa, the question of color raises no insuperable barrier, seeing that with chameleon adaptability we are able to offer white colored men and women for *Hamlet, The Doll's House* and *Second Mrs. Tanqueray*; brown men for *Othello*; yellow girls for *Madame Butterfly*; black men for *The Emperor Jones*. And underneath and permeating all this bewildering array of shades and tints is the unshakable precision of an instinctive and spontaneous emotional art.

All this beyond any doubt will be the reward of the "gift of laughter" which many black actors on the American stage have proffered. Through laughter we have conquered even the lot of the jester and the clown. The parable of the one talent still holds good, and because we have used the little which in those early painful days was our only approach, we find ourselves slowly but surely moving toward the most glittering of all goals, the freedom of the American stage. I hope that Hogan realizes this and Cole and Walker, too, and that lastly Bert Williams the inimitable, will clap us on with those tragic black–gloved hands of his now that the gift of his laughter is no longer tainted with the salt of chagrin and tears.

—1925

FAREWELL TO ABRAM HILL

LOFTON MITCHELL

[Excerpted from *New York Amsterdam News*, Saturday, Dec. 20, 1986]

"People become stars when they die. And they are never dead as long as they are remembered."

This oft-quoted African saying has poignant meaning when we remember Abram Hill, playwright-director, scholar, and Black Theatre pioneer. He departed this life October 6, 1986 at the age of 76, but his name remains on the lips of theatre people everywhere. He parades across our minds at all hours, reminding us of the contributions he made to our lives and careers.

Memories erupt, volcano-like, pouring lava-like rivers down the mountainside and into the sea of youth. The 1930's were sinking into the 1940's when Dick Campbell, Muriel Rahn and the Rose McClendin Players produced Abram Hill's play, *On Strivers Row* in the basement of the 124th Street Library. A 21 year old simple Cat from Harlem who bore my name said: "This hilarious play will live on and on!"

Hill later joined with Frederick O'Neal and others, organized the American Negro Theatre, and presented this play a number of times. Recently, there was a successful production at Roger Furman's New Heritage Theatre and Mrs. Jesse H. Walker spoke of another revival. The 21 year old had been replaced by a 67 year old man who wrote Hill: "I told you so!" ...

On Strivers Row is a wonderful satire about people who strive to live in Harlem's famous community. Hill's play deals with the Van Striven family. They are pretentious, more middle class than middle class itself. At one of their swanky affairs appears Joe Smothers, a jive-talking, swinging Harlem hipster, hired by Mrs. Van Striven's adversary to break up the party. And all hell breaks loose. No cursory outline can do justice to this work.

Full appreciation of Hill and his colleagues demands an overview of more than 350 years. This overview has been repeated endlessly, yet we — and others — constantly forget it. We get into long diatribes about "us" needing to "get it together", not "being ready" and endless et ceteras. Writer Alice Childress put it bluntly: "The trouble with us was slavery. The trouble with us is still slavery."

ZORA NEALE HURSTON'S COMIC VISION

LYNDA M. HILL

"Language is like money," according to Zora Neale Hurston. By exchanging words for actions, and vice versa, black folk write and talk themselves into situations requiring original responses to old problems. "No matter how joyful or how sad the case there is sufficient poise for drama, "Hurston explains in her essay "Characteristics of Negro Expression."[1] Laughter is a bridge between comedy and tragedy for there is no humor without a pathetic side nor any tragedy so sad it contains no irony.

Hurston's life along with the plays and musical revues she wrote and produced supply anyone intrigued by the possibility of a new dramatic style with enough plots, songs, jokes, games, sermons and spells to fill stages all over the United States. Romance, tragedy and comedy are condensed into scripts stitched together to resemble the "little plays by strolling players" she observed while doing field work as an anthropologist among black people, from the sawmill camps of Polk County, Florida, to the Bahamas, to the Harlem streets. Hurston set out to create shows that would dazzle audiences from New York to Los Angeles, from Chicago to Orlando. And to a large extent she succeeded. Although mainly known for her fiction and folklore, Hurston strove, above all, to write for the stage as well as to direct and to perform in spectacular renditions of daily rituals that shape relationships among workers and bosses, worshippers and preachers, gamblers, lovers, and family folk. The ordinary existence of black people, to Hurston amounted to a type of theatre —what I call "the drama of everyday life." Her career as a playwright began in the 1920s. Between 1931 and 1934 she wrote, directed, and performed in musical revues. During 1935 and 1936, she was a drama coach for the Negro Unit of the New York Federal Theatre Project, and in 1939, while director of a drama program at North Carolina College in Durham, she explored collaborating with the Pulitzer-Prize-winning playwright Paul Green on John de Conqueror, a play that never reached fruition.

Her plays explore human tragedy without reverence or sentimentality. In *Color Struck* (1925), the comic tinged with a pitiful scandal shows how white American beauty standards have damaged the central character, Emma. A black woman who refuses to believe she is lovable because of her dark skin, Emma punishes her suitor John with caustic remarks that become self-fulfilling prophecies. Her sarcasm allows the spectator to see her self-hatred destroy her chance to win a Cakewalk contest she and

John had worked so hard to join. The dance, thus, serves to illustrate how artistic self-expression, particularly performance, has the potential to deepen one's character, to increase one's understanding and maturity. In *The First One* (1927), Hurston parodies the biblical legend of Ham that circulated during antebellum times to cajole blacks into accepting slavery as part of God's design. In her typical playful style, Hurston creates a whole family of "Hams"—musicians and dancers who fail to concede that being black is a curse, even though Noah meant for it to be. *The Fiery Chariot*, a one-act skit as part of Hurston's musical revues, lampoons the unquestioning devotion black folks allegedly have to God and the white man. *Polk County, A Comedy of Negro Life on a Sawmill Camp* (1944), which Hurston co-authored with Dorothy Waring, dramatized the treacheries the hard-working folk must endure, then escalates into a romance culminating in the style of a classical comedy. Hurston's musical revues *The Great Day* (1932) *From Sun to Sun* (1933), *All de Live Long Day* (1934), and *Singing Steel* (1934) spin through a folkloric world of children's games, work and ceremonial rites set one day in a railroad camp. "The Court Room," a skit included in J. Rosamond Johnson's Broadway musical *Fast and Furious* (1931) and Hurston's own *Jungle Scandals* (1931) were in the musical comedy style popular during the twenties and thirties. Finally, *Mule Bone, a Comedy of Negro Life* (1931), which Hurston co-authored with Langston Hughes, combines hilarious anecdotes from Hurston's folklore collection *Mules and Men* (1935) with a witty parable, mass hysteria, and the broadstyle of blues humor Hughes used in his plays. Although the collaboration led to a dispute over who owned the rights to the play, a 1991 Broadway production of *Mule Bone* has ensured that Hurston's notoriety as an innovator in the theatre shall always be remembered. And how remarkable that a small-town African American woman born in the nineteenth century (1891) has made such a mark on twentieth century black theatre that her legacy promises to reverberate into a new millennium. The circumstances surrounding Hurston's birth and death add a mystery to her life. Only recently did we learn she was born in Notasulga, Alabama, rather than in Eatonville, Florida, where she spent her childhood, until Alice Walker placed a headstone on Hurston's grave in 1976, her renowned books had faded from the public's memory. Within her 69 years Hurston was educated at Howard and Columbia Universities, received numerous awards, including the Guggenheim, published two folklore books, four novels, an autobiography, many stories and articles; made films, taught, and in general lived as if she might never see another day. She had so many ambitions to squeeze into a finite amount of time, she turned back her clock approximately ten years. Critics might say she lied about her age, which is the common way of scorning a person who, like Hurston, would hardly admit her year of birth, much less admit it was at least ten years earlier than she had ever reported. Showing how age is only one of the many artificial qualities of life we take for granted, Hurston had a talent for pointing out the absurdities that make human existence worthy of ridicule. The fame and obscurity characterizing her persona are a major reason black producers, directors, playwrights, and actors now look to her as a source and an influence for their work. Witness the recent productions, in addition to Mule Bone, adapted from her autobiography, folklore and fiction. One that stands out, *Spunk*, a spectacular blues piece George Wolfe adapted, brings to life three of Hurston's short stories in a poetically choreographed collection of scenes. Spectators get a close-up of what Hurston means by "the boiled down juice of human living." Although Hurston had planned to write a play by the name of "Spunk," as with her other theater ventures remaining unfulfilled, she never realized her dream. She has, however, given the world a generous offering from that "great big old serving-platter" called folklore. As artists continue to feed themselves from the abundance found in Hurston's gift, they are likely, as she believed and as Wolfe has done to "take the universal stuff and season it to suit themselves."[2]

1 Quoted from Hurston, "Characteristics of Negro Expression," in Lynda Marion Hill, *Social Rituals and the Verbal Art of Zora Neale Hurston* (Washington, DC: Howard University Press, 1996) 243.

2 Quotes in this paragraph are from Hurston's unpublished essay "Folklore" which she wrote for the Florida Folklore Project of the WPA Federal Writers' Project; see *Social Rituals* 77 et passitn.

RECREATING BLACK FOLKLORE: TELLING LIES ON SOUTHERN PORCHES AND URBAN BACKYARDS

JEFF NICHOLS

Writing the Words

No one listens to words anymore
And how are we to hand down the tale?
Sometimes I am this lone woman
standing in a field where only words
survive
realizing that I also will never be
a flower but at least I am
soil
I plant words and bring up myself
even if no one sees me I can be the
history of migrations
coming through the city pavements
reminding them where home really is

Brenda Abbey

Zora Neale Hurston was one of the few southern born Afro–American writers who consistently mined literary materials from southern soil. Hurston, outstanding novelist, anthropologist, and folklorist, was the most prolific black woman writer in America between 1920 and 1950. She published more books than any Afro–American woman before her *Jonah's Gourd Vine* (1934), *Mules and Men* (1935), *Their Eyes were Watching God* (1937), *Seraph on the Swanee* (1948) and her "autobiography," *Dust Tracks on the Road* (1942).

Zora Neale Hurston was raised in Eatonville, Florida, an all–Black village in central Orange County. When Hurston writes of Eatonville, the store porch is all–important. It is the center of the community, the totem representing black cultural tradition; it is where the values of the group are manifested in verbal behavior. The store porch in Zora's language, is the "center of the world." To describe the porch's activities she often uses the phrase "crayon enlargements of life" — "when the people sat around on the porch and passed around the pictures of their thoughts for the others to look at and see, it was nice." (Hemenway 239).

By the time Hurston wrote *Their Eyes were Watching God* or perhaps in the act of writing it — Zora Neale Hurston discovered one of the flaws in her early memories of the village: there had usually been only men telling lies on the front porch of Joe Clarke's store (Hemenway 238). It is these "lying sessions" which imbue the novel humor. Hurston is without a doubt a writer gifted with an ear tuned to African American idiomatic expression. It is this natural gift combined with cultural myopia which caused her to be extremely critical of her contemporary, Richard Wright: "Wright's inability to accurately portray the black southern dialect; since the author himself is a Negro, his dialect is a puzzling thing. One wonders how he arrived at it. Certainly he does not write from ear unless he is tone deaf." (Saturday Review, 1938)

In the review of *Their Eyes*... Wright claims:

> ... Miss Hurston voluntarily continues in her novel the tradition which was forced upon the Negro in the theater, that is the minstrel technique that makes the white folks' laugh... She exploits that phase of Negro life which is "quaint", the phrase which evokes a piteous smile on the lips of the "superior" race. (New Masses, 1937)

A major difference between the works of Wright and Hurston is their impetus for writing. Where Wright attempts to enlighten his reader, Hurston chooses to enlighten her characters. Hurston's character–based writing is a tradition inherited by the playwright August Wilson. Wilson, the most celebrated and widely produced twentieth century African American playwright, has completed six of a ten play series which chronicles by decade the experiences of African Americans. Born and raised in Pittsburgh, Wilson uses this northern city as the backdrop for most of his plays, *Fences*, *Two Trains Running*, and *Seven Guitars* to name a few. Like Hurston, Wilson has an amazing ear for recreating African American idiomatic expressions which retain a southern flavor in its urban setting. Wilson, a dramatist who usually deals with serious subjects is also quite humorous when he has his characters continue the tradition of southern "lying" sessions in northern backyards. In his most recent play, *Seven Guitars*, the character Canewell, best described as a folk philosopher, provides a rich source of humor when he gives an elaborate speech about how to tell roosters apart from each other. While it is not mentioned specifically, it is clearly the case that Canewell honed his craft for storytelling not in an urban poolhall or juke joint, neither locale provides the right audience or ambiance, but instead on a southern porch reminiscent of Joe Clarke's store porch.

Notes

Hemenway, Robert. *Zora Neale Hurston: A Literary Biography*. University of Illinois Press: Urbana, 1980 pp. 238–239

Hurston, Zora. "Stories of Conflict" [Review of *Uncle Tom's Children* by Richard Wright}. Saturday Review, April 2, 1938, p. 32.

Wright, Richard. "Between Laughter and Tears." *New Masses*, Oct. 5, 1937

LANGSTON HUGHES' *SIMPLY HEAVENLY* AND AFRICAN AMERICAN HUMOR

EUGENE NESMITH

> Humor is laughing at what you haven't got when you ought to have it.... You're really laughing at the other guy's lack, not your own. That's what makes it funny—the fact that you don't know you are laughing at yourself. Humor is when the joke is on you but hits the other fellow first—before it boomerangs. Humor is what you wish in your secret heart were not funny, but it is, and you must laugh. Humor is your own unconscious therapy.
>
> Langston Hughes, *The Book of Negro Humor*, p. vii

From the beginning of the African–American experience in America, humor has been not only a necessary tool for survival and a form of entertainment, but also a way to confuse, challenge and ultimately subvert white supremacy. African–American humor, like the humor of other ethnic groups, emanates from the social and political predicament of the group; for African Americans, their predicament has been based on their status as outsiders, which has allowed them the opportunity to expand their comedic talent by performing one way for the dominant culture and another way for their own.

Blacks were funny for whites by exhibiting childlike, innocent behavior, a misuse of language, shuffling and appearing confused because that was how whites wanted to perceive them. According to Mel Watkins, in his wonderful book *On The Real Side: Laughing, Lying, and Signifying*,

> This perception of Negroes, to a great extent, dictated racial relationships, directed and often limited the course of black advancement, and influenced nearly every phase of day–to–day living involving blacks. It also defined the role that black Americans were compelled to play if they were to move unimpeded in society. Out of it, an uneasy pact emerged. Whites presumed that Negroes were still naively adjusting to a superior culture, and blacks ritualistically re–enacted the scenario for their own benefit and well–being. White Americans clung to this illusion well into the twentieth century.

With the creation and development of the Simple character, Langston Hughes was able to develop an authentic style of black humor that rejected the artificiality and the absurdity of the dominant culture's preconceptions of blacks as inferior. Unlike the humor of minstrelsy and early films, which portrayed comedic blacks as shiftless and naive to please the white audience, Hughes' Simple was a common man who spoke his mind. He was simple minded but he was also a man who was trying to understand his place in the world. Hughes' characterization of Simple challenged the perception of the common working black man as a childish buffoon, incapable of taking care of himself.

Langston Hughes introduced readers of his weekly *Chicago Defender* column to "My Simple Minded Friend," who later became Jesse B. Semple or Simple on the 13 of February, 1943. Simple subsequently became very popular. Throughout the next 25 years he made regular appearances in Hughes' column. Hughes' play *Simply Heavenly* was inspired by *Simple Takes A Wife*, one of the collections of Simple stories and Alice Childress' play *Just a Little Simple* (1950), which was also based on the Simple character. It opened on May 21, 1957 at the 85th Street Playhouse to mostly favorable reviews and closed after fifty performances, and then re-opened on Broadway at the 48th Street Playhouse on August 20, 1957, and ran for sixty-two performances before it closed on October 12th.

A folk play with music, *Simply Heavenly* is a comedy about everyday life in Harlem with the songs forming an integral part of the story. The time is described as the "present," meaning 1957. Hughes paints an affectionate picture of the Harlem community through the fondness and respect that the characters show for one another. Families frequent the bar and there are even kids who come into the bar, in which a lot of the scenes occur. The play is constructed as a series of vignettes revolving around Simple's relationships with women; his wife Isabel (who does not appear in the play), his girlfriend Joyce, his landlady, and the other woman Zarita. The action takes place in three locations: Simple's room, Joyce's room, or Paddy's Bar, a neighborhood hangout.

The plot is simple and straightforward. The play opens with Simple in his small rented room after having just come home from work. His landlady asks him to walk her dog. He refuses until she points out that he is late with the rent again. After walking the dog, he visits Joyce who immediately begins to talk about marriage. Separated from his wife, Isabel, for five years, he has nevertheless been unable to afford a divorce. Also, he doesn't want to pay for a divorce for a woman whom he doesn't love. Although he has been going out with Joyce for three years, they haven't had sex. Joyce offers to help pay for the divorce but Simple is too old fashioned to allow her to do so. Joyce is presented as idealistic and angelic, rather than as a complex individual. Zarita, the other woman, is loose and carefree, the antithesis of Joyce, and a temptress whom Simple can't resist. In the process, there are ample occasions for Hughes to demonstrate the humor of the situation through the antics of the three in combination with the various characters in and around Paddy's Bar.

The Simple sketches established Hughes as one of the preeminent writers of African American humor. Simple's appeal is that he gives voice to the desires and aspirations of the little people. In general, African–American folk humor, much like the blues, served as a tool to help African–Americans overcome the burdens of slavery and oppression. Simple serves as an affirmation of the African–American ability to avoid bitterness and confront racism and oppression on their own terms. Continuing to believe in the goodness of mankind, Simple appreciated the life and culture of the Harlem community. The duality of blacks communicating one way with whites, and another way within their group continues to exist until this day.

THE ELECTRONIC NIGGER

ED BULLINS

The Electronic Nigger (A Tragi–Comedy), one of my most comedic plays, was written from the outset to be funny, i.e. to be a comedy. Ironically, I conceived the piece in a moment of anger, one evening on the campus of Los Angeles City College. I was taking a creative writing class, and after that evening's session, walking off campus with Bill Harris and Pat Cooks, I said: "I'm going to write a story about that guy . . . I'm going to call it *The Electronic Nigger*."

And that's how the idea which became a play was born. As easy or as inspiration–targeted as that. The "guy" of my statement was the prototype of Mr. Carpentier, as described in the notes of the play:

MR. CARPENTIER: A large, dark man in his late thirties. He speaks in blustering orations, many times mis–pronouncing words. His tone is stentorian, and his voice has an absurdly ridiculous affected accent.

The student who was to become Mr. Carpentier had routed my friends and me another night. We had spent nearly three hours painfully listening and inadequately rebutting him, and this is how it had been for the past month since the semester had begun.

I do not know or remember what happened to Mr. Carpentier after that night. He was a survivor; apparently he is still out there somewhere, intellectually riding roughshod through the Los Angeles Basin terrain, the scourge of campus career students. But his tragicomic memory is captured in this funny, sad play.

Why tragicomedy? Well, Mr. Carpentier is a lost soul. He substituted it for a metaphorical transistor. The promise of the future technological paradise of man on earth and among the stars he swallowed whole in a warped way. That culture was real; while, the culture of his familial origins was bogus. In response to an appeal to his cultural and racial humanity, Mr. Carpentier says:

"Sir, I am not black nor your brother . . . There is a school of thought that is diametrically opposed to you and your black chauvinism . . . You preach bigotry, black nationalism, and fascism! . . . The idea . . . black brother . . . intellectual barbarism! . . . Your statements should be reported to the school board—as well as your permitting smoking in your classroom."

Great Judge Clarence Thomas' ghost! The future is upon us. How tragic. And at once, how funny.

The protagonist's inept straightman is...

MR. JONES: A light–brown–skinned man. Thirty years old. Hornrimmed glasses. Crewcut and small, smart mustache. He speaks in a clipped manner when in control of himself but is more than self–conscious, even from the beginning. Whatever, MR. JONES speaks as unlike the popular conception of how a Negro speaks as is possible. Not even the fallacious accent acquired by many "cultured" or highly educated Negroes should be sought, but that general cross–fertilized dialect found on various Ivy League and the campuses of the University of California. He sports an ascot.

So Carpentier's foil for the night is an early–sixties "new breed" Los Angeles Negro scholar. Actually, the characterization is a cross–fertilization of 1961 Ronald Everett (nee Karanga), early Shelby Steele and Robert Allen.

It is soon apparent that Jones is no match for the self–assured Carpentier. Even while Jones makes black humanity and feel good statements, they register as hollow, without foundation and weak, against Carpentier's technocratic determinism.

MR. CARPENTIER: [*Oblivious.*] The new technology doesn't allow for the weak tyranny of human attitudes.

MR. JONES: You are wrong, terribly wrong.

MR. CARPENTIER: This is the age of the new intellectual assisted by his tool, the machine, I'll have you know!

MR. JONES: [*Furious.*] Carpentier!... That is what we are here in this classroom to fight against... we are here to discover, to awaken, to search out the human values through art!

MR. CARPENTIER: Nonsense! Nonsense! Pure nonsense! All you pseudo artistic types and humanists say the same things when confronted by truth.[*Prophetically.*] This is an age of tele–symbology... phallic in nature, oral in appearance.

MR. JONES: Wha'... I don't believe I follow you. Are you serious, man?

And the beat goes on.

The play begins with a description of its setting: "*A classroom of a Southern California junior college... Modern decor. New facilities:... Light green blackboards, bright fluorescent lighting, elongated rectangular tables, seating four to eight students, facing each other, instead of the traditional rows of seats facing toward the instructor. The tables are staggered throughout the room and canted at angles impossible for the instructor to engage the eye of the student, unless the student turns toward him or the instructor leaves his small table and walks among the students . . . It is seven o'clock by the wall–clock . . . A* NO SMOKING *sign is beneath the clock . . . The bell rings."*

Some denizens of this place of supposedly deep thinking are already in attendance. "MISS MOSKOWITZ [*An aging professional student.*] *drinks coffee from a paper cup.* LENARD [*A fat white boy.*] *munches an apple, noisily,*" Soon "BILL [*Twenty–two years old. Negro.*] *comes in the back door to the room*; SUE [*Twenty years old. White.*] *enters the other* [*door*]. Bill and Sue somehow, incidentally find seats next to one another. Finally, "JONES *enters puffing on his pipe and smoothing down his ascot.*"

"*The bell rings.*" Jones begins by introducing himself and laughing nervously at nothing that is particularly funny. He announces the name of the course, English 22E, Creative Writing. A conflict starts between Lenard and Miss Moskowitz concerning the numbers on their little I.B.M. cards, as Mr. Carpentier enters unnoticed and surveys the room, as if he has it under surveillance.

By the time Mr. Jones has mellowed out this first class conflict, Carpentier has launched his attack:

CARPENTIER: Sir . . . I just arrived in these surroundings and I have not yet been oriented as to the primary sequence of events which have preceded my entrance.

This first short speech by Carpentier is so unnerving to Jones that he does not ever regain full control of the class again. And Carpentier plows straight ahead through each obstacle, though the students at first attempt to save Jones.

BILL: Just take a look at your card and see if . . .

CARPENTIER: Didn't your mother teach you any manners, young man?

BILL: What did you say, fellah?

CARPENTIER: Don't speak until you're asked to . . .

MR. JONES: Now you people back there . . . pay attention.

MISS MOSKOWITZ: Why, I never in all my life . . .

MR. JONES: Now to begin with . . .

SUE: You've got some nerve speaking to him like that. Where did you come from, mister?

MR. JONES: Class!

CARPENTIER: Where I came from... *mon bonne femme*... has no bearing on this situational conundrum... splendid word, conundrum, heh, what? Jimmie Baldwin uses it brilliantly on occasion... "

So through bullying, bragging and blustering, Carpentier beats down their resistance. He tells them in his special way that he wants to learn to write fiction, while claiming to be already a successful writer: "... you can find my name footnoted in numerous professional sociological–psychological–psychiatric and psychedelic journals... " To Jones' objections, Carpentier announces that he is "a Sociological Data Research Analysis Technician Expert... penology is my field, naturally, and I have been in over thirty–three penal institutions across the country... in a professional capacity, obviously... ha ho ho."

Yes, Carpentier does laugh at himself sometimes. But somehow his self abnegation seems sinister. He claims to be creating a new art–form. Socio Drama. But his is not the same sociodrama that Edwin Wilson defines [*The Theatre Experience*, McGraw–Hill, Inc., 6th Ed., 1994] "as educational therapeutic methods"... in which "parents and children, students and teachers, or legal authorities and ordinary citizens—explore their own attitudes and prejudices."

No, Carpentier's methods for his art are more direct: "The only way one can get the naturalistic speech and peer group patterns and mores of children recorded accurately...

MR. JONES: [*Begins a string of "Oh God's" rising in volume until* MR. CARPENTIER *finishes his speech.*] Oh God, Oh, God, Oh, God, Oh, God, OH, GOD!

MR. CARPENTIER: ... is to scientifically eavesdrop on their peer group with electronic listening devices and get the actual evidence for any realistic fictionalizing one wishes to achieve.

MR. JONES: [*Scream.*] NO!!!

MR. CARPENTIER: [*Query.*] No?

MR. JONES: [*In a tired voice.*] Thomas Wolfe once said...

MR. CARPENTIER: [*Ridicule.*] Thomas Wolfe!

MR. JONES: "I believe that we are lost here in America, but I believe we shall be found."... Mr. Carpentier... let's hope that we Black Americans can first find ourselves and perhaps be equal to the task... the burdensome and sometimes evil task, by the way... that being an American calls for in these days.

MR. CARPENTIER: Sir, I object!

MR. JONES: Does not the writer have some type of obligation to remove some of the intellectual as well as political, moral and social tyranny that infects this culture? What does all the large words in creation serve you, my Black brother, if you are a complete whitewashed man?

The satiric environment of *The Electronic Nigger* is charged with comic potential. The characters Miss Moskowitz, Lenard, Bill, Sue and Martha (an "attractive negro woman" and c.p. time arrival) all serve the play well.

Miss Moskowitz is my favorite. Obviously a cliché, she transcends her sub–middle–brow pretensions through revealing her vulnerability—her humanity. She is first seen at RISE, drinking coffee from a paper cup. Although never stated in the play, Eating and Drinking are not allowed as well as Smoking. In this setting depicting somewhere beyond a High School but not a fully evolved college which dots the twentieth century American landscape like educational stations for the marginally and dis-advantaged working poor, breaking minor rules is a stance of the rebel and independent free–thinker. Hence, Miss Moskowitz is no mere subur-ban mall crawler; she, probably a substitute social worker during working hours, views herself as slightly gifted with vision, endowed with a sensi-tive soul and huge heart. Though she has a propensity for confusion.

Her first words in the play:

MISS MOSKOWITZ: [*Confused.*] Why...I don't see any numbers on my card.

For which, Mr. Jones obviously ignores her.

MR. JONES: [*Extinguishing pipe.*] Good...now that everyone seems to be-long here who is here, we can get started with our creativity...ha ha...

But this lady protests:

MISS MOSKOWITZ: [*Protesting.*] But I don't have a number!

At which point, Lenard snatches the little I.B.M. card from her which almost starts a physical fight. And just as Jones quiets them, Mr. Carpentier makes his previously mentioned attack.

Of course there is significance in the computer cards and the little numbers on the little cards. In the junior and senior educational head-quarters of our country, attendees are numbers which can be punched up or downloaded. And now, in the transistor age, so many times those num-bers represent surplus labor pools and statistics statistics statistics.

Yes, *The Electronic Nigger* has been one of my favorite plays. I guess I view it as one of a handful of personal bests because it evokes painful chuckles while it shreds conventional reality. In it, some things seem al-ways off kilter, always not as they could be. It is a very California play. Hence, a quintessential America play.

CONTRIBUTION: A DOSE OF SOCIAL PROTEST

FLORANTÉ GALVEZ

Dark comedy, like satire, can be the most wicked form of theatrical art. When written and performed skillfully, the form can tap into our deepest desires or touch our most intimate fears with the strike of a sledgehammer or the pierce of an ice pick, directly reaching our funny bones. In our realm of the black experience, dark comedy, added with a dose of social protest, can also be cathartic.

Ted Shine's *Contribution*, first produced in 1969 by the Negro Ensemble Company, is a testament to the power of dark comedy's presence in the legacy of the black theatrical experience. The play is presented as the third one–act installment of *Contributions*, Mr. Shine's comic trilogy about what it means to give of one's self to the struggle for black liberation. As the most popular in the series, *Contribution* is set in the genteel southern home of Mrs. Love amidst the turmoil of the 1960's civil rights movement.

The play opens with Mrs. Love singing:

Where he leads me
I I I I shall follow
I I I I ' L L L go with him

This familiar spiritual, which grows in importance late in the play, sets the tone for what becomes a lesson in false stereotypical perceptions. These perceptions are focused in the age–old battle between traditional versus modern values. At the center of the conflict is Mrs. Love, an elderly, wise and seemingly content septuagenarian who has worked a life of domestic servitude for abusive white employers. Also, at the center is Eugene, her young, brash and naive grandson. He is nervously preparing for a sit–in demonstration at a segregated lunch counter. Eugene is representative of the mid 1960's civil rights activist — clean cut, dedicated, idealist and energetic for protest. Though his intentions are noble, he rudely expresses disdain for his grandmother's antiquated ways. Eugene views her as a stereotypical "tom"/"mammy" figure. He just cannot understand why she continues to smile and bow before white society in this age of militancy. He arrogantly dismisses his grandmother as a useless dinosaur who cannot keep in step with the demands of the struggle. Before he leaves, Mrs. Love sets him straight, reminding him of the struggles she has endured to provide for her family. She also reminds him that he has benefited from her works.

Once he leaves, Mrs. Love's neighbor, Katy arrives to relate the news of the strange death of the town's racist sheriff. Later, Eugene returns to announce that the lunch counter is now integrated, due to white reaction to the mysterious death. They attribute this to "Black Voodoo." Then, in an extended monologue of righteous fury and emotional liberation, Mrs. Love gleefully speaks of her unsung contribution to the movement through the creation of her special cornbread recipe, most devilishly prepared. This hilarious monologue is the essence of *Contribution*, for it ties together the social/historical burdens of oppression, suppressed black rage and the question of what true radical protest is all about. Truly, the audience will find new meaning in Mrs. Love's spiritual, which may be considered as an anthem for a different brand of cultural liberation.

As dark comedy goes, *Contributions* works because, despite its potentially disturbing subject matter of murder as retributive catharsis for four hundred years of oppression, the play is most definitely funny. Shine carefully crafts the story early on in such a serious tone that one is shocked, almost embarrassed to laugh, but can't help it, once the rapid comic transition is made.

Because Mrs. Love draws so heavily on her personal history as a long suffering African–American woman, it is hard not to identify with her pain and rage. I am suddenly reminded of portions of Clay's monologue in Amiri Baraka's *Dutchman*. In beautifully stylized poetic and stinging language, Clay philosophically alludes to the possibility of the cultural and physical murder of white society. Still, it is talk and Clay is murdered, partially because of his failure to act. Mrs. Love plainly and simply has acted on this urge. As if led by some spiritual force, like an angel of death, she will take her philosophy and apply it. She will apply it, just like Junie, the reborn Vietnam veteran of George C. Wolfe's *The Colored Museum* who will continue to act on his urge to end human suffering.

The haunting strains of Mrs. Love's spiritual will leave the audience to reflect on whether or not her actions are insane and wrong, or justified within the realm of the madness of America. Yes, the question remains after the laughter is long gone.

TEMPORALITY, IDEALISM, AND THE COMIC IN OSSIE DAVIS' *PURLIE VICTORIOUS* OR...FROM GREENS TO CHITLINS

DR. PAUL JACKSON

PURLIE: [*In reference to the implications of kissing a white woman.*] Yeah! And what you supposed he'd a done to mean if I'd a kissed his? (*Purlie Victorious*, p. 61)

MISSY: [*In reference to Ol' Cap'n's anger.*] He's dangerous, Purlie. We could get killed if that old man was to find out what we was trying to do to get that church back. (*Purlie Victorious*, p. 11)

LUTIBELLE: [*In reference to her origin.*] I reckon I ain't rightly got no Maw and Paw, wherever they at...and nobody else that I knows of. You see, sir—I been on the go from one white folks kitchen to another since before I can remember. How I got there in the first place—whatever became of my maw and paw, and my kinfolks—even what my real name is—nobody is ever rightly said. (*Purlie Victorious*, p. 26)

PURLIE: [*In reference to his origin.*] ...And I thought of the black mother in bondage...the black father in prison...and of momma...how she died outdoors on a dirty sheet cause the hospital doors said—for White Folks only. And of Papa...who brought her tender loving body back home...and cried himself to death. (*Purlie Victorious*, p. 68)

Ossie Davis' *Purlie Victorious* (1961), the comic tale of a community of poor sharecroppers trying to win back their church from the dishonest, lecherous, and racist Ol' Cap'n, occupies a pivotal moment in African American history. In 1961, Negroes, [later Blacks, 1968, and currently African Americans, 1997] intoxicated with an idealism reminiscent of the period that fostered the Harlem Renaissance were poised for political and cultural change. Many events such as the monumental successes of Brown vs. the Board of Education (1954), the montgomery Bus Boycott (1955), Lorraine Hansberry's *Raisin in the Sun* (1959) and the Frankel production of Jean Genet's *The Blacks* (1960) encouraged African Americans to believe that change was imminent, or at least plausible. Semiotically, one could argue or believe that white racism in the United States could be confronted and beaten, that the "Youngers," after some prudent editing for their Broadway opening, could live anywhere they chose, and that European colonialism could be purged from African soil. It is in this political climate that Davis dramaturgically historicized and realized several aspects of African American experience in *Purlie Victorious*.

The location of comedy or the nature of the comic in the theater of African Americans — especially in relation to *Purlie Victorious*, is related both to the idealism of the early sixties and the material position of African Americans. African American comedy [comedy written by an African American, and in performance, primarily received by an African American audience] embraces the sardonic, the real, the ideal, the meta-real and that which is utterly impossible and/or ridiculous. Furthermore, that which is comic, materially and culturally, is more equally temporal. A line that might be hilarious at one moment might foster dead silence one month later. Consider the temporality of two of Ol' Cap'n's lines,

OL' CAP'N: "In the beginning God created white folks and he created black folks," and in the name of all that's white and holy, let's keep it that way. And to hell with Abraham Lincoln and Martin Luther King. (*Purlie Victorious*, p. 48)

OL' CAP'N: [*In reference to the Negroes' church Big Bethel.*] Then — ain't one thing left to do with that ramshackle dung-soaked monstrosity — that's burn the damn thing down. [*Laughs aloud in triumph.*] (*Purlie Victorious*, p. 79)

Purlie Victorious reflects a benign idealism — an idealism that would prove ephemeral at best. The bombing of the church and subsequent deaths in Birmingham (1963), the assassination of Malcolm X (1965) and of Dr. King (1968), and the urban uprisings that would close the decade would dramatically transform the political and cultural mis-en-scene.

Dramaturgical evolutionary signs of change were first. Lutibelle, who "wouldn't pass unless the people she loved could pass too" would hang herself [Sarah] in a mental institution in Adrienne Kennedy's *Funnyhouse of a Negro* (1964), and Reb'n Purlie, feeling empowered enough to deliver his sermon to Ol' Cap'n directly, the whore Lula, would lay dead on Leroi Jones' (né 1934) later Amiri Baraka's (changed in 1968) subway car in *The Dutchman* (1964). The idealism inherent in Davis' worldview would "grow a 'fro" and Gitlow and Missy would be told to "get black or don't come back." In short, the "greens" were burning on the American stage. [Even now the temporal idealism of Davis' "comedy" is highly sensitive. I recently directed Purlie Victorious at Spelman College in Atlanta, Georgia (February 1997), and the recent (late 1990's) rash of church burnings gave me pause. After much hesitation and discussion, I reinstated the church lines. However, I could not bring myself to include the reference to Dr. King. Often there was a profound silence in the audience when Ol' Cap'n made his threat against the church.]

Linked to the issues of temporality and African American political idealism are the issues of African American community and comic form. in an african american setting and before an African American audience, a group that is increasingly forced to be at least bi–cultural in order to survive, African American comedy simultaneously disrupts and embraces European aesthetic principles of comic form, recognizes West African performance ceremonies and signifies specific African American communal rituals and practices. Irony reigns. At a given moment, African American comedy can remind one of an Aristophanic or B. Jonsonian comedy, a Ghanian rite of transition, an A.M.E. morning service, or a Brechtian/DuBoisian lehrstuck/lecture. [Reb'n Purlie has at least seven sermons, before the final funeral ode for Cap'n Cotchipee, and the play sings with the musicality of the African American trope of call and response!]

Now that we, African Americans, are increasingly enjoying the chittlin' circuit in great numbers (and our sages are theoretically vexed by its drawing power) it is important to recognize and remember the greens (s) pastures from which these new swine dramas grew. It is also timely to reconsider ossie Davis' *Purlie Victorious* and its multi-textured, multi-layered and ideal dramaturgical moment when change seemed possible.

All references are from:

Davis, Ossie. *Purlie Victorious, A Comedy in Three Acts*. Samuel French, Inc. New York, NY. 1961.

This paper is for my student, Pamela Jackson.

PERCEPTIONS COLORED

KAREN A. MORGAN

The fact remains that *Five on the Black Hand Side* the Place's newest production, is an inferior play, amateurishly written, amateurishly directed,
on stage only because of its blackness and taking up space that might
have been used, money that might have been spent on an artistically
valid play that was, God help it, written by a white man.

Women's Wear Daily, Martin Gottfried

WOMEN AND MINORITIES NEED NOT APPLY!

December 10, 1969, *Five on the Black Hand Side*, a new play by Charlie
Russell opened at St. Clements Church (W. 46th St.). It was produced by
American Place Theater, noted for its presentation of experimental works
and directed by Barbara Ann Teer, actress, dancer, director–founder of
the one year old National Black Theater in Harlem. The run — 62 performances. A very good run, considering the time, the place, some . . . critics.

Five on the Black Hand Side, now in an elaborate production at the
American Place Theater is simply in the wrong house in the wrong part
of town . . .

NY Times, Walter Kerr

NEGROES GO HOME!

"We rehearsed uptown, taking the production downtown at the last possible moment," says Ms. Teer. Uptown was the one year old National
Black Theatre on 125th Street and 5th Avenue. Theresa Merrit, who
played Ruby, remembers, "It was a warehouse. We had to walk up all
these steps, it was dirty, had to get a broom, sweep, there was no heat . . .
But, Barbara had a dream and it came true. It's wonderful to see Barbara
Ann Teer have her dream come alive. Today, I look at the place with
pride." (The place, the National Black Theatre Institute of Action Arts, a
multi–million dollar performing arts complex.)

Barbara Ann Teer's direction sensibly accentuates the amiable eccentricities of Mr. Russell's racy and lively Harlem, but equally manages to keep
those eccentricities within certain limits, so that the acting has a grace
and a pace to it and never slips into caricature.

NY Times, Clive Barnes

Ms. Teer rehearsed 'uptown' to give the cast a feel of Harlem. In Harlem, they visited barbershops, local hangouts and various places in the community. "Charlie lived the Black experience. He listened and saw Black people as beautiful. His context was culturally indigenous to the traditions, folklore of Black people," says Ms. Teer. Thus, as director, this was her attempt to give to the cast a view from the writer's eye.

This experience of the actors ranged from Broadway to inarticulate. At one end of the spectrum was Ms. Merritt (later, *The Wiz* and the TV series, *That's My Mama*), who came to the play having just completed a Broadway revival of *Trumpets of the Lord* with Cicely Tyson at the Brook Atkinson Theatre: "I lived in Queens and had previously done mostly Broadway musicals, not a lot of black plays. *Five on the Black Hand Side* gave me an opportunity to do a black play and to work with peers that I adored. We had a damn good cast." At the other end, Tchaka Almoravids played the character, Fun Loving, and came from the community. He was a member of the National Black Theatre. "He had problems articulating, to the point that we often couldn't understand what he was saying," says Ms. Teer. "But," she adds, "he had a natural rhythm, a preacher's rhythm, and we worked with him."

> The barbershop characters are perhaps the most fantastic and marvelously antic folklore figures ever put on a stage...Fun Loving, the world's greatest Avenue aristocrat whose extended rap should stop any show...
>
> *Manhattan Tribune*, Clayton Riley

> ...and Tchaka Almoravids defining his style as Fun Loving, provide comic turns that are nothing less than classic.
>
> *Village Voice*, Dick Brukenfeld

ONE NEVER KNOW, DO ONE!

Charlie Russell was quoted in the original program guide as saying, "People are so unused to blacks writing comedy, that some people who read *Five on the Black Hand Side* did not know it was a comedy." Theresa Merritt didn't remember thinking of the play as a comedy at the time. Thinking back, she feels the play has the same type of satirical, issue–oriented humor as *Day of Absence*. "Comedy was a thing that we were allowed to do. As in minstrel shows and traveling shows like the Silas Green Shows of Ma Rainey's day. Like Buck and Bubbles, Butter Beans and Suzie, we entertained. Barbara Ann Teer states, "The play is not about comedy. It's about Black lifestyles. Black people are funny. It comes with the territory."

It is a novelty to come upon a black play that contains no anger these days ...

New York Post, Richard Watts, Jr.

It is comparative rarity in the black theatre, a middle–class comedy ...

NY Times, Clive Barnes

The character is the first Negro matron I have seen on a stage who is drawn with affection and no sentimentality whatever ... but there is more fun in it than anything else I've seen Off–Broadway this season, and in the midst of all the flap doodle there is a sense of people at a time and in a place.

New Yorker, Edith Oliver

LAUGH, AND THE WORLD LAUGHS WITH YOU

Charlie Russell's play is essentially an installment for a Fifties television series (Let's admit it, *Amos N' Andy*, exactly) ... There is a daughter, too, and she is about to marry an equally idealistic black man named Marvin (I once met a black dentist named Irving, but never heard of a Marvin.)

Women's Wear Daily, Martin Gottfried

MAMA, I'M CONFUSED!

This is a play about the affirmation of life in a Black family (hence community) and of the generation gap. It is not an angry play, as has been the case of Black plays of late, nor one bemoaning the fate of one's people. Rather it's a play simply told full of fine little absurdities of Black community life and one which speak (almost completely) through its characters.

Show Business, Joyce Tretick

Out of the shifting ambiguities of black theater, the characteristic genre piece that seems to be emerging is the exploded naturalistic play, part put–on, part agit–prop, in which a cutting edge of militancy is balanced by a sense of iron which humanizes a social situation that would otherwise be largely unavailable for art.

Newsweek, Jack Kroll

Remove the label on *Five on the Black Hand Side* and what's left is a standard comedy shifted to the black community, the same community that until relatively recently had to filter its outer image and interior fantasies through movie and television personalities almost exclusively white.

Wall St. Journal, John J. O'Connor

LOOK, RED BLOOD!

"The issues that I'm raising happen between blacks. This is about the internal life of blacks, not their relationship to white people. But it's equally pertinent for whites and blacks. I'm not one of those writers who aspires to be universal. But I do think that if I discover the truth about a particular man, then I have discovered the truth about men. I'm talking about some very basic things in this play. On one hand it's a celebration of a total style of life, the joy of black life. But I'm also talking about values and attitudes. I'm talking about hypocrites . . . Any person can understand that. I hate to call it a morality play, but it's about values."   — *Charlie Russell*

"The play was always well attended and the little, old ladies, (we called them blue–haired ladies), would come to the matinees and laugh, feeling happy when they walked out. Charlie was a funny man in his own way. He had a dry humor. Adults, could identify with the issues. The play brought up hair, going natural. It was a big thing back then. It also brought an awareness of Africa. It was a delight to many people. We did-n't know too much about Africa and the regalia and all. The show caught on. As I remember it was favorably reviewed. We had the blue haired ladies, learning about black life, about black families. Everyone seemed to laugh in the right places."   — *Theresa Merrit*

THE APPLAUSE OF ONE RESOUNDS FOR ALL!

At the American Place Theatre, the blacks in the audience stamp their feet and talk to the stage. The experience is speaking to part of their soul, and the white audiences — many for the first time — get intimations of their parochial feeling for the world.

Village Voice, John Lahr

However for some young black members of the audience at a recent pre-view, the effect was electrifying. Here, for a change, they were listening to lines directly connected with their own experiences, and they let loose with many a shout to the cast of "Right on" and "Say your piece."

Wall St. Journal, John J. O'Connor

Barbara Ann Teer stated that everything in the play was a slice of life and audiences responded favorably. They related. The issues observed in *Five on the Black Hand Side* were not new then and are still being examined within the scripts of today's writers: the cry for more black ownership on 125th Street in Harlem; a woman of color taking a stand (before women's lib became colloquial); the nationalists in the play, would today be labeled Afro centric; and Charlie Russell touched upon a bi–racial relationship before Spike Lee explored *Jungle Fever*. *Five on the Black Hand Side* was presented with love, from its writer, from its director, from its cast. It was presented with pride, veracity and spirit. Ms. Teer states, "there is dignity in spirit."

I LOVE IT WHEN A PLAN COMES TOGETHER!

Generally, I don't recommend plays, believing the best route is to present my impressions and viewpoint; the reader will take it or leave it from there. But this is something else. In showing how politics begin at home, merging revolt with reconciliation, *Black Hand Side*, doesn't cop out, it deals playfully. It's a loving, fun play and a Fun Loving play, a play for theatre buffs and for people who've given up on theatre. At a time when there's scant cause for joy in the land, Charlie Russell's writing and Barbara Ann Teer's beautifully orchestrated production celebrate the possibility of change and human renewal. It's not the only thing comic drama can do, but it's basic. And it inspires the kind of feelings you want to share with friends.

Village Voice, Dick Brukenfeld

DEAR GRANMA GLADYS

TIA DIONNE HODGE

May 4, 1997

Dearest Granma,

I was sitting under a tree the other day sort of waiting for my life to happen (as always) when I saw a couple walking around the campus green. I've seen them here before several times, holding hands and smiling as if they're on their first date...just walking...walking and talking as if it was something new. At least that's what it seemed to me from my shaded spot under the sycamore. She reminded me of you—the woman—with her blue cotton dress, polka-dots dancing as bold as can be, and silver hair shining under a matching cap. She had your walk too! Strut she could, and I swear I wanted to run up and hold on to her...maybe study her hands like I did yours when I was little. Remember that? Remember how I'd sit for as long as you'd let me...watching the hands that Momma said could love like an angel but set tea for the devil, if Grandaddy wasn't acting right. I watched those hands. Watched them and pretended that they were mine sometimes. And, I guess, that that's where I am right now. Pretending that my hands are yours...pretending big and whole because something is happening, Granma...something big, something big and moving. Moving inside, moving outside...just moving. And I wonder if those hands can help me.

Don't worry. Things are going well. At least I think so. Classes are fine...got an 'A' on my history paper, and I really think I'm on my way to becoming...becoming, well, something. But what? Momma says I should go to Pre-Med, Daddy says engineering, Uncle Booker says advertising, and Uncle Gideon—you know what he says—but President seems, well, I don't know. What do you say? What would Grandaddy say? Heck, what does Ms. Monday say? She always seems to have the scoop before everyone else does. Yes, I know I was supposed to be asleep in the living room, but who could sleep with all that laughing going on...the singing, the chanting, the gossip, and the stories! Who could sleep while folks were laughing out my history in the next room? Who could let it all go by without holding on...holding on with the same hands that give me five, on the black hand side...up high, down low, and sometimes too slow?

Maybe that's it? Sometimes things are just too slow. Maybe even myself...sitting under the sycamore waiting for my life to happen.

Sometimes I sit through lunch just waiting for life, love and happiness to jump up and bite me, but what I've come to expect is the occasional bite of a fire ant. And the itch, Granma! Oh, the itch! Want to scratch at it all day...Want to do something. Be something...and get on with it. But what? I sit, and scratch while my friends decide to go with braids, waves or weaves, perms or texturizers, or just cut it off and go natural like you did. They want to talk clothes and cars, men and music all for the sake of "keepin' it real." But how real can you get when the future's itching and the ants are biting? We are all a part of the new computer age. Folks are trying to catch a ride on that information highway—hitch-hiking with thumbs up to the sky, but being rundown by fast moving technology... too busy dancing to that new step, I guess.

Then again, I could be too serious. It's hard not to be. With the American Dream flashing by on television with the help of glorious surround-sound, I seem to be encased by could be's and should be's if I, of course, buy now! from the "them" out there that call us Generation X... the same folks that marked that spot with a baby boom. Not that I'm picking on Momma and Daddy's generation, but things are different. I don't check Negro, or Colored, or Black, or Afro-American on my financial aid papers. I check African-American, but I can't cash that check in for the American dream...or can I? With sound-bites snapping at my ankles and downsizing knocking on my future, the only thing I can hold on to is the stories and sounds that seem to paper the walls of my mind. The laughter...the memories of what was an what changed.

Anyway, I'm just ranting and raving because I think the hardest thing for me to admit is that I want to be a writer. I want to put all I've got into these fingers...I want to grab hold of pretending—big pretending—as if my hands were your hands tap-tap-tapping away at the new world with picket signs and a list of demands. Man! My Granmama making bread rise and the world stand on end! Do you think Grandaddy would approve? Do you?

Well, I should get going. Class starts in ten minutes and I have to meet James at the library. Have I told you how perfect he is? He has so many ideas. So many wonderful ideas. I can't wait for you to meet him. You'll love him! As always, I love you with all my heart. I miss you, Granmama. I miss you all the time. Oh, before I forget, please say hello to Ms. Ruby for me, Breck, Gillette, Jean Nate and her family, Ajax and Wildroot. I'll be home to visit at break!

Love always and a little on the side,
Charline

P.S. Ouch! Darn, another ant.

CONSCIOUSLY POLITICAL: AN INTERVIEW WITH CHARLIE RUSSELL

PAMELA FAITH JACKSON

The genesis of the play started when I did some work for some people at a theatre, like a play doctor. I went in to do some revision. They liked my writing which established a relationship and they asked, "Why don't you write a play?" I said, "Fine." At that time I had *Five...* on my mind — not really — but I was just thinking about writing something. I wrote the first draft, gave it to them, and they were really impressed, but they wanted to do a musical.

There was a guy named Luther James. At that time I was a member of the Harlem Writers Guild and that was during the era of John O. Killens and Rosa Guy, Clayton Riley, Lonnie Elder — it was really a vibrant time — there were others that I didn't mention, but it was great! James came to the workshop wanting plays; he was doing a series of plays in Boston at the time. I had the first and second act then, so I rushed to finish it. Then *Five...* came.

It wasn't a conscious thing, "I'm going to write a comedy." I didn't set out to say I'm going to write a comedy.

Are you a funny man?

Yeah. I am. I set out to write this play and I wanted it to be funny. And these guys were funny. What I wanted to do consciously was mix comedy and the political thing. Cause it was very consciously political all the time. Now I didn't know any people like that, but I knew what the issues were at the time. I was at City College when I wrote it, and it was the whole thing about campus life that was happening; women's lib — that was happening. So, I just wanted to make the play contemporary.

You seem to be a sympathizer of women?

No, I wouldn't say that. I'm not a sympathizer. I believe in being fair. It's like I'm going to be as fair to the women as I am to the men. On the other hand, I never had any problems with women's lib either. Because I was always for that. I think like a lot of brothers, a lot of stuff was going on I didn't even know. Like women couldn't get bank accounts — they couldn't do this... women could hardly do anything. What?!!! You had to have somebody to sign for you? I didn't know that! Because there have always been strong women in my life. I never saw guys as better than women when I was coming up. Everybody was out there trying to get up. It wasn't like this lady worked and this lady didn't work. Women were taking care of business whatever they were doing.

Did you have a strong mother?

Yeah, yeah. Like a lot of other guys, my mother was probably . . . certainly in my early development . . . THE person in my life. But she passed away early. It's like somebody gives you some things and you run with them for the rest of your life. She was heavy on education and wanted you to be somebody, you know. And determined that you would have a life better than hers, you know. Typical good mother.

Five . . . . is a different kind of play. I'm not saying it's better than any play but its a different kind of play. It is political; it is comedy; and the other element that makes *Five* . . . work — its about the culture. Its about rapping, its about folklore and those elements make it work also, you know. That's a very significant thing.

So anyway getting back to the story, this guy comes, I finish *Five* . . . I send it to him . . . and he doesn't like it. So he tells me, "Man why don't you write another one." In those days I could whip that stuff out. So I said, "Fine." And they did the next play up there in Boston . . . *Men are not Made of Steel*. Louise Gossett and Moses Gunn were in it.

So, now I got this play and I run into this guy, Woodie King and he said, "What you doing?" and I say, "Nothing!" He said, "Man what have you written lately?" and I say, "Aw man, I just got this old play with me nobody wants." And Woodie took it to American Place Theatre.

So how did the National Black Theater connection happen?

This was during the sixties . . . during the time when everything was going on . . . So I met Lonnie Elder, who wrote *Sounder* and *Ceremonies*, at the American Place Theatre. Lonnie was a friend of Bobby Hooks, Douglas Turner Ward, Barbara Ann Teer, . . . they were all friends. I thought it was a good idea to be attached to the theatre. At that time there was NEC, New Lafayette, and Roger Furman's theatre. I had worked with Barbara before as the director of the play I mentioned at the beginning of our interview that I had revised. She is a great director . . . and visionary even, I mean in terms of getting away from European–centered plays and getting into this form of ritual. So that was visionary, and I was happy to be a part of that. There were so many creative people around her. Not just actors, but people would just flock up there during the time I knew her.

Mr. Brooks is a universal character. The play has been produced all over the world . . . like Jamaicans will say . . . I know he's Jamaican, he's got to be Jamaican . . . and other third world people will say I know somebody like that . . . my uncle . . . .everybody knows this guy . . . .bombastic! . . . .controlling! . . . and we set him up — he's a bully . . . .I mean he has his good points . . . .everybody is against this guy . . . Its like I hope he gets what he deserves, and so when Mrs. Brooks comes out everybody says, "yeah" . . . The play is still being done.

It could be updated but it doesn't need to be. It's what it is. I'm not boasting because a lot of time has passed now. It's a classic. A period piece. It's the sixties, when you do it, let's do the sixties cause that's what it is. We have the culture . . . we have the African gowns, . . . we have the Afros . . . we have the music . . . .we have the folklore . . . this is just what was going on.

I like the way it is. A lot of people have come to me and said update it and they try it, but to me it captures the time period.

Where does the language of Fun Loving find its genesis?

I never take credit for that. Whenever it comes up I say, "No, I got that from Rap Brown."

I knew Rap Brown; we used to visit each other's house in New York. So, one time we were on the phone talking stuff. I say, "Man, where you get that stuff?" I'm into folklore. He says, "Man that's just some stuff we made up . . . all the cats sitting around made it up." Just like blacks made up Shine and Signifying Monkey, etc. So I said, "Man let me write it down." So he gave it to me on the phone. I ask him if I could use it in the play and he said, "okay."

The Clarice Taylor connection?

Clarice Taylor played Mrs. Brooks. And I also knew Clarice from The Negro Ensemble Company. She did the movie and the play. She created the part. She is a wonderful woman, great actress, great person. I really got to know her more when we did the movie.

What's the transition like from the stage to the big screen?

Different writers will give you different points because it could be a bitter experience. To me it was ideal except for the money. I'm not saying I was a poor boy and they took everything, because I had an agent, but it's not set up for a writer to make any money their first time. I got paid. They bought the rights from me and then they hired me to write the film script.

It was great was because of my producers, Brock Peters and Michael Tolam. Michael Tolam was on the Board of Directors of American Place Theatre and he saw the play about three or four times and loved it because he liked my writing. He asked, "Why don't you write a film script for me?" And I don't know whether it was him or me, but we agreed, "We got something! Why don't we make a film out of *Five ...*!" That's how it started and he got Brock Peters involved.

Because Tolam loved the play so much, and since he and Brock were the producers, I didn't have to have any fights about anything. He would be arguing sometimes against me, "No no no keep that! Don't cut that!" Creatively and artistically, it could not have been better. Financially, I didn't know what I was doing.

How long did it take to write?

It took me about six months to write the film script.

In terms of the writing, what were the mental adjustments?

With that project it was a thing of cutting, just basically cutting. They are different mediums. Plays are driven by dialogue, but a movie is visual. You don't want a lot of dialogue because you can see all the stuff. I don't have to describe it, I don't have to tell you anything, ...you see it. So, mainly it was cutting dialogue and as they say, "opening it up." I'm not confined to that one set. I can go outside on the roof. I can get Mr. Brooks walking down the street. I can get him in the barbershop ... It was a visual experience.

AN INTERVIEW WITH TED SHINE

PAMELA FAITH JACKSON

I don't think I deliberately set out to write a comedy. I wanted to write a play dealing with the problem that I certainly was experiencing and felt very much about at the time. I think all African–Americans were caught up in the movement, and we saw some horrible things taking place. Some things that made us all very very angry, and so to release that tension I chose to do so through my writing. I guess I had a flair for comedy because most of the plays that I've written have been comedies. I tried my hand at tragedy when I was in college, and it turned into a farce, so I stuck with what I felt I could do best. And really its just an outgrowth of the characters.

Where do you get your sense of humor?

Well you mentioned something yesterday, I sort of tied it in with Langston Hughes who titled one of his works *Laughing to Keep From Crying*. And again you sort of laugh to smother the hurt that you sometimes have. I guess I see humor in situations or the irony in so many situations and that comes through in the writing. If you look at people, and what we do, often it borders on the ridiculous. So I guess I observe these things and use them.

You ask about the irony of the name, Mrs. Love? And that name really came out of the clear blue sky. I guess when I was working on it, years ago I had asked a roommate to give me the name of someone he knew and respected very much. So he chose a school teacher that he was very fond of, a high school teacher. And I sort of liked the name; he had given me her full name, but I just used the last name. I may have used it again in another play, or at least made reference to her because I've had people who have said, "Oh, I had a teacher named Ms. Love." Well, if you're from the particular town that's probably who it's in reference to. But again I thought it was sort of ironic to use Mrs. Love with this particular character. Something else that I wanted to include into her language. It is so easy for actors to portray certain characters in a stereotypical manner, and I was trying to avoid that. It still happens. I've seen it where she's played as Mammy, and that was certainly not the intent.

In amateur productions you run the gamut in terms of characterization. I was trying to avoid stereotypes so I did little things in it hopefully that would give the actor some clue as to what they might do. And I guess language too came in there. She is a militant and I was looking for the irony in the relationship between the boy and the old woman. The old woman is brave and active so that her militancy has always existed. The boy is a frightened demonstrator. He is just the opposite of her. He presumes the role of militant, but in reality he is afraid. He's afraid to exert himself until after the fact.

When we kill the sheriff, are we killing just the sheriff?

No. I think it was a symbol of the racism that was so pronounced during that period. It was the sheriff, it was the members of the mob who were the followers of the sheriff, or who rode at night and burned houses or who shot into houses, blew up churches—that whole conglomeration of racists.

When I think about food and killing a master I think of slave master. So, I thought pre-1860?

Yeah, that was one of the ways that slaves revenged themselves.

Do you think that people in 1960 might have? Or was that a take from . . .

I don't know if it went quite that far, but I've heard some horrible tales involving food that people have alluded to.

So, when Mrs. Love says, "I'm justified," does she really believe that?

Oh, yes, yes. She has suffered and has sought revenge, and I'm sure she will justify it biblically.

"Where He leads me, I will follow." What does this song mean to her?

I think here she is looking again at that symbol of the hot spot at the moment where the trouble is involving the civil rights movement. The worst of the areas would be where she would go next.

Is she a symbol for all of us to get up and do something?

In a broad sense I would say yes. But everybody isn't going to be that . . . you've got some complacent people, and . . .

In the neighbor, Katy Jones?

Yes, yes, she becomes that representative of that complacent type who is just basically afraid. And that was sort of interesting when I saw one of the New York productions of it (it wasn't the Negro Ensemble Company), but I guess the production following that. The young lady playing the neighbor had some difficulty trying to figure out who she was and what she was all about. And I told her that the key to her character was fear. And when she thought about it, her performance then began to sparkle. Before she was sort of searching and nothing was clear, but once she got a key, a hook into the role through that word it changed completely.

The word black comedy, what does that mean to you? Is this a black comedy?

I suppose you might label it that. Here its a comedy that we laugh at but it contains very gruesome material. Quite often in dark comedy the ending is unhappy; I think here the ending is sort of triumphant, at least for the focal characters. But the act, the irony of the act is gruesome.

How do white audiences react? My first time seeing it was three seasons ago. I was sitting next to white people and they were quiet. And then they burst out laughing.

They see the humor in it. One of the ironic things was some years ago in Santa Barbara California a white group of senior citizens did it. They sent me a letter afterwards, I didn't get to see it. I think the man who played Eugene was in his eighties and there was an elderly woman doing the grandmother — they were all retired people, and I couldn't quite understand why they wanted to do it. They had a little drama group that performed plays and they wanted to do *Contributions*. I told them yeah, go on.

That's strange, but I guess not. The play kills racism—but to be that old and to be that forward thinking...

...Or to get a better sense of how African–Americans felt at that time. I would imagine that most of them didn't know African–American and had never come into contact with African–American and certainly didn't know how they felt about them other than what they saw on television. And sometimes you don't get a valid picture.

Do you feel that people can appreciate this piece now?

I think so. It's constantly being done. I base it on the productions of it.

What made the trilogy happen?

Well the producer wanted a full evening. So she ask for two other plays to go along with it. *Contribution* was first. That was sort of ironic how the play came about. I had written the play and literally had put it in a trunk. Allie Wood had directed another play of mine at the Negro Ensemble

Company, and he called and asked if I had a companion piece. He said, "Give me something short and something with a small cast and get it to me right away." So I went through a stack of plays and I found *Contribution* and I said, "Well it only has three characters and I won't have to do any re-writes." I thought it was solid enough to send and I wouldn't have to do too much. He didn't do it, but the script was there. I forgot about it until I happened to see Douglas (Turner Ward) who said, "You know we're touring your play this Fall." I said, "What?" and that's how it came about.

Where were you when you wrote it?

I was here in Texas. I was teaching at Prairie view at the time. I was constantly writing. I had an agent, and I would send her material, but it wasn't until Allie Woods got that script and the people at the Negro Ensemble Company read it and Alice Childress had *String* and Derrick Walcock had *Malcochon* that they gave us an Evening.

Do you remember the day you sat down to write? Was it a long process? Any advice for young writers?

No, because at that time, I was just turning plays out rapidly and I was doing one–act plays really sort of as exercises. I was involved in other things. It was difficult for me to set aside a block of time to do a full length play, so to keep my hand in it I was doing these one-acts, and I ended up with a trunk full of them. Really, they were exercises and I never really thought of having them done. I was really working on the longer more serious pieces.

I keep looking for ironies and incongruities and hopefully something that does more than merely entertain. I think that comedy is for me probably, and for many writers, the best tool to bring about change. I don't feel that audiences like to be preached to but if you can amuse them and let them see how ridiculous our behavior is, then they are more apt to correct it.

DIRECTOR ON DIRECTING: AN INTERVIEW WITH L. KENNETH RICHARDSON

PAMELA FAITH JACKSON

Let's start with Don Evans and Crossroads. He had done *One Monkey* . . . in Trenton maybe a year before we did it at Crossroads and he sent the play to me and I read it and I was in stitches. Don is a very frank man and what he did was take a classic genre like restoration comedy and adapted it to a contemporary black theatre format, I guess you might say. Or "adapted it to the black experience." What he did was to take a character like Ms. Malaprop who of course mispronounces words in her attempt to impress people with her level of intelligence and he transposed that kind of character to black middle class America. Which I thought was perfect . . . absolutely perfect. In her attempt to keep up some kind of guise, Ms. Malaprop is just mispronouncing and misusing words all over the place, and I just found that to be hysterical. I think what has drawn me to Don's work is that he is making social commentary, you see — and particularly Black social commentary. That's what grabbed me . . . that behind the work there was a mind. Behind the work was a particular vision of what Black theatre could be and I've always been attracted to writers who are smart. And I think . . . what do some of the great comedy writers say, "Tragedy is easy. Comedy is hard." And I agree with that.

Do you think that is why we have fewer comedies in the canon?

No, I think that black playwrights, when writing plays dealing with society and American society, find it almost impossible not to be humorous. Particularly when it comes to black people. We have sort of used humor to keep our head above water; otherwise we drown. You look at our situation in this country, from the start, its not been an easy road to say the least, and I think that humor has allowed us to keep on keeping on.

And so, when you think back to some of the classic drama of the sixties and seventies like *The River Niger*, people went to see that play and you heard waves of laughter in the theatre. If you walked in midway not knowing you would say, "Oh did I step into the wrong play? I thought I was going to see this award winning drama." But Joseph Walker writes in that tradition of finding humor in the serious, you see. And from the very beginning that first image of the grandmother coming down the steps as the sleepwalker, coming into the kitchen, making a cup of tea, then opening her eyes looking both ways to make sure nobody's watching her, reaching behind the refrigerator, getting her whiskey, putting it into the tea, replacing the whiskey, stirring the cup, and then all of a sudden going back to be a sleepwalker as she walks up the steps got rolls and rolls of laughter out of the audience. And that was just a pantomime at the beginning of the play.

So it is part of our culture. It is part of who we are, and I think that we broke ground in many ways in terms of how rich the humorous observations in those "serious" plays were. So, if you were an outsider you would really wonder, "Am I at a comedy or am I at a drama?"

Now, what's interesting about that is that black audiences as you well know are shall I say almost the navigators. If you are "an outsider" to the black experience, if you go to the theatre and there's a large black audience, they become the navigators into the experience. They in many ways let you know it's okay to laugh. We laugh at the irony; we sometimes laugh at the tragic.

Now let's fast forward to 1996 to the *Colored Museum* and particularly to the one segment called *The Gospel According To Miss Roj*. Now Miss Roj taught us about the significance of the snap. And what she/he said was that we recognize the truth when we hear it and the (*) snap queen just punc(*)tuates it for us. Or acknow (*) ledges the fact that was the truth. Did you get it (*)? The truth (*) just went by. It's like a comet (*). Catch it. And because we live in darkness so much, the society lives in darkness that whenever there is light, let's acknowledge it. And so when blacks in an audience hear those kind of truths (*), our snap in many ways is a laugh, a chuckle, it's a recognition to say I hear that. I heard that.

It's a recognition. An oppressed culture will strive to be recognized, and now, I think what black people are realizing in the theatre is that it's important that we recognize it. Not necessarily that the predominant culture recognize it, but that we recognize it. Because if we acknowledge it, the world will acknowledge it. All that we're doing is saying, "There it is. There it goes. Catch it before it goes. That was a brilliant moment." It's gone. We acknowledge it because they're fleeting. They are fleeting moments when the writer really zeros in on those truths, on those pearls of wisdom. You find a lot of that time is couched in comedy. That it is a comic's reference. That it is a funny moment. That it is a hilarious scene in that the writer has been able to pinpoint a frailty, pinpoint some absurdity, pinpoint a stereotype, pinpoint a ridiculous preconception...

I am a child of the television generation and sitcom, the good ones, the pioneering sitcoms. And so I think that growing up as a child I had my finger on the pulse of what is funny. What is humorous about the human journey. You're right when you talked about its medicinal purpose. There

(*) indicates snap.

is no question. Sometimes a playwright can make a very serious point in a humorous way, and it resonates in a way that when we laugh, we are recognizing what the playwright's message is. And usually, it is a serious message.

Let's now go back to *One Monkey Don't Stop No Show*. We're talking about the middle class black experience and how it is perceived as being an experience of holding up fronts. Because you are middle class, because you are black, you must talk a certain way, you must look a certain way, you must live in a certain neighborhood, your house must be furnished in certain ways, you must listen to a certain kind of music, you must read certain kinds of books, your kids must go to certain kinds of schools. And so what Don Evans does is sort of skews those kinds of universal experiences. So, the idea that the "Black experience" is something unto itself is a little misleading. Yes, there are certain subtleties that black people understand in ways that other races probably don't quite understand. But the primary difference is that the characters have dark skin, and that primary difference is a very superficial difference. .

The humor is very rich. We have a tremendous tradition in humor in the minstrel show. There is humor in almost every art form that we have ever been involved in — the tap dancer has a sense of irony; he has a sense of comedy in his work; he has a sense of tragedy in his work; the dancer, the painter, the novelist, the photographer, and on and on and on. I think that has existed in our work for years and years and years and I think it exist in the work of artist regardless of what color you are.

When you chose actors, was there anything special about those people?

Again, I think that you have to be very bright to do it well. Of course you always say "good actors" but I look for the actor who is willing to expose himself or herself. Roxanna [Carter] had to expose herself...

She was Myra Harris.

Yeah... [*chuckles*]. It was wonderful to see her expose that part of herself. The woman who wants everything to be just right and yet everything falls apart every possible moment of the day. And she's trying to keep up a front, because basically she is a good old southern gal, but she's tried to recreate herself. But at every moment something is falling apart. The make–up is not quite right; the wig is a little askew; the dress gets stuck in the door and eventually she comes revealing to us that she knows exactly what her husband needs. She's going to keep him on his Ps and Qs and she's not going to give it all up to him because he must not feel that he has her in the palm of his hands. And that's so funny. Those kinds of asides are what drew me to Don's work because they are so classic. What a way to involve a theatre experience by making those kinds of winks to the audience and letting them know I know you're here and I'm going to fill you in on something so that when a scene happens later on I'll be able to look to you, wink, and you'll know. And that's what's great!

We did it in the old building at Crossroads on the second floor. At the beginning of September in 1980...it was hot...there was no air conditioning and the best we could do was open our back door; we had fans hanging upside down in the ceiling.

Hmph. That felt like Lil Bits' house, didn't it?

You see what I'm saying? [*We have a good laugh.*] The people were in the theatre two hours and forty–five minutes and they were sweating, but they didn't care because they had ball. They forgot that it was hot. It all became this wonderful experience — the fans flopping, and people laughing and taking off their jackets and unloosening their ties was all a part of the experience.

That's like the club too, isn't it. Second floor club/bedroom.

There you go, you see. So it was wonderful to be in that kind of experience. And I will say to you that that was one of the early productions at Crossroads that began to become a trademark for what Crossroads was about in that it became a community of artists and a community of members exchanging ideas. That's when it became...and I think that's when we began to define Crossroads by that kind of performance and that kind of exchange between audience and actor. And one of the best ways to do that was through humor. In the old configuration, there were probably sixty seats, and I'm telling you, you couldn't have been any closer to the actors on stage in this L–shaped formation. That was before we did our first set of renovations.

In many ways we were defining a comic playing style. These were all things that had already been done. *Showdown Time* was done maybe two years before. *One Monkey* had been done in Trenton. But here we were a young professional black theatre with a new generation of artists and we were sort of defining a style.

Douglas Turner Ward said something very interesting when he was here in Los Angeles at my Blacksmyth's Festival last summer. He said that we tend to re–invent the wheel in Black Theatre. I felt that to be a very incisive statement.

We are re–inventing the wheel he calls it. And I understand exactly what he's trying to say because he's saying the wheel has already been created. And I think that all that we did at Crossroads is kept it spinning. We didn't invent it, we just kept it spinning. We were taking it to another level, you see. And we were infusing it with our energy and particularly in a regional theatre environment. This was not New York. This was not sort of savvy New York audiences, this was regional theatre outside of New York. These were people many of whom who had gone to the theatre and then again many of whom who had not. And then mixing them together and also mixing black and white and so it helped to create a style of playing and particularly a style of playing comedy and playing Don Evans' plays. I always went for the real. I felt that if we simply went for the real then the humor would play very easily.

Don't go for the laugh?

Absolutely. And it's a cultural specific. We can be a very humorous people. There is something about when we perform for one another that's very funny. And it's not always funny, ha ha. But it's funny. It's humorous.

Michele Shay is doing that in the August Wilson piece.

You're exactly right.

She twitches her nose . . . she slows down the dialogue a step behind everybody else's. It not necessarily on the page, or in the script. It's what she is doing with those words.

There you go. You know what it is? Again, I'll go back to the *Colored Museum* to the beginning of Miss Roj. "God created black people and black people created style." That's it. STYLE. So it was fun to work with actors on scripts like these . . . on Don Evans' script. We did *One Monkey*, we did *Show Down Time*, we did *Sweet Daddy Love*, after me Crossroads did *Spooks. Love Song for Miss Lydia* which was a bit more dramatic. And then of course *piece de resistance* was Mr. Wolfe's play. It's a comedy that comes out of the baby boomer generation.

So he could write it in retrospect.

Yes. That's the comedy of the hip generation. That's the comedy of the Jimmie Hendrix, Sly and the Family Stones, Jackson Five, Motown Generation. That is the comedy of the black panther generation. That's the comedy of the Amiri Baraka generation. That's the comedy of the SHAFT generation. And I will tell you that when I read it the first time I can remember it like it was just yesterday. The play appeared on my desk and I said very interesting title. I took it home and was literally blown away. I had to stop and go, "I don't believe [Wolfe] said that." Okay? All right?

ME TOO! [We chuckle.]

It was dangerous humor. It was provocative humor. It was do I want to do this kind of humor.

Am I brave enough?

Right. Am I brave enough kind of humor. And I knew Pamela that it had come to me for a reason. I knew that at every turn of the page. I said there is probably no other director more suited to do this than you.

Why? Other than the things you've already talked about, what made you think that you could make this work and people would accept it?

I felt that there was a part of me in terms of my creativity as an artist that had not been fully explored. That's because I felt that I was having, in some ways, to adapt myself to the words and ideas of other people. And all of a sudden something came along that just flowed through me like my own blood. It was just a symbiotic, and it's interesting because after we left New Brunswick, George wrote the piece called *Symbiosis*. That was developed in that summer between New Brunswick and New York, but there was a symbiotic experience you see. I was with this writer every step of the way. It felt like a relay race when you pass the baton on. You know they say the real good relay runner knows how to pass that baton. You must know how to pass that baton and it has to be done in rhythm. The runner is running up on you and the other runner who is going to get the baton starts to run and there's that moment of symbiosis. There's that moment where it just gels. You put it in that hand and you are gone; you are one. It's like one person is running all four legs or however many legs of the race. When I read *Colored Museum* I said, "God, I'm all up in this script." I too at some time have just wanted to scream at all of the momma on the couch plays.

Its interesting, Pamela, because there was a backlash that a lot of people don't want to talk about that has been swept under the rug, but there was a backlash. There were people who felt that this was a negative depiction ...

Attack?

... attack on black people and black culture. And I sort of understood. When someone like a George Wolfe comes along and someone like me who is so willing and so excited about doing the production, I think that you sort of want to hold on to your territory. When young turfs come along and say we are going in a different direction. It was never an attempt in any way to try to take anything from anyone because I had tremendous respect for those that had come before. Doug, Woodie King, and the list of writers that I couldn't even begin to call out to you. We knew at Crossroads. We modeled our programming and our theatre after these great institutions that had come before us... ten, fifteen, years before we hit the pavement. So in many ways this was a Valentine. It was a Valentine because what I was saying was, "Guess what everybody, we are ready for this. We are strong enough...

And we can laugh at ourselves.

...and we can laugh at ourselves. Again, I'm not talking about how others see it. I'm saying this is ours. Ultimately this is ours and once we acknowledge that it is ours then we can allow everyone to come into the room. But I wanted there to be that acknowledgment. This is something that probably very few people know... but it was Ron Milner who first brought me to George Wolfe.

From Detroit? How did that happen?

I ran into Ron Milner and George who had a piece at Playwrights Horizons and Ron said to me, "Lee, you need to know who this man is." Ron was the one who introduced me to George. So you see that tie there. It was one generation passing the baton to the next. I'll be the first one to say it, "We ran with it."

I'm glad you did.

And now I'm ready to pass it too. You know I got a few more years but I want to pass it on. I want to have these chi'rens in a room so I can talk to them the way I'm talking to you on this phone. I haven't had that chance to do this. People need to hear the stories. I need to have some young directors on each hip. I get it with the actors because I direct but I need to have young directors on each hip. We need these opportunities to pass down the information.

Now we'll continue with *Colored Museum*. I was scared and excited at the same time. The fear was I knew it was going to shake people up because we all know there are those people who consider themselves to be the keepers of the gate. And I knew that by me coming up to the gate and bang bang bang banging on it that there was going to be some uncomfortable folks.

In terms of the visuals and theatricality, where did you go in your mind as a director? What did you think?

Well, when I say to you it was symbiotic, I knew. I just trusted after a point; I just simply trusted my own imagination. I said, "Lee, you have prepared yourself, you have been preparing yourself for thirteen years." I started as an actor, I did almost everything in the theatre. I was now producing and here came this piece and I said, "Lee, you can't be any more prepared for this so just go with it. Don't try to screen and second guess yourself just let it flow." We had a huge design team because there were a lot of things that we were responsible for. There were slides, there was music, set, lights and costumes. Just simply making that turntable work at Crossroads was a feat in itself. It sounded like the IRT.

Did you do it manually?

Oh yes. I'll tell you a funny story. There was a long flight of steps from the basement at the Memorial Parkway location up to the second floor where the theatre was and you would get this gust of wind sometimes that would come shooting up those steps and through the theatre. Sometimes we would leave the door to the theatre open because even though we had air conditioning it would just get too close. So we'd leave the theatre door open and keep the lights out. One day when the sliding doors (two sets of sliding doors on stage right and stage left) opened, the designer had this very thin white material that continued around the circle all the way upstage of the doors. Behind this white material were the people on the wench. When this burst of wind came up it blew the material away and you saw these guys. It was like in the *Wizard of Oz*, don't pay any attention to the man behind the screen. They were just going around and around sweating with their shirts off, they were just turning and turning.

The second funny story was when L. Kenneth Richardson debuted as Miss Roj. I covered for Robert Jason who originated the role. He got cast in *Hamlet* directed by Zoe Caldwell and the rehearsals conflicted with two of the performances. And so, I had to go on. Pamela, imagine the kid in patio pants. I remember distinctly being backstage waiting to come on as Miss Roj and as the exhibit just prior to Miss Roj was finishing up the door to the theatre opened and about fifteen people squeezed into the entranceway. Who were these people? All my friends. They all squeezed in to see Lee do Miss Roj. *The Gospel According To* ... But you know what, I had a ball.

You can cry on that too though.

Yes, you can. Some of it was just downright painful. It was such a purging; an experience that was purging your soul because Miss Roj is as funny and as smart and as witty as she is pained. Because they look at her and say look at that faggot, look at that tall black faggot and he/she has had to deal with that for most of his life he decides to be the drag queen. And, that's a lot of anger and that's why he tells us don't let me drink too many rum and cokes. My demons are coming. He knows that they're going to come out. That's part of the ritual. You get the humor, but guess what its going to leave a bitter taste in your mouth. And I will tell you particularly in Reggae Montgomery's performance in New York it was breathtaking. To see him after he purges, after that anger spews out like so much vomit. To see him pull it all up to say the next time you see me on the street you'll think twice about throwing those remarks my way. He pulled it up and the tears were right there at the edge of the eyelid and that tear did not drop.

It was a blessing. If I never do anything as breathtaking as that I will have had that opportunity.

Where did Party *go? What is the freedom about?*

Symbiosis and *Party* were new. We didn't really have an ending in New Brunswick, so I think that George realized that he needed to somehow take this incredible energy and resolve it somehow. So that's where I think Party Girl comes from. Party Girl is all of that energy. Party Girl is all that contradiction as she says. Party Girl goes uptown and is partying with the divas and the divos. She is having a ball and realizing I'm in sync with everybody, but don't define me because I'm going to be the one who's going to really defy definition. Realizing that I got all of them and I got all of me, and I'm moving forward with it. I'm not going to let you define me because I'm going to be like quicksilver. I'm like a shooting star. You can't even catch me. One minute I'm here...the next minute....

I remember doing it in Baltimore when we were at Center Stage. Elia English did Party Girl. We were in rehearsal and I will tell you she levitated. She got that "Tear the roof off the f— , tear the roof off the motherf— . She got that P funk up in her. She got that P funk thang and she levitated. Girlfriend went some place and got dizzy. Girlfriend's energy got so intense that she got dizzy and again what George is saying is that it can overwhelm you. You got to make your piece with it because it's so powerful.

Our experience and our lust for life and our ability to absorb and the fact that we are like mediums for this kind of psychic spiritual "dark" energy that if you don't make peace with it, it'll take you somewhere. It takes a lot of those characters to different places... It takes Miss Roj, it takes Miss Pat, it takes the two wigs, it takes the man in *Symbiosis*, it takes La La Amazing Grace, it takes the people in *Last Momma on the Couch* ... it takes you!

I think what he does so brilliantly is he says, "The source of your joy is also the source of your pain." And that's what makes us unique as individuals because it all swirls together in the same body at the same time. You have to make peace with it otherwise it can destroy you. The pain is the thing that also fuels you. Just as much as the joy. You've got to make peace with that and you've got to accept that those two things can co–exist. And that's why I'm saying to you the minute it gets a little bit too serious, chuckle a little bit.

George in this play defines what comedy has meant to Black people in America.

That's right and that's what he was saying and I think that may be where people took a wrong turn was that in Miss Pat, he's not laughing at slavery, he laughing at the absurdity of it. The absurdity of the basketball appearing. The absurdity of tap shoes. The absurdity. In other words in that piece he says I got to laugh to keep from crying because you can't explain it... there's no rationality. What he did was he freed us by taking it to a level where we could look at it objectively and I think that's what all good artist do is give us an objective viewpoint. And so Miss Pat comes out and she's Mary Tyler Moore dipped in chocolate.

What do you think about Danitra Vance?

I thought Danitra was about as brilliant as you can get in a role. Ms. Danitra, God bless her soul, taught me something in that. She taught me to trust. She taught me not to worry. She taught me to have faith in my instincts and then to allow her, to allow artists to take the kind of food that I give them and let them eat it up and turn it into energy and turn it into brain food. That's what she taught me.

HM! She's still living then.

Oh she is. She is ... We're not going to even understand the phenomenon called *The Colored Museum* for another 50 to 100 years. When they look back at it there're going to go my gosh this was a watershed experience in 1986 in that little town called New Brunswick, NJ. And let's not forget that it was a black theatre that brought it forth. It was a black theatre that introduced George Wolfe to the world. Lest we not forget.

Danitra taught me to trust. We couldn't get Miss Pat for some reason.

Miss Pat wasn't working and we knew that was what we called the entrée into the world of *The Colored Museum*. And I remember in previews Joe Papp would come and watch and remark, "Wonderful show, wonderful show, but fix Miss Pat," and that's all he would say. And so finally we're in rehearsal, because of course during the previews we were continuing to rehearse. And finally Danitra looked at me and George and said, "Let me try something." And of course trying to hold on to the reins I said, "Well what are you going to do?" She says, "No no. Let me just try something." Well what we had was a comedian with a lot of experience in front of an audience and so on one particular night she stood there and said the line, "And no drums will be allowed on board." And here's where the improvisation began, "Repeat after me. No drums." And she then kind of conducted the audience to say, "No drums" and then what happened?!! She opened it up to us and baby they took it and we were gone. You understand. You hear what I'm saying. Baby, that was Danitra. People were sitting there going this is funny but should I laugh at this...Oh my God... You know the Celebrity Slave Ship...Oh my God...And this woman in this little pink outfit from the 1960s with this little flip wig. God, this is hysterical, but I can't laugh. Someone might see me. But when she said "Repeat after me, "No drums." The mouthing of those words allowed people to go AAAH.

From that point on Danitra and I had an understanding. And I'll never forget her. That is my story about Danitra. There is no one to play Miss Pat, there is no one to play Normal Jean that could in any way get any deeper.

I said to the actors, "This dialogue is rich, this story is rich so don't allow yourself to go for the cheap laugh. Allow yourself to live inside of these characters and trust me it will be funny because it is funny. But allow yourself to live." I did not want it to be sketch comedy...one little bit after another little bit after another little bit which it could have easily been. And it is a very fine line that you straddle with the style in *Colored Museum*.

Again, what we were doing was keeping the wheel spinning. Didn't they do that with *Day of Absence*?

YEAH.

Here's my *Day of Absence* story. I was a senior in high school in 1968 and it was at a time when all of the major universities were trying to snag as many black students as possible because they didn't have many on their campuses and the government was starting to clamp down and say, "You've got to integrate these campuses." So I was invited to spend time at a number of schools. One of them being Dartmouth, where I spent a few days. One night I went off into a student center into a room where there were television sets and I sat down and saw what looked like black people with white face on and I said what is this. I looked around and there was nobody in the room but me and I said, "Did somebody spike what I had to drink for dinner?" And I sat and I watched and I said, "They are black, cause that's black skin, but what are they doing? And I sat there mesmerized again, by the wit, by the intelligence, by the humor, by the tragedy, by the on–the–nose–observation of race relations in America.

Doug has to realize that in many ways he is the Godfather of *The Colored Museum*. That's what he is! He wrote that play almost twenty years before *Colored Museum*. Think about it! That's what it is . . . it really is. It's taking something which has been the source of so much pain and turning it into a joyful celebration without demeaning it, without de–valuing it. And George, I don't know if he consciously knew that he was doing that, but that's what he was doing. When you have those two wigs arguing who's going with this woman to tell this man off you know you're in that world of *The Day of Absence*. You're in that world of "SATIRE."

I had a conversation with Doug last summer, about this very point, and I think he agrees that there is definitely a line between *Colored Museum* and *Day of Absence*. I want to see what the next line is going to be, and what is so so important is I hope we are somewhere nurturing our next genera- tion of comedy writers. Okay? Again, I think you have to realize that cer- tainly *Colored Museum* pre–dated *In Living Color*. It pre–dated that kind of freedom to laugh at ourselves and to use black culture as the target of that kind of very sharp humor. It pre–dated all of that.

Ultimately *Colored Museum* is a party. It's a celebration. That's what George tried to do with the television production. It's a party. We're all here to have fun. And when you do it in those small spaces like Crossroads, and at the Public you get that kind of thing. And then to come out here to the Taper and play in front of seven hundred people and to literally tear the roof off the sucker, tear the roof off the mother sucker . . . I thought we were going to go off into outer space. I thought the roof was just going to fly off into space because the energy was so high.

It's supposed to go there because it's cathartic.

It's supposed to go there you see, but you have to be very careful. You have to straddle that line because you want to have the audience laugh with, not at. Realize, you see. I would always tell the actors you've got to be smarter than everybody else. You got to be a couple of steps ahead of everybody else. Don't go for the cheap laugh because then the audience will feel like they're past you . . . that they've run a race and they've just trampled you. Go for the more difficult laugh. That's where the play has to spin. It has got to be the complete madness of allowing for hair and texture of hair to dictate your sensibility . . . to dictate your choices in life. To feel like you are a slave to texture of hair is maddening and that's what he's getting at. And so at first it's funny, "Child, you see her . . . girlfriend . . . no you won't! I'm going . . . No you won't Ms. Thing. People are laughing and going crazy cause it's like being on some kind of mind/mood altering trip that you're in. What kind of universe are we dealing with here? But at the end it's the madness. It's always that madness.

You remember the soldier, Junie. He saves people's lives by killing them. Is he an angel of death or an angel of mercy? What is he? It's that madness that goes through Lala. Finally it breaks and consumes La La. See, I believed very much that there was an arc in this play and it went from Miss Pat all the way to La La, and La La broke and was destroyed by it. And so what has to happen, there has to be a rebirth and that's the egg and then who comes out of the egg? Party Girl.

Defying Logic and Limitation! . . .

So you see there is an arc to that play. It isn't just eleven unrelated skits. It starts off a lot of fun and we think there are no consequences, but eventually we get to *Symbiosis* and then right after *Symbiosis* is *La La's Opening* and that's when we have the breakdown and the mirror crashes and she has to face herself and realize that its been a fraud because she's been fronting. She's been trying to completely deny the pain and has created La La Amazing Graze, who has a French accent and who has this revolutionary past, but it's all fake. So she breaks. When the little girl comes to her and she mirrors the little girl, we are in essence letting that melt away like so much snow, like so much ice and then left in that little snow is a little seed and that seed blossoms in Normal Jean. And it blossoms in a regular little old colored girl.

NOTES ON THE CONTRIBUTORS

Ed Bullins

Playwright, Professor, Acting Director of the Center for the Arts at Northeastern University in Boston, MA.

Jessie Fauset

(c. 1886-1961) Author/educator. *Comedy American Style* (1933)

Floranté Galvez

Playwright; wrote and directed his first film,*Sister Sessions*; Assistant Professor at SUNY Oneonta

Lynda M. Hill

Author, "Social Rituals and the Verbal Art of Zora Neale Hurston"; Assistant Professor, Temple University, Dept. of English

Tia Dionne Hodge

Recent 1996 graduate from Case Western Reserve University with a MA & BA in English. She is the first recipient of the Louis Kent-Hope Award for Excellence in Creative Writing and Poetry awarded by the Adrienne Kennedy Society, and a two-time winner of the Nemet Scholarship for Excellence in Creative Writing.

Dr. Paul Jackson

Author; professor, former department chair Spelman CollegeTheatre Department, Atlanta, GA

Lofton Mitchell

Playwright, black drama historian, essayist, and teacher. Author of "Black Drama: The story of the American Negro in the theatre"

Karen A. Morgan

Playwright, *And the World Laughs with You*, produced by Crossroads Theatre Company

Eugene Nesmith

Assistant Professor, English Dept. City College of New York; Director-Annual Langston Hughes Festival Theater at CUNY

Jeff Nichols

Yale Graduate; History teacher at The Dalton School in New York City

L. Kenneth Richardson

Producer, Director, Crossroads Theatre Company co-founder , Rutger University M.F.A.; Founder/Director of BLACKSMYTHS, The Black Playwright's Festival